American Sports
and the Great War

ALSO BY PETER C. STEWART

Early Professional Baseball in Hampton Roads: A History, 1884–1928 (McFarland, 2010)

American Sports and the Great War

College, Military and Professional Athletics, 1916–1919

PETER C. STEWART

McFarland & Company, Inc., Publishers
Jefferson, North Carolina

LIBRARY OF CONGRESS CATALOGUING-IN-PUBLICATION DATA

Names: Stewart, Peter C., author.
Title: American sports and the Great War : college, military and professional athletics, 1916–1919 / Peter C. Stewart.
Description: Jefferson, North Carolina : McFarland & Company, Inc., Publishers, 2021 | Includes bibliographical references and index.
Identifiers: LCCN 2020054840 | ISBN 9781476681054 (paperback : acid free paper) ∞
ISBN 9781476640440 (ebook)
Subjects: LCSH: Sports—United States—History—20th century. | Military sports—United States—History—20th century. | Sports and state—United States—History—20th century. | Male athletes—United States—History—20th century. | World War, 1914–1918—Social aspects—United States.
Classification: LCC GV583 .S74 2021 | DDC 796.097309/04—dc23
LC record available at https://lccn.loc.gov/2020054840

BRITISH LIBRARY CATALOGUING DATA ARE AVAILABLE

ISBN (print) 978-1-4766-8105-4
ISBN (ebook) 978-1-4766-4044-0

© 2021 Peter C. Stewart. All rights reserved

No part of this book may be reproduced or transmitted in any form or by any means, electronic or mechanical, including photocopying or recording, or by any information storage and retrieval system, without permission in writing from the publisher.

Front cover: Hobart "Hobey" Baker (left) poses with a football in college; Baker's crashed SPAD S.XIII biplane that he was testing on December 21, 1918, the day of his intended return from France (photographs courtesy of Princeton University)

Printed in the United States of America

*McFarland & Company, Inc., Publishers
Box 611, Jefferson, North Carolina 28640
www.mcfarlandpub.com*

Table of Contents

Preface	1
Introduction: Before America Entered the Great War	5
1. Professional Baseball	9
2. College Baseball	20
3. Military Baseball at Home and Abroad	35
4. College Football	54
5. Professional and Military Football	85
6. Track and Field	104
7. Basketball and Volleyball	119
8. Golf and Tennis	135
9. Rowing, Swimming, Yachting and Motorboat Racing	144
10. Boxing and Wrestling	149
11. Auto, Motorbike and Bicycle Racing	160
12. Ice Hockey and Other Winter Sports	164
13. Equestrian Sports	168
14. Gymnastics, Lacrosse and Soccer	173
15. Potpourri: Archery—Trapshooting	178
16. The Inter-Allied Military Olympics	183
17. Legacy of the War	193
Appendix: Records, 1916–1919	199
Chapter Notes	205
Bibliography	221
Index	225

Preface

The commemoration of the 100th anniversary of American participation in the Great War created much interest. This book surveys athletics, focusing on colleges and the military. My interest in this war started when I watched a Memorial Day parade around the end of World War II. An old man who had served in the Civil War led the parade while sitting in a convertible, followed by a large group of veterans of the "Great War" on foot. In my academic career, that war became a focal point. As a college instructor, I taught the history of American sports. This project brings together two long-term interests.

It took several years to gather and analyze enough sources to make more than general assertions. How to organize the material into a coherent body proved a problem. Based on a critic's idea that readers might prefer one sport, I took up each major sport in turn, starting with baseball, followed by football and track. Ensuing chapters deal with two or more sports. One summarizes several not previously covered. A chapter focuses on the Military Olympics held in France in the summer of 1919. The last chapter summarizes the contribution of athletes, connects sports with the political culture and briefly compares sports in the two world wars.

The Great War affected nearly every sport to varying degrees. Some major league baseball players volunteered to fight the Germans and a few avoided being drafted by working in industry and being paid for playing for these companies. The war also affected college athletics. Considering that only a little over 5 percent of college-age men went to institutions of higher education at the time and less than 1 percent of Americans had graduated from such places, one might assume they would have played a minimal part in the conflict. Such was not the case. Over 50,000 current collegians and thousands of former students volunteered in the spring of 1917 when Congress declared war. Many more joined the military over the next year. Yet, although the war cut into athletics at colleges, it did not end them as many had predicted.

Conflicting scores abound. Reporters for student or local newspapers or those who produced college yearbooks often decided championships. It was not so critical to know who won but that contests took place, though at a reduced rate. The number of semi-pro and amateur non-collegian baseball and football games played by those not in the military also fell. But the overall number rose as the military used sports to keep up morale while having recruits reach a high level of physical readiness.

About 250,000 men attended colleges and universities, with their overall registration 20,000 fewer in 1917 than in 1916, roughly 40,000 replaced by women and more freshmen than usual. A report taken just after the war came up with about a thousand institutions above high school level counting women's colleges, professional and normal schools (for prospective teachers) and many small colleges. My database on athletics now has over 900 of those that admitted men and might qualify as colleges, not including vocational schools. This list includes several institutes for Native Americans and about 75 historically Black institutions, only a few of which had yearbooks or campus newspapers. Much more needs to be done to understand the role athletics played at these places.

In the fall of 1918, the Student Army Training Corps (SATC) ran at 500 "real" colleges, a few others being veterinary, medical schools, etc. About 150,000 entered this program on 1 October. Most of the 500 schools have more data than those without the SATC. West Point, the Naval Academy and four Quaker schools, even with no SATC, have full records. I started my pursuit of information about athletic activity with results from annuals produced by the Spalding company, which contained the records on several sports. I then delved into yearbooks and newspapers, adding to my database, state-by-state.

How the military employed sports can be discerned by looking over volumes on the Library of Congress website, which, when I started, numbered a few hundred but now contains several thousand. A few of these deal with athletic activity of individual military units, sometimes including scores. The official army newspaper produced in Paris during the war contained many items of interest. Daily newspapers on the home front had sports sections, though nowhere near the size of current ones, where the public learned about the results of such competition. In addition, newspapers in cities near army camps produced "Camp & Trench" editions. Coverage was not uniform; often an issue mentions an upcoming event, but a subsequent one fails to follow up.

Most reporters strove for accuracy and I have relied on their findings. Yet it is quite likely that perceived facts occasionally were inaccurate. Reported deaths of athletes, for example, could later prove untrue. Reporters often refer to major leaguers playing for military baseball nines. In reporting on football, the college represented was of utmost importance.

The accuracy of some of these was occasionally suspect. Many reporters at urban newspapers wanted prize fighting made legal and were happy when the military trained recruits to box. In some states reporters often decided the winner of matches, thus allowing illegal betting to continue. Reporters and yearbook contributors expressed their points of view about the war and a range of other matters. They also gave athletes and teams nicknames, which were sometimes less than appropriate. They admired Native American athletes and tended to be more liberal-minded than politicians regarding black Americans.

I would like to thank the staff of the Old Dominion University library for securing microfilm copies of several newspapers. The Library of Congress website proved useful in finding newspapers from several smaller cities. Several hundred yearbooks appear online for a small annual fee. Dozens more exist in digital form, along with many campus newspapers. Newspapers, yearbooks and campus magazines are not cited in the bibliography, citation notes sufficing. In the last few years trips to about sixty college archives filled in gaps. I plan to keep up this research and thereby add to the database, which one day might find its way into a digital collection. These trips confirm my belief that archivists are very important people. And I thank them all.

Introduction
Before America Entered the Great War

The connection between sports and the military did not suddenly appear with U.S. entry into the Great War. In 1897, the U.S.S. *Maine* won a title just months before it sank in Havana harbor, killing the winning pitcher who also served as a black fireman. Just before entry into the Great War, Fort Totten (N.Y.) won an East Coast football title over Fort Adams (Newport). In the 1915 Atlantic Fleet championships, the U.S.S. *Wyoming* overcame the U.S.S. *New Hampshire*, 6–0, a back from Buffalo plunging for the only score, the winners thwarted by a left-footed punter and former naval boxing champ.[1]

The creation of pro baseball leagues of corporations in the 1870s and 1880s meant the sport became part of the capitalist culture. In the 1880s the Young Men's Christian Association (YMCA), under the umbrella "Muscular Christianity," used sports to acclimate young men to urban and industrial life. In the same decade, athletic clubs organized the Amateur Athletic Union, which supervised track and encouraged several other sports, such as basketball and swimming. Also, in the 1880s, higher education created what became its favorite sport, the NCAA (National Collegiate Athletic Association) transforming American football into what exists today just a few years before America entered the Great War. In the spring, collegians sustained intercollegiate competition in the National Pastime and rowing, both predating football by a generation. The military also promoted these as well as pugilism, which derived from a "Sporting Fraternity," whose members embraced a violent and sometimes illegal lifestyle. A more refined type emerged in the 1890s but gambling remained at its core. Boxing and the military became linked well before World War I. In January 1917, the Army heavyweight title fought in Mexico went to Private Rufus Williams, an African American infantryman.[2]

In 1916, the Red Sox won the World Series over Brooklyn, with Babe Ruth peaking as a pitcher, the National Pastime recovering from the challenge of the Federal League, whose brief existence forced owners to raise salaries. After Dave Fultz started his baseball career with hometown Staunton in the Virginia League in 1894, he went to Brown University where he played baseball and football. After his major league career ended, he became a lawyer and in 1912 organized the Baseball Players Fraternity, which claimed over 1,200 members. When Fultz called for a strike about the same time Germany resumed torpedoing American ships, Grantland Rice said if the strike took place it would be as if France suddenly invaded England or England assaulted Russia. Most players broke pledges before spring training.[3]

In 1916, the New York press rated Columbia, 18–1–1, Tufts, 20–2, Harvard, 21–3, and Syracuse, 19–3, as the best college clubs in the East. Illinois stood first in the Western Conference (the Big 9), Missouri claimed the Missouri Valley, Auburn the Southern and Texas the Southwest. In the summer of '16, as the U.S. ramped up pursuing Pancho Villa, a national-guard league near El Paso had field artillerists from Massachusetts leading other Bay State units and Rhode Island artillerists.[4]

In the fall of '16, infantry Blues from Richmond (Virginia) and light artillery Blues from Norfolk, getting ready to move to the border with Mexico, took to the gridiron against small Virginia colleges. When the Norfolk Blues reached the border, they lost by a lot to the 2nd Texas Infantry. On the last Saturday in November, these Texans, with nine Longhorns and two Aggies, mauled Missouri artillerists, 60–0, at Laredo. On New Year's Day, with six Longhorns and three Aggie backs, they scored fifteen touchdowns against a New York regiment at Corpus Christi.[5]

That November, playing on Saturdays and Sundays at Rio Grande Park in El Paso and nearby camps, Michigan's 32nd Division (mostly from the Kalamazoo area) led one division at Fort Bliss, at 5–0. A North Carolina eleven, previously undefeated but twice tied, fell to Ohio field artillerists, led by a West Pointer. In the championship at El Paso on New Year's Day, '17, in the high school stadium, before several thousand, including nine military bands, Michigan rolled, 41–26, over the Ohioans. Almost all attending wore khaki, while civilians picnicked nearby.[6]

Inter-collegiately in the fall preceding American entry into the European war, Colgate's battering of previously unbeaten Brown left the Pitt Panthers, coached by Glenn "Pop" Warner, and West Point as the only two undefeated in the Northeast. Georgia Tech, under John Heisman, tied Washington and Lee, rendering suspect any rating as the nation's best, even with a record 222–0 over Cumberland University. Ohio State, 4–0 in the Big 9, 7–0 overall, should have had consideration. All the other major colleges and universities lost or tied at least one. The new Texas coach received praise for not losing heart when many joined the army in response to Villa's

Introduction 7

raid in New Mexico. His eleven led the Southwestern Intercollegiate Athletic Conference, 6–1. Baylor, 3–1, with a win over Texas, claimed a share of the title. A Wisconsin mining school canceled its first game because the coach and five players were still on the Mexican border.[7]

The boxing arena at Camp Cotton in Texas compared favorably to the Sporting Club of London in being "bohemian, cosmopolitan and exclusive." Some 2,500, including a colonel who was a judge in Boston, saw a pro take on one from Massachusetts. The Texas attorney general said the matches were illegal but admitted he had no authority in the camp or on the Bliss reservation. Not wanting to challenge local law, the military moved the next fight on a Sunday to Juarez. Bouts took place in the picturesque sand hills of New Mexico, north of the Rio Grande in an arena with no roof but with benches and a ring. Almost all the spectators dressed in olive came from Texas on an improvised trolley or in autos or trucks from the motor pool. Chaplains sanctioned this activity for improving morale.[8]

Riders from Fort Bliss played polo at El Paso's Rio Grande Park on Sundays, the Freebooters having an edge. Pershing aide First Lieutenant George Patton, who placed fifth in the Stockholm Olympics in 1912 in the military pentathlon, scored for the winning cavalry in a match in Mexico.[9]

With "physical preparedness" the theme at the NCAA meeting in December 1916, Maj. Palmer Pierce called for physical fitness to infuse the curriculum. "Pathetic" described the condition of 3,200 collegians at Plattsburg, Missouri's, officer training the previous summer, even though most came from schools "that rank athletically—if turning out successful teams be considered a criterion—second to none."[10]

Stanford University and the University of Washington planned to suspend all intercollegiate contests as soon as Congress declared war on Germany. The Oregon Aggies hoped to continue, but nearly all the leaders in every sport pledged to some form of service, and all the football regulars committed to the Reserve Officers Training Corps (ROTC), created as part of the preparedness program in 1916. Stanford considered giving a degree to an all-round athlete who passed the exam to be a signal officer at San Diego even though he had over a month left in the semester. In February, the Naval Academy suspended sports, then reversed that decision. Prestigious institutions of higher learning, especially in the East, considered stopping all athletic programs, figuring most athletes would volunteer for service in the event of war.[11]

Around the time relations with the Germans headed south with the resumption of unfettered submarine warfare and disclosures of a plot to have Mexico attack the U.S., Franklin Roosevelt, Assistant Secretary of the Navy, organized fellow yachtsmen to make their craft and themselves available in the likely event of war. Tillinghast Huston, part owner of the

Many, however, were needed in other work. And the war reduced interest in pennant races, especially in smaller communities.

The high minors (Class A with two leagues and AA with three) came through '17 not even losing or transferring a franchise. The Pacific Coast League even lengthened its season, teams averaging over 210 games. Two of six shortened seasons in Class B as the Northwestern stopped in mid–July, a rainy spring and high travel costs to Montana influencing the decision. The Three-I's eight clubs lost about $25,000 and its president urged all leagues below A to cease after the 4th of July. Two in C folded in May followed by one just after the 4th of July, another surviving about two more weeks. Among eight leagues in D, six failed to reach the end of the schedule, compared to one in twelve the previous year. The North Carolina League closed at the end of May, prodded to do so by the governor, a Greensboro reporter tiring of that worthy's "utterances on the subject."[4]

Among African Americans, the Capital City League (Nashville) survived '17, four clubs playing once a week, sometimes on Sunday. One club had infielders valued at $1,000 and charged fifteen cents admission, attendance in the low hundreds. A league nine played outsiders. Rube Foster, from Chicago, scouted for potential talent.[5]

Sgt. Hank Gowdy, catcher for the Boston Braves, received much praise when he volunteered for the U.S. Army in 1917. *Library of Congress: LC-DIG-ggbain-17478.*

1. Professional Baseball

Reporters spilled a lot of ink determining the draft status of major leaguers. Jack Barry, player manager of the Red Sox, and several others passed physicals. Two "Mack Men" (Philadelphia Athletics), likely candidates for conscription, volunteered in August. Among Pacific Coast Leaguers, a one-time ace looked liable, marriage to a vaudeville star not exempting him. Davis Robertson, a Giant, volunteered but failed his physical due to an old football injury. Marriage might exempt another Giant, but he would "serve without quibbling."[6]

Brave catcher Hank Gowdy of the Ohio National Guard infantry soon became a sergeant, his picture often appearing in newspapers. The press also had a lot of interest in Brave shortstop Walter "Rabbit" Maranville and Leon Cadore, a Dodger, who went to Camp Upton after receiving a $50 gold watch from his mates. On furlough, he occasionally won for Brooklyn, going overseas in '18. White Sox pitcher Jim Scott signed on for officer training at the Presidio. Working his way toward a captaincy, he cheered for the Sox in the World Series, after which owner Charles Comiskey sent him a full share of the earnings.[7]

In July 1917, Ban Johnson said the draft doomed the World Series even though his league had lost less than twenty players and the National League even fewer. Comiskey said that if his White Sox won the pennant, the World Series would go on, whether Johnson wanted one or not. Comiskey also subscribed $100,000 to the Liberty Loan and donated to the Red Cross. After volunteering his talents to the Secretary of War, Johnson called for exempting 288 players from military service. John Tener, President of the National League, and nearly everyone else rejected the idea.[8]

The White Sox beat the Giants in six, even though Robertson, batting .500 in the series, saved one game, described as like the "Miracle of the Marne," the "mysterious agency" that stopped the Germans, when Paris was "almost in their grip" in 1914. French commander "Papa" Joffre must have done "a Davy Robertson," who "snatched victory down out of the sky," then tripled and scored the winning run.[9]

Over the winter, more entered the military, so that by January, the American League had 52 and the National League 23, rising to 86 and 49, respectively, before the start of the '18 season. These numbers would likely not ruin the season. The Red Sox lost the most, but Harry Frazee, the new owner, made deals through the winter, picking up the few talented players left on the A's.

The Senior Circuit felt the effects less, the Braves losing Gowdy and Maranville. Cincinnati would likely lose pitcher Fred Toney, who would either be in the army or in jail for evading the draft. Toney said his mother's farm could not even rent for $100 a year. His brother suffered from dysentery. "If they ain't dependent upon me, I don't know who they are dependent upon." A jury failed to find him guilty of draft dodging, but in a plea deal he briefly went to federal prison prior to the '19 season for taking a consenting woman over state lines for illicit purposes.[10]

When Bob Shawkey's wife ("Tiger Lady") refused to say she needed his income, being "through with him," he enlisted, pitching for the League Island Navy Yard, also losing for the Yankees, though only yielding three hits. For missing his assignment for the Yard, Chief Yeoman Shawkey went to sea and watched the surrender of the German fleet.[11]

Through the '18 season every few days the press reported players drafted or volunteering. When the Dodgers traded Casey Stengel, the talkative outfielder joined the Navy, serving not far from where he had recently been playing ball. In the off-season, the Cubs paid a princely sum for Grover Alexander and then negotiated a costly contract with him. Fearing being branded a slacker, he tried to enlist in the navy, but an army officer, noting that he had all winter to do that, said he would soon be in the army. After a special day put on by the Cubs, he went to Camp Funston supposedly as a clerk to make him available to pitch, a status possibly condoned by General Wood, camp commandant. Instead, he trained in Texas for the field artillery and went to France, as a sergeant.

Eddie Collins, second sacker for the White Sox ($15,000 salary) and an old Athletic, joined the Marines in early August. Playing in the Main Line League and working at a supply depot in Philadelphia, he made $30 a month. Yankee Wally Pipp, who signed up for aviation at MIT and went to Pensacola to secure his commission, had not completed the program at the time of the Armistice. A one-time Giant third sacker signed on for aviation and received many perfumed notes from female admirers.[12]

Just before the '18 season started, about 25 percent of potential major leaguers were in the service. The American League ranged from Boston (13) to St. Louis (6). In the National League, Pittsburgh (11) led with Philadelphia (2) the least. In the Junior Circuit, over 50 percent of those under contract in March '18 ended up in the military. Detroit led with 25 which likely explains its fall in the standings. After the war, a reporter figured the American League had 150 serving, the National League 103 (Brooklyn 18– Cincinnati 6), 42 being drafted, 22 volunteering for the army, 32 for the Navy and 7 for aviation. A reporter, assuming a link between the demise of most minor leagues and the number in military service, came up with about 1,100 pros (both majors and minors) "with the colors" in the spring of '18, a bit over half the 2,000 or so in that profession.[13]

With over a thousand in the service, many volunteers, and the rest registered, pro baseball was doing its part. Griffith raised thousands to send bats and balls overseas (one shipment went to the bottom of the sea thanks to a German torpedo). Baseball capitalists invested in Liberty Loans, donated to the Red Cross, or, like the Atlanta Crackers, sent $2,000 to the government in the war tax.

Americans remained confident as the Sammies, named in honor of Uncle Sam (later called Doughboys), helped blunt the German offensive that spring. This "International Ball Game" included the Kaiser halted in "bleeding Belgium," as Johnnie Bull pitched, helped by French fielding. Russia "pinch hit," while Italy and Romania "each laid down a perfect bunt." As the Allies batted at Verdun, Uncle Sam warmed up to pitch "such speed and curves that he will strike out Kaiser Bill." An American would soon hit "one down to Hindenburg" and beat "his throw to first" as Admiral Sims swept U-Boats from the sea and "Pershing, sliding into third—spikes the Crown Prince on the knee." After Uncle Sam "goes in/they'll be building baseball diamonds in the City of Berlin."[14]

As the '18 season neared, the Germans, having struck a deal with Russian Communists, were bringing several hundred thousand troops from their Eastern Front to France. Allied forces, now in the Archangel area to help the Whites against Reds and Germans, forced the latter to keep a substantial force in the East. But their troops moving to the Western Front and the general weakening of both France and Britain meant the U.S. had to draft far more than the original number to create an army (counting Marines) of about 4,000,000 and a navy of about 600,000. The War Department tightened exemptions. A third draft, effective in September, enlarged the pool by subjecting all aged 18 through 35 to the draft, those between 18 and 21 being phased in and age 31 kept for a time for the high end. All pro baseball, it was predicted, would in time only be played by Methuselahs.[15]

In May, the administration coined the slogan "Fight or Work." One could avoid the draft by farming, mining, building ships or engaging in other military-related work. The absence of baseball as an essential occupation caused a writer to rail that it was a victim "of an unwarranted attack, when pool rooms, movies, vaudeville and theaters are passed up without a word." An accompanying cartoon singled out racetrack and pool hall attendants as "non-essentials." Baseball was no "slacker" nor "non-essential."[16]

Only Jim Dunn, owner of the Cleveland Indians, defended the fight or work policy. The president of the Giants, Harry Hempstead, argued that the sport not only collected receipts for the government and helped the Red Cross and raised money for bats and balls for troops overseas, it also gave workers a chance to be in the open air and "take their minds off weightier matters." Even those who did not attend games talked about them. Its value as a "tonic could not be overestimated."[17]

The chair of the National Commission, August Herrmann, thought pro ball "unequaled" for "relaxation, diversion and recreation." Writing to Provost Marshal General Enoch Crowder, chief enforcer of the work or fight rule, Herrmann claimed that the mandate would crush an industry that had over $8,000,000 invested, the leagues standing to lose 258 of 309. Of 531 reserve players on 1 October of the previous year, 81 already volunteered and another 63 drafted, proportionately more than most businesses. Average annual pay for volunteers topped $2,500, that for the draftees slightly less. While Herrmann understood Crowder could not make a wholesale exception, he should consider the impact, including on those players who worked in other industries for almost half the year.[18]

The magnates waited for Crowder's order to be interpreted, especially after a New Jersey board exempted a Yankee pitcher. A June meeting considered allowing furloughed military to play if they received permission from their commander and the team had fewer than 23 on its roster. They complained about rising railroad rates, now operating under the control of federal managers.[19]

Tener made an issue about Rogers Hornsby, when the board at Fort Worth classified him 1A, no matter who depended on him. In a brief, Clark Griffith argued that draft boards should recognize the marital status of one of his catchers and not mandate he find acceptable employment. Baker decided in favor of the boards, and married players had to find suitable work, if their draft board said so.[20]

The business manager of the Boston Braves, dealing with the Brighton, Mass board, argued that conscription should not impose major financial hardship on the registrant, dependents or employer. Having few skills besides playing ball even though he had gone to Amherst College, catcher John Henry had no hope of being paid near his salary (over $500 a month). The Brighton board majority said the family could fall back on income related to a business. A minority thought Henry might suffer financially, but they believed he was not doing critical work.[21]

A reporter thought Baker's decision and Wilson's acquiescence a blow to the nation's psyche, pennant races and the World Series being the very "soul" of the country and so important to the military. The previous spring, the writer found support not seen in the nation's capital, where opponents of the game could be found in un-essential jobs, especially at newspapers. "Teaming millions" wanted its continuation. Witness the thousands of soldiers and sailors "rollicking and laughing" watching the White Sox play the Yankees or naval crew at a ball game in Boston. One editor supported Baker's decision but recommended that 236 major league players exposed to the draft go to France to entertain troops.[22]

When it looked like the "fight or work" order might immediately end the major league season, the owners asked the War Department to hold off call ups until 15 October. Although Crowder was unconvinced that the rule would ruin the game, he and Baker agreed not to implement it until

1 September. The decision pleased Herrmann and Johnson found it acceptable. The commission shortened the season, leaving the World Series in doubt, resolved when local boards held off calling up participants. Even with this agreement, the loss of players and war news reduced attendance. After considering ending the season in mid–August, the owners, with attendance dwindling, limped to the end of the month.

Boston, the best fielding club under manager Ed Barrow who quit the presidency of the International League when it looked like it would merge with the American Association, copped the series. Playing "Dead Ball," with near flawless fielding, they hit about .200, with Ruth holding the Cubs scoreless before they broke through late in his second game. The teams combined to score 19 runs in six games. Going into the series, the Red Sox averaged .253 (14 homers) against the Cubs .269 (19 homers). Ruth led the Sox in average (.300) and home runs (11).

The first three games, all played in Chicago to keep travel expenses down and help the nation's over-burdened railroads, attracted far fewer than the first three games of the '17 series. The disbursement plan gave 60 percent of the receipts of the first four to the players, after 10 percent was siphoned off to the National Commission. After four games, owners received the lion's share from remaining contests. Even before the series, players grumbled about not receiving the usual $2,000 for winners and $1,400 for losers. Threatening a strike in the fifth game, Harry Hooper (Sox) and Leslie Mann (Cubs) negotiated over the phone with Herrmann, who, even though he came up with the idea of having such a playoff in 1903, seemed willing to end the series immediately. After the game was supposed to start, the crowd at Fenway building to about 25,000 and a riot likely should it be called off, convalescing soldiers attending for free and the public condemning the players, they gave up. The Cubs eased out a 3–0 win, sending the series to the sixth game, won by the Sox, 15,000 or so paying to watch.

Receipts of six games yielded about half that of the previous year. The players shared almost $70,000 from the first four games, while the teams took about $46,000, the national commission keeping about $18,000. Payments to the six other teams in the first division of both leagues, a government tax and other expenses accounts for the remainder. The winning Red Sox each received about $1,100, the losing Cubs 67 percent of that amount. Fred Thomas, on furlough from Great Lakes, took in $750, playing far less than half the season for the Sox. The owners tried to cut losses by not paying after 1 September (contracts normally ran to the middle of October). Although they lost the case, the owners weathered the problems brought on by reduced attendance, inflation and paying players after the season ended.

In 1918, the minors started out with ten leagues, only the International League surviving, as players leaving for the service or to the majors intensified fan disinterest. The Virginia League (the only C level) lasted into July, two Norfolk Tars going to the nearby Navy Yard to play ball. In the Northwest, a new six-team Pacific Coast International League suspended in early July. Two weekday contests drew in the low hundreds, management blaming the inadequacies of local trolley service. Tacoma hoped to use Camp Lewis as a home field, but the military nixed that notion. That left military nines and a private ship-related business, which, with several former Tacoma Tigers, vied against Seattle steel clubs. The Queen City (Seattle) Giants, remnants of the league, lost to a Camp Lewis nine. In March '18, a manager in the Capital City League in Tennessee predicted a good season in what turned out to be the lone press coverage of the local Negro league that year as many Nashville blacks went to war.[23]

When the Southern League folded, managers Norman "the Tabasco Kid" Elberfeld, the firebrand of the Little Rock Travelers, Charley Frank, president of the Atlanta Crackers and Carleton Molesworth of the Birmingham Barons, received YMCA training. They ended up in charge of programs in the military camps of Shelby, Gordon and Greene.

In Newport, Rhode Island, the semi-pro '17 Trojans, with some minor-leaguers, lost 4–1 to the Cincinnati Reds, bested the Yankees, edged a fort in Boston Harbor but were shut out by the Newport Naval Reserves, a '17 Yale grad doing the honors. The Trojans, returning in '19 after missing a year, lost to the Cardinals, Braves and Red Sox.

In Richmond, Virginia, in '16, pursuing Villa disrupted local baseball as several joined the military. In May '17, the Amateur Commission forecast few losses because the schedule would end in August before draft call ups and married men would probably be exempt. Fewer teams and leagues showed up in '18. Battle Axe (a shoemaker) featured ex–major leaguer John Boehling, who later joined the army at Camp Lee. His future regiment and Battle Axe split decisions against each other before he switched uniforms.

Washington, D.C., had over fifty semi-pro clubs in '16, the Clarendon A.C. (Alexandria) and a railroad club vying for the lead. In '17, with a smaller number contending, Clarendon again won, this time over the Cardinals (Alexandria), who also split with the Newport News Shipbuilders after the Virginia League folded. The area lost half its amateur leagues between '16 and '17; more disappeared in '18.[24]

After an active '16, no semi-pro or amateur teams surfaced at Bemidji in Minnesota in '17. In '18, on the 4th of July, with most regulars in the service, in its only known game of the season, Bemidji, with Alexander John "Rube" Schauer on the mound, shut down Red Lake, 1–0. After working on ships in Duluth in '18, Schauer resumed his pro career with Minneapolis in '19.[25]

The idea of hiring major leaguers as semi-pros in shipbuilding seems to have been hatched the previous winter, with the blessings of industrialist

Charles Schwab, who later took charge of the Emergency Fleet Corporation, which controlled all American ship construction. When "Shoeless Joe" Jackson took an industrial job, knowing the Greenville, South Carolina draft board was about to send him into the army despite his several dependents, Comiskey said he would ban him from baseball. Jackson said he was through with the majors and would build ships. When Jackson, pitcher Claude Williams, centerfielder Oscar Felsch and a backup catcher took shipbuilding jobs, the "Old Roman" tore up their contracts.

The Reading Steel Casting Co., in the only city in the state allowed to play on the Sabbath, winning 17 of 19, overcame Harlan, 6–5, in 10 innings for a title. In late September '18 it had pitchers Williams and Babe Ruth as well as Rogers Hornsby and Joe Jackson. Such "hippodrome amusement" seemed not to qualify as "arduous military work," a critic thought. The national game was losing respect as a "national tonic" and prominent players were revealed as "timid, shirking, self-protective and slacking."[26]

Not all who played in these leagues did so to avoid military duty. In the six-team Steel League playoff, Joe McCarthy, recently with the Louisville Colonels (suspending in late July) and exempted from the draft due to dependents, tripled in the tenth (batting about .100 overall), for Steelton. Game receipts went to the Soldiers' Tobacco Fund. Some quit when another company stopped paying a baseball bonus, but "four patriots" received praise by continuing to play.[27]

Reporters mistakenly assigned pros to these places. A Yankee supposedly went to a steel plant in Maryland but ended up in the army assigned to a training battalion in Kentucky. George Sisler, a young talent from the Browns, was said to have signed with a shipyard but became a second lieutenant, representing Camp Humphreys at a track meet. He was about to head to France to join Branch Rickey, Ty Cobb and Christy Mathewson in chemical warfare, when the armistice ended the fighting.[28]

Two thousand Philadelphians steel workers walked off because several Mack Men, including outfielder Rube Oldring, wore fancy duds and drove to the yard in fancier cars. An inquiry blamed the strike on labor agitators. None were foremen and all did the same work as anyone else. Some rode to work in Oldring's "flivver" because they lived five miles from the yard on a route not well served by trolleys. One of them, waking at 4 a.m., took two trolleys to reach Oldring's house. Another former Mack Man claimed they were "doing more for their country," toiling with no let up and facing dangerous conditions than those "near the old homestead." Munitions plant managers wanted those physically fit and were paying up to $200 a month. They could only play outside work hours.[29]

Another commentator agreed a few players and agents who enticed them deserved "shafts of hostile criticism," but Chief Bender and Hans

Lobert, experienced machinists, worked on holidays and Sundays, the latter required to play at times. Neither Lobert nor Bender were at a playoff, working on ships that Saturday afternoon. Other writers thought such entertainment somehow built ships faster.[30]

The vice-president of the Emergency Fleet Corporation predicted the same situation would not exist the next year, which turned out to be the case because the fighting in France ended. Major league owners complained about plant managers persuading players to break existing contracts. It was almost as if a new Federal League might be in play. Reporters figured owners would crack down in negotiating contracts.[31]

Other "shop" teams, with impressive fields if photos are any indication, played colleges, military squads and other businesses. A Massachusetts firm (23–14–1) lost to a college but beat a fort and Camp Devens. A Worcester company had a 45-year-old catcher whose major league career spanned the first decade of the century and a lineup sprinkled with refugees from the N. England League. A dry dock company in Baltimore, where amateurs predominated, save for Joe Judge, just starting his career with the Senators, won 37 and barely lost to Babe Ruth's All-Stars at Oriole Park in the fall. Ruth had a deferment but also joined the Mass Home Guard.[32]

In New Mexico, Copper League clubs gave several former minor leaguers bonuses, but they had to work eight hours a day, with the weekends off. Fort Bayard, the fourth member of the league, sans a permanent lineup and fewer pros, were the weakest.[33]

After yielding but one run in the decisive game for the Red Sox in the World Series, Carl Mays went to Washington University (St. Louis), getting up at 5:30 a.m., peeling potatoes and washing dishes for over 400 military in vocational training, finishing at 7:30 p.m., for $1 a day. "With the Red Sox I pitched one game in four days, two hours' work and I received nearly enough to pay off this entire unit." He agreed with Sherman that "war was hell."[34]

In the year following the end of the fighting in France, Johnson caused a court case when he sought to stop the sale of Mays to the Yankees. The owners cut the normal schedule by fourteen games. The eventual pennant winners—the Cincinnati Reds and the Chicago White Sox resumed the October classic, the Reds winning in eight games. The betting-bribing scandal, suspected at the time but rejected as impossible by Comiskey, did not fully come to light until 1920. Dave Fultz, returning from France, became the president of the International League as the minors and majors squabbled about their relationship. Only 16 minor leagues now belonged to organized pro ball compared to 26 in '16. Two associations disbanded, in '19, suggesting that post-war problems affected the minors. The Armistice in November did not mean that pro ball would revert to pre-war conditions come the next spring, even though many hoped the players would be back by Christmas or at the latest by spring training. A general encouraged Ban Johnson to think that most stars would be sent back early, but several did not make it back for spring training.[35]

How did the public react to steel leagues refugees? Writing from Camp Gordon, Major von Kolnitz of the White Sox pointed out that "the Shoeless One" had a failed investment and his mother, wife and two children depended on him. Besides, "patriotic Americans" worked in the yards. A Chicago waiter said he would "holler my head off at him… He quit 'em last summer, didn't he?" A restaurant manager asked "why shouldn't he play for 'em? He worked in a shipyard, didn't he, just to earn enough money to support his wife and parents? Didn't thousands do the same?" Owner Comiskey, considering their behavior a betrayal at the time, said he wanted them "out of organized baseball forever." By February, as spring training loomed, the three stars and Comiskey reconciled—more or less, but Comiskey got his earlier wish (no longer wanted) when they were among the eight banned from baseball because of the betting/bribery scandal in the 1919 World Series.[36]

Griffith reported that fans donated $148,969.92 but he only spent a little over $95,000 purchasing and sending some 3,100 sets of equipment, each one of which included a catcher's mitt, mask, chest protector, first basemen's mitt, base bags, along with a dozen balls, bats, etc., plus $2,000 worth of boxing gloves, ending up with $1,059.02. The failing of the bank where he put the money caused the discrepancy.[37]

Gowdy was not happy when his division, one of the first to arrive in France, remained in Europe, part of the Army of Occupation. He not only did not make it back for spring training, but he also lost about a month of the season, finally appearing in Boston, where the mayor and president of the league honored him, in response to which "Hammering Hank" said, "Holy cow!! This is great!"[38]

2

College Baseball

As Congress discussed declaring war in early April 1917, delegates from prestigious Northeast colleges planned to shut down athletics. Harvard had already cancelled its schedule until the end of the war, but President Wilson and Secretary of War Newton Baker urged the retention of sports to develop "iron muscles" for hand-to-hand fighting. Major General Wood told collegians "stick to their present duties until "the government calls for men." A Naval Academy official advised copying West Point and carry out athletic schedules unless the War Department ordered otherwise. The current "agitation" was "well meant but misdirected enthusiasm."[1]

After the war, a contributor to the California yearbook chided several prestigious schools for consigning "intercollegiate athletics to the limbo of the past," but the administration at Berkeley, being "saner and more farsighted" sustained and encouraged sports after the declaration of war.[2]

In August, 1917 an official at Indiana University approved recent decisions in Minnesota and Wisconsin to re-instate intercollegiate activity. The Hosier also agreed with Princeton prof Joseph Raycroft, who thought athletics helped physical growth, encouraged self-subordination and promoted co-operation, all qualities needed in warfare.[3]

Yale, so-so in '16, after announcing it would end the program while on its southern excursion in '17, split with Harvard, playing less than half the usual. Although losing to Navy, the '18 Eli overcame four others, along with a 4–0 record against the other two of the "Big Three" (Harvard, Princeton and Yale). In '17, Trinity (Hartford) cut out all except games on Saturday so as not to interrupt military drills, losing all. In '18, the Blue & Gold managed one game—with Wesleyan, a 5–17 loss.[4]

The four-team Maine State League kept two contests against the other three and plugged in military teams to replace foes like Harvard. Bowdoin claimed the '17 title (the War Department delayed calling up several potential officers), replaying and again winning an apparent earlier victory when they used an ineligible pitcher. The captain/ catcher of '16 perished in a plane accident in France. The '17's sophomore right fielder died in an airplane accident near Pensacola. Colby took the championship in '18 and Maine occupied first in '19 as it had in '16. Even with many in the military, all four competed through the war. Bowdoin won over naval reservists twice in '18.[5]

St. Anselm's, a student noting that not playing ran against the wishes of the military, claimed the New Hampshire title in '17 (Dartmouth and New Hampshire State not participating). The school played about half the usual twenty games, under Manchester policeman John "Phenom" Smith, an ex–major leaguer, most well-known for developing Christy Mathewson. The Blue & White increased play in '18, repeating as state champion with a win over Dartmouth. New Hampshire State did not play in either '17 or '18.[6]

Playing at least 15 in '17, the '18 Brown University faced two military nines as part of a smaller schedule. R.I. State, which lost thrice and ended '17, tried to revive in '18 but could not. The Mass Aggies axed '17 after a win over R.I., reported themselves "missing" in '18, returning "to active duty" in '19. A student blamed William Hohenzollern (the Kaiser) for the disruption, branding him an "also-ran" who "ducked for the showers" when the going got tough.[7]

In '18, Harvard lost all seven to the military and two to Yale. Although losing to Penn before 8,000 in '17, Holy Cross increased the number played and the percentage won, reaching a 22–1 in '19, possibly the nation's best. Tufts, 20–2 in '16, did the opposite, reducing the number played and gradually lowering the percentage won, falling to 3–4 in '19. In '17, Amherst fell just shy of matching '16, reducing more in '18. Amherst and Williams, the two that started intercollegiate baseball in 1859, split two in each season in the four-year span. Williams got in 16 in '17, but in May '18, 100 ROTC went to Plattsburg, ending the season after the Amherst game.[8]

Princeton, 13–9 in '16, canceled soon after its start in '17 as half of its 1,600 students volunteered. Rutgers cut back in '17 and had a few more in '18, a still greater number in '19, almost as many as in '16. Seton Hall did a little better in ten games or less for all seasons. Stevens 6–4 in '16 and 2–5 in '17 before giving up due to a lack of interest, improved in '18, the post-war above .500 in 11.[9]

Columbia, possibly the nation's best in '16, played twice in '17, a few more in '18, losing more than winning, hinting that top players were in the service. Colgate, 8–7 in '16, ended '17 after losing to West Point as athletes went into the service. In '18, Colgate lost nearly every game, some after commencement. Fordham, so-so in 13 in '16 split six, nine canceling in '17. In '18, they were 9–6, against colleges in 28 contests. With returning servicemen, the '19 Rams, 14–6 against collegians, beat Holy Cross (its only loss) and a battleship. Future Hall of Famer, infielder Frankie Frisch, the

BASEBALL TEAM

Standing:—Fr. Brock, Halloran, McNamara, Sweetland, Donovan, Buckley, Frisch, McLaughlin, Devlin, Coach, McMahon, Mgr. *Kneeling left to right:*—Lefevre, Gleason, Eustace, Keough, Finn, Cap

Fordham Baseball Squad, 1919. Frankie Frisch (standing fourth from right) missed the two previous springs, probably for military service. He did play varsity football in those years. *Courtesy Fordham University Archives.*

"Fordham Flash," did not play baseball in '17 or '18, presumably in military service.

Cornell, 13–9 in '16, canceled early in '17, ran one over .500 in 11 in '18, about the same in '19, a win over Penn before 7,000 the high point. Syracuse, 19–3, in '16, won over Navy in '17, others canceling. Few scores show up for '18, more lost than won in '19. St. Lawrence, 4–3 in '16, shut down in '17, their coach in France on hospital duty. With no experienced players, they managed about .500 in a few in '18. The '19 season was even thinner, losing to Fort Ontario (Oswego) home and away. Union College, 7–4 in '16 ran about the same in '17, losing to Vermont but easing by the Catamounts after the latter sent four to the service. In '18, 5–6 against colleges, Union lost twice to Pelham Bay Naval Training.[10]

West Point, a 10–8 in '16, recorded eight games in '17. In '18, coached by Hans Lobert (ex-Phillie third sacker), with Elmer Oliphant starring in occasional playing, Army went 10–5 against collegians and 4–2 against the military, including one over the Jack Tars who tended the submarine nets protecting N.Y. City. In '19, the Naval Academy allowed Army to use students who graduated well before June and went to war in '18. They returned to fill in their coursework in '19. Despite the re-enforcements, Navy won.[11]

A writer emphasizing the negative described '17 as "one of the most disappointing" seasons ever as major universities canceled or curtailed schedules. Pennsylvania, retaining competition, exhibited at least as much patriotism as did those who quit. Had it not been "for the efforts of the red and blue" there might not have been much to record. Praised for staying the course, Pennsylvania, after a weak '16 and 8–4, with J. Howard Berry in the infield in '17, slumped in both '18 and '19.[12]

Haverford, with intercollegiate baseball recently started, suffered from the war. The only college to field a cricket eleven routinely, the Quakers played nearby country clubs. After a Southern trip in '17 (0–9), they suspended baseball right after the war declaration, resuming with a brief schedule for '18 (0–4). The Scarlet & Black managed one win out of seven recorded in '19. Cricket lost most all that season, when its captain elect went to France with Friends Reconstruction, a humanitarian organization that, among other activities, built temporary shelters for the French. The team picked another captain coming back from France from the same work.[13]

Penn State in '17 played 18 (7 cancelled). The Blue & White ran above .500 in a dozen in '19. Pittsburgh in '17, won most except when the Panthers sustained a 0–28 loss when two pitchers became ineligible for playing on another team. That is the last heard about Pitt baseball until 1920. Lehigh, 18–5 in '16 and 19–5 in '17, canceled trips in '18 and cut back to eight encounters, doubling that in '19, mostly wins.

Swarthmore, which ran 10–6, including one over Michigan in '16 canceled those against Michigan and Stanford in '17. The next two seasons came in with about half the usual number, mostly wins. Susquehanna, 1–10 against colleges in '16, "suffered" in '17 and '18, the post-war year a bit better. Villanova, which won most in a brief '17, split with two large military camps. Washington & Jefferson came in a bit above .500 in '16, well below that in '17, while they made "the world safe for democracy." A '19 "irregular varsity," 0–3 versus colleges, followed a "death knell" in '18. Thiel College found it hard to keep the game even without a war because seasons usually only had a month of baseball weather.[14]

Among Pennsylvania's normal schools, Bloomsburg, which in '16 outscored seminaries and a few colleges, lost to two other normal schools in '17. The '18 clobbered the same twice, nothing reported for '19. Indiana Normal, with a complete '17, overcame a small college twice. A full '18 showed wins over two small colleges and a split with another, but like at Bloomsburg, nothing surfaced for '19. It is likely that many went into the service in the summer of '18 and did not make it back to campus for '19.

Carlisle Institute did not play much in '16 or '17; in '18, in its last year (closed as the buildings housed convalescing soldiers) it had a handful of wins and losses. Muhlenberg, which had no program in years, drew up a schedule for '17, only to have its trustees stop athletics and start military drilling.[15]

In D.C., historically black Howard University had scores only for '16, mostly wins. Catholic and Georgetown in '17 stopped in April, the latter's athletes joining a local amateur club. Gallaudet carried on a bit longer. Georgetown in '18 (a former star falling from a plane at Pensacola), won most except two to the Naval Academy. A 15-3 in '19 challenged as the best in the S. Atlantic.[16]

Maryland State, which lost a lot in '16 and canceled 11 in '17 (1-5 versus colleges), won over a radio school and an army signal team in '18, its one win in seven versus colleges coming against St. John's, whom they had not beaten in five years. The '19 Farmers won 14 of 17, vying with Georgetown as the best in the South Atlantic. The cadets at St. John's (Annapolis), taking two over Maryland in '16, lost two to Washington College, which won the state title. The Naval Academy, which did not compete for state or S. Atlantic titles in any sport, went 16-8 in '16 and lost 2 of 3 before canceling '17. The '18 Midshipmen lost only a couple of a baker's dozen. A win against Army in '19 made up for the loss against West Point in '16, the last time they played each other.

Winners of the Eastern Virginia Intercollegiate Conference in '16, William and Mary's varsity scattered into the military, with three losses in league play in '17, the same in '18, regaining the crown in '19. Richmond College, after disbanding, had a successful '17, repeating as champion in '18. With five of 11 lettermen leaving Randolph-Macon (two for aviation), the Jackets lost to Richmond before forfeiting in '17, 1-5 in conference in '18, similar in '19.

Roanoke College, in '17, won over Haverford and two Virginia small colleges and lost three to Virginia Tech. The coach went to Camp Lee in '18. Bridgewater, after re-instating the sport in '16, ran a 1-7 in '17, playing one college. The war taking so many players in '18 it plowed up the ball field and planted crops.[17]

VMI lost several in '17, the trend continuing in '18. Virginia's Cavaliers in '17 stopped on 12 April, following an extra-inning loss to UNC at Greensboro before some 6,000 as players headed to Fort Myer for officer reserve training. The Cavaliers resumed, at 7-3, in '18. Virginia Tech, possibly 16-8 in '16 and 9-1-1 in '17, scheduled 28 in '18, but went 8-4. Washington and Lee, which split four in '17 and had a "year of inactivity" due to "the late unpleasantness" in '18, won 11 of 12 in '19, losing only to Maryland State. Three of five historically black colleges have scores for the war years. Two others likely had teams. Limited coverage indicates that Virginia Union University won the most.[18]

2. College Baseball

Among colleges for blacks in North Carolina, Bennett College (Greensboro) likely won the state's Intercollegiate Athletic Association in '16. Biddle University (Johnson C. Smith) likely prevailed in at least one war-year. N.C. A&T (Greensboro) won 9 of 10 on a trip into eastern Carolina in '17 before the war declaration, losing the lone college encounter to Shaw at Raleigh in 14 innings.

The Wildcats at Davidson, 16–4 in '16, best in the state, fell off a bit but remained competitive. Guilford College, 10–0 overall in '17 won the state title (5–0). The Quakers claimed the same the next year, a 12–2, though losing a close one to UNC. In one win, after a scoreless tie for 16 innings, rain ended the affair just after N.C. State scored twice in the first half of the 7th to take the lead by a run. State split with Trinity and Wake Forest in '17 and '18 running about .500 over twenty games against collegians in '19. UNC, below .500 in 18 games in '16, did about the same in '17. The title evaded these Tar Heels in '18 even though they won over Guilford and Elon because the two were the only N.C. teams encountered, too few to merit a state title. The Trinity (Duke) schedule dropped a bit in '17, even though not very ambitious in '16, .500 or just below both years, slightly improved for '18. The post-war schedule and wins ballooned, losing a playoff to UNC, the first time the two played each other in over twenty years. A Trinity reporter gave UNC the state title. Wake Forest, so-so in '17 and '18, also claimed the '19 title, defeating UNC and splitting with N.C. State and Trinity.[19]

In West Virginia, Bethany College, which lost most of fewer games in '17 and '18, hoped for a positive result in '19 only to cancel the season when all 250 students walked out when the administration expelled over fifty men who refused to join the ROTC. During the war, those who argued for all male collegians being required to have military training usually won the college debates. Now in the spring of '19 patriotic service seemed less a necessity, though Secretary of War Baker favored the idea.[20]

In '16, Marshall, slightly better in state than either West Virginia University or West Virginia Wesleyan, fell twice to West Virginia in '17, when Wesleyan claimed the state with two over West Virginia University. In '18, the university claimed the state, 14–4, overall, many against Northeastern nines. In '19, Marshall beat the alumni of Morris-Harvey and other obscure opponents, losing twice to Wesleyan, which had no losses in state. The university at Morgantown had no state competition that year, 8–2 versus schools elsewhere. Fairmont State Normal (4–3) ended '17 prematurely when the "back to the farm" movement put "the quietus upon all sports."[21]

The Colonels of Kentucky State played about a dozen in '16, 7 in '17, 9 in '18, and 13 in '19, the middle two over .500. A normal school that upset Transylvania in '16, had the impression that the losers won the Kentucky State Association title, but Centre and Kentucky State could have triple-tied with Transylvania. In '19, Kentucky and Centre probably tied for state honors.

Tennessee, with over thirty institutions, at least 21 with intercollegiate baseball, had the University of the South (Sewanee), which cut its schedule in '16 because of fever in Alabama, played once in '17, split with Vanderbilt in '18, with nothing detected for '19. The University of Tennessee split with Kentucky in '16, lost to the Colonels in '17, split in '18 and lost to them twice in '19. The Volunteers also yielded to Maryville College in 11 innings in '17. Nothing shows up for Vanderbilt for '17; in '18 the Commodores overwhelmed a normal school, losing 4 of 5 others. A brief '19 barely broke .500. Maryville, with no membership in any conference and whose players may have earned money in summer ball, were 8–6 in '16 and 5–6 in '17, losing twice to Lincoln Memorial. In '18, going 9–10–1 overall, they lost 3 of 4 to Lincoln, which ran 14-straight in '17. In '18, "like woods on fire," the Rail Splitters lost only two, one to Maryville in 14 innings, the schedule roughly the same as in '17. Tusculum, at 14–7 against colleges in '16, saw far less action the next three years.[22]

After a 14–4 at one point in '16, Auburn, the likely Southern champ in '17, ceased in early May. In '18, the Plainsmen, possibly second in the South, tied Mercer for first in the Quadrangular League (3 Georgia colleges and Auburn). A pitcher in '16, Marcus Milligan, using an alias, helped Portsmouth (Virginia League) in '16 and '17 and in '18 perished in an accident at a Texas army airfield. Alabama ranked first in the Southern Intercollegiate in both '18 and '19.

Millsaps led other Mississippi colleges in '16. Miss A&M (State), 13–3–2 in '17 (5–0 in state), placed high in Southern standings. Ole Miss, losing three to State in '17, had the best record in the state in '18. Losing 3 of 4 against State in '19 likely again reversed the championship.

Georgia Tech split 16 in '17, about the same the next year in 18 (6–6 in the Quadrangular whose four colleges played four times against the other three). Mercer, which won a couple over Northerners before the war declaration, won about a half dozen after that in '17 against top Southern nines, achieving roughly the same in '18 and '19. The Baptists, tying for first with Auburn (7–5) in '18 in the Quadrangular, canceled with Floridians for "military reasons." The university at Gainesville suffered a "painless death" in '18, apparently the same condition at other Sunshine State schools.[23]

Oglethorpe, which lost thrice to Palmer College "pros" in '17, ran about .500 in '18, dropping 3 of 4 to Clemson (one at Ponce de Leon Park in Atlanta). With future major league outfielder Absalom H. "Red" Wingo on the mound, they took 2 of 3 from North Georgia Agricultural College), which was probably 7–3 in '17 and came out of its "cave" in '19. The University of Georgia claimed a high rating when they took 3 of 4 from Georgia Tech at season's end in '17 and won over Auburn and four times over Tech in '19.[24]

Clemson's Tigers, after losing more than half in '16 in well over twenty contests, had about the same number in '17, with a winning record. A smaller number in '18 possibly clinched the state. The Newberry newspaper gave the '17 title to its Indians, noting six wins (.750) was better than Presbyterian's .714. Furman's Purple & White Hornets, strong in '16, with fewer wins in '17 and '18, made 23 errors in two games in '19 but ended up above .500. The Presbyterian Blue Stockings sat out '18 and fell short in '19. Wofford's Terriers vied with Furman for first in the state in '19. South Carolina, a bit over .500 in over twenty in '16, reduced in '17, losing to Newberry and 3 of 4 to Clemson. Erskine College Seceders, named for an 18th century split among Presbyterians in Scotland, won most of their recorded scores for '16 and lost most in '17, running about .500 in '18 and '19. The Citadel, following a respectable '16, canceled most in '17 and lost several to the military and the one college encounter in '18. Still reeling under the "ravages of war," the Cadets in '19 lost to Naval Training and five colleges. Recovery in 1920 brought a state title. The '17 College of Charleston fell to the Navy Yard and two colleges; the '18 lost to a receivership and a training camp; '19 won even fewer.[25]

Southwest Louisiana in Lafayette won the state's small-college title in '16 and '17, few scores surfacing in '18 or '19. Lacking a stadium in '18, Tulane won against a manual training school and Spring Hill. By '19, the Greenbacks had a more normal agenda, yielding 2 of 3 to LSU, splitting four against Spring Hill. Louisiana State, winning about half in over twenty in '16, had fewer games in '17, '18 "somewhat disappointing," 19 slightly better.[26]

In Arkansas, Ouachita Baptist, 12–8 in '16, claimed two titles in '19. Hendrix College did not contest the state but disputed the association title, noting their split with the Baptists, and a record in conference about the same as Ouachita's. In '18, Hendrix ran 14–2–1, so the Bulldogs were likely the champions of both leagues. The university at Fayetteville went intramural during the war.

Okla. A&M, which lost 2 of 3 to the Indians at Chilocco Institute before war "swallowed all athletic possibilities" in '17, split with Phillips University and lost several to Okla. and the Indians in '18 and four to the Natives in '19. The Okla. Sooners lost to the Indian school in '16, 2 of 3 to the Natives in '18 plus all four to Phillips. Had Chilocco athletes, with what looked like swastikas on their uniforms, been in a league with the state's major colleges, they would likely have been champions.[27]

In the Lone Star State in '17, Rice Institute lost two close ones to Texas and canceled on 1 May. Baylor canceled on 20 April '17, the Bears 1–7 in '18. The Longhorns, a perennial power, won three state titles (numbers 5–7), rising to 20–1 against colleges in '19, dividing two with Kelly Airfield. Texas State Normal, at Commerce, 9–5–1 in '17, the year it became a public college, with many in officer training, curtailed '18 after a loss to Texas Christian.

Michigan State got in at least eleven in '17, before "confusion" brought cancelations. Michigan, which axed '17, won the Western Conference (Big 10 which it recently rejoined), at 9-1, in '18. Kalamazoo College, which posted little for '16, nothing for '17 and lost more than it won in '18, carried 12 of 13 in '19 for the Michigan Intercollegiate Athletic Association title.

Minnesota was the only Western Conference university not playing inter-collegiately during this era. Carleton (Northfield) headed toward a strong showing in '18 and St. Thomas (St. Paul) won most in '17 and '18, several leaving for Camp Dodge. In '17, the war took away the "more adventurous" at St. John's College. St. Olaf's had six experienced at the start of '18, but eleven signed up for the military, 2-7 the result. Winona Normal, inter-collegiate for the first time in '18, with but few men, lost the only one played against a college.[28]

The commissioners that oversaw Wisconsin college athletics ended sports in May '17 but then changed their minds. The main university, after compiling 25 in '16 and winning over four small colleges, losing to Notre Dame, in '17, canceled the Big 9 schedule. The '18 Badgers lost to Notre Dame twice, winning over three small schools, 1-6 in the Big 10. La Crosse Normal canceled baseball even after winning all in '16 in a small schedule. Track was becoming more popular and the lack of talent contributed to a lack of interest. Only River Falls Normal seems to have been a big proponent of the national game among small colleges in Wisconsin.

Chicago went 5-4 in the Big 9 (5-2 against small colleges plus two over Japanese collegians) in '16. In '17, the Maroons, with only one small college opponent, split ten against teams backed by banks and other businesses. The Conference record slipped to 2-8. In '18, the Maroons did better in a briefer schedule. In '19, Chicago was the only one to come close to undefeated Michigan (about breaking even in the Big 10), winning over a Great Lakes nine and a small college.

Northwestern, 1-8 in Conference in '16 and 4-4 in '17, when Paddy Driscoll hit a homer and a triple to down Purdue, had little for the next three years. After winning the title in '16., the '17 Illini, 2-4 on a 2,500-mile "jaunt" in the South, placed second in the conference. They also toured the South in '18, unlike most other northern nines (again second in the Conference) and repeated the same standing for a third time in '19. In '17, versatile George Halas was one of two "shining lights."[29]

In the Little 19 Conference (Illinois), Wesleyan had a standout '16, 9-0-1. In '17, with no experienced players, most becoming soldiers or farmers, they went 0-6. At McKendree the national game "never had the popularity and support" enjoyed by basketball. Only a couple of colleges made it

The "Shining Light," George Halas, outfielder for the University of Illinois, 1917, a star in three sports. *Courtesy University of Illinois Archives.*

to season's end in '17 amid "wholesale cancellations." Augustana won a few before several left to farm. Bradley Institute (Peoria) put baseball "into the background" in '18, military drilling taking three hours a day. In the Little 5, Monmouth, which played few in '17 and possibly a 4–2 in '18, claimed (unconfirmed) the title over Knox when Lake Forest, Lombard and Beloit suspended until after the war.[30]

Indiana University had about as many results in '17 as in '16, improving to 5–4 in Conference in '17, nothing for '18. A Purdue coach directed athletics at Camp Taylor and the best pitcher joined the aviation corps in '17. The Boilermakers, 7–5 in Conference in '16, fell to 3–5 in '17 and 1–5 in '18. Notre Dame, not a member of the Conference, after winning well over half in '16, 7–5 in '17, about the same in '18, jumped to 10–4 in '19, improving against Western Conference foes.

DePauw played through the war, 11 in '17, the same as in '16, 13 in '18, losing most encounters with Wabash, which was likely the best among small colleges in '16. Wabash also dominated Franklin for the war years. Franklin revived in '19 but lost to State Normal, which claimed the overall title when Wabash failed to schedule the teachers at Terre Haute. One who played three different positions for Franklin in '16 as well as in the line for football died in France leading a raid.[31]

In Ohio, war "shoved baseball" aside in '18 at Kenyon. Ohio Wesleyan played a full slate in '18, losing three to Ohio State (two close). Miami University, which split six before ceasing in '17, got in four before the "war jinx" took over in '18. Ohio State, 4–2 in '16 in the Western Conference for second place, won the title at 6–1 in '17, third in '18. Ohio State ruled over smaller Ohio Colleges, 6–0 in '17 and 5–0 in '18, with possibly one loss in both '16 and '19 out of a number that was not much greater than during the war.[32]

Iowa's Simpson College, 3–4 in '16, lost several in '17 before eight players left to farm, the Red & Gold eventually losing almost every experienced player to the service. With "serious war conditions" prevailing in '18, Iowa colleges "abandoned baseball." In '16, Coe College, 2–5, yielded twice to Highland Park, supposed state small college champ, a questionable issue. The Patriots lost to Cornell in '16 and twice to the same in '17, but they took 2 of 3 in '18. Coe won all three over Cornell in '19, not relegating baseball "to the past" like at other state schools. In '16, Cornell College lost 1–0 to Highland Park, which may have used a Central Association pitcher, but subdued Chicago and split with Iowa and later overcame Highland Park.[33]

Dubuque College (Loras College), for whom Urban "Red" Faber pitched in '09, ran 8–4 against colleges in '16. The Purple & Gold avenged a loss to Highland Park in '17, part of a 6–4. Only one college result showed up for '18. St. Ambrose (Davenport) ran 6–5 collegiately (5–1 with others) in '16, 6–2 against colleges in '17 (3–1 others). In '18, they lost to St. Viator's but upset Notre Dame, competing for the Midwest Catholic title, also winning over infantrymen. After a so-so '16, Grinnell canceled when the military took all starters, plus the coach who went to Fort Snelling, closing the program through '19.[34]

Morningside (Sioux City), which got by several South Dakota and Minnesota nines in '16, claimed the Iowa title in '17. The lack of a field prevented home games in '18 and '19, though they still won against state clubs. Iowa Wesleyan (Mt. Pleasant), winner of few in '16, gave up "temporarily" in '17 as players prepared to be army officers. In May '18, they got in one game.[35]

Iowa University, 3–5 in '17 and 2–3 in '18 in the Western Conference, did not reduce the 16-game schedule, adding Notre Dame in '18 with whom they split. They also usually beat small colleges and split with Iowa State, which ran 0–4 in the Missouri Valley in May '17, just before play ceased. Ames, in '18, when the conference numbered but three, lost six to Missouri, downing Kansas twice.

Kansas had eight veterans to start '17. The Jayhawkers who cut back during the decline in the Missouri Valley in '18 and '19 hoped to revive in '20. In '17, Kansas State, even though only losing one key player—to Fort Riley—played but half the schedule, losing to Missouri twice. A full-range appeared for '19 amid concerns about the lack of baseball in valley schools.[36]

St. Mary's, a Jesuit school near Topeka, claimed seven straight Kansas small college titles in this era. Due to "unsettled conditions" in '18, Bethel took on mostly high schools and turned to track in '19. Fairmount College (Wichita State), around .500 in a small '16 schedule, "found hard rowing" in '17. Students lacked interest at Ottawa, few paying to watch a low quality of play, as chief rivals withdrew. Despite the negatives, a sufficient number tried out, so Ottawa went ahead with the '17 nine-game schedule only to have war declared, and with two more colleges withdrawing and several players going to Fort Riley and others into farming, it canceled the rest after losses to St. Mary's and Haskell. Nothing surfaced for '18, '19 or even in the 1920s. In February '17, following a mediocre previous spring, students at Kansas Wesleyan voted not to have baseball, focusing on track instead. At least a half dozen Kansas schools that became junior colleges after the war developed football and basketball but not baseball.[37]

The Missouri Tigers ended '17, 9–1 in conference, Valley titlist like the year before. The '18 season ended after Missouri (9–2) oozed one out in the mud, so far ahead of Kansas and Kansas State (the only other two left in the Missouri Conference) that officials called off the rest. The Tigers did not field a team in '19, possibly caused by a three-term system replacing the two-semester model. William Jewell started '17 with a pitcher striking out 23, then the Cardinals forfeited two to Tarkio. No state small-college title appeared because of the loss of participants. Warrensburg (Central Missouri State), with few in '16 did away with '17. Girardeau Normal (Southeast Missouri State) lost three pitchers and their catcher to the service, 5–2 in '17 (4–3 in '16), "adverse circumstances" forcing a re-organization in '18. Someone remembered President Wilson calling athletics a "contribution to the national defense."[38]

Nebraska tried to revive its program during the war, after ceasing six years earlier when the conference banned athletes from playing in any summer leagues. Now with the rule rescinded, the Cornhuskers lost a couple and a cold rain canceled two against Creighton, ending '18 for both. After a supposed nine-year lapse as "as baseball fever" swept the land in 1920, the Cornhuskers took to the field.[39]

Arizona University, winners over the New Mexico Aggies twice in '17, regretted not playing Chinese University (Honolulu) as in '16. One wonders whether they knew these Hawaiians did not represent an educational institution. In '18, the Wildcats yielded to Tempe Normal, champs of the Salt River Valley, getting the better of Tempe thrice in '19 along with a loss to some cavalry. In New Mexico, the Aggies (Las Cruces), after splitting with the university at Albuquerque and overcoming the School of Mines in '16 (losses with Arizona), ceased until well into May '19. The university, winners over an Indian institute in '16, lost to a business college, the Chicago Cubs and the mining school, overcoming a railroad nine, in '17.

The Denver daily gave the university at Boulder the state title in '17. Sacred Heart (Regis) punished the university, Colorado College and the Teachers in '18, suggesting the prep school suffered less from the war. In '18, Denver University took two each from Colorado College and the State Teachers, splitting with Colorado and the Ore Diggers (School of Mines), giving the Ministers the Rocky Mountain title, even though they never played Montana or Utah. Colorado institutions had brief schedules even with no war, only Colorado University recording even ten games a season.

Idaho University, which won most of 16 in '16 (5 over Montana), losing four to Washington State, dropped off a bit in '17 in the Eastern part of the Northwest Conference. After a win or two in '18, students exhibited little concern in '19, when they had three lopsided losses and were no longer in the Northwest Conference. War was not helpful to these Vandals.

Montana played all these seasons, losing to Washington State twice in '17. The next year, the Grizzlies lost to Washington State thrice but also inflicted the latter's only loss. In '19, they split with Washington State (two canceled by the flu) and defeated Montana State four times. Nevada had a couple lettering in baseball but no scores. Wyoming didn't put a nine on the field until 1920, although it considered starting one in '17.

At the university at Salt Lake City, with a thin schedule in '16, "patriotic sentiments paralyzed" all athletics in '17, but in '18 the Crimson won a state title, splitting with the Utah Aggies and bettering Brigham Young University twice. The outfield in '19 had two Romneys.[40]

2. College Baseball

The Dakotas got by—barely. After winning 5 of 6 in '16, splitting with the Aggies, the Flickertails of North Dakota have no scores. Sharing the state title in '16, the Aggies in '19 were "informal." After 3–4 in '16 and 0–2 in '17, Jamestown College, considered turning "away from childish games," but continued, with few scores. Dakota State Normal (Ellendale) played in '17 but calls to military service ended '18. Valley City Normal, maybe the best among normal schools, played only local nines after the war. South Dakota, 3–4 in '16, had nothing for three years. Northern Normal (Aberdeen) split two each with Ellendale Normal and Jamestown in '17, amid a "gradual decline of interest." Dakota Wesleyan (Mitchell), running against the trend, probably went 10–0 (few colleges) in '19.[41]

Stanford and California (Berkeley) usually had full schedules, playing athletic clubs (some semi-pro), only a few against collegians. Cal did about the same in '17 as '16, most played before the war. In '18 the Bears won 3 of 4, thus not necessitating a fifth against Stanford. After subduing Stanford twice in '17, Santa Clara split with the Cardinals in '18, downed some infantry and sailors from Mare Island, losing to a sanitary train. In '19, in addition to a close loss to Cal, the Catholic school took 2 of 3 from Stanford, splitting with Mare Island. In '18, Stanford won over officers, a field hospital, a sanitary train and infantry, all located at Camp Fremont next to the campus, losing 3 of 4 against Cal, the season ending in early April, all sports suspended.[42]

At USC, the Law School produced the only intercollegiate club, losing twice to Cal and Stanford, even to a high school. The coach moaned about the bad field and the lack of student support. In '17, the lawyers overcame a small college, split with Cal and lost to Stanford. The president of the law school said the decline from 650 in '17 to 150 students in '19 compelled his institution to "forego all athletics." Even so, a supposedly non-existing nine split with UCLA.[43]

Washington State overcame Montana in 3 of 5, Idaho in 4 and Whitman in 2, claiming the Northwest Intercollegiate Conference '16 title. State won all six in that conference in '17. Among the 107 athletes who joined the service by February '18, 15 played baseball. Yet that spring, State again dominated the Northwest. The post-war brought the Cougar Crimson & Gray into the Pacific Coast Conference, where a 1–5 put them just above Oregon. In '16 Washington ran below .500 in its first year in the Pacific Coast Conference, rising to first the next season. After a blank in '18, the undefeated Seattle school won the Coast title in '19, when Californians would not come north.[44]

Oregon lost seven to the Spokane Indians (pros) and a couple to the University of Washington for '17, taking 6 of 8 from the Oregon Aggies in '18 for second in the Western Division of the Northwest Conference. The

Aggies "abandoned" '17 and ran a Conference 2–6 in '18. In '19, the Orange and Black placed second in the conference (4 losses to Washington). In '16, Willamette University claimed a state small college title. Thirty-eight athletes joined the initial wave (mostly the National Guard), eight from baseball, the season kept alive by whipping the Oregon state pen. Six games showed up for '18, including against an Indian school and the state pen; '19 only had two games, both over the Natives.[45]

Nationally, the number of programs ran well over 600 for the era (1916–1919). Scores in '17 fell to just below 60 percent of the '16 level to about 50 percent in '18 and rose to around 70 percent in '19. Although the number of programs remained low in '19, those that fielded teams had fairly full schedules. Among the 500 colleges that had the SATC in the fall of '18, about 400 had records for at least one of the four seasons of the era. That 80 percent fell short of intercollegiate football, which for the same institutions ran over 90 percent for the same time. College baseball received less coverage in the press.

While the Northeast and the South had about as much collegiate baseball as football, only about 40 percent of Michigan, Minnesota and Wisconsin colleges had teams in '16, the percentage falling in both '17 and '18, the number of games coming back a bit in '19. Ohio, Indiana and Illinois had close to 60 percent participating in '16, falling to below 40 percent in '17, even lower in '18. The Missouri Valley ran a bit above 50 percent in '16, falling to just over 30 percent in '17, even lower in '18, a modest increase in '19. The gap in the Midwest is simply too great to allow one to think collegiate baseball would have prospered had war not been underway.

Only a few contests between colleges and the military took place in '16, the number rising in '17, even more in '18. Among the future 500 SATC schools, the number of losses to military units ran slightly below wins. Colleges took most of fewer games in the other years.

3

Military Baseball at Home and Abroad

Creating an army of over a million conscripts (a number that would rise over time) plus a smaller number of National Guardsmen consumed the better part of a year, with a draft in the summer. The training camps they were sent to sometimes contained up to 50,000 people. They were scattered through the country, with a greater proportion located in the South, which annoyed Northern members of Congress.

In addition to these posts (16 for the national guard and the same number for conscripts), the government created 32 army airfields and a few dozen smaller camps, usually for some special purpose, such as Camp Greenleaf in northern Georgia for medical training. The War Department added forts to those defending the coastline. The number of training grounds for Marines and the Navy also increased. Almost all these installations had organized athletics. Most large ships usually fielded teams but on occasion even those with small crews competed.

Army ball grew as rapidly as the nation's recruitment. In '18, as Uncle Sam started spring training, the War Department figured about a million (an exaggeration) would play. The statistically minded figured they would wear out 50,000 balls, with about 4,000 company-level clubs. Each company would receive a dozen balls from the government in the hope that the men themselves could come up with a similar number. Later, the government sent 70,000 baseballs and 3,000 bats to the camps. Dr. Joseph Raycroft, president of the Eastern Intercollegiate Athletic Association (Basketball) and Princeton professor, led the army. Walter Camp, the "Father of American Football," directed similar efforts for the navy.[1]

At the end of July '17, an "athletic clan" of naval reservists at Newport, R.I. included four each from Yale, Dartmouth and Cornell as well as one each from Princeton and the Naval Academy. In '18 they tied Pittsburgh a day after the Pirates played a 20-inning scoreless game with the Braves, lost to a Cincinnati pitcher with a brief stint in the majors, tied Hartford which had a Pirate pitcher and overcame Cleveland at Newport, 3–2, neither Ray Chapman nor Tris Speaker playing on a Sunday afternoon, resting up to play the Red Sox a doubleheader on Monday. They also downed Bumpkin Island twice, overcame a fort in N.Y., losing but 1 of 9 against nearby naval training. In '18, five forts along Narragansett Bay had a league. In '19, a six-team city league had two civilian teams and three military plus Coast Defense, which, drawing from several forts, won the Southeast N. England army title. A fleet of destroyers with one team competed outside the league as did the crew from a cruiser.[2]

At Camp Devens in '18 (the 76th Division), inter-regimental competition kept the men amused and in shape. The Brigade formed four twilight leagues—the National, American, Southern and Federal. The camp had a second baseman who had a brief time with the Braves and a Cub catcher. Hal Janrin (Red Sox) led the mostly minor leaguers and a few collegians.[3]

Shortstop Maranville served at the Boston Navy Yard. Jack Barry (Red Sox) enlisted along with Herb Pennock and at least four other Sox, along with a St. Louis Brown and a "Mack Man." The yard eked out a 2–1 over Devens. Some 40,000 showed up for another encounter, donating to Naval

Walter "Rabbit" Maranville, shortstop of the World Series–winning Boston Braves in 1914, served in the Navy, playing baseball in several locations, starring in football for the *USS Pennsylvania*. *Library of Congress: LC-DIG-ggbain-17330.*

Welfare. The commandant then disbanded the squad, cancelling a game at Braves Field. Maranville requested sea duty, the others also re-assigned. Women with equal qualifications took their jobs at the yard.[4]

Secretary of the Navy Josephus Daniels turned down a request from a Mass Congressman to let Barry play with Boston while on furlough. Later, Daniels must have ended his edict about playing on furloughs because Gunner's Mate Maranville, on a 10-day furlough, played for the Braves after going to Europe twice on convoy duty. Before returning to sea, he excoriated major leaguers in the Steel League. Secretary Baker had no problem with army personnel on furlough playing in major league games. Outfielder Sam Rice, stationed at Fort Terry (Long Island), got a critical hit for the Senators against the Yankees on a five-day furlough.[5]

Just before his furlough in '18, Rice helped his fort crush an academy and Norwich All-Stars, 13–1 and 20–1, respectively. Sam went 4 of 6 in one and was the winning pitcher in the second. Nearby, the crew from a cruiser eased by All-Stars, which also played naval reservists. The local sandlot clubs were likely not a full strength because many were in the service, but they routinely played one of the teams from the forts or naval nines from New London on Sunday afternoons in a picnic setting.[6]

The Naval Radio School (Harvard) won the '18 Navy title for the Boston area, besting its chief rival at Braves Field on a Sunday in September, the winning pitcher a former collegian. Radio, 21–10, in winning the trophy, played a mix of military and community nines, losing 2 of 3 to Bumpkin Island, a naval training station in Boston harbor.

In the battle for supremacy in New York's naval district, the U.S.R.S. *Granite State* yielded to a transport unit, composed mostly of former collegians. Jeff Pfeffer, after a stint for reservists at the Municipal Pier in Chicago, beat the Cubs while on furlough for Brooklyn in '18. He shut out a New Jersey army camp for a Brooklyn receiving yard at the Polo Grounds. Phillies and Reds laced the camp lineup, while the yard featured former Dodgers, including Casey Stengel, who drove in the winning run.[7]

Games occupied "every level space" until dusk at Camp Dix. Harry "Socks" Seibold, won three but, when this former Mack Man was missing, his unit lost. The regiment "makeshift" nine lost to a brigade that represented those at the camp not part of the 79th Division. A company from a signal battalion met a depot brigade, which took a 1–0 lead in the sixth, a medic/umpire inciting calls of "robber" from his own men, whence he gave way to another officer who made even worse decisions. Yet they won. Then it was off to France, where they strung wire and trained carrier pigeons.[8]

Around D.C. in '17, Jack "Dots" Miller (Cardinal) who set a record for marksmanship at Parris Island arrived too late in France to shoot Huns because a general sent him to Quantico, the new marine base, where he and

Justin "Nig" Clarke (catcher for the Indians), a Chicago Cub, plus a couple of Southern Leaguers, went 16–1 (the loss to Camp Meade), sometimes at Griffith's park. The military guarding the White House did not lose once in fourteen up to early September '17.[9]

The 319th Infantry Regiment, 80th Division, located at Camp Lee (near Petersburg Virginia) acquired Cleveland pitcher Eddie Klepfer, a couple of other ex-major leaguers plus several from various minor leagues along with collegians from Brown, Ohio State and Pitt. Camp competition produced 600 games in four weeks, one 16-team league playing mostly on Saturdays and Sundays. The 319th sent a "crack team" to Pittsburgh, the home for many of its players. A steel company yielded 2–0 even though fortified by recently retired Honus Wagner as first baseman.[10]

In July '18, Camp Lee included Molly Craft, a Washington Senator, and John Boehling, the two Virginians each hitting a homer off the other. Craft yielded nary a run to Camp Humphreys (Belvoir) with the help of Virginia Leaguers and collegians from Pitt, Georgetown, Notre Dame and two from West Virginia University.[11]

In the Fifth Naval District, six teams played twice weekly at Norfolk's Red Circle Park, run by the War Camp Community Service, composed of local leaders and military officers. On a national level that organization was one of seven (the YMCA, YWCA, Knights of Columbus, Jewish Welfare Board, American Library Association and Salvation Army), all part of the United War Work Campaign, whose symbol was a white circle, with a blue star in the middle, surrounded by a red border.

Win Clark, directing athletics at the Navy Base, coached the Base Runners, with no major leaguers. The Minesweepers, managed at the start by Davy Robertson, had a Mack Man, a pitcher and infielder from the Cubs and a Dodger catching. The Saints (St. Helena) had William "Doll Baby" Jacobson (St. Louis Browns) and catcher Norm "Home Run" Glockson, briefly with the Reds. Two Mack Men led the Naval Air Station. The Saints, 25–3, led the standings on Labor Day. A Saint win over the Sweepers on a Sunday attracted 6,500.

Clark's 5th District All-Stars defeated a club that included Maranville at Yorktown before several hundred sailors on a Sunday and shut out the Philadelphia Navy Yard before losing to the 4th Naval District picked team. On Labor Day, the 5th battered Boehling and Camp Lee. In September, Great Lakes beat the 5th before 30,000 Bluejackets in Chicago. Chief Petty Officer Paddy Driscoll (a Chicago Cub in '17) had six hits. In '19, the base led the first half over a receiver ship, airfield, navy yard, army supply base and naval hospital, but the aviators won the rubber game of five for the title. The undefeated U.S.S. *Pennsylvania* won the '19 Atlantic fleet championship, Maranville not yet released for spring training.[12]

Relations between community leagues and the military were not always cordial. The Charleston City League dropped Fort Moultrie, amid complaints about "overseas" trips to the fort, the soldiers only wanting to play at the fort (once even failing to appear there). A meeting, to which officers from the fort were invited but failed to attend, removed it from the league.[13]

In April, Camp Jackson (near Columbia, South Carolina) had a short-timer with the A's, an outfielder from the Southern Association, a first baseman from Ohio State, a Carolina Leaguer, second and third sackers from the Texas League and an International League catcher. Later, someone asked a recent draftee who "looked like he could pitch," if he wanted to. N.Y. Giant Rube Benton struck out 25.[14]

Camp Gordon, a few miles from Atlanta, had high turnover, as elements of the 82nd went out early and units form other camps came and went. One Gordon squad was composed of one from the American Association, another from the International League, four from the N. England League, three from the Connecticut League and a catcher from the New Jersey League. They had a hard time getting everyone together, the men on the shooting range or drilling. They lost to the Atlanta Crackers but won over the staff of the federal prison on the latter's grounds.[15]

A Gordon team, with different personnel, outscored the Atlanta Crackers, 13–12, Oglethorpe's "Red" Wingo holding Gordon after the Atlanta starter yielded ten runs. J. Howard Berry, training to be an officer after ambulance duty, made a game-saving catch in the outfield. After initial training in Camp Travis, 25 "fine looking" Creek volunteers from Haskell Institute (led by a Carlisle athlete) challenged anyone who would play them. Camp Gordon's black champs planned to play the Atlanta Cubs (non-military) on the Morris-Brown campus, hoping to avenge another battalion's loss.[16]

In early August, Gordon ousted Camp Sevier, which had Southern Leaguers and Ohio State League pitchers. As part of a double bill, Camp Jessup (a transport and repair center in downtown Atlanta) downed Fort McPherson before a big crowd. "Packed stands" at Ponce de Leon watched Gordon shut out McPherson and Jessup dispose of a regimental nine which earlier lost to Camp Hancock and Cadore, 4–0. Gordon, adding a Cleveland backup shortstop as Major von Kolnitz slumped to .214, won over camps Greenleaf and McClellan, the latter for the second time, 16–0.[17]

Camp Wheeler (near Macon) had Majors and Minors, the former with infantry, three artillery companies and engineers. The Minors had supply, sanitary, ammo trains, three machine gun battalions, headquarters and a signal battalion. An infantry company, with many from Atlanta, led the Major standings. A Wheeler nine (Dixie Division, the 31st, mostly

Alabamans) racked up 20 of 23 in '18, losing only to Camp Jackson (a Pirate pitcher) and naval training twice, playing colleges, military and community clubs. Members included two from Auburn, two Texas Leaguers, a S. Atlantic Leaguer, an Atlanta Cracker, a world amateur champ (Maxwell Club of Detroit) and a short timer with the White Sox.[18]

In late February '18, an "old Mack man" in the 28th Keystone Division shut out Hancock (near Augusta). The Senators defeated field artillery, 7–0, à la Walter Johnson, who also shut down one regiment over 16-innings. A diarist who ran practice for Walter Camp Jr. at Hancock lost that job when he became despondent over the death of a baby at birth, the illness of his wife back home and the death of a friend.[19]

In Florida, Carlstrom and Dorr airfields opened early in '18, squadrons vying for supremacy. At Dorr, one squadron obtained "proprietary rights" and another overcame All-Stars that combined four other posts. On Independence Day, Carlstrom shut out Dorr before 5,000 "howling fans." In August, officers from Carlstrom and Dorr flew to Bradenton, believed to be the first such use of planes, where Cardinal Lt. Marvin Goodwin, who a few years later died in a military airplane accident, served a shutout, after which transfers forced re-scheduling.[20]

At Camp Joseph E. Johnston, near Jacksonville on the St. Johns River, quartermasters in training had little time for athletics, most of them there but for sixty days, but the athletic director received donated equipment and organized a team from the enlisted men, several of whom had pro experience. The chief concern seemed to be the sandy soil.[21]

The '17 World Series attracted a lot of interest in the 29th Blue-Gray Division at Camp McClellan in Northwest Alabama. The signal corps set up telegraph lines so that a report on every play could be announced by megaphone to the "living field of khaki" that occupied the slope. Because many of the men came from New Jersey, the crowd likely favored the Giants.[22]

In the spring of '18, at Camp Sheridan, near Montgomery, field artillerists mostly from Akron, becoming too fixated over overcoming another club, failed to respond to a call to duty, whence the commander confined them to camp for three days. When they moved to Fort Benjamin Harrison, a lack of interest upset devotees of the National Pastime.[23]

At Beauregard, Louisiana, in the spring of '18, 65 tried out for the base hospital as engineers defeated a nearby Baptist school and some semi-pros. The 39th Division (Delta—Ark., La. and Miss. guardsmen) edged artillerists, 2–1, after nixing a naval station. A N. Orleans Pelican gave up but one run in a win over Camp Shelby on 4 July. That September, with new personnel, the ordnance depot, at 16-3-3, shut out infantrymen who came from Panama where they had been protecting the canal. A private and one-time lefty for Cleveland and N. Orleans anchored the club.[24]

3. Military Baseball at Home and Abroad   41

Reports from 28 Southern facilities (Camp Wheeler and Fort Moultrie among the missing) for July '18 showed baseball leading all sports with 10,623 games, reaching 736,953 servicemen. Oglethorpe was the busiest, Gordon second, followed by Jackson, Parris Island, Shelby, Johnston, Hancock, Wadsworth, Sheridan, McClellan, Sevier, McPherson, etc.[25]

By '18, Camp Greenleaf in northern Georgia had seven diamonds on the drill field. Camp Pike (North Little Rock) had 122 teams in the spring of '18. Guy Morton (Cleveland) managed the camp club that included a Yankee pitcher and at least two other major leaguers. They bested Funston twice. So many came that the owner of the Little Rock Travelers added seats to the camp stadium until they held 5,000.[26]

In Bisbee, Arizona, in '16, fans took a trolley over the mountain to see semi-pros miners and military nines on Sundays. Infantry from Camp Harry Jones shellacked the Copper Queens and ran a streak over another mining nine, a combined team doing better against them. All-Stars (miners) beat soldiers from New Jersey. Labor unrest and confining Industrial Workers of the World (so-called "Wobblies") at the ballpark in '17 perhaps prevented games on the 4th of July. Locals reined in cavalry, who suffered a "bootless drive on Verdun." In July '18, the semi-pro titlist clobbered the colored cavalry from Fort Huachuca when the latter's pitcher, the "Black Thunderbolt," fell ill.[27]

Camp Cody, near the border with Mexico, with Western and Three-I leaguers, played a series against Fort Bliss in December '17, garnering the first two, losing at El Paso, but taking the series with a Sunday win. When Cody claimed the Southwest title, personnel at Fort Bayard, with a minor leaguer at nearly every position, complained. At Cody, a machine gun company won eight straight in the fall in '17 and 49 (a disputed number) more the ensuing spring before losing to the 34th Division (Sandstorm) picked nine. By September '18, Cody only had 3,000 personnel remaining compared to 25,000 at its peak as the denizens of Deming awaited the 97th Division and whatever contests it might offer.[28]

Military police won the first half of the league at Bliss in '18. Toward the end of the second half, the 15th Cavalry, ran ahead of other cavalry and artillerists that included ex–Texas Leaguers. Engineers, tops in the first half, had so many leave they fell into the cellar and suspended. After defeating Camp Harry Jones twice quite handily, while the 24th Infantry split with the same. Bliss then played these African Americans, including boxer and agile second-sacker Clarence Ross. In two weak end series, they split, one winning on a Saturday, the other on a Sunday. In the third, played at Bliss, the two again divided, then went for 12 innings, 7–7, when the visitors had to catch the train to Columbus.[29]

Camp Bowie (Fort Worth) ran an inter-regimental tournament in late

March '18, a sanitary train downing the favorites, with a Yankee catcher and one who once pitched for Connie Mack, along with a few Texas Leaguers. The 36th Division planned to have a team represent it, but no scores surfaced. Writing from Bowie, a former El Paso city leaguer reported in October that his company remained undefeated and close to a regimental title playing as many as three games a day. The next year a report from France from another El Pasoan, claimed his field hospital won the Bowie title and were still winning "over there." At Camp Travis in Texas in July '18 almost 12,000 played in hundreds of games.[30]

In '18, Camp Dick (near Dallas), with the help of a Texas League owner, led the six-team Inter-Aviation League, followed by others including two airfields that were tied for last after an encounter at Fort Worth's Panther Park. Kelly Field, (San Antonio) amassed a 42–8, a loss against engineers in training in the 7th Division near Corpus Christi ending a nine-game streak.[31]

Members of the supply co. of a regiment in the 88th Division (Midwesterners) thought no company team better at Camp Dodge. A depot brigade won 27 of 35 against independent and military clubs, three over Fort Riley. Field artillerists downed Des Moines of the Western League as well as Camp Grant, the last on 4 July '18.[32]

The Greater Omaha All-Stars, from the only league left in the city for those over age 19 in '18, upset the local navy recruiting office, staffed with minor leaguers and a major leaguer or two. Those Recruiters (19–2) overcame Camp Dodge, 3–1, on the Sunday before Labor Day. Dodge supposedly had a major leaguer (really his brother), at least three other major leaguers, plus five from the minors backing a college pitcher from Chicago. Only one major leaguer played. Recruiting had a White Sox pitcher, a supposed Yankee (Omaha shortstop) and two others familiar to local fans. Earlier, locals lost to a hospital from Camp Dodge led by Tom Sheehan. Infantrymen at Fort Crook (mostly former Omaha amateurs) yielded in high-scoring affairs to the best in the Greater Omaha, raising $1,500 for the fort's hospital athletic fund.[33]

At Camp Sherman (Ohio), the '18 spring started out with an ambitious program ruined by a quarantine. As troops making their way to New Jersey detrained in upstate N.Y., one battery beat another handily. As they awaited transport into the war theater, the chaplain arranged for a series.[34]

In April, Camp Custer (Michigan) had minor leaguers and one major leaguer. The 85th Div. (Mich./Wisc.) beat Camp Grant twice, with two from the University of Michigan and one from Notre Dame, plus pros from the American Association and a future major leaguer who hit three homers in a game.[35]

In August, Great Lakes, 30–8 in '18, with at least nine major leaguers, defeated the 5th Naval District and an Atlantic Fleet club that included Maranville. Red Faber, recovering from a loss to an army club when a batted ball struck his hand, won before 16,000; he also lost, 2–1, to a Pirate and Camp Grant in front of 10,000. Grant then bested the Lakes, sans Faber, to enhance a claim as the Midwest military champs.[36]

Before the flu became rampant, the military put together a league of Jefferson Barracks (St. Louis), Great Lakes Naval Training and camps Custer, Dodge, Funston and Sherman, starting after Labor Day. The Barracks overcome a Great Lakes regiment in Illinois before 6,000, losing to an ex-Red. Over 17,000 Cardinal fans saw the Barracks play reservists from Great Lakes. The Barracks had a six-team league, each team having at least one pro.[37]

Camp Lewis in '18 had two 10-team leagues—the American and National—which used fourteen of the camp's forty diamonds. Captain Scott ran the program, along with a minor league manager/owner and a lieutenant in the military police. Lewis had thirty pros including major leaguers. One regiment had seventeen well-equipped teams and a field with a grandstand, bleachers and a clubhouse with the amenities. A nearby Washington fort had robust competition for its championship. Its picked team lost to All-Stars from Tacoma's semi-pros.[38]

In Los Angeles harbor in '17, Fort MacArthur lost to "tar babies" of the Coast Naval Reserve, brothers from St. Mary's College the winning battery, before 500 sailors and soldiers. In September, a naval training station overcame the fort.[39]

When the Coast League capitulated in July '18, the manager of Balboa Park (San Diego) increased the military schedule, building on the rivalry between his sailors and the subbase at San Pedro, endowed with a Tiger and a few other pros. A six-team league among the Los Angeles shipyards had just begun, when orders from D.C. cancelled a Sunday game between the base and shipbuilders. San Diego naval training posted a 78–10 record, including two shut outs of Camp Kearny. An "All Majors" team at Los Angeles had outfielder "Wahoo Sam" Crawford.[40]

Duffy Lewis's Naval Training (Mare Island) lost two in March '18 to Mare Island Marines and later a five-game series to the same, even though a National League lefty stymied the leathernecks. Duffy's team included at least four respected major leaguers. Plans for them to play Great Lakes for a naval championship fell through when flu forced personnel to sea.[41]

On the other side of the Atlantic in June '17, a crowd in blue and khaki watched teams from destroyers that had recently landed in Britain. Villagers gawked at the men on their way to a field located near a backdrop of green-topped cliffs, where the Greys overwhelmed the Blues, the former with a Pacific Coast League pitcher with a sharp curve. Teams played on fields bounded by hedges and stone walls. The day the first American soldiers landed in France, crews of the ships that brought them carved out a diamond, donned uniforms and treated a crowd to an example of the American pastime.[42]

Convalescing Canadians and Americans in London played a match at Queen's Club in June to benefit widows and orphans of Canadian soldiers. The Lord Mayor of London threw out the first ball. Bantering among the players, aimed at the umpire, puzzled the largely English audience. The Canadians won. In late July '17, destroyer crews conducted a championship series before American and British naval personnel. The leading club finally tasted defeat after eight wins, when their opponents rallied for two in the last of the ninth. The winners received a silver cup earned the previous season at Guantanamo. In the fall '17, British naval officers considered having the "Grand Fleet" (100,000 strong) play baseball, sailors thinking cricket wasn't "belligerent enough." An officer who had played in America thought the skills and experience needed were too high, but it might help cement the "entente cordiale."[43]

At Nottingham in front of 4,000 for the benefit of the British Y, a duke threw out the first ball, hoping the game would further cement "the friendship of our two peoples." Those watching enjoyed the "staccato shouting" of the soldiers. The noise of the relatively small crowd exceeded that made from the larger ones on Cup Final day at the Crystal Palace.[44]

Americans fell to Canadians, the English champions for two years, at Swansea before 15,000, receipts for the British Prisoners of War Fund. Australians, who only had a broken pole to practice with, bested American engineers in early May. A naval air station blew up some Canadians in warmups for the regular season to start at Chelsea on 18 May. Grenade throwers edged depth bombers in 11 innings, with Admiral Sims throwing out the first ball to his army counterpart outside London before some 7,000. British and American khaki mixed with shades of blue worn by British and American sailors along with colorful dresses of the women.[45]

In late May, a U.S. Army outfit, with three wins, led the Anglo-American League, overcoming a section base on Decoration Day, several women sitting in the royal box with Sims and his aides. One army club used so many against "mast-climbers" that listing them would give Germans an idea of American strength. The games on Saturdays and holidays ranged from 1 May through 24 August, with admission eight pence (16 cents) for standing room and a shilling and six (36 cents) for a grandstand seat, netting $15,000 for British war charities.[46]

With a British dirigible hovering, a crowd (estimates as high as 70,000) including three from royalty plus Winston Churchill, spent a pleasant 4th '18 at the Chelsea football grounds in London, receipts for war charities.

Lefty Herb Pennock struck out fourteen for winning Navy against dental surgeon, former Detroit Tiger and Federal Leaguer, Captain Ed Lafitte, who yielded but five hits. Previously, Army nines dominated at Liverpool and Hyde Park.[47]

In late July at Hyde Park, a largely English crowd watched a mostly African American club which had whites pitching and catching. The crowd, detecting no differences in skills, enjoyed the banter the blacks provided. Their physical appearance and agility reminded the audience of the black boxers who fought in Britain over the years. Authorities permitted the use of the park, a decision that complimented the sport and the nation that produced it.[48]

The 840th Aero Squadron, trained in Texas, overwhelmed another squadron on an English football field in May. A week later they edged the same on a cricket field and then suppressed a third squadron. Several wins came against three Canadian cadet schools in different English cities. They finally tasted defeat at the hands of the 186th Squadron before 5,000, receipts benefitting the English Red Cross. Arriving in France near the end of August, a depot nine of the 840th, with an electrician pitching and a "demon little right fielder" who "shagg[ed] down balls" at the "back of the tents," edged infantrymen of the 26th Division. After losing to a pro field artillerist, other engineers dismantled depot when Frank Walker, a Tiger outfielder who led Newport News to a Virginia League title in '16, slugged a homer and a triple.[49]

Combat engineers for the 26th, reaching France in late '17, got in in a couple of games in March '18 as they dug trenches near the front. Officers from Fort Sheridan eked out a verdict over counterparts from the Presidio. The first gas and flame regiment to reach France played while in training and holding off Germans in the British sector, the games promoting Anglo-American unity. Writing from "somewhere in France," a handball player reported that he was now playing baseball "between acts" on a diamond near one of Napoleon's stone barracks and underground cells dug at the time of Roman occupation.[50]

In the spring in France in '18, an infantry company that claimed the Mexican border championship in '16, yielded to engineers while a naval air station downed a dirigible station. On a Sunday, French folks roared as a medical repair shop dominated a searchlight division, losers' hits as scarce as "Huns in Paris." while on another diamond Red Cross drivers overcame a YMCA club. Motor mechanics clobbered some Marines and naval aviators bombed aviation technicians, as engineers took down transporters, a Tri-State Leaguer starring. The 85th Division had a 10-team league, two field artillery units vying for the lead. When an artillery brigade in the 41st Division (several western states) showed up at a camp in the spring of '18 for further training "diamonds sprang up as if by magic," headquarters capturing the title. As part the Army of Occupation, they continued to play.[51]

An Army and Navy League in France with twelve teams playing on Sundays at a Racing Club at Colombes. Another site, starting in April, attracted thousands, a section base tied for the top. Military police won a playoff but were ordered out of the area. Scattered references show a wide variety of occupations including chief quartermasters, camouflage engineers, base censors, search lighters and medics. Thousands of games in July involved over 100,000 soldiers.[52]

Engineers out of Camp Grant who reached France early in the '18 spring were soon playing with "much gusto." The French, especially younger folk, were interested in the sport. "Considerable money" changed hands among the military especially at the finale on the 4th of July.[53]

After combat, an R.I. artillerist rested at a chateau, when suddenly the commander announced a recall to action near St. Mihiel. It was akin, he sighed, to slugging a long hit to center field, with the bases loaded in the last of the ninth, rounding third base heading for home only to be told by the umpire you failed to tag second base.[54]

At a chateau near Lorraine medics at a base hospital unit out of Allentown, Pennsylvania, found baseball useful in helping soldiers suffering from shell shock as they roamed a 40-acre estate. A supposed pro pitcher would be unable to play for a time because a bullet had "beaned" him. The Pennsylvanian who had become despondent at Camp Hancock saw a hospital nine overcome "crack Canadians" on a Sunday. A little later, cavalrymen won a 16-inning affair over the hospital where he was being treated, having been gassed and shot in the foot. In a wheelchair, he got permission for someone to push him to the park to watch the best game he had ever seen.[55]

An ambulance driver out of Michigan, serving with the French, recalled "swearing like a baseball player in July," as he endured heavy enemy artillery in rescuing wounded soldiers. In a quiet sector near Verdun, they crossed a river to "play the great American game every afternoon for three or four hours." French soldiers got a kick out of seeing Americans slug the ball and run the bases.[56]

On the 4th of July, field artillerists in the 35th Division won in a grove near a chateau west of Paris, awaiting a move to the main artillery training farther north. An infantry regiment in the 4th Division, once at Camp Greene and now intensively training before moving to the front, shut out other infantrymen. Other artillerists, some starting out at Fort Totten, played before a French crowd, bands playing the national anthems of both countries. Soldiers also played before 20,000 at Rouen, where a pharmacist reported a loss, but the holiday had been a great treat. His B-rated nine were "awfully good."[57]

Still other field artillerists won 2,000 francs in bets in May, prevailing on the 4th on a rough field and securing vengeance from another battery on Bastille Day (14 July), the Knights of Columbus distributing prizes. On a roadside field, a third battery rebounded on the 12th just before the offensive in the St. Mihiel sector when baseball ceased because the soldiers were getting "enough exercise, without having to play games to work off surplus energy."[58]

Army ambulance drivers helping the French military prevailed over a hospital, then defeated a French eleven, 4–1, in soccer, drinking wine afterwards. They bested another French team, 2–1, on Bastille Day. After hazardous duty in the St. Mihiel sector, they swam the Mosel and lost to engineers, unable to overcome a lieutenant who had not very successfully pitched for Connie Mack. Inter-squad contests produced so much feuding they turned to soccer and defeated some more Frenchmen.[59]

An observer out of Camp Funston thought the African American Pioneers (probably the 809th), "a fine bunch of fellows" who dug trenches, were "crazy" for playing within a quarter mile of the fighting. Occasionally, a German shell exploded in the French pasture where they were playing. One section base had a labor battalion with four or five who played either pro or semi pro for a range of African American nines. Their leader was Sgt. Otey Scruggs, a pro who also played with a regiment in the Philippines.[60]

Other engineers (road builders) who reached France in mid-winter, bested infantry and ambulance drivers, winning "beaucoup francs" between 5 May and 14 July '18. They ousted ordnance, split two with artillerists, yielding to fellow engineers and winning over a truck company on Bastille Day. An "Old Men's" game among officers produced three casualties.[61]

The Y created a league of thirty teams, even allowing games every Sunday, with as many as eight going on simultaneously, all within a 50-acre field (site of the 1900 Olympics). A paid admission accessed all contests. Claude Thomas, "the Indianapolis Iron Man," who was less than spectacular in four games for the Senators in '16, supposedly won fifty times pitching in or near Paris.[62]

Raymond B. Fosdick, chair of the War Department's Commission on Training Camp Activities, touring France in the summer, saw servicemen playing at every chance, even after harrowing days, whether in Paris between American soldiers and sailors or the next day, close to trenches, playing until dusk, knowing they would carry out an attack the next morning.[63]

Some 60,000 or so watched a contest with bats made from saplings and a round stone off the beach wrapped with taped rags for the ball. Flannel shirts covered with old shoe leather tied by twine became a catcher's mitt. Elsewhere, a captain of artillery who had packed plenty of balls and bats on leaving America, described "the worst sand lot you ever saw," a hurriedly prepared diamond still containing stumps. "Every bit of spare time," his "He-Men" played ball.[64]

In an August game, Johnny Evers, in charge of the Knights of Columbus program which included supplying equipment, after playing for an ambulance nine in the Paris League, praised the talent. Having taught the game to some French military, he thought it might become popular in France, at least more so than in England where it competed against cricket.[65]

Lieutenant Harry McCormick of the Giants claimed soldiers did not like the "hanging back" and were "incensed" over those making munitions or ships continuing to play. McCormick thought the owners should have followed Huston's lead and wholeheartedly joined the war effort. Evers supposedly also expressed negative comments but later denied ever saying soldiers were hostile to major leaguers.[66]

After the '18 major league season ended, St. Louis Cardinal manager John C. Hendricks, a "100 percent American and patriot" hoping to hit a homer for the United War Work campaign, headed to France to join Evers. Major league umpire Jack Kerin coached in the Rhineland, where they even played by moonlight. Evers urged umpire Hank O' Day to help. Did O' Day plan to take up Evers' offer? "Hell, no. They're trying to end the war over there. If I'd go over where Evers is, the war would go on." Bill Friel umpired some 500 games for the Knights of Columbus, his reward—apparently—an Italian bride.[67]

Christy Mathewson discussed playing a world championship in Rome, pitting pros in the military versus the winners of the World Series. Another idea would send two big league clubs, largely composed of those over age 31, to play each other. In the spring of '18, the director of all overseas Y instructors, told Mathewson that American soldiers wanted him in France. Matty thought Honus Wagner would be a better choice but would go if really needed. Fearing a French negative reaction to so many non-essential personnel, the director quietly dropped the idea.[68]

YMCA Field Secretary Elwood S. Brown, who organized the Far Eastern Olympics, reached France in April '18. With the end of the fighting in sight in the middle of October, Brown wanted "athletics for everybody," that would demonstrate America's spirit of play and manly stature." These championships would be followed by Olympics for the armies of the Allied nations. Brown and Fosdick advised Pershing to promote a program even in the winter to combat the restlessness sweeping through the army, most of whom thought they should be headed home. They convinced the general that the men participated in the war as patriots, not professional soldiers. Pershing asked the Y and Knights to intensify their efforts. Fosdick, who was upset with the Y for not reducing its religious role, making it necessary for the Knights of Columbus and Jewish Welfare Board to do more, urged Pershing to rely on the military itself to promote athletic activity.[69]

Between January and May '19 the AEF conducted indoor and outdoor baseball, basketball, boxing, three types of football, quoits, sitting up drills, tennis, track and field, volleyball, wrestling, tugs-of-war and cage ball. "Informal Games" drew some 11,310,401, as thousands took part on multiple occasions. Baseball attracted the biggest number of regular sports with over 3,000,000, some 105,350 playing in January and 1,300,000 in May. Indoor baseball drew a total of 2,342,896, with 646,066 in January and something over half that number in May. Ten sports had championships, taking place on the sodden fields of France, on islands in the Rhine near castles on cliffs, in Luxembourg, on the Kentish coast of Britain, even in Italy. The Army distributed 58,963 baseballs, 14,385 gloves, and 12,646 bats.[70]

After wintering over in a village, a "crafty" company (80th Division) reached "the heights of their glory" near La Mans in the spring '19. Pennsylvanians included a wounded first baseman, a wounded shortstop who attended a university in France; a POW private, a corporal "slightly gassed" and a sergeant assigned elsewhere when the company lost so many advancing against the enemy in the Argonne.[71]

As the 80th Division awaited orders to head home, an infantry regiment commander thought playing ball helped the men become "quite American" again. Among field artillerists of the 80th (W. Virginians) one company took the regimental title before "howling fans" on the "high flats" at Brest. The historian would not give the score, joking (one assumes) that an umpire may have been on the take. A day or so later, on the same field, they passed cootie (lice) inspection and headed home.[72]

In February '19, baseball got underway in southern France, Marseille shutting out La Rochelle. A field hospital (88th Division) in the Riviera League had "Long Tom" Sheehan plus five others with major league experience along with an equal number of minor leaguers. Marines overcame Cannes, the southern France titlist. "Nig" Clarke caught for the winners.[73]

The 88th Division won over the 6th and 36th divisions, 8–1 overall, a lone loss part of a split with the 7th. In their final game they beat St. Nazaire Marines. The 36th Division had one infantry regiment with over 70 teams, 16 in a league. Artillerists entertained the king and queen of Belgium with an exhibition. And although missing cleats, the division, with pros, overcame the 6th in April.[74]

An engineering regiment had four leagues, the Y supplying equipment but no uniforms or shoes. When these roadbuilders encamped on their way to the coast in '19, starting in late March, teams nicknamed the Bolsheviki and Red Guards played each other, ending at Le Mans, where 3,000 watched one contest.[75]

The 321st Infantry (81st Division) never lost, starting in '17 in Camp Jackson, featuring Cpl. Charles Franklin "Whitey" Glazner, a future National Leaguer pitcher. Diamonds materialized in "every available spot" near Le Mans, the main embarkation center. A regiment of the 79th Division near Nantes lost two to the 809th Pioneers. Lt. Col. Huston's engineers were too busy to play until '19 even though in France since late '17. Eddie Kaw, trained at Camp Humphreys and later a Cornell gridironer, proved a talented left fielder. Awaiting departure, they overwhelmed other engineers, before 18,000.[76]

In May '19, the French University Baseball League opened, Paris defeating Lyons. A one-time Harvard pitcher allied with a Princeton catcher for the winners, the ex-president of the Federal League directing affairs. League All-Stars lost to the 36th Division.[77]

On the Rhine, the 342d Field Artillery, 89th Division, had Grover Alexander, three other major leaguers, two from the high minors, plus collegians put together by a major at Camp Funston. Alexander pitched occasionally, once for five innings for prison guards, allowing two hits, before 10,000.[78]

So, who won the AEF title in 1919? Mostly amateurs from the Chicago area organized from remnants of the 86th Division (Blackhawk) and representing the embarkation center at Le Mans. They took 2 of 3 from a 3rd Division nine.

After fighting in France ended, Brooklyn pitcher Cadore, a lieutenant with the black 369th regiment, received a medal in helping capture 1,000 Germans. In N.Y. harbor, Dodger teammates met his ship before it docked. In response to a reporter's question, he said that even though his regiment had several stars, they had only been able to toss balls around in the trenches, not having enough room for games.

Camp Gordon reduced its force below 12,000 in February '19, but its units still competed with Camp Jessup and Fort McPherson, colleges, the Crackers and guards from the federal pen. In late May, Camp Benning (Columbus, Georgia) edged Camp Jessup, 5–4, when Josh Cody (Vanderbilt) bungled a play, the game featuring five catches by Benning's director of athletics, Elmer Oliphant. Later, on leave from the army, he played for the Atlanta Crackers, returning to the service as a coach at West Point.[79]

One estimate claimed over 95,000 played in Europe along with the same number in the military who never crossed the Atlantic. An official with the National Baseball Federation, founded a few years earlier and ready to replace pro baseball should the war continue into the summer of 1919, believed that as many as 100,000 more would be playing that spring than in 1916, a 50 percent increase. The war, it seems, had made the world "safe for baseball." That 300,000 played for semi-pro, sandlot or other

"The Big Serb" Corporal John Miljus, who was nearly blown up carrying a stretcher, later suffering gas inhalation, played for Brooklyn in '20. *Courtesy National Baseball Hall of Fame.*

amateur clubs the year after the war is not likely. Indeed, they probably did not even recover the '16 number.[80]

Several major leaguers died in the war. Corporal Ralph Shaman, who batted 37 times for Connie Mack in '17 and captained Camp Sheridan's nine in '18, drowned in an Alabama river. Larry Chappell, with three major league teams over four years, died helping the sick in San Francisco. Lt. Eddie Grant, a Harvard infielder who played in nearly 1,000 major league games, ending his career in '15 with the Giants, died rescuing the Lost

Sgt. Charles "Gabby" Street fought for 48 days in the Argonne. While giving first aid, he inhaled gas and a machine gun bullet grazed his nose as he squirted liquid fire into the Boche, before shrapnel hit him. He later managed the World Series–winning Cardinals. *Courtesy National Baseball Hall of Fame.*

Battalion. Bun Troy lost his only decision pitching for Detroit in '12 and his life from wounds in October '18, while Alex Burr (Williams College), who once appeared in a game for the Yankees, perished from a plane accident. Minor and Negro leaguers also died in the service. Pearl "Specks" Webster, who died in the pandemic, was the only black pro to receive much publicity.[81]

Several major leaguers dealt with serious wounds. Sgt. Joe "Moon" Harris fractured his skull and broke both legs and three ribs when a vehicle overturned in France. Unbelievably, he played for Cleveland in '19. Cleveland pitcher Lt. Eddie Klepfer (Camp Lee) and Lt. Joe Jenkins, the White Sox catcher, both injured in the war, had little playing time in '19. Pvt. Hugh S. "Cotton" Miller, a former Phillie, Federal Leaguer and recipient of a distinguished service cross, recovered from a shoulder injury but then an explosion broke his leg. Cpl. John Miljus also sustained injuries as did Gabby Street.[82]

Captain Christy Mathewson returned on the *Rotterdam,* "bigger and stronger than ever." Accounts mentioned him being ill in France but nothing about ingesting gas working for Gas and Flame. He died of lung disease a few years later. Major Percy Haughton, owner of the Braves, arranged for Branch Rickey, president of the Cardinals, to join him in France, where Rickey contracted pneumonia, recovering after the Armistice but losing a chance to kill Germans, akin, he said, to "bunting in a 9–0 game."[83]

4

College Football

With the Declaration of War and knowing thousands planned to leave school, some even before the end of the spring semester, college administrators cancelled spring practice, intending to drop the fall schedule. In late May, Secretary of War Newton Baker, who wanted physically fit officers, called for keeping collegiate competition. In August, 160 delegates at a NCAA meeting in D.C. urged colleges to cut pre-season coaching, training tables and paid coaches. Above all, do not interfere with military training. They did not call for easing transfers or stop conferences from banning freshmen on varsities.[1]

After deciding not to have football, the "Big Three" changed their minds—sort of. Concerned about words like "hysteria," Harvard, Princeton and Yale would not officially have teams, but when fall came, so did "Informals," whose losses would not count. This decision produced a poem with the line "in days of old, when Yale was bold/And Harvard picked up scores abnormal, they didn't squirm at every turn and call their puny teams informal."[2]

Not taking aspersions lightly, Harvard's officials made sure the press knew that its top fifty athletes went into the service. Of its first eleven from '16, all were in the service at Plattsburg for officer training, with the Naval Reserves or driving ambulances in France. Only 6 of 73 (all sports) varsity "H" the previous year returned that fall. Because conscription only took age 21 or over, one might assume most freshmen and sophomores might come back, but only 2 of 31 returned from the frosh eleven. Princeton had 15 of the '16 squad in the service, plus six captains of varsities, many of whom had taken part in military training on campus the previous spring, 90 percent with commissions. Even before the end of May, 44 of 50 Princeton lettermen had committed to military service.[3]

As the '17 season closed in on its Thanksgiving finale, a reporter lamented that few had a team that approached "its former prowess." Untested youngsters and the less athletic replaced "the real blood, bone and sinew of Young America." Another columnist contended that when stars joined the colors, mediocre athletes improved. Maybe the typical squad was not the usual caliber, but games were enjoyable. A North Dakotan reported that a "fighting spirit" created by the war "permeated the gridiron," producing a "season out of the ordinary."[4]

Obviously, the war profoundly affected collegiate football, at least in the short term. The differential in scores from one year to the next between traditional rivals varied by as much as 150 points, some schools losing almost all experienced personnel, others incurring fewer losses. Anyone gambling on the outcomes, particularly on point spreads, had a very hard time.

Most major schools played about as many in '17 as they had in '16, even with the loss of a few prominent programs. The number of programs dropped a little over 15 percent, the number of games less than 10 percent. Colleges with less than 200 full-time students also fielded teams but not at the level of major institutions. Bigger schools were expected to play about two-thirds the number in pre-war years in '18. The number of programs, almost reached the target, but influenza, which caused the cancelation of most October games, cut the game count by over 50 percent.[5]

With new draft rules taking effect in '18, it looked like football could not be played in any meaningful way, the minimum age at 18, the number of current collegians in military service expected to top 100,000. The administration established the Student Army Training Corps (SATC), paying collegians the same as privates ($1 a day) to prepare most of them to be officers to lead the second wave of conscripts. Some 150,000 took oaths on 1 October.

In September, the War Department seemingly banned football for the SATC, drilling and studying requiring too much time. Chicago's Amos Stagg, who must have noticed workmen underneath one of the stands creating barracks for the SATC, grumbled that West Point only drilled an hour a day. Moreover, college players made excellent officers, witness several of his former players already overseas and the '16 Minnesota eleven, all now officers "giving a good account of themselves in France." Earlier, "Hurry Up" Yost (Michigan), from a lengthy list, highlighted two majors with the Rainbow Division (42nd) in France, from the '03–'05 squads, one each from '07 and '08, lieutenants from '15 and '16, along with a former tackle in the regular army "breaking up" the "mass plays" of the Huns and an All-American guard in '10, a lieutenant machine gunner. Four recent players, including Pat Smith, were in aviation.[6]

So many protests reached Congress that the War Department denied ever telling anyone not to play. Games between neighboring schools could be played but none that required being away from campus more than from noon to taps on Saturdays. Practice would be limited to no more than an hour and a half counting bathing and dressing. The directive encouraged playing and avoiding contests that brought large revenues. The War Department finally allowed four games in November, two possibly being well away from campus.

One government official thought that all physically able collegians should play intramurals at least. Columnists recalled the old chestnut attributed to the Duke of Wellington that Britain won the Battle of Waterloo because of cricket at Eton. American football served even better, developing muscular strength, speed and "bottom," keeping one's wits a vital byproduct. French battlefields resembled football fields more than baseball diamonds. Germans, it seems, used an old "guards-back" perhaps a "triple-tandem." The Allies resorted to "quick, slashing, concealed balls" and unexpected thrusts. In the war, the Huns kicked off, the French fumbling. Smashes through the left side of the Allied line almost allowed the Germans to score at the Marne, but the Allies held, though they failed to make a first down.[7]

As the end of the fighting approached, Wilson asked United War Work to raise over $170,000,000 (the final number went over $200,000,000) to provide a "Cheer-Up Fund" for the troops. Receipts of collegiate and military games for the week of November 11–18 would go to the fund. Revenues from at least one other should be donated to charity.[8]

Had they only had to deal with the machinations of the War Department, the season would have turned out much like '17, but starting near the end of September and lasting through October and into November, the flu became more lethal, appearing in a more virulent form in Midwest military installations. It sporadically reappeared in 1919, killing nearly 59,000 Americans in the service, over half of all military losses. About 675,000 Americans died from its complications.

In '17, "informal" Harvard relied on military opponents and scheduled more games for '18. Yale's captain went to Pensacola for training. Quarterback Chester La Roche also applied for air service, the mayor of Boston hoping he would "fly as well against the enemy as you did against Harvard in the Yale Bowl last fall." The Eli "Informal'" didn't do so well and Yale didn't field a team in '18. Princeton played military exclusively in '17 and one college in '18. Other than Vermont and Trinity, no one else went "informal." The latter lost to Yale but overcame Vermont, scheduling mostly nearby military. The "SATC regime" in '18 lost to Amherst as half the regular team went to Camp Lee.[9]

Vermont, 4–5 in '16, loser of its only one in '17, had a scoreless tie and a loss in '18 and went 3–6 in '19. Middlebury, 5–2 in '16, 1–5–1 in '17, had flu reduced '18 to two ties and two losses, followed by 4–3 in '19. Norwich, a loser to Middlebury in '16, played them in '17 and '18 (a win and a tie), overwhelming Fort Ethan Allen. After being commissioned as a second lieutenant at Plattsburg, the Middlebury '16 backup quarterback graduated dressed in khaki in '17 and perished not quite a year later at Chateau Thierry, serving the Ist Division as a machine gunner.

Colby won the Maine state title in '16, 2–0–1, Bowdoin in '17, 2–1, although at least six joined the service. Bowdoin and Maine tied, 2–1, in '18, the latter undefeated in '19. Between 1916 and 1919 the four schools played Fort McKinley regularly, two other forts occasionally, along with nearby naval reservists. In '18, with 145 SATC to help field a team, Bates, returning four from '17, did not win any games, losing by a touchdown or less to the three other Maine colleges and to the Portland Naval Reserves, who had an end from Bates. German-born Albert Adam, a man of "high principles" who had been in the army for four years, "feeling that the team represented the SATC unit more than the college" kept his job as its coach but had a SATC member replace him as team captain. Of about 500 SATC at Maine, three were athletes, with six in naval training (the football captain one). A student commentator did not think the SATC did much for Maine football. Military deaths included a transfer from Susquehanna, from pneumonia in France the day of the Armistice and a Class '20, next to his ambulance, from shell fire. At least 3 of 7 from Bowdoin who died in France were first or second-string Varsity (one from '17 and two from '18).[10]

New Hampshire, playing some Maine schools, downed Fort McKinley in '17 and '18, dunking the crew off a cruiser in '17, losing to reservists at MIT in '18. In '17, despite the loss of veterans to the Ambulance Corps, with two back from the previous year, plus seventy inexperienced, including freshmen, Dartmouth went 5–3 (5–2–2 in '16), beating West Virginia and Penn State and 2–3 against colleges, when the SATC represented Dartmouth in the flu season. Recovery in '19 brought 6–1–1.[11]

Brown, 7–1 against colleges and loser to Newport Naval Reservists in '17, lost to Camp Devens and the League Island Navy Yard in '18, winning 2 of 3 from collegians, the one over Harvard, supposedly making them some sort of champion. One of R.I. State's few wins in '17 came against Fort Kearny, located a few miles from the campus, its previous year's captain leading the fort. R.I. did not play in '18. Chief rival Connecticut, which did not play in either '17 or '18, started off '19 badly when a flying tackle killed one of them returning after a stint with the Harvard Radio School.

Texan Benny Boynton, leading the Purple of Williams (7–0–1 in '17), with sixteen from '15 in the service, started naval aviation training in Philadelphia in '18. With the "Purple Streak" back, they were 6–2 in '19. Of the 25 from Williams killed in action or dying from combat wounds, at least ten had played on the varsity. In addition, the quarterback in '00, a sergeant, died at an army camp from the flu. A frosh fullback in '13 who also briefly pitched for the Yankees in '14 died in an aviation accident in France.[12]

With the help of ten from the SATC, Boston College in '18 shut out three military elevens, one at Braves Field and split with colleges. Holy

Shellfire killed Captain Belvidere Brooks, captain and quarterback '09 for Williams College, as he stepped out of a cave, 22 August 1918. *Persons Photograph Files College Archives and Special Collections Williams College.*

Cross, 4–3 in '16, winning over small colleges, went 3–4 in '17, losing to top programs, the same pattern in '19. In '18, they won over Tufts and WPI. The Mass Aggies, 3–4–1 in '16, posted nothing for '17 or '18, 5–2–1 in '19. Boston University, with no field nor campus, had an SATC eleven in '18, eight of whom formed a nucleus in '19 when the school, now with an athletic fee, created its first official eleven, registering 3–3, playing at Braves Field and Fenway Park.[13]

Springfield, winners over four N.E. colleges and losers to Army and Colgate in '16, had a scoreless tie against artillerists from Maine and a lopsided loss to the U.S. Ambulance Corps in '17. The flu season brought a win over Fort. McKinley and a loss to Newport Naval Training. Tufts surprised Harvard at the beginning of '16 and Indiana at the end followed by a reduced '17, a loss to Harvard the only result in '18, with notable wins as in '19. Worcester Poly, which rarely won, blew up a Devens' ammo train in '17, the "military regime" and flu complicating '18, followed by a no-win '19.[14]

Lt. Bradford Turner, Williams fullback, '11–'13, died on the Hindenburg Line, 27 September 1918. *Persons Photograph Files, College Archives and Special Collections Williams College.*

The U.S. Military Academy, 9–0 in '16 and 7–1 in '17 (with the loss to Notre Dame), played once in '18 (a win over Mineola Aviators). In '19, they went 6–3, with losses to Syracuse, Notre Dame and the Naval Academy. After upsetting Brown at the end of '16, Colgate, with Michael Hayes, future KIA and Distinguished Service Cross recipient, yielded to Brown by a point and to Syracuse by a lot more in '17. An alumnus blamed the SATC for Colgate having no team in '18. The N.Y. Teachers College tried to create one in '16, but polio forced a school closure that fall. In '18, its SATC played several Albany independents. The school did not follow up with an official eleven in '19.[15]

In '17, Fordham crushed Camp Wadsworth (New Yorkers coming back from South Carolina) and downed other military elevens, losing to Georgetown and Rutgers. Four drove ambulances, while the quarterback, an end and a tackle joined the naval reserves. In '18, half back Frankie Frisch, probably after aviation training, captained the largely SATC (Frisch not a member), which won 4 of 5 against colleges, losing to Camp Merritt (New Jersey). Fordham had no eleven in '19.[16]

In '16, Syracuse only lost to Pitt. The '17 Orange practiced twice against an infantry regiment, 7-1 (losing to Pitt) against collegians, including Nebraska, a surprising opponent given the problems with rail transit. In '18, wins over army aviators and Naval Transport (Hoboken) flanked 3-1 against colleges (Michigan a loss). In '19, Syracuse, 7-3, punished Pitt.

Rutgers University, 3-2-2, in '16, tied Washington & Lee, black end Robeson not playing against Southern whites. In '17, with at least nine in the service, the Scourge overcame Fordham, won five over small colleges and the military, losing to Syracuse and tying West Virginia. The '18 won four, a loss to Great Lakes, 14-54, attributed to the "Hooverized training table" (meatless days ordered by food administrator Herbert Hoover), a lack of subs and the lake men striking ankles from the rear. Stevens Institute of Technology, 5-0-2 in '17 and 7-0 in '19, did not play in '18.[17]

In '17, Lehigh's "not informal kind" went 7-2 (6-2-1 in '16). The Brown & White, not too afflicted by flu in '18, split four with colleges, losing to Rutgers, Penn State and 2 of 3 to the military. Carlisle fielded an eleven in '17 although 29 (football and track) signed up for army, 6 for navy and 5 for engineering. Little Thiel College, which had a hard time breaking even most years, split two in '18 with 97 in SATC, losing a former team captain at Belleau Woods and at least two other gridironers to the flu.[18]

In '17, Pop Warner had few returning, but freshmen filled in, the undefeated Panthers not playing Georgia Tech for the national title. Pitt blew away the Golden Tornados in '18 at Forbes Field before a big crowd. Pitt partisans were convinced a one-point loss to the Cleveland Naval Reserves could be attributed to a timer stopping play prematurely. Southerners cheered the Pitt loss, with Richard "Moon" Ducote, a Plainsman and an All-Southern back, starring. Pitt's athletic director criticized Cleveland Indian Ray Chapman, now in the backfield for the Reserves who harassed a ref to prevent off-side calls against his teammates. In 1920, he would become the only one who ever died from injuries in a major league baseball game. The number of those who perished playing the National Pastime averaged about 28 each year during the preceding decade; football killed about 18 annually, 1 or 2 being collegians.[19]

The University of Pennsylvania '16 squad produced an ensign, a first lieutenant in ordnance, a sergeant, a hospital staffer, a first lieutenant at Camp Dodge, a dental reservist, plus all-round J. Howard Berry, who served on the Mexican border in the summer of '16, joined the university's hospital unit and had officer training at Camp Gordon followed by an assignment at Camp Hancock. In '17, the 9–2 "Big Quakers" beat Michigan, their only two losses to Georgia Tech and Pittsburgh. In '18, though three registered too late, its SATC sank a battleship, splitting two others with nearby military, nine played in total.[20]

After an 8–2 in '16, the center for Washington & Jefferson returned after ambulance duty, in France, most all from the previous year still in the service. In '17, the Presidents played the same number as in '16, including one over Camp Sherman. In '18, they edged a normal school, losing to Geneva College and Pitt, outpointing Camp Sherman. The post-war ran 6–2. Sol Metzger, no longer coaching there, wrote columns about football and coached Camp Dix without pay in '18.[21]

Swarthmore in '18 (the coach, an SATC surgeon), gave the patch work Navy Yard a battle before yielding. The Little Quakers were 6–1–1 in '16, 6–2 in '17, a "husky war baby," 4–2 in '18 and 7–1 in '19. Haverford won three in '19, better than '17 but not as good as '16. "Abandoned" described '18, athletes going elsewhere, the SATC not on campus as Quaker pacifism prevailed.[22]

After winning 8 of 10 in '16, a 4–4 in '17 against colleges (a win over Army Ambulance), Penn State replaced their coach who went into the service with Hugo Bezdek, the Oregon coach who also managed the Pittsburgh Pirates. In February '18, State had 100 lettermen in the service, including 31 in football. Bezdek's eleven tied a military unit, then lost to Rutgers and Pitt, barely getting by Lehigh. With several military veterans in the lineup the Blue and White lost only once in '19.[23]

Indiana Normal, 6–0, with wins over three other normal—Edinboro, Mansfield and Kalamazoo (Michigan)—in '17 after 8–1 in '16, played no other teachers in '18 and lost narrowly to Washington and Jefferson. Waiting out flu for four weeks, they ended against a high school and an academy. It turned the '19 season around with wins against California and Mansfield, earning the normal school title, at least in the mind of one observer. Mansfield cut its schedule in half in '18, even though the SATC brought 35 out for the team. It bested a small college in upstate N.Y. after a complicated trip.[24]

Shippensburg State Normal, victor over Millersville Normal in '16, 2–4 overall, subdued the same in '17, losing to Bloomsburg Normal amid "decidedly discouraging conditions." Too few men returned for '18, disappointing fans as the SATC also did not appear. Scores showed up in '19. Two other normal schools, East Stroudsburg State and West Chester State, had football only for '18, the SATC providing personnel, both playing high schools and splitting a pair with each other.[25]

In '18, after officer training in Iowa, Fritz Pollard, the black back from Brown, took charge of the SATC at Lincoln University. With an inexperienced squad, Lincoln outplayed an athletic club, black elevens from camps

Dix and Upton and SATC's from Hampton Institute and Howard University (before 2,500). The next year ('19) Lincoln had a scoreless tie with Howard, which lost to Hampton in '16 and '17 and won over the same in '18, and '19. A tie between Howard and Lincoln (both undefeated) in '19 likely meant the two co-championed the Colored Inter-Collegiate Athletic Association.[26]

In '17, Gallaudet subdued soldier interns at a hospital and tied an artillery eleven, 1–3 versus colleges. In '18, the deaf students overcame Army medics and three small colleges before submitting to VMI. The '19 version won over four small colleges, naval gunners, tied Catholic and lost three, including to Delaware, which was so-so in '16, '17 and '19, the SATC sustaining that pattern in '18.

The U.S. Naval Academy did not play Army in '17 or '18. Losing to Army in '16, the Midshipmen improved in '17 under Gilmour "Gloomy Gil" Dobie, with a loss to West Virginia The only loss in a full '18 was to Great Lakes Naval Training Station when a Midshipman on the sideline tackled one headed for a touchdown. The '19 proved a success by virtue of a win over Army. In March '19, Commander Jack Dalton, a drop kicker who almost single-handedly beat Army in '10 and '11 (Camp first team All-American), died from pneumonia as his ship brought soldiers back from France.

The South Atlantic Intercollegiate Athletic Association supervised only track, but reporters and coaches chose the best eleven and an All-S. Atlantic squad from many D.C., Maryland, Virginia and North Carolina colleges. Georgetown, which beat Fordham but lost to Navy in '17, wiped out a host of military foes in '18 with its SATC. In '19, after pummeling the Navy Base (Norfolk) and a Portsmouth athletic club, they prevailed over Navy and Washington & Lee, but losses to Boston College, Georgia Tech and the University of Detroit weakened their claim to be the best in the S. Atlantic.

At first it looked like Catholic and G. Washington would have second seasons without football in '18. The former, however, recruited enough SATC to tie the Gunners School at the Navy Yard and American University chemists. In '19, it lost to the Hampton Roads Naval Base, tied Quantico Marines and flew over some aviators, losing all but one to collegians.[27]

After tying for first in '16 (4–1–2) Hampden-Sydney claimed the Eastern Virginia Intercollegiate Athletic Association in '17, even though a new coach never came, the captain joined the army and the number of students fell below 90. In '18, with only two with experience, one serving as coach (with a hospital unit in '17), the Tigers won 2 of 3 and either tied Richmond for the title or won it outright. In '19, the Garnet & Gray tied Richmond.[28]

Richmond, with a player coaching for a time, went 4–1–1 in the conference in '17, also overwhelmed by Washington & Lee. The '18 stood 1–1–1, or a 2–1–1, Randolph-Macon failing to give a 24-hour cancelation notice, giving the Spiders a possible forfeit. In '19, even Monk Younger, the new Tiger coach back from France, admitted that the Spiders were better than his eleven although they both had the same record. Randolph-Macon, with 140 students (half the '16 eleven in the service, 43 for the school), won but one in conference in both '16 and '19 and none in either '17 or '18.[29]

With only a win and a tie in conference and one with St. Helena Naval Training in '16 and 2–4 in conference in '17, William & Mary in '18 lost to Virginia Christian (Lynchburg), Richmond and the Sewanee A.C. (Portsmouth). In '19, they started with an eleven, all of whom had served in the military, six in France. Fluke-like losses to Randy-Mac and Hampden-Sydney prevented a winning season.

Emory & Henry re-instated intercollegiate ball in '15, thereby making the school "a real American college." In '17, they lost by a lot to VPI and two others, winning over Virginia Christian. Nothing surfaced in '18, the post-war bringing wins over an athletic club and Carson-Newman, a loss to Maryville College and another stomping by VPI.[30]

Hampton Normal Institute, with Native Americans, beat Howard, Lincoln and Virginia Union University in '16, possibly ranking tops among historically-black schools. Beating Petersburg Normal, Lincoln and Howard in '17, they lost most in '18 and ran about .500 in '19. Virginia Union was likely best in '17. Still led by quarterback Henry Hucles, now in the SATC, Union easily overcame a Camp Lee eleven but did not do so well otherwise; an improved outcome took place in '19, with Hucles playing and coaching.

The university at Charlottesville started '16 losing to Yale, when Alan Thurman failed to return in time from France, where he drove ambulances. In '17, the athletic committee insisted on keeping freshmen ineligible for the varsity, so Virginia Cavaliers fielded only a frosh eleven. Thurman and other Cavaliers were already at Fort Myer, including Robert "Bobbie" Gooch, another ambulance driver and a quarterback in '15, who in '16 received the Croix de Guerre for running through a German barrage trying to save a wounded companion. Another member of that backfield, Eugene Mayer, a Camp's 3rd team All-American, perished from pneumonia at an army camp in Florida in October '18. Mr. Jefferson's university planned to renew football in '18, against UNC, possibly even VPI, whom the Cavaliers had not played since '05, but flu and/or the freshmen rule ended those plans.[31]

A fullback and captain from '16 and a punter represented VPI at Myer, the school carrying out most of its regular schedule in '17. In '18, it eased by N.C. State in Norfolk and swept seven to claim the S. Atlantic Conference title, overcoming Camp Humphreys, where hundreds died from flu that October. Honorary Tech captain William "Monk" Younger, with his mates "in spirit", also captained a hospital eleven in France, composed in part of University of Virginia Cavaliers. The '19 Tech squad, disappointed when Younger chose not to return to school, had a few from '18 along with a '16 starter back from France and Coast Artillery and a former Norfolk Blue. An '18 halfback died from an accident at Pensacola.[32]

After tying Rutgers and Georgia Tech in '16, Washington & Lee, under William C. Raftery, with the "smallest, youngest and most inexperienced" squad ever, lost to Tech in '17 by about 60. In '18, the SATC lost to Staunton Military Academy—by about three touchdowns. The Generals, 9–1 in '19, avenged themselves against Georgia Tech by a field goal and nailed Navy, losing to Georgetown.[33]

In '17, VMI played for the first time at West Point, where the versatile Oliphant punched holes in their line. In '18, losing their coach to the service, scouring the campus for players and taking a drubbing from the Naval Operating Base near Norfolk, the Cadets won over Gallaudet. Flu and travel restrictions cancelled three. They also fell by about the same score as W & L to Staunton Military Academy, which also wiped out Quantico marines and aviators near Richmond. Although losing to University of Virginia and N.C. State in '19, VMI dominated VPI and UNC, 6–2 overall, acquiring the nickname "Flying Keydets."[34]

In '18, after not playing in '17, UNC mixed in SATC, including freshmen, to pass Camp Greene's Remount and Camp Polk tank corps officers in '18, 4–3–1 in '19, beating N.C. State in their first encounter in years. Petitions from Trinity (Duke) alumni stationed at Camp Jackson in '18 calling for resuming football, canceled in 1893 to satisfy Methodists, helped restart the program in 1922.[35]

Following a mediocre '16 and an improved '17, N.C. State in '18, with flu wiping out five weeks as officer school took several, were ground into the mud by Georgia Tech and fell to VPI and even Wake Forest. In '19, after weary months against "a mighty foe on the world's greatest gridiron," college colors replaced "olive drab" and the "thump of punted balls" the sound of exploding shells. All state's starting eleven in '19 were military veterans. Of those in France, one served eighteen months as a sergeant; another, a machine gunner with the 81st Division, incurred wounds helping Brits on the Hindenburg Line. A field goal carried state to a win against VPI before a small crowd in Norfolk.[36]

In West Virginia, only Bethany played all four years, one win in each—'16, '17 and '18—and a 3–5 in '19. Marshall College, 7–2–1 in '16, mostly against small colleges, failed to score in 8 of 9 in '17, tying Morris-Harvey, which Marshall manhandled the year before. Not playing in '18, the Big Green won all nine in '19. At West Virginia University, 8–2 in '19 (losses to Pitt and Centre), dropping football in '18 created "long faces" among fans. The program did well in '16 and '17, a loss to Wesleyan notwithstanding. In '19, the latter had six

4. College Football 65

lettermen, five of whom helped defeat West Virginia in '17, when Wesleyan also lost, 7–8, to Penn State (a broken-field score in the last half-minute).[37]

The cause of the commotion in the Blue Grass State—aside from the war and flu—was the school in Danville, the student body growing during the war from about 120, including several Texans, Centre only lost once over the two war years. Alvin "Bo" McMillin starred for five seasons ('17–'21), '18 not counting against eligibility. Camp listed him a first team All American in '19, second team in '20 and '21. Others cited him in '17 for state honors, All-Southern in '18. He also excelled in basketball and track and lettered in baseball. He later received a degree when his military coursework (naval service) belatedly counted. Centre went 9–0, in '19, amid later disproven complaints from a W. Virginian about him being a professional, reciprocated by the Kentuckians concerning a Mountaineer. In 1921, the "Praying Colonels" preyed on Harvard, then unbeaten over two years.

In '17, Georgetown College walloped Kentucky Wesleyan, among five wins, losing to Camp Zackary Taylor and Centre. Following a 4–1–2 in '16 and a 3–5–1 in '17, the "SATC and FLU busted up Kentucky football," allowing no home games. Recovery in '19 meant romping over Georgetown College, a loss to Centre and a season-saving win over Tennessee.[38]

Most athletes at Tennessee, undefeated in '16, living up to their nickname, went into the service. The Volunteer replacements only played military in '17, losing to Virginia artillerists from Fort Oglethorpe and a Camp Gordon eleven. In '18, their regular SATC with mechanics in training endured a wipeout loss to Vanderbilt. The SATC also lost to army champion Camp Greenleaf but battered bakers from the fort, the post-war year a 4–3–2.[39]

After losing one game each in '15 and '16, Vanderbilt went 4–3 in '17, humbled by Georgia Tech (0–83). Two losses to military units were followed by a blowout over Tennessee's SATC and easy wins over Auburn and Sewanee in '18. The next year, bringing Josh Cody from Camp Jackson, produced 5–1–2. Lieutenant Irby "Rabbit" Curry, who died in aerial combat against elite German flyers in August '18, captained '16 as a third team Camp All-American.

In '16, Sewanee (the University of the South), once a premier program, romped over four small colleges, 2–2–1 against bigger schools. With 75 percent of their athletes in the service, '17 brought four wins and a tie, then a 4-touchdown loss to Centre ("words fail me," a student remarked) and a closer loss to Vanderbilt. In '18, the Fighting Tigers had easy wins over an academy and Oglethorpe and a poor showing against the Commodores. A 3–6 (wins over an academy and two small colleges) ensued in '19.[40]

Among Tennessee's smaller colleges, Maryville usually won about half the time, the SATC losing to Tennessee, though completing 14 of 21 passes in '18. Union University (Jackson), in addition to winning one against a normal school in '17, lost to the Jonesboro Aggies and were so-so against high schools and a military academy. The "premiere halfback of the world" with his "infectious ready smile," Joe Guyon, coached the Bulldogs in '19, when they lost to Vandy but downed the normal school again.[41]

An Atlanta reporter considered Fisk University (Nashville) the black champion in '15, giving greater significance for Morehouse's win over Fisk in '16. That year Fisk vanquished a couple of Y's, Walden, West Virginia Institute and a Mississippi school. Fisk "suspended intercollegiate athletics on account of the war" in '17 but students organized a team and whipped Walden. Some sources rank Morris-Brown as the best black college in '15 and '16, in the Southern Intercollegiate, with Fisk securing that honor in '17 and '18, followed by Talladega in '19.[42]

Alabama Poly (Auburn), winning most in '16, ran about the same in' 17, tying Ohio State and vanquishing an Ohio military eleven, losing to Georgia Tech by a lot. The Plainsmen lost 5 of 7 in '18, three courtesy of army camps. The '19 collegiate went 7–1 plus one over the 25th Division from Camp Gordon. The university at Tuscaloosa, 5–3 in '16, overcame an Ohio ambulance corps, an institute, plus three colleges in '17 (tied Sewanee), losing to Vanderbilt and Camp Gordon. After a blank in '18, the post-war year yielded but one loss—to Vanderbilt. In '18, Birmingham Southern (a merger) hurdled over Howard (Samford) and Camp McClellan's officers, humbling some aggies and small colleges, losing to others in '19. Spring Hill (Mobile), 4–2 in '16, lost to an institute and Tulane, eased by an academy and Howard and plowed through one of the Aggie schools in '17. The '18 Purple & White trailed Tulane, lost by a point to Gulfport Naval Training, tying Gulfport's reservists. They improved to 3–3–1 in '19.

Stetson University (Deland), routing Rollins twice in '16, resumed after a two-year lapse, in '19, overcoming some All-Stars and flyers, losing twice to Southern "hirelings" and Florida. They then cruised to Cuba (losing to athletic clubs in basketball and football). Florida, 0–5 in '16, went 2–4 in '17, shut out by Auburn, Clemson and Kentucky. After idling in '18, the Alligators ambled, 5–3, in '19. Southern College, splitting with Stetson and rolling over Rollins in '16, flayed Florida in '19 and Stetson twice. Rollins College (Winter Park), losing to Stetson and Southern in '16, recorded nothing for '17 or '18. Playing for the town team in '19, students at Rollins lost twice to Stetson.[43]

In '17, under John Heisman, Georgia Tech, using freshmen, crushed two separate colleges on the same Saturday, playing each half a game. Then the Golden Tornados punished Pennsylvania and whipped the Washington and Lee Generals so badly that coach Bill Raftery inferred that Tech had a lot of experienced players. Irate Atlanta reporters replied that 16 of 22 Tech lettermen from '16 had joined the military. Late that season, Tech clobbered Auburn. A reporter wondered if Raftery still "wouldn't be surprised" should the Plainsmen beat Tech. In '18, Tech proved no match for Pitt. In '19, the Panthers prevailed once again and W & L trumped Tech with a field goal.[44]

Oglethorpe College, with seventy students (20 out for the team), had little chance against Camp Gordon or even Dahlonega in '17, but in '18, "blessed with" 300 SATC, the Petrels downed Dahlonega and Chattanooga at Atlanta's Grant Field. The Camp Gordon machine piled up a big lead, but the crippled Petrels stopped them on eight plays within the one-foot line. Oglethorpe also played Non-Coms from Gordon twice, losing because of unfair officials, finding revenge at home. In '18, flu closed North Georgia Agricultural College (Dahlonega) for three weeks, the SATC interfering, yet after beating one of Georgia's numerous A&M schools and Oglethorpe, the Mountaineers only lost at Camp Gordon by a touchdown in a huge stadium amid a cold wind.[45]

Georgia (Athens), 6–3 in '16, with at least fifteen volunteering for the military, gave up in '17 and '18, resuming in '19 (4–2–3). Mercer College (Macon), outscored 7 to 214 in '16, lost at least three (0–174) in '19, when the Orange & Black resumed, emphasizing football for campus spirit. The crimson-clad Cyclones of Gordon State overcame a couple of the state's A&M's in '16 and '17. Several hundred from one of these aggie schools went into the service, perhaps explaining why few scores came up in '17.[46]

Among historically black Georgia colleges in '16, Atlanta University lost 1 of 4, winning against Tuskegee. In '17, Atlanta lost to Morehouse and Tuskegee but downed Talladega and Morris-Brown. Morehouse ran over the other black colleges in Atlanta in '16, also taking both Talladega and Tuskegee and capping it off with a win over Fisk. The SATC plus vocational units, though present on a few of these campuses, did not encourage football in '18.

Louisiana State University, 7–1–2 in '16, broke even in eight in '17. After giving up '18, LSU went 6–2 in '19. Southwest Louisiana Industrial Institute (Lafayette) lost to LSU and Spring Hill College in '17, winning six. The '18 won over Louisiana Industrial and some engineers. The preponderance of SATC was so great at Tulane in '18 that, renamed Camp Martin, they played mostly military, beating Shelby and Beauregard, losing to Pike, and tying the Pensacola Aviators, slipping in a customary win against Spring Hill.[47]

Miss A&M went 7–1 (the loss to Auburn) in '17, even though ten graduated, most of them entering military service. With seven underclassmen also enlisting, only two lettermen remained. In '18, the Bulldogs looked solid, with seven returning but flu felled two starting ends and three others went to officer training. In November, after losing to Payne Field, a win over Camp Shelby hinted at improvement, but in a second match against Payne, in Memphis, to raise money for War Activities, a fumble gave the airmen the ball, whence they drove the length of the field for the only score.

The Aggies then crushed Ole Miss at home and at Oxford. Ole Miss, which excused '18 (1–3) on relying mostly on frosh, took pride in holding Payne Field, 0–6, at West Point, Miss., the aviators drawing from 1,500 in four different squadrons.[48]

In '16, Miss. College (Clinton) downed Miss. A&M, Ole Miss and three small colleges, losing to LSU and Tulane. An abbreviated '17 produced four losses to big programs. After complications from the SATC and games only against aggie schools in '18, the Gold & Blue went 3–5–1, in '19.[49]

In '19, a reporter assumed football would resume its ascent in South Carolina started in 1913 when Furman, Newberry, Presbyterian and Wofford took the field. Erskine joined the next year. A critic urged one who drove ambulances in France not to play because he "might get hurt," ironic advice given the recent past. Only the College of Charleston had no team in this era. Presbyterian was the only one not to play in '18. Claiming the South Carolina title in '16, Citadel won over the Navy Yard in '17 and tied naval training. In '18, the Bulldogs lost to the Yard and to the crew of a cruiser and in '19 to Georgia, edging a hospital ship. Clemson, the Tiger cry heard in France, ravaged an army camp in '18, with no losses to South Carolina colleges and shut down Davidson (losing to the same in '16 and '17), succumbing to Camp Hancock and Georgia Tech. In '19, they tied for the state title with Furman, which in '18 shot down the same infantrymen twice before losing to Georgia Tech 0–118. The Baptists again gave way to Tech, more respectably in '19, when a mainstay of the SATC squad showed up along with one from the 81st Division.[50]

At the University of Michigan, where officials canceled everything but changed their minds in '17, Yost with a few holdovers, went 8–2 overall and humbled Chicago, Ohio State and Syracuse in '18, 1–4 in '19 in conference. Wisconsin had three regulars in '17 but most lettermen and frosh (about 20) from the previous year were in government service. Half-way through the season, the Badgers looked formidable, but their captain went into artillery, six others already in the military.[51]

In '17, Minnesota, with a "bright outlook," even with many in the service, forged ahead like the Italians "only to fall back in utter rout at the critical juncture" (a close loss to Wisconsin). The next year a quarantine was lifted just 24 hours before the Iowa game, the Gophers losing 6–0. They also lost to the Chicago Naval Reserves, possibly the best in the country, which had never trailed anyone before a Minnesota touchdown. A '15 All-American end and Marine captain wounded four times, Bert Baston, was 1 of 3 Minnesota varsity captains commended for heroism.[52]

After contending for a national title in '16, Ohio State counted 5 of 18 regulars back, several in the officer reserve corps, the state militia or farming in '17. Near season's end State tied Auburn after a lengthy trip into the

South. After the season, several enlisted, offsetting rumors of opposing the war, though three failed physicals. The next year brought few positives, '19 yielding a much better result.[53]

At Chicago in '18, seven went to Waco as infantry officer trainees. Stagg ran many practice games, disposing of Crane Junior College, but in a return scrimmage, Crane held Chicago to a scoreless tie, showing just how far the "Poor Old Maroons" had fallen. At least two former players died in the service, one in the Argonne, the other, who also played baseball and basketball, from wounds.[54]

Following so-so seasons in '16 and '17, Bob Zuppke at Illinois in '18, with only one who had played the year before, used frosh, apparently an abundant crop, for the Illini only lost to Great Lakes. Only a loss to Wisconsin blemished the Orange & Blue in '19, giving them the second straight Conference title. Ralph Chapman, a guard for three years, All-Western for two, captain and All-American in '14 (Conference champs) died in action.[55]

Northwestern, in '16, with senior Paddy Driscoll, only lost to Ohio State. The first year of the war brought back only two with experience and a lopsided loss to Ohio State. In '18, after holding Great Lakes in a scoreless tie before Driscoll took over at quarterback there, the Purple yielded to the Reserves of the Municipal Pier and split two in conference. A narrow victory over Indiana provided the one conference win for '19. At least two died in the war, one in an accident, the other KIA.

Purdue won only one conference game between '16 and '19, though tying Indiana. In '18, outside the conference, the Boilermakers lost to DePauw, Notre Dame and Great Lakes, but they held a parade that included 3,000 soldiers, women in nightgowns and a pep talk from the coach to set up a win over Chicago. The spirit associated with football was far from dead in Lafayette. At least one former player died during the war, at Camp Taylor from the flu.[56]

Indiana University in '17 clobbered several small schools as well as Purdue. The abbreviated '18 produced a loss to Camp Taylor, a decisive win over Fort Harrison. As fans grumbled about being "doormats" in the Big Ten, the '19 eleven produced losses to Centre, Notre Dame ("like an Allied tank in Flanders mud"), Minnesota and Northwestern (a field goal in the last minute bettering a safety). The Hoosiers then gave Bloomington much to cheer about by upsetting Syracuse.[57]

Iowa, 0–67 v Minn. in '16 and loser to Great Lakes, Nebraska, Wisconsin, even Grinnell in '17, fared better in '18, though the Hawkeyes again lost to the sailors. They shocked the Cornhuskers, whom they had not beaten for about two decades. A win over Coe had a nary a spectator due to flu. Illinois won the next even though the game had to be moved to Iowa because flu still raged in Urbana. Before 7,000, the Hawkeyes stopped the "Minnesota Shift" for the first win over the Gophers in years. Some thought an ensuing win over Northwestern and 2–1 in the Big Ten ranked them above Michigan (2–0). Victory over Iowa State gave them the usual state title. Although outplaying "the Dodgers" (Camp Dodge), the Hawkeyes settled for a scoreless tie. Eckersall reported that an officer from southern Missouri, an area known for its racism, raised no objection playing against African American freshman "Duke" Slater. He even received plaudits after helping the tackle stand up after a rough play.[58]

Notre Dame, in '16, only lost to Army. In '17, the Irish, under former assistant, Knute Rochne, tied Wisconsin and lost to Nebraska but overcame West Point and Washington & Jefferson (6–1–1). The flu season brought a briefer schedule, versatile back George Gipp and two easy wins, ties against Great Lakes and Nebraska, a win over Purdue and a loss to Michigan State. The next season brought an untarnished account, including one over Army.

Monmouth (the North Shore), usually tops in the Little 5 (Beloit (Wisc.), Lake Forest, Knox and Northwestern College, sometimes Armour Inst.), did not retain the title even with six returning in '17. With the SATC in '18 the Red & White may have played once, a loss. In '19 with only three with at least a year's experience (Northwestern returning 11, Knox 14 and Beloit 22), Monmouth went 1–2. The program sustained at least one war death, a lieutenant from wounds.[59]

Knox College (Galesburg), 4–1–2 in '16 and 4–2–1 in '17 (1–1–1 in the Little 5 each year), lost to Municipal Pier and Northwestern University in '18, tying quartermasters and nudging Northwestern College (Naperville) in the only conference game. Going 8–0 overall in '19, Knox secured the conference title (3–0), not playing Northwestern , which posted 7–1–1 in '16, a 5–1 in '17 and (5–1–1) in '19, a 2–0–1 yielding second place in the Little 5. Lake Forest, rare winners in '16 and '17, with the end of the SATC (100 students) impending, it became imperative to schedule at least one collegiate contest. Every student donated $1, but the eleven lost to the YMCA College from Chicago. Few positives ensued in '19.[60]

Augustana College (Rock Island), resumed in '17 (the first since '04); the "Terrible Swedes" undefeated in four in '18, went 1–2–3 in '19. Augustana was one of several colleges under the auspices of the Evangelical Lutheran Synod, which in '16 refused to change its anti-football policy. Possibly the war altered its official position, for several such schools resumed the sport in '17 or '18.

James Millikin University (Decatur), 8–0–1 in '16 and 7–1 in '17 and undefeated in 9 in '19, sustained '18 (with many SATC), winning over an airfield and three small colleges, losing only to Illinois. In contrast, a cartoon at Shurtleff College, with 51 men in '17, depicted a tombstone which read "Here Lieth the last Remains of Shurtleff's Athletics." The equipment

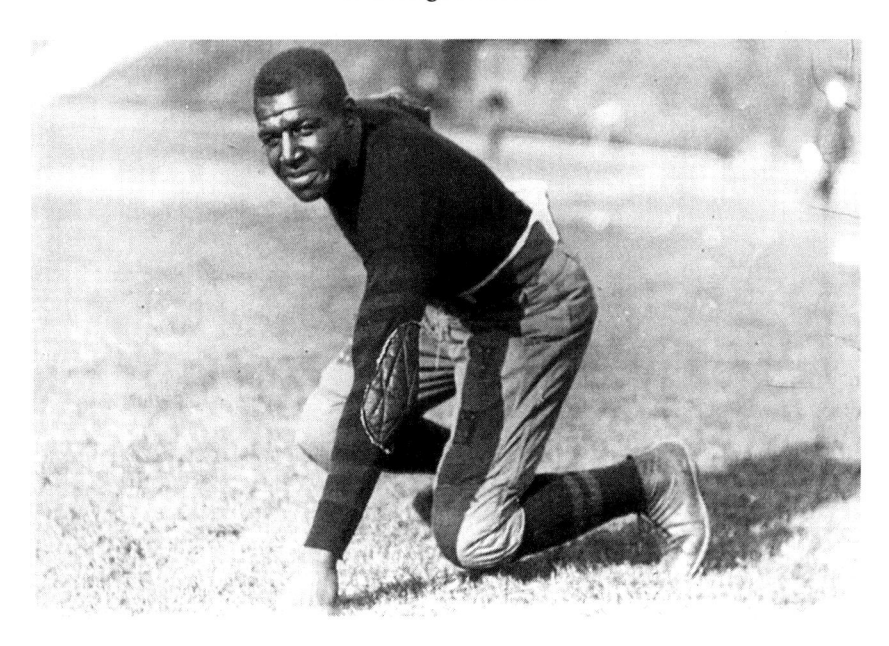

Iowa University's Fred Slater, pictured here as a senior, played against Camp Dodge in 1918 as a freshman. After leaving Iowa, he played in the National Football League. Frederick W. Kent Collections, the University of Iowa Libraries, Iowa City, Iowa.

went to Camp Taylor. After losing two in '18, the Bisons rose to 7–0–1 in '19. Carthage College, with less than a hundred before SATC added 125 in '18, had no coach and 75 cases of flu. An officer described a loss to Lombard as army football, where Carthage lost four to injuries and Lombard six, ten standing for each side at the end.[61]

Wabash, slightly better than DePauw in '16, lost to the same in '17 and '18, tying them in '19. Rose Poly (Terre Haute) got by Wabash in '17 but not DePauw. Losing to DePauw in '16 and '18, Franklin College humbled Hanover whenever they played, the Gold & Blue also tying Purdue in '19. Earlham College (Richmond), less than so-so in '16 and '17, with no SATC went intramural in '18, and, with "several old men back from war service," 3–2 in '19. In '17 Butler College (Indianapolis), usually so-so, defeated Camp Taylor, coached by a former Butler mentor. Word of the result reached a former player in France. The Bull Dogs, mediocre in '19, became the Indiana small college titlist in '20.[62]

In '18, Ohio University found the SATC and SNTC (Student Naval Training Corps) a "colossal" undertaking. Even worse, a player broke his neck. The victim, who started as a student in '13 and dropped out to teach school, returned as a senior with the SATC, his death considered a war loss, six for the school, at least one other an athlete. The press claimed no collegian died playing football in '18 apparently discounting the SATC. The Green & White went 7–1 in '19.[63]

Miami University, 7–0–1 in '16, undefeated with two ties in '17, went 4–0–1 in '18 after the flu abated, losing only two in '19 and leading the Ohio Conference from 1916 to 1918, Oberlin and Wooster vying in '19. The College of Wooster disputed the title in '17, undefeated with three scoreless ties. The Black & Gold went 6–1 in '18, reeling off seven in '19. Mt. Union, a frequent winner in '16 and almost the opposite in '17, considered itself a "hotbed of patriotism" in '18 by which time some 200 were in the service, about the same number of SATC coming to campus, yielding a 5–1 in conference followed by a winless '19. Otterbein fans blamed the SATC "regime" for the 0–5 in '18, offering no such explanation for the 1–7 in '19. After an embarrassing '16 when the first string was exiled for fraternity hazing, Oberlin went 5–2–1 in '17, the epidemic producing havoc in '18 (1–4). The Crimson & Gold lost but one in '19. War dead included the football captain of '01, a tackle from '08 and one each from '12, '13 and '14.[64]

The Ohio college conference held up remarkably well during the war. With sixteen members in '16, '17 and '18 and seventeen in '19, they only played three fewer games in '17 compared to '16 and about a dozen fewer in '18 compared to '17, around a 20 percent reduction from the previous year. All 16 had the SATC but only three played military units other than fellow SATC.

Playing at least seven in flu-ridden '18, Albion lost to Michigan State but waylaid the two Kalamazoos, Hillsdale, the University of Detroit and a couple of military clubs. Detroit lost only to Michigan in '17, winning over Camp MacArthur (Mich. men) and 8–1 in '19 (the loss to Tufts). In June '17, a committee at Hope College, which had no football for at least two years, voted, 8–7 for its "re-enthronement" but no crowning took place because so many entered the service. The "royal game" returned to "its rightful place" as "king of athletic sports" in '18 when the SATC brought "lively adherents" who overcame Kalamazoo College by a point but were wiped out by Western Mich. Normal (Kalamazoo).[65]

Michigan State lost to Michigan and Notre Dame in '16 and bested some small colleges (but not all) and tied South Dakota State. With a lot of inexperience, the Aggies lost a bunch to colleges, both large and small and to Camp MacArthur in '17. Fortunes revived in '18, with wins over three small colleges and Notre Dame and three losses to the Big 10. The post-war year brought 4–4–1.

After a loss to Notre Dame in '16, Alma College, with only about a hundred men, upset the Aggies and downed five small schools in '17, after losing to Camp Custer Officers narrowly. They then disposed of Kalamazoo College via a passing attack, never practiced when the loser's scouts were watching.

Thus, they posted a 4–0 in the Michigan Athletic Assoc. In the '18 fall exactly 101 men were expected to show up but 49 joined the service. Everything depended on 100 or so SATC. The lieutenant in charge, after calling for athletics, changed his mind and the campus woefully awaited basketball so students would have "greater interest in college work." In '19, under a new coach, the Maroon and Cream fell to Kalamazoo, the only conference opponent.[66]

In '16, in Minnesota, Carleton, surprised Chicago (losing to Cornell of Iowa) and won four in '17. A combined Carleton–St. Olaf fell to Minnesota in '18. Another loss to Cornell appeared in '19. St. Olaf (Northfield) revived football in '18. After working with Carleton and dealing with the flu, St. Olaf came up with its own eleven, winning one of three versus Carleton.[67]

Hamline University (St. Paul), winner of 2 of 3 against Dakota elevens in '16, fell to the North Dakota Aggies in '17. In '18, Hamline's SATC mauled Macalester but submitted to St. Thomas before flu closed the program, the Red and Gray strong in '19. St. Thomas, 3–2 in '17, lost to Minnesota (not by a lot) in '18, tying a military eleven, when the coach went into the service and the best player to officer training at Camp Pike just before the last game—a win over Macalester. That Presbyterian school lost to Hamline and St. Thomas every time they played each between '16 and '19. Macalester won three from Gustavus-Adolphus (evangelical Lutheran) from '17 through '19, tied River Falls in '16 and '19, lost to the same in '18. Someone at Gustavus-Adolphus attributed the end of the anti-football policy of '05 in '17 to rule changes and because 11 Lutheran schools were now playing inter-collegiately.[68]

In Wisconsin, Beloit College, 0–4–1 in '16, collapsed against Carleton, the university and Marquette in '17. The flu season brought another loss to the university before they rousted riders from Camp Grant and ripped Ripon. The Black & Gold 0–3 in '19 in the Wisconsin Intercollegiate, also lost its only game with the Illinois-based Little 5 to Northwestern College, not to be confused with the Wisconsin school with the same name. After going 6–1 in '16, not playing in '17, and losing all four games in '18, Ripon went 4–0 within the state in '19, taking the Wisconsin Association title. They were followed in the standings by Carroll (3–1), Lawrence (1–2), Beloit (0–3), and Northwestern (0–2), respectively. Marquette University, so-so in '16, went 8–0–1 (tying St. Louis) in '17 after which almost the whole team entered the service, seven in aviation. In '18, the Hill Toppers' SATC outpaced Ripon, tied Carroll's SATC and lost to Lawrence (later overturned). The post-war brought a winning season and Earl Bodine back from France, another from naval service and a third from digging for gold in the Klondike.[69]

In '16, 22 tried out at Eau Claire Normal, but defective anatomies prevented putting an eleven on the field. In '17, when the number of males fell to 19, 15 put on "moleskins determined to do their best" even though most had never played. They lost by tons in two tries but exhibited persistence, if not courage.[70]

The University of Nebraska went on, even with the loss of 17 from '16, 11 being commissioned as officers at Fort Snelling's officer training. Holdovers included two rejected for Snelling and four others, plus sophomores, enough for the Cornhuskers to retain the Missouri Valley in '17 under Coach Ed Stewart, winning over Kansas and Notre Dame while losing to Michigan and Syracuse. In '18, with Stewart at Camp Gordon, they won one of two in conference, losing to Camp Dodge, tying Notre Dame and deflating Omaha balloonists. A 3–3–2 in '19 featured a win over Syracuse.[71]

In '18, Missouri practiced 250 hours (an exaggeration given SATC rules) but never played. Kansas split four, including two in conference, Nebraska overcoming the Jayhawkers by nearly three touchdowns. Kansas State beat Iowa State and lost to Kansas. With one win (over Drake) and no losses, Washington University prevailed over Nebraska, thereby claiming the Missouri Valley Conference title. Iowa State was competitive save for '18 when they lost all three, including one to Camp Dodge.

Sol Butler, an African American quarterback and the "greatest football player that ever donned the moleskins" at Dubuque German College and Seminary ("German" was dropped from the name in '16) ran 35, 65 and 95 yards in one game, once circling his goal posts and loping the length of the field. Only Cornell College could keep up in '17, when the Blue & White blasted Buena Vista, 125–0. The next year La Crosse upset Dubuque as its SATC, including Butler, humbled Grinnell and another college.[72]

A separate school also known as Dubuque College (now Loras

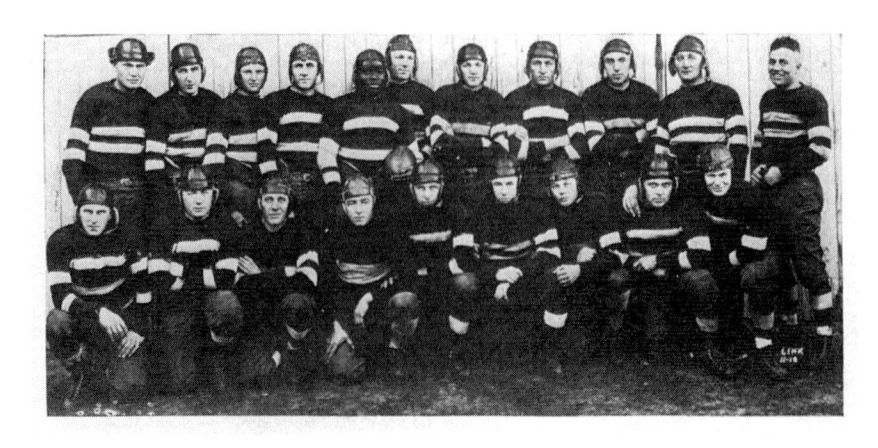

Sol Butler (fifth from left, back row), captain of the Student Army Training Corps team at Dubuque College and Seminary, 1918. *Courtesy University of Dubuque Archives, Special Collections.*

4. College Football

College), after challenging for a Western Catholic title in '16, with wins over St. Ambrose and St. Viator's and tying Creighton, lost to Creighton and St. Ambrose in '17, and then had an SATC officer cancel '18. Morningside (Sioux City) battled close with Notre Dame in '17 and '19, the Methodists making mincemeat of several smaller colleges. Coe College (Cedar Rapids), which won at least four in '16, suffered a "severe blow" from the war in '17, with a much more lopsided loss to Grinnell but had a drop kick overcome Grinnell in '18 among six played, overcoming the flu. Nearby Cornell, 5–3 in '16 and below .500 in '17, also played six times, absorbing two wipeouts from naval reservists at Great Lakes and Cleveland along with others to colleges, as eight went to an army camp just before the start of that season.

The Kansas Intercollegiate Athletic Association (15 colleges) played 15 percent more games in '17 than in '16. The College of Emporia, so-so in '16 and 7–2 in '17, somehow overcame "the irregularity of schoolwork on account of the flu and the S.A.T.C" in '18, playing the required minimum of six, all wins. These Crimson & Gold Presbyterians went 8–0 in '19, for another title.[73]

Ft. Hays Normal, 4–1 in '16 in conference, went undefeated in '17 for the title, edging Emporia Normal, also untainted by defeat. The SATC proved unhelpful in '18. In Topeka, Washburn College, below .500 in both '16 and '17, improved to 3–0 in conference in '18, the Sons of Ichabod hustling past Haskell and ambulance elevens. A 7–1 in '19 ranked second in the conference. Fairmount Normal (Wichita St), 6–2 in '16 and breaking even, with two ties in '17 (five lettermen, ten now dressed in khaki), had six return in '18 but "Uncle Sam" enlisted several. With the SATC akin to "being vaccinated" (an unwanted necessity), a 1–4 resulted. The Wheat Shockers also found foraging hard in '19. After that season, the Baker University eleven, winning about half, planned to work in mines during the Christmas vacation not to break a strike, they claimed, but to prevent suffering of the sick that winter. At Ottawa University, which usually fell below .500, Ken Cassidy, a '16 quarterback (also the top debater) with the Rainbow Division (42nd) in France received a Croix de Guerre and captaincy for fighting for three days even though wounded. Four of fifteen conference members failed to play in '18, even though the only program without the SATC was Friends University, with Quaker connections.[74]

Playing on a higher level than the Kansas Conference, Haskell Institute (Lawrence) sent 16 Native Americans of its '15 and 11 of its '16 squads into the service, winning 6 of 10 in '17, losing to Notre Dame. In '18, nearly all the males left in school played, recording only one win, followed the next year by a tie with Creighton with eight wins and no losses.[75]

Cape Girardeau Normal (Southeast Missouri State), 5–1, subdued St. Louis University in '16, the latter returning the favor in '17, the Sagamores

3–2. Flu cut short '18 after a win, resumed later with an SATC win. In '19, the "Heroes of Argonne" lost most, the standoff with Shurtleff reminiscent of the trenches of Flanders.[76]

Drury, 3–3–1 in '16, had no defeats in '17. The flu year brought a crushing loss in the only contest, the post-war 4–2–1. William Jewel (Liberty) only lost one in '16, likely giving the Big Red at least a tie for the Missouri Intercollegiate A.A. In '17, Jewel gave Missouri University all it could handle, then went 4–0–1, almost the same for '18 save for one more loss and 3–2–1 in '19. Wesleyan 3–3 in '16, claimed the state, 7–0–1, in '17. At 10–0 (8–0 conference) the Possums returned to prominence in '19, following a reduced '18. St. Louis, after a losing '16, won more in '17, tying and winning over different aviators and one of the Great Lakes' elevens in '18, yielding to neighboring Washington University, which beat the Missouri School of Mines at Rolla all four years. The Brutes of Warrensburg State Normal (Central Missouri State Teachers), after their best season in '16, slumped in '17. Football proved incompatible with "Uncle Sam's monstrous war plans" in '18. At least 160 joined the military, twenty "paying the purchase price of liberty in full," including five "old Normal gridiron heroes" and two more from '15.[77]

Creighton (Omaha), which shut out St. Louis University before 15,000, only lost one (Denver by a point) in '16, losses for '17 coming against Dakota teams. Flu canceled one against Colorado's Miners, both undefeated in '18. The post-war brought at least three wins and two ties—Marquette (9,000 at Rourke Park) and Haskell. York College won the Nebraska small college title in '16 and '19, outscoring opponents, 187–0 in the former, when four Panthers made the All-Nebraska small college first team. Although the SATC showed up at several schools, few fielded elevens in '18. Nebraska Wesleyan started '17 pulverizing Peru Normal, then lost the rest when nine went into the service. "War conditions" ended football except for a possible exhibition in '18, only a loss to York marring conference play in '19. Winless in '16 and not playing in '17, the absence of the SATC made football impossible at the University of Omaha in '18. The next year brought improvement, splitting four with colleges plus a tie and win over a nearby fort.[78]

Arkansas (Fayetteville) punished small schools and lost to four bigger ones in '16. In '17, the Razorbacks whipped two Missouri schools, Hendrix, Kendall and LSU (a loss in '16), tying Okla. and losing to Texas. The flu year brought a loss to Camp Pike depot, a 0–103 loss to Okla. (3–2 overall). Arkansas, 3–4 in '19, included a 7–63 loss to Kendall and a one-point win over the Sooners. Ouachita Baptist College, 4–2 in '16 went 4–0 in '17 including over a military hospital, 83–0. In '18, after downing Camp Pike's hospital and the 112th Ordnance, Ouachita claimed a title after four other Arkansas colleges refused to play. In '19, with at least three war vets, the

Baptists pulverized a small college, downed Henderson-Brown and edged Hendrix as well as state normal, yielding to the Jonesboro Aggies.[79]

Hendrix College (Conway), 0–2 versus big schools and 6–1 against small ones in '16, revenged a loss to Henderson Brown, lost again to the Razorbacks but by a lot less in a smaller schedule in '17. In '18 the Bulldogs crushed Little Rock and edged Henderson Brown, 0–1–1 versus the military. With their coach back from two years as an army officer, Hendrix went 6–2 in '19. Arkansas Baptist, in Little Rock, won at least four in '17 over other African American institutions.

In '17, Okla. State overcame Kendall (Tulsa University) and shut out Okla. (losing to both in '16) on Thanksgiving to even up its record at 4–4. The next year, with 350 SATC, the Aggies, with a 116-pound quarterback, took Haskell by a touchdown and Kendall by a lot more. Texas and Okla. proved too strong. In '16, the Sooners wrecked the Aggies, 41–7, which pales compared to scores against smaller schools, but the Sooners lost four to bigger schools and edged Arkansas. The '17 version piled up points against small schools including Kendall, taking Texas and Missouri but losing to Illinois by 44 and to Okla. State and Camp Doniphan, not scoring on Arkansas. The '18 squad came up 5–0, with 103 points against Arkansas. In '19, the Sooners, 5–2–3, lost by a point to Arkansas and to a revived Kendall College.

Kendall in '16, undefeated in 11 games, romped over at least six small colleges and edged Okla. A&M. The next year, with almost all, including Native Americans in the service, replacements tied one in a winless season. Kendall got by a normal school in '18 but not the Aggies and Arkansas. In '19, they bull-dozed some Baptists (152–0) and at least three Okla. normal schools as well as Arkansas, tying Aggies and stopping the Sooners.

Central State Normal (Edmond), possibly a 9–2 in '16, fell to East Central State Normal (Ada), in '17, 2–4 overall. Central lost to Okla. and Okla. State, as usual, in '18, but, with six back from '17 and one from '16, the Bronze & Blue downed Ada by 70, with only Alva Normal scoring on them—on a fumble. That ranked them fourth in the state, behind Phillips and ahead of Kendall, the SATC keeping the Okla. "gridiron game on a par with previous years." Several experienced players at Edmond received training at Fort Sheridan in the summer to lead the SATC. The coach supervised construction of barracks on campus. A former captain at Ada, Harry Jones, had an army camp in Arizona named for him when an errant bullet fired by Mexicans fighting each other killed him.[80]

Phillips University, mediocre in '16, got by Okla. A&M in '17, only losing to Okla. In '18, the Haymakers won 3 of 4, again losing to the Sooners. Only a tie with the Aggies tarnished the '19 season. A reporter, contending that "All Prominent Oklahoma College Athletes of the Last Half Decade" were in the service, listed the Aggies with 94, Central 49 (35 football), the

Sooners about 50 (half in football), Southeastern Normal at least 20, and a Methodist school adding 11.[81]

The university at Austin first in the Southwest in '16, even though losing to Baylor, fell back in '17. The Longhorns, undefeated in '18, overcame the Aggies of Okla. and Texas, Rice, SMU and about as many military elevens. In '17, undefeated Texas A&M took the conference. In '18, the Aggies, in addition to losing to Texas and bumping Baylor and Southwestern, raided an army airfield and defeated elevens from Camp Travis and Camp Mabry. The post-war season went 10–0 for a title.

Baylor challenged Texas for the '16 Southwestern championship, beating the Longhorns but losing to the Aggies, 3–1 in Conference, 9–1 overall. The Bears repeated the same against the other two Texas powerhouses in '17, tying Southern Methodist and losing to Texas Christian. The '18 lost to two airfields and four Texas colleges. Recovery in '19 brought 5–3–1. Rice, not a member of the Conference in '16, lost to Texas but otherwise had two ties and six wins. The '17 Owls eased past Illinois medics and a field hospital, along with six collegiate wins, only the Aggies besting them. Rice, which smashed SMU and downed infantrymen, two aviator elevens and tying Camp Logan in '18, only lost once in '19—to Texas.

Southern Methodist, 0–8–2 in '16, improving a bit in '17, secured a couple in '18, along with three losses in the first conference season. The Mustangs broke .500 in '19, 2–0–1 in conference. Southwestern University (Georgetown) found '16 tough in and out of the conference, losing all three of the former and one to the latter in seven. The '17 version did about the same, with no affiliation with the conference. In '18, the Pirates beat Baylor and lost to the Aggies. A 2–6 ensued in '19.

Texas Christian University (Fort Worth), 6–2–1, losing to Baylor and Southwestern, in '16, only lost to Rice in '17 in seven collegiate matches, disarming field artillerists and ambulance drivers, losing to infantrymen. The flu season brought a close loss to an airfield and Texas, winning over three colleges and two normal schools. The post-war Horned Frogs recorded another over North Texas Normal, then a string of losses—to Decatur Baptist, among others.

The Texas School of Mines (El Paso), winner over infantrymen in '16, also nailed the New Mexico Aggies but lost to New Mexico Military Institute (Roswell) by 79. With no scores for '17, its SATC lost to cavalrymen, a hospital and some engineers at Rio Grande Park in November after flu abated in '18. The post–SATC won over drivers from Fort Bliss and a high school, losing to the University of New Mexico and the school at Roswell. Trinity University (San Antonio) lost to four of the Lone Star State's bigger institutions in '17 and to Daniel Baker College. After 6–1 in '16, losing only to TCU, Baker "retreated into the clouds caused by the European war," giving "heroic service to the country's flag." Although the war did not kill the "old Daniel Baker spirit," a "renaissance" came with obstacles, as eight opponents outscored the once successful Hillbilly program, 0–479, in 1920.[82]

In topsy-turvy '17, in the "Farmer' Revenge" New Mexico's Aggies rolled, 110–3, the chastened losers not accepting varsity letters. The university had no returning coach and sixteen of the previous year's squad were in the service, only one left with any experience. The previous year the Aggies lost to them by over fifty, when several Hill Dwellers returned from pursuing Villa two weeks before the Thanksgiving showdown. Otherwise, the university at Albuquerque blasted the mining schools of New Mexico and Texas in '17 and '19, tying Colorado Ore Diggers in '19 when they went 3–0–2.[83]

The New Mexico College of Agriculture and Mechanical Arts (Las Cruces), in '16 apparently had some still pursuing Pancho when they lost to the university, but in '17, after annihilating the latter, they lost to New Mexico Military Institute and won over the 7th Cavalry. With no team in '18, the '19 lost to soldiers from El Paso, New Mexico University and the University of Arizona. New Mexico Military Institute (Roswell) downed the Aggies, a normal school, two small Texas colleges in '17 and tied New Mexico and the Aggies, with two wins in '19. No reports surfaced for '18.

Losing to Whittier, Rice and USC in '16, Arizona outpointed the New Mexico Aggies and the Texas School of Mines, along with some infantrymen. In '17, a field goal from an officer at Camp Harry Jones beat them as did USC again, the Wildcats taming the Aggies, Whittier as well as some field artillerists. With no scores for '18, the post-war brought easy wins over Tempe Normal, the Indian school in Phoenix, some soldiers, Texas Miners, Occidental and Whittier (a forfeit), the only loss to Pomona.

In '17, Denver, 6–0 in the Rocky Mountain Conference, which banned frosh, claimed the title though the Utah Aggies also did not lose any but won two fewer. In '18, with flu pruning the schedule, the Ministers defeated Colorado College, the Aggies and the Buffaloes but lost to the Teachers of Greeley and the Miners of Golden. In '19, they tied the Ore Diggers but lost at least five others.[84]

In '18, Colorado College, runner up in '16 and 2–3 in '17, persisted mostly with freshmen (355 SATC), flu reducing the schedule to three, winning over the university, being buried by Ore Diggers, fans sitting two feet apart. This record did not detract from having a freshman on the All-Conference and two others honorably mentioned. A loss to Utah and a tie with Colorado marred '19.[85]

The Colorado Aggies (Fort Collins), winner of the state and Rocky Mountain in '16, went from 6–0–1 to 0–7–1 in '17. They lost both Conference games in '18 but got by the Teachers. In '19, they returned to the '16 form, a loss to Colorado College notwithstanding, outscoring Utah, which ranked second in the Conference. Looking like the potential Rocky Mountain winner in '17, with seven back, the Buffaloes at Boulder endured a lopsided loss to Colorado St. Ore Diggers at Golden lost by a lot to Colorado College in '16 but held the Aggies to a scoreless tie. Blasting the Aggies in '17, they fell to Denver. The '18 dominated Denver and Colorado College to claim the state. Even though flu had not shown up in either place, Greeley health officers would not allow folks from Golden to come their city. When the contest finally took place, it was at Golden, the Teachers losing. Officials talked about allowing only SATC to watch. Game receipts likely went to United War Work even though fear of flu delayed the game.[86]

Going 4–0 in the Rocky Mountain, the Utah Aggies (Logan) ran second to Denver in '17, after a poor '16. The reversal included beating Utah by two touchdowns after losing to them the year before by over forty. The Aggies did not play in '18 because SATC started late and sent 397 to camps out-of-state. In '19, they went 5–2. Scattered scores for the Salt Lake City university showed a 3–2 in '16, a 2–3 3 in '17, not playing in '18 and 4–1 in the Rocky Mountain in '19, Utah, led by a Romney, lost to the Aggies of Colorado and won over those from Utah, part of a 5–2, the same as the Aggies.

Nevada started a program, losing all five in '16 and more in '17. When flu felled the coach, the '18 season ended abruptly. The post-war year brought an 8–0–1 with dominant wins over Mare Island, the College of the Pacific and Santa Clara, which was taking up football again.[87]

Wyoming (Laramie) struggled to find traction in the Rocky Mountain Conference, winning once in '16, none in '17, no scores appearing for '18, finally winning several in '19. In '16, Idaho struggled against strong opponents in Oregon and Washington but won three in a week. The Gem Staters fell by competitive scores to strong Northwest elevens in '17, then whipped Whitman and Montana. The Silver and Gold succumbed to Mare Island's Marines in '19 but otherwise did okay.[88]

Montana State, after a productive '16, lost to Denver, tied the Colorado Aggies and Utah, losing to arch-rival Montana in '17. After its SATC could not play in '18, the post-war brought 0–3 in the Rocky Mountain and a tie with Montana before 5,000. Montana prevailed over most opponents in '16, less so in '17. Nothing but flu showed up for '18, the hangover carrying over to '19. Students at Billings, which usually played high schools (a scoreless tie with Montana Wesleyan in '16), were "bitter" about not being able to play in '18 even though they practiced a lot. After a herculean effort, they tied Billings Poly in '17 only to have the State Board of Health cancel four games when scarlet fever invaded Helena. They tried again in '18, when flu cancelled all save a close win over a nearby small college and an academy.[89]

The Flickertails of North Dakota flirted with an undefeated '16, a loss to South Dakota State tarnishing the season. The next year brought more

4. College Football

losses than wins, a blank for '18 even with an SATC, a modest recovery in '19. North Dakota State (Fargo), missing a half dozen pursuing Pancho, 2–3–1 in '16, improved in '17 and drew a blank in '18. Under a new coach who served as a military engineer in France, they only lost one, tying South Dakota State in '19. Fargo College lost to Jamestown in both '16 and '17 but reversed course in '19, conquering the Vikings and wiping out Wahpeton after losing to the same in '17.

Valley City Normal, 1–4 in '16 and 2–2 versus colleges in '17, had no football in '18 because it had exactly one man on campus, 83 in the service. "King Winter" canceled all but one in '19. In '16, Jamestown College rang up six shutouts, five over normal schools and one with Fargo College. Over a third of 68 on the military honor roll at the end of '17 were athletes. Quarterback Kennedy Wanner, small, fast and durable, full of pep and the coach's "right-hand man" (the team captain), attributed his being the first Jamestown collegian to attain a first lieutenancy to football. Wanner and an end on that '16 squad perished in France in the fall of '18.[90]

The Jackrabbits of South Dakota State claimed the Dakota titles for '16 (3–0), '17 (2–0) and '19 (4–0–1), "WE BEAT THE U," the slogan. About 5,000 came to the '17 win over North Dakota State, a scoreless tie with the same in '19. The boys from Brookings also grounded the Flickertails of North

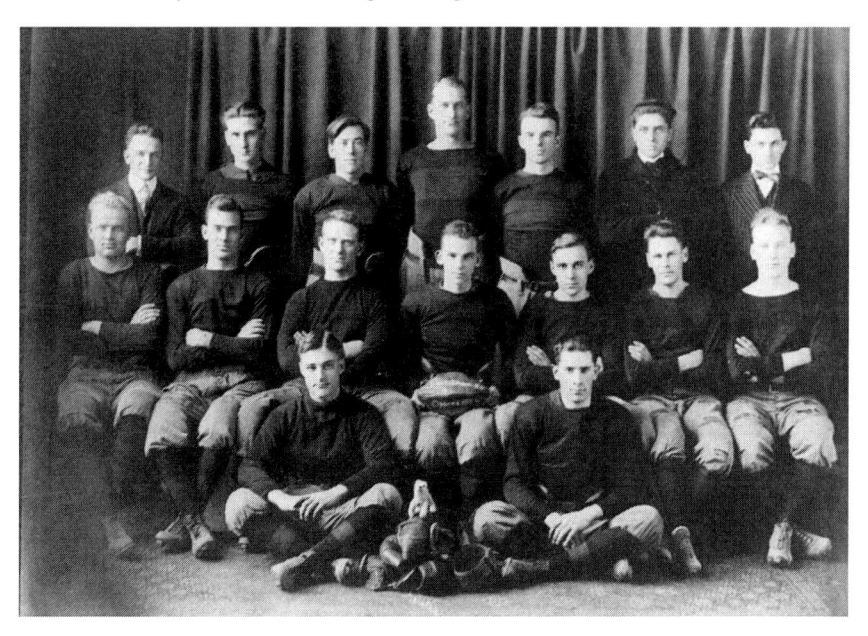

Kennedy Wanner, football captain at Jamestown College in 1916, seated on floor on the right, was killed in action, 1918. *Courtesy University Archives, University of Jamestown, North Dakota.*

Dakota University in '16, '17 and '19. Yankton College, after losing to three small colleges in '16, went 6–1 in '17 and, after giving up '18, ran 7-straight in '19. Dakota Wesleyan (Mitchell), which had a 64-yd. field goal in '15, waited for three to return from the Mexican border for the first game in '16. The coach of the 4–4-1 Blue & White of '17 went to Camp Sherman. The '18 loss to South Dakota University, was one of few played, '19 going 3–4–1.[91]

In '16 and '17, South Dakota University had a hard time against Western Conference foes as well as Notre Dame, 1–2 in '18, with 35 minutes of practice a day, flu a problem. The Coyotes also had a disappointing '19, but fans could reflect on a 3-sports star at Camp Dodge in '17, a '12 varsity transfer to Syracuse who became and war hero and Gene Vidal, a drop kicker at West Point after graduating from South Dakota.[92]

The University of California replaced rugby with football in '16, the coach praising the return of the "red-blooded American sport." The Bears got by Whittier but lost at least three. Mare Island Marines mauled them in '17 as they went 2–2 against colleges, including one over the University of Washington, a "mere shadow of the former football machine" not adapting as well to the war as Berkeley. In '18, the Bears went 3–2 with the military, 4–0 over colleges. They were 5–2 versus colleges in '19.[93]

Stanford and Santa Clara resisted efforts to be rid of rugby, both with unblemished records against athletic clubs and a thriving rivalry with each other. The Red & White, 9–0 in '16, and 9–1 in '17, beat the Cardinals in the former year and lost to the same in the latter. In '18, the Missionites won all three over Stanford's SATC, the proceeds of one going to the United War Workers. Two Stanford players from before the war were killed in action in France in '18. When the officer of the SATC at Cal allowed non-military to play as Stanford and Cal planned to renew their football rivalry, the president at Palo Alto made it clear that the SATC did not represent Stanford. The Cardinals lost to Cal by a lot, but in the ensuing February, the Cardinals got revenge, in rugby, 21–8. Otherwise in '18, Mather Field, Mare Island and USC humbled its SATC, the post-war bringing more success as the school formally resumed intercollegiate football. Santa Clara restarted the gridiron game in '19, winning over two naval ships, splitting with an athletic club and losing to Nevada and Stanford.[94]

Occidental College, which tied Cal in '17 (2–1 versus the military), suspended practice in '18, when only 3 of 90 escaped the flu, in spite of which Oxy won over USC, going 2–2–2 against colleges. In '19, Southern Branch Normal (UCLA) lost to high schools, the Oxy frosh as well as a naval crew. After downing Southern Branch in '16, Throop College endured shutouts against Oxy, Pomona, the Sherman Indians and L.A. State Normal, yielding to Whittier by a point and Redlands by a couple of touchdowns in '17. After not playing in '18, the Orange & Black ran off wins against crews off two battleships as well as Loyola, the Indians, Redlands (7–6) and Whittier but gave way to Occidental and Pomona.[95]

In '16, Cal Poly (San Luis Obispo) split two with a high school. In '17, with 41 in the military, including most of the experienced athletes, Poly prevailed over Coast Artillery from Long Beach described as "grown men" from Stanford, USC and Colorado, "equal to any American football squad." Poly, however, lost the rematch when "like wolves upon the fold," the artillerists ate up the Green & Gold. Even though 138 Poly students were in the military by the fall of '18, the press thought the school could play, even without an SATC, but no one would play them.[96]

In '17, although the top player returned from military duty, Washington tied Oregon State and lost to Cal and Washington State. The University of Washington SATC took care of business against a naval ship, overwhelmed a small college, beat Oregon State, losing to Oregon. The next year, the Seattle school bested Washington State as well as Cal but lost to Oregon before 10,000, doing well against two naval opponents and walloping Whitman College but failure to play the Aggies meant they had no real chance for any Northwest or Pacific Coast championship.[97]

In '17, guided by William "Lone Star" Dietz, Washington State tied officers of an infantry regiment from Camp Lewis, at Tacoma and won six over colleges. The football program sent 34 into the military. The varsity SATC, under another coach, accompanied by 600 fans (flu abating) lost by a point to Idaho at Moscow after overcoming Gonzaga's SATC a week earlier. Flu prevented a game with Washington. An officer at Mare Island hoped to send Dietz and State players to Quantico, but the Corps rejected the idea. State's athletic board refused to renew Dietz's contract when they heard he was not a Native American. The next June, after a hung jury, he served a brief sentence for evading the draft. Later, he coached the Boston Redskins, the team with the same nickname that moved to the nation's capital.[98]

Willamette (Salem) lost by a lot to Oregon in '16. Only wins over Chemawa showed up for '17 or '18, victories over three small colleges in '19. Oregon Agricultural College (later State), splitting eight in '16, overcame a field hospital from Vancouver in '17 as well as Oregon and Idaho. In '18, they again vanquished Vancouver, losing to a Camp Lewis eleven and Oregon in the only college contest (5–4 in '19). Oregon, in '16, corralled Cal but yielded to Mare Island, the Oregon Aggies and Washington State in '17. In '18, with no coach, the SATC Yellow/Lemon, half with the flu, lost to an athletic club, the rule about time being off campus cancelling two games. Even though three went to officer training, Oregon won over shipbuilders and the Depot Brigade (Camp Lewis), led by a former Oregon frosh. Wearing weird-looking uniforms, Oregon beat Washington at Seattle for the United

War Work campaign. In '19, with a Mare Island fullback, Oregon lost only to Washington State in a full slate, later yielding to Harvard in the '20 Rose Bowl by a point, though statistically ahead of the presumptive best team in the nation.[99]

Several conferences, sanctioned by the NCAA, did not count '18 against eligibility. In a related action, the Big 10 let no one play varsity in '19 who had not registered before entering the service, thus preventing Northwestern from making freshmen from Great Lakes eligible. The Southern Intercollegiate in February '19 threw out the season. The Atlanta press claimed Guyon and Strupper would have one more year at Tech, but neither came back.[100]

What was the overall impact of the SATC and related military units on college-level football? In addition to training potential army officers from 150,000 men on over 500 campuses, vocational programs for those without a high school education appeared at about 100 places, a dozen of which (Historically Black schools) had no regular SATC. Over ninety naval and a dozen marine units also operated, all at schools that had the SATC. While many criticized the mixing of military oranges with academic apples, it may well have saved several institutions of higher education. It certainly produced more games (225 discovered so far) than would otherwise have taken place in '18 without it.

At least 700 football programs existed between 1916 and 1919 at over 900 institutions. More programs and scores will eventually come to light, bringing the percentage well above 80. Over 90 percent of the 500 "real colleges" with the SATC had intercollegiate football between 1916 and 1919. The overall number fell but only by a small amount in '17. Conferences varied greatly in dealing with the flu in '18. The Rocky Mountain and the Missouri Valley had deep cuts while the Southwest cut the game count by about 20 percent as did the Ohio Conference.

Most reporters thought military elevens dominated collegians, but in scores gathered thus far, colleges had a substantial edge in about 100 games in '17, lost less than 40 percent of the contests with the military in '18 and dominated in '19 in far fewer contests. Games between colleges and the military in '18 were for the most part two military clubs competing against each other. What explains the ability of collegians to hold their own against older and tougher military men? Colleges often played against only officers or units smaller than regiments like hospital corpsmen, bakers, etc. In '18, both the SATC and the regular military faced limited times for practice. Many older men could not regain their touch after a long absence from the field.

5

Professional and Military Football

Starting in the 1890s, collegians introduced football to the YMCA, high schools, prep schools and athletic clubs. The Y lost interest, but community clubs not connected with the Amateur Athletic Union first started paying collegians in 1892 and by 1916 several dozen pro teams operated from New York across the Midwest. Owners of major league baseball teams considered using their stadiums as gridirons.

In '16, in any given Sunday in the fall, Midwestern pros competed, including Pine Village, a community of a few hundred that won Indiana titles more than once. That season, a W & Jefferson back helped Hammond overcome Detroit. In '17, a number of teams dropping out, Hammond lost to the Detroit Heralds but, adding Driscoll, downed Davenport, then overcame a Chicago club, when a "knocked out" Paddy drop kicked a field goal from the far side of the 50. They later ruled Racine and Wabash, losing to Pine Village, which they had defeated earlier. Reporters gave Hammond the Indiana pro title.[1]

In '18, with Driscoll in the service and flu a factor, only a few came to fewer games. The post-war ('19) brought George Halas, after his stints at Great Lakes and with the Yankees. Dominance over Gus Dorias and the Fort Wayne Friars gave Hammond the state title. Earlier, the principal owner of the football Heralds, who also owned the Detroit Tigers, refused to play in a "light rain" annoying the crowd and Hammond's owner who returned gate receipts. Hammond later harnessed the Heralds, 7–6. After rocking the Rock Island Independents before 7,000, Hammond tied Thorpe's unbeaten eleven, but 12,000 saw a drive after a Driscoll fumble give Canton a win at Hammond.[2]

In '17 the Rock Island Independents won seven, losing twice to the Minneapolis Marines, several of whom signed with Rock Island to help down Davenport. In '18, 5–0, about half the usual, the owner ended the business because it was not a "paying proposition." In '19, they rang up 9 of

10, losing only to Hammond after flattening Fritz Pollard and Akron on the mud and ice. Thorpe's Canton crowd turned down a challenge for $10,000 raised in one day.[3]

Disagreeing that the war ruined football, a columnist focused on the large number of teams at all the army camps and wherever soldiers are stationed." Another editor observed that football, formerly restricted "almost exclusively" to a small number of colleges and high schools, was "now gaining widespread popularity" because "every recruit who ever played on a team is now playing in camp and teaching others." It might well challenge baseball as the National Game.[4]

At Camp Funston (89th Division), the 342nd Field Artillery put eight on the divisional squad in '17 as the camp eleven defeated Great Lakes and Kendall College, losing to Illinois before 30,000 at Fort Riley, winning 7 of 10 under Dr. Paul Withington, a former Harvard athlete. Another battery won all games within the regiment, scored on only once, and tied a signal battalion. In early September '17, the camp and nearby Fort Riley had forty fields supervised by a lieutenant from the Springfield Y school. Most of the 88th Division (Minn.) received training at Dodge through that cold winter of 1917–18. The 352nd regiment, with heavy scoring won the camp title. A 3–0 Camp Dodge victory over Funston in '17 injured eight for the losers, seven for the winners.[5]

At Camp Custer in '17, Captain W.J. "Birdie" Gardiner, out of Carlisle, coached and captained officers in an infantry regiment in the 85th Division, who kayoed Kalamazoo College, the Heralds and Great Lakes before surrendering to Camp Grant, winning 5 of 6. In the Heralds game, with Eckersall refereeing and reporting, the pros injured one of Gardiner's men in an out-of-bounds tackle. Shifted to fullback, Gardiner drove his head into the stomach of the rivals' biggest player, forcing him out of the contest. Before the showdown between Camps Custer and Grant (won by the latter by a point), an English officer and veteran of trench warfare spoke in horror about the brutality as he watched Camp Grant practicing.[6]

In '17, Camp put Gardiner on his All-Service eleven. One of the guards, Clinton "Cupid" Black of Yale was now with the Newport Naval Reserves while the other from Michigan was now with Fort Sheridan. Harvard men were the half backs. Fullback Pat Smith temporarily served at Great Lakes. Camp's list of 33 Military All-Americans contains only four that had not played in college, three on his third team. Five came from the army on his first team, four with the navy, plus one Mare Island Marine (Beckett from Oregon) and an army aviator. The second team had seven army, two naval reservists, one from Great Lakes and a Mare Island Marine. The third team consisted of nine in camps plus two from navy elevens. No Southern camps or naval installations were included on any lists because they were still competing at the time Camp made his selections.

In '17, a company of railway engineers, with about 1,200 enlisted at Grant, came away with the championship amid a lot of betting. The weather did not cooperate, equipment was hard to come by and military matters interfered, but the regiment managed several games with a "high standard of efficiency." The camp eleven took 3 of 4. In '18, forty men who had played in college and/or pro showed up to Camp Grant's first practice, those of the previous year with the 86th Division overseas; the new players included top Chicago high school stars, a pro halfback capable of punting the ball 60 yards who had recently stopped Thorpe's aggregation. Marquette's captain would quarterback the club.[7]

In '17, at Camp Sherman Ohio (83rd Division), a supply company won one regimental title, over a battery which had never given up a touchdown, when a novice accidentally fell on a ball. When the regiment fought a scoreless battle with a field artillery, lineman "Fat" stopped the foe on the goal line. The camp's '18 lost to Camp Taylor, 0–40 (Louisville), which included a Cornell '17 abetted by a Notre Dame '13. Taylor lost to Sherman in '17, tying Hancock while losing to Centre in '18, overcoming Indiana and taking down camps Shelby and Grant at some point.[8]

In '17, about 10,000 fans ($20,000 divided among twenty teams to buy equipment) probably did not see a drop kick in the fog by a former Dartmouth star in a Dodge win over Funston at Omaha. Eckersall called the kick wide, the umpire ruling it inside the posts. Dodge went undefeated until all-star Iowa collegians beat them, 6–0. None of that squad were still in camp in the fall of '18, most of them off to France with the 88th. With different athletes, the director announced that both officers and enlisted men could compete. Collegians came from several prestigious programs, including three from Carlisle.[9]

In '17, 10,000 at Stagg Field (Chicago) saw Pat Smith and a halfback from St. Olaf ease Great Lakes past Fort Sheridan's seconds. Selfridge Field (U.S. Air Service), near Detroit, had Smith in '18, an All–New England tackle (Maine), an All-Ohio (Case), an Armour Institute quarterback, a Yale Informal plus several other collegians. With twenty minutes of practice, they lost to naval reservists from River Rouge and later to the Heralds. They advertised their games by dropping leaflets on University of Michigan fans.[10]

A battery of field artillerists, 29th Division, in training near Fort Oglethorpe overcame the University of Tennessee at Knoxville in '17. Near the end of November, possibly the same or other Virginia artillerists, transferred to Camp McClellan. In '16, it had supposedly won all its games, according to the Atlanta press, which did not mention the loss to the Second Texas of the Norfolk Light Artillery Blues. The margin of one battery's win over Tennessee was about the same as the 38–0 verdict over the Volunteers secured by Gordon a few weeks earlier over the same, but the camp easily vanquished the Virginians.

Gordon, fifteen miles from the center of Atlanta, started the '17 season with a lineup sifted from a hundred recruits, included Kirke Newell, a quarterback from Auburn '13, plus six former Georgia Bulldogs, a guard from Vanderbilt, a center from Pitt, thirty overall, only three with no college affiliation. They rolled over Oglethorpe College. Later, Newell fell on a live grenade, the heroic action described in the press as if the Plainsman covered a fumble. Camp Jackson (South Carolina), with two Eli, a Cavalier (Alan Thurman) and a Commodore (Josh Cody, third team All-American), along with those from Washington & Lee, South Carolina and three North Carolina institutions, shut down the vaunted Gordon "Steam Rollers" 10–0, also humbling Hancock and Wadsworth. Thurman became a first lieutenant in the 371st Regiment, composed of black draftees from South Carolina who fought with the French. Camp Hancock in '17, under Walter Camp, Jr., had an All-American lineman from W & J, a fullback from Brown, plus other collegians.[11]

At Gordon, the '18 season brought Sgt. Strupper, who quarterbacked players from Dartmouth (a supposed All American), a Carlisle Olympian (Lt. Frank Mt. Pleasant), a Missouri Tiger, a Texas Longhorn just to mention a few. In an outing in October, they overwhelmed Oglethorpe College before 20,000, civilians discouraged from attending due to the flu. On the eve of a showdown with Tech, Coach Ed Stewart (Nebraska) argued that "All-American and all-star talk is simply bunk, pure and unadulterated." A Princeton Tiger left school ten years earlier. Mt. Pleasant was in his thirties. Major Albert von Kolnitz starred long ago at South Carolina. Tech, even though it had nine from '17 in the service (only Strupper came to Gordon), had thirteen return to school. Stewart strongly advised soldiers not to bet on the upcoming contest. After being wiped out by Tech, Gordon yielded to Camp Hancock, as J. Howard Berry avenged a loss incurred by Pennsylvania against Tech and Strupper in '17. Hancock in '18 had collegians from Dartmouth, Minnesota, Texas, etc.[12]

The field at Camp Greenleaf near Fort Oglethorpe in northern Georgia was in a natural amphitheater at Chickamauga Park in '17. This camp for medics won the army Eastern title in '18, using a "steam-roller attack" and an "impregnable defense," downing Camp Dix, 34–0, at the American League Park in D.C., witnessed by Baker and army brass. Greenleaf had three All-Americans and included a Pitt Panther or two from '17. The road to the championship brought victories over Auburn, Vanderbilt, Hancock Ordnance, McClellan and Gordon. That they played Dix, which only won one (tying Camp Upton, which won at least four times, the same number achieved by Camp Devens), remains an issue.[13]

5. Professional and Military Football   89

Camp Shelby (Mississippi) remained undefeated in overcoming the fort at Pensacola, in a "ragged" contest in November '17, a Notre Dame quarterback making big yardage on a punt return. The next year, Shelby shut out Park Field at Memphis, helped by an Ole Miss punter. In that Thanksgiving showdown, Shelby faced aviators that sustained four major injuries, plus minor injuries for everyone else against Payne Field the previous Saturday, a "gory affair," when "every time the two teams would crash, somebody wouldn't rise." To cover positions, non-officers could now play. A captain out of Nebraska who had coached in Tennessee quarterbacked Kid Elberfeld's Shelby.[14]

In '17, Camp McClellan (Anniston, northwest Alabama) set aside Wednesday and Saturday afternoons and all-day Sundays for games. Engineers claimed the camp title but were beaten by infantrymen that had not found much chance to practice but had several former college stars. Gordon whitewashed the camp eleven, which also lost to Greenleaf and Camp Sheridan, both by a lot. Chaplains for the 29th from New Jersey, Maryland, and Virginia bragged about a win on a Sunday.[15]

In '17, Fort Root (near Little Rock) had some notable Southern athletes serving as officers, including a former quarterback at LSU and a one-time captain of Tulane. Camp Beauregard (Louisiana), with a Virginia Poly back from Europe in '18, a lieutenant from a small college in Wisconsin, one from Jewell College and another lieutenant from Washington, had little trouble crushing a nearby college.[16]

Kelly Field, near San Antonio, claimed the Southern Department army airfield championship in '18. Infantrymen edged field artillerists from Camp Scurry, 13–12, before 5,000 on Thanksgiving at Laredo. Those artillerymen had at least four batteries playing each other, sometimes on Sundays.[17]

In '17, Camp MacArthur (Waco, 32nd Division) followed the tradition of the Michigan national guardsmen near El Paso the previous year in claiming an Army championship in '17, but given the lack of scores and balanced schedules, that claim appears mythical. They did subdue Camp Bowie (Fort Worth) that likely included Longhorns and Aggies and lost to the University of Detroit. Camp Bowie had at least three artillery companies, one of which won over an infantry regiment, another infantry regiment smashing these field artillerists before 4,200.[18]

In the New Mexico desert near Deming that '17 Thanksgiving, the "Giants" from Cody, with ten nights practice, overcame Fort Bliss at El Paso's stadium, 9–7, winning on a safety, before 14,000 screaming fans. Officers at Bliss at first designated a cavalry regiment to represent them, then, on learning that Cody was sending a picked team, they created one from all personnel. Cody, composed mostly of enlisted non-collegians from Iowa, brought 1,500 supporters, by train. The coach and best player for Bliss, Captain Alex "Babe" Weyand (Camp 2nd Team All-American in '13) starred for West Point on an undefeated eleven and another that only lost to the Notre Dame passing combine of Dorias and Rockne. He later received a Purple Heart, a Silver Star and a promotion to major.[19]

That fall at Bliss, the 7th Cavalry shutout an athletic club on a Sunday at Rio Grande Park, later sustaining injuries in beating medics. Field artillerists rolled over an ambulance unit and tied infantry before some 3,000. On Christmas Day, the 7th had the only two touchdowns in beating a sanitary eleven. Fort Douglas claiming wins over the University of Arizona, 3–0 and some miners, challenged Bliss but no game materialized. With players from Yale, Harvard, Cornell and Chicago, Douglas matched up well with nearly any other eleven. Whether this fort was the one located in Utah to confine dangerous Germans (alien enemies) or refers to one of two forts near Douglas, Arizona is unclear.[20]

In '18, Bliss secured revenge against Cody on Thanksgiving, 19–0, inclement weather keeping the crowd down to 8,000. This time Cody, now home to the 97th Division, had players from Harvard and one each from Minnesota, Purdue, Texas and Virginia. Bliss more than matched that assemblage with two from Texas and one each from Lehigh, Princeton, Nebraska, Colorado and Kansas.[21]

Bliss divided into American and National leagues. Field artillerists (ravaged by flu in October) called "Gunners," two cavalry ("Riders") and two engineer companies ("Builders") played twice on Saturdays and once on Sunday mornings usually on parade grounds. On a Sunday afternoon, thousands from the garrison and hundreds from El Paso gathered for the game in January between one of the Builders and the 7th Cavalry, the former copping the title.[22]

On a Sunday in January '19, at Columbus, New Mexico, the 24th infantry (African American) came up with a regimental champ but at Nogales, Arizona, the 25th Infantry upset the 24th, 26–0, in a Southwest championship for black soldiers. The 25th, having recently moved from Hawaii, also overcame the 10th Cavalry twice that fall. In the real war, the 10th fought Mexicans and German agents.[23]

Camp Kearny (near San Diego) had a field that ran two miles, five hundred yards wide, the ground softened to reduce injuries. The Grizzlies (40th Division) counted on using San Diego Stadium, built for the 1915 Exposition and capable of seating 39,000. The commander believed football helped train for trench warfare, the specialization of each position and reliance on teamwork key points of comparison. Utah grounded the Grizzlies' field artillery, 7–0, at Kearny in '17, the losers overcoming submariners in Los Angeles in January 1918. In San Diego, in February, the Grizzlies "pawed their way to the service title," upending artillerists called "He Men." A leg fracture to Fred Thomson, the loser's best defender, made the task easier before 8,000 including actress Mary Pickford, who kept the time.[24]

Camp Lewis, which opened in early September '17, near American Lake not far from Tacoma, with close to 40,000 personnel, had fifty officers managing twelve teams in 132 games. The 362nd took a seemingly commanding lead, over a sanitary train. In the last contest, however, the 362nd fell to the 316th, a sergeant scoring all its points. When the latter won three postponed games, the race ended in a tie, but because the 316th loss had been a forfeit, officials gave it the title.

The Camp Lewis All-Stars (91st Division) started with seven from the University of Washington plus several from Oregon and other western states. Early in October officers at the camp overwhelmed enlisted. One of the camp teams played a scoreless tie with medics from Eugene, five of whom later moved over to the divisional squad. In the middle of October, officers of one regiment played a scoreless tie with Washington State before 15,000, at Tacoma's Stadium. Enlisted and children paid 25 cents and others twice that amount, which raised $2,000 for the regiment to buy athletic equipment. Lewis overcame a nearby fort, but despite heroics by a quarterback out of North Dakota, it lost, 13–0, to Mare Island in the Tacoma Stadium before some 25,000 (half in uniform), setting another attendance record. Thanksgiving Day, Lewis overcame University of Washington naval training (Seattle), 14–13, when a wet wind drove an extra point try off course. Inclemency kept attendance low, with most of the audience 8,000 sailors. In December, teams from Lewis filleted one of the three forts defending the Columbia River before 10,000 at the Camp and overwhelmed the Chemawa Indian School (Salem, Oregon). Lewis sent "a real team" to Pasadena to play the Marines again, but Mare Island won at the Rose Bowl on New Year's Day '18 and were thereby ranked "Best in the West."[25]

Before facing Lewis, undefeated Mare Island crushed California. Johnny Beckett, the captain of '16 Oregon that had bested Pennsylvania in the Rose Bowl, led the Marines. Other collegians (one each from Occidental, Nebraska, Montana, Utah, Washington and Washington St.) plus five from Oregon (subs from UNC, Minnesota and Michigan), abetted him. As he warmed up to play USC, Beckett asked the name of the high school on the other side of the field.[26]

A company of engineers at Camp Meade had three scoreless ties, 1–2 against other engineers. Within a few days of their arrival in September, one infantry regiment in the 79th Division, after intramural play, with no winner determined because of the lack of a playoff, lost to another infantry regiment. A Princeton Tiger coached one of these but his eleven lacked prominent collegians. A picked team, along with supporters entrained to

Philadelphia, where many came from, to represent the division against Camp Dix, the Jersey post prevailing. An army lieutenant, formerly captain and quarterback of Colgate, scored two touchdowns. Fourteen colleges had representatives on the two combatants.[27]

Naval Gunners planned a playoff against Quantico Balloonists for the last week of December to determine the best military eleven in the D.C. area in '17, but rain forced cancelation. A proposed New Year's game could not be played because one team had already disbanded. After the flu abated in '18, a league consisting of aviators from Anacostia, Chemical Warfare (Camp Leach, American University), army medics, soldiers from Camp Humphreys, Barrack Marines, Seaman Gunners and the Gun Factory vied. In December, the last mentioned, buttressed with collegians including a fullback from Illinois, remained undefeated after five. They played on Sundays and occasionally used Griffith's ballpark. "Gassers" from Chemical Warfare lost to Catholic University, 7–6, possibly having run out of the non-mustard variety.[28]

In '17, on the last Saturday in November, Pitt shut out a regiment (most of whose members hailed from western Pennsylvania) from Camp Lee at Forbes Field, even though the Panthers were shorthanded, having played on Thanksgiving. The losers beat Bethany College.

Camp Lee in October '18, seemingly ignoring the flu, utility workers, truck drivers, laundry workers and veterinarians vied. In December, a black battalion scheduled Virginia Normal and Industrial (Virginia State), but no score showed up. Possibly the same lost to Virginia Union University by four touchdowns. An ammo train from Camp Fremont (California), with a half-back from Oregon, clobbered a battalion. They all finished up on the first day of the New Year. No divisional eleven apparently took the field.[29]

In Newport News in late November '17, an aero squadron (Langley) lost 0–62, to artillerists, receipts going to the Red Cross. The captain and coach of the airmen came from Georgia, the army leader from Northwestern, seven from Washington and two from Washington State, other colleges also represented. Artillerists included two from Okla. State and Okla. and one each from Nebraska, Michigan State, Notre Dame and Butler. An aero squadron near Richmond, had representatives from Arizona, California, Kansas, South Dakota State, Mt. Union and twins from West Virginia University, etc.[30]

In '17, a Colgate collegian led aviators from the training camp at Mineola, Long Island over Fort Slocum to win the N.Y. Athletic Club's Metropolitan District Army and Navy Posts League title at Garden City. In September '18, at Mineola's Aviation Field, a former coach at NYU started practice, knowing that many candidates including college stars would be redeployed almost daily. In a well-advertised affair, Camp Upton beat the aviators at the Polo Grounds, after a previous scoreless tie between the two.[31]

5. Professional and Military Football 93

At Camp Devens in October '17 infantrymen took on a machine gun battalion, a one-time Dartmouth fullback coaching the former. Other contests pitted the only cavalry in camp against an ammo train with a former Springfield Y-back, the previous year's captain of the Norwich University frosh and former students at other N. England small colleges also contending. Percy Haughton, former Harvard coach and owner of the Boston Braves, took over at Devens and arranged to play the Boston Navy Yard, under another Harvard man, with receipts going to the war camp community fund. When R.I. field artillerists moved to Mass, one battery bested Headquarters, a mere corporal scoring the lone touchdown. A schedule had to be curtailed because the 26th "Yankee" Division headed overseas. The All-Camp Devens '18, champs of the Northeast, which overcame Brown University, aviators from Garden City, Camp Merritt and tied Harvard Radio School, included athletes from at least eleven different schools.[32]

In Hawaii, on a Sunday in '17, Fort Kamehameha rolled over artillery, the speed and deception of a back the deciding factor. At Schofield Barracks, in one of the "best games ever played," infantry overcame artillery, 16–13. After a few games, the 4th Cavalry stood last in a six-team Oahu League that had four military, a Y and an athletic club. Fort Shafter, with 1,200 personnel, created an eleven too late to join even though they had experienced collegians. The death of a Kansas Aggie (a broken rib puncturing his heart) for Kamehameha in a win over the cavalry in early December, ended fort football. Hawaii's first football death was just a few days before, in a high school match.[33]

In his year-end report, Camp, who appointed directors of athletics at naval installations, determined that the war had increased the number of games played and people playing. At the bigger bases, as many as fifteen teams played regularly. Even more might have participated if enough equipment could have been found. Former collegians who had gone into business were returning to the sport. Young men with limited previous exposure were now involved.[34]

Among naval units, despite the flu in '18, 8 of the 13 teams in the First Naval District League, covering Mass, New Hampshire and Maine, played at least once in October. The Radio School at Cambridge (Harvard) humiliated an ammo depot. Bumpkin Island's only loss came at the hands of the Radio School, whose players came from nine states, including an end from Washington State, a quarterback out of South Carolina, a back from Washington University (St. Louis), and a center who had never played before. At Soldiers Field in Boston in '17 the Charlestown Navy Yard shut out the League Island Marines led by Harvard's Eddie Mahan, when an intercepted pass set up the winning score.[35]

Shortly after the Armistice, Radio lost to Devens but nailed Newport

Naval Training, 21–6, which shut out a nearby fort twice in '17, the loser tying the Providence Steam Rollers, a future version of which would reign as the champions of the National Football League (1928). Providence lived up to their name on a Sunday in early November, rolling over Fort Greble which in '18 took the Narragansett Bay Coast Defense title. The training station even played a team composed of those taking care of victims of the flu, encamped outside Newport. The Newport Torpedo Station yielded to the aerial-minded Rumford Navy Rifle Range, 20–0, before about 5,000, standing several rows deep on the sidelines.[36]

In '17, after downing Maine's Artillery, the 2nd Naval District's Newport Naval Reserves, led by Clinton Black, overcame the Boston Navy Yard to win the N. England Service title 7–6 at Cambridge and ran a scoreless tie with Devens at Braves Field on Thanksgiving. This "remarkable aggregation of college luminaires," with at least three All-Americans, found out they were less than "invincible" against the "giant negro" Robeson and Rutgers. In one contest they raised over $2,000 for widows and orphans of naval men. The champions of a six-team league in Eastern Connecticut turned out to be the squad from the submarine base at New London.

In the 3rd Naval District, Charles Brickley, a Harvard great from a few years back, easing into the game after being vaccinated, led Hoboken Naval Transport over the U.S.S. *Arizona*, 10–0, on the Stevens Institute Field in '18. Syracuse and Rutgers proved too much; a camp in New Jersey (probably for signal corpsmen at Monmouth) submitted.

In the 4th Naval District, the League Island Marines lost to Allentown Ambulance and Camp Meade before cruising past Camp Lee in '17. In '18, after a win over Penn at Franklin Field in late October, the crowd restricted to students due to the flu, most of the Marines transferred, so, Byron Dickson, a former coach at Penn and several other Pennsylvania colleges, re-organized his squad, keeping a few marines, adding personnel from Naval Training and the Navy Yard. With the '17 captain from Swarthmore, the rest mostly all Pennsylvania collegians except a walk-on who became the team leader, the Navy Yard overcame Lehigh, Swarthmore (Ben Boynton in his only game), Brown, Georgetown, the Charleston Navy Yard and Camp Hancock, led by Lt. J. Howard Berry.

In the 5th Naval District, St. Helena Station (Norfolk) in November '17, with a right halfback out of Rutgers, the left one from Villanova and the fullback from Swarthmore (others from Fordham, Minnesota and Dartmouth), sank the new Naval Operating Base, 18–6. In late August, Win Clark organized a squad from naval reservists at the unfinished base. Prospects included one each from Syracuse, Michigan and Texas, plus several from small colleges.[37]

In '18, a first team '16 All-American center, Bob Peck (Pitt), led the

Hampton Roads Operating Base along with collegians from at least nine other colleges and universities. The coach helped the U.S.S. *New Hampshire* win the Atlantic Fleet title the previous year. The base only lost to the Naval Academy, with one tie, in nine. In '19, an eleven combining Naval Training, St. Helena and a nearby receivership won the Eastern naval championship. Quarterbacked by Joel "Black Star" Wheelock, an Oneida who played over eight years at Carlisle, the Base rolled over the Philadelphia Navy Yard and tied Newport Training. A second contest, in Norfolk, tied in regulation, Wheelock passing and runners circling ends making it 25–6 in overtime. The "splendid aerial offensive" and "Heisman shift" turned back the U.S.S. *Pennsylvania* for the Eastern navy title.[38]

With the War Camp Community Service as sponsors, about 4,000 from Pensacola saw the nearby Naval Air Station soar over army aviators from Montgomery, 33–0 on Thanksgiving, '18. The score would have been even more decisive save for the defensive efforts of one from Carlisle. A few days earlier, at the municipal park, 2,500 ("a big crowd") witnessed Naval Air ease by marines, 9–0, in the "cleanest and fastest game in years," the sailors led by a Nebraska Cornhusker. The Air Station also played a scoreless tie with Tulane's SATC.[39]

Around San Diego in August '18, officers at the Naval Training Station, Army Aviation Camp, Naval Aviation Station, Navy Base and Fort Rosecrans and infantrymen created a league. Based on a successful previous season, the athletic director thought football would go "over the top." The naval station's top player from the year before returned to help a newcomer Carlisle quarterback, plus two Longhorns.

The U.S.S. *New Hampshire* won four in '17 and a fifth in January '18, receiving the trophy in February. The U.S.S. *Michigan* claimed the next title, when, led by an Indian "chief," they sank a crew that had previously dunked three ships and a Naval Hospital staff. One wonders why the U.S.S. *Illinois* missed out, because it won $2,000 in bets, taking the Division 1 title with a drop kick against the U.S.S. *Kentucky* and submerging the U.S.S. *Ohio*, 7–0. One of their supporters complained that no one would bet against them after the first game, but another claimed he approached the Illinois crew while it was in the Norfolk Navy Yard willing to wager several thousand dollars, but only when Illinois scored against the *Ohio* were they willing to put up even $200.[40]

Just before Thanksgiving '18, the U.S.S. *Pennsylvania* overcame the U.S.S. *New Mexico* at Prospect Park in Brooklyn, 20–0. Rabbit Maranville scored two touchdowns for the former, one on a pass reception, and two extra points. The shortstop, who also liked to box, played for the Radio School in the fall of '17 at quarterback and right end. In '19, the *Pennsylvania* surprised the U.S.S. *Arizona*, 18–0, in Brooklyn to remain undefeated.

Coached by a former Naval Academy player, they knocked off the U.S.S. *Utah* in Boston and cruised past the U.S.S. *Nevada* to secure the Atlantic Division. Aspirations to capture the Eastern naval championship went asunder when they fell to the Hampton Roads Operating Base in D.C., with Josephus Daniels and Franklin Roosevelt among the spectators.[41]

Two of the most powerful military teams in the country—the Cleveland Naval Reserves and the Great Lakes Naval Station—never played each other in '18, flu causing a cancellation. Cleveland edged the best college, Pittsburgh 10–9, because of a missed extra point and questionable refereeing and/or time keeping. Chicago's Municipal Pier also put in a claim for the mythical military title, its chief athletic officer pointing to a 6–0 win over Cleveland.[42]

After a shaky start (ties against Northwestern and Notre Dame), Great Lakes cruised, beating the Naval Academy and six others, routing Rutgers, 42 scored by Driscoll who set his feet as if to punt, then ran "rings round" the defense. Critics complained about his playing for pay for Hammond, but the military refused to ban pros. The Lakes' line averaged close to 190 pounds, including two guards and a center from Notre Dame, a tackle from Michigan State and another from Minnesota. The ends, though not considered the same caliber, included Ensign George Halas, a versatile athlete at Illinois. Using an "Atlantic States" style of ball, it passed or punted only when necessary.[43]

Mare Island Marines, Mather Field Aviators, Rockwell Field Aviators and Balboa Park Sailors vied in the West. No scores surfaced for the San Pedro Submarine Base, but they must have had a team. Rockwell Field, with no stars, had won six-straight but soon withdrew. Balboa Park Naval Training, fresh off a win over the U.S.S. *Oregon*, won the Southwest Service '17 title on 1 January '18 over Utah artillerists stationed at Camp Kearny before 15,000 (receipts for the Red Cross). Mather's aviators, mostly collegians coached by Pitt All-American quarterback Jimmy De Hart, defeated California and Stanford on two successive days but seems not to have challenged military elevens.

Mare Island, with seven from Washington State, won the West after the flu abated, ringing up at least ten victories. Just as they ruled over Camp Lewis and the 91st Division the previous year, the Marines disposed of the current camp occupants, the 13th Division, which had downed two athletic clubs, an Ohio military camp that specialized in training marksmen and sailors at Mare Island. With Dietz from Washington State at the helm, Mare Island Marines crushed Mather Field in the middle of December and struggled to overcome Balboa Park on Christmas Day at Vallejo. Of Dietz's All Pacific Coast Military (all collegians), chosen after the Rose Bowl, 6 of the 11 vied for Mare Island (4 from State, 1 from Gonzaga and 1 from

5. *Professional and Military Football* 97

Oregon). Mather Field had 1 from State and 2 from the Big 10. The University of Washington sent one to Camp Lewis, while the Oregon Aggies contributed one to San Pedro's sub-base.[44]

The Rose Bowl clash between Mare Island and Great Lakes, on 1 January '19, proved anti-climactic and the dope a bit inaccurate, the Sailors punting twelve times, Driscoll passes effective. The Marines kicked the same number but averaged much less yardage. Driscoll made one field goal in two tries and had a couple of good runs from received punts. The Marines had no penalties, the Gobs losing fifty yards. Great Lakes lost two fumbles, the Marines one. A reception and an interception by Halas proved critical. A day or two earlier, the press revealed that the eventual losers had several weakened from fighting flu and others sustained injuries in the last two contests. The winners were stuck on a train in the mountains for a time, held up by volumes of snow caused by the coldest winter on record.[45]

After the '18 season Camp singled out two Great Lakes linemen, to go along with Driscoll at quarterback, with Halas on the second eleven for the All-Service squads. The other eight places on the first eleven went to players for Granite State, Chicago Naval Reserve, Camp Greenleaf, League Island, Mare Island, Mather Field, Camp Devens and Hoboken Transport. Again, the Deep South seems shortchanged.

American football showed up in France about the same time as the Sammies in the fall of '17. Infantrymen of the 26th Division, after eating turkey, downed engineers with a field goal. One losing officer, upset with the calls of the chaplain, ran onto the field as a bugler for the other team played Officers Call. On the first play, someone knocked him out, and the bugler trumpeted Taps. In early December, two platoons of the 101st vied in hobnailed boots, Buckets of Blood waylaying Cut Throats, the names summing up the affair.[46]

Field artillerists from the 42nd Division, mostly from Illinois and the Upper Midwest, after brief training at Fort Sheridan near Chicago, came to France in the fall of '17, among the first American forces. As they received further training that Thanksgiving, one of the national guardsmen died of pneumonia, and in his honor, his brother serving with the Y, organized a game between two battalions.[47]

In March 1918, reporter Eckersall thought it appropriate that a Michigan wing man from early in the century, known for his high, long punts was now serving as a major in France directing artillery barrages. He also described a one-time guard on the Chicago elevens of '07 and '08, possessing little natural talent but endowed with pluck, now serving in France as a first lieutenant.[48]

In early May '18, in the hills of Lorraine, the Reading (Pennsylvania) Militia was the first to carry a machine gun over a hill in a raid on German lines. On their return, the men, draped in mud and blood, but with no deaths, looked like they had just played football. In May in France, "gladiators of the gridiron" held a spirited contest at their training camp. The men, however, would have to wait for cessation of the fighting for a real chance, even though Harvard grads had sent balls over via the Red Cross. Two hundred fifty were for rugby and 559 for soccer.[49]

In assessing athletics at the camps as its graduates began to take on the Huns, a writer praised the Commission on Training Camp Activities for alleviating "trench crouch," when muscles stiffened in the neck and shoulders from constantly bending forward to keep one's head below the parapet. Evers, who compared trenches to coal mines infested with rats as he evaded German shells, asked for 500 uniforms in September. The Knights of Columbus came up with $200,000 in equipment along with $100,000 more for rush orders. Having seen soldiers at the front playing football with rags tied together, Evers made sure that outfit received real balls. Between 1 August and the end of '18, American football had over 610,000 incidents (the number playing times the number of occasions played). A slim rugby program netted but 13,700, while soccer came close, at 527,500.[50]

On 11 November '18, the day of the Armistice, crowds in Paris yelled "Vive la France," their noise and glee surpassing that of fans in America's big colleges winning over their most important rival. Celebrating the Armistice and the Thanksgiving that followed, field artillerists in the 85th Division battled. One infantry regiment of the 89th Division (Michigan) "nearly won" against another. Around Thanksgiving, artillerists of the 86th Division (Wisconsin, Illinois, etc.) staged a championship, one company prevailing by a point over the headquarters of another in a "haphazard" affair. Four from headquarters sustained injuries, while three backs for the winners fell, one returning with a broken rib. The losses meant giving up trick plays, the lighter players digging deeper, as headquarters, with more collegians, drove close to the goal line several times, only to be stopped, two place kicks blocked. This regiment had just finished preparing to advance to the front when the armistice took effect. A championship enlivened the ranks. Thousands of francs changed hands. Officers of the 88th Division, in building esprit de corps, had a range of athletics, every branch of the division taking part through the winter. A star at Minnesota reflected on his escape from a German prison in the Black Forest, walking some sixty miles to freedom.[51]

The 47th Coast Artillery, out of Virginia, had men from every state. Coming too late to take on Germans, an eleven from six batteries and headquarters "slipped, slid and skidded," in containing a "whirlwind halfback" (a sergeant). In competition among the batteries, the lightest averaging 147 pounds did not lose, making another battery pay thousands of francs on

Christmas Day in a field surrounded by vineyards. None had reputation as collegians and officers only coached. In the 318th Infantry Regiment, 80th Division in the Burgundy region, amid a "restless air," a "grueling" match produced a champion.[52]

As military engineers settled in northeastern France, one company yielded to the heavier headquarters in the morning before their Thanksgiving meal. As an infantry company in the 78th Division rested at St. Quentin after fighting beside the British, they tossed a football around. One officer still had rheumatism caused by breaking his ankle playing at Camp Dix a year earlier.[53]

Some field artillerists for the 26th Division, after training west of Paris and fighting at Chateau Thierry, settled at Burgundy after the Armistice, where, boredom threatening, they took up football—in January. When they returned to the village exhausted, limping and "plastered from head to foot with liquid mud," the people rushed "to the doors in amazement. Surely these Americans were mad!" Word came that they would soon be headed for Le Mans and home, but breaking "the monotony," a battery won "a desperately fought game," a large sum changing hands among "the sporting element." The French watched in horror as Americans splashed "about in the muddy pasture" and pondered why they tormented themselves.[54]

Other field artillerists of the 26th Division (R. Islanders) played on Thanksgiving, pitting those representing various batteries and other units, each with a football to drive toward opposite goals. The melee damaged clothes, skins and tempers. An All-American at Yale coached one battery. Orders to move toward the coast in January prevented another contest, but they practiced a lot in the mud and appreciated the French "mothers" who dried their togs overnight. "Time never dragged."[55]

A battalion celebrated Thanksgiving by "crawling around in the mud for a couple of hours" before eating roasted ox in the rain. Once the men settled down in Northeastern France, seven helped the divisional team tie the 36th Division, but then the 29th lost out via a lucky drop kick.[56]

Near the end of November, a battery of field artillerists deflated the 840th Aero Squadron, 36–0, led by Michigan Aggies. Fifteen turned out for the airmen when they had a scoreless tie with Wisconsin artillerists. John Frey, a quarterback who helped make Xavier's (Cincinnati) effort to renew football in '16 successful played in all the games for artillerists of the 37th Division. "December passed very quickly because of football," he reported to his college.[57]

Lt. Col. Huston's engineers started in the fairgrounds near Detroit with an end from Michigan, a "colorful Indian from Carlisle," as well as Eddie Kaw, a future Cornell All-American. Relieved of work near Bordeaux in January, a Kaw-led company, behaving like "plutocrats of ancient Rome," won the regiment title and eased by other engineers, fans standing 10–20 feet deep.[58]

Pershing divided the season in two. In the first part, the 36th Division won the championship of the First Army, downing the 78th, 38–0, on Christmas Day and taking the 80th on New Year's Day, 28–0. That Christmas, St. Nazaire's Services of Supply bested Bordeaux, 17–0. Its marine captain, Harvard's Mahan, kicked a field goal from the thirty to seal the win. Coach Eddie Hart, a Princeton '10, kept practicing despite rain. In the showdown in Paris on a Sunday in January, not far from where politicians discussed peace, no "paix" prevailed as the faster St. Nazaire prevailed over the heavier 36th, on a muddy field. The tall, black-haired Mahan returned a punt 65 yards for the first touchdown, recovered a fumble and fired a long pass to the five, from where the other halfback bucked it over in two tries.[59]

Another St. Nazaire eleven (a section base) overcame a team that had a former lineman and captain for Georgia. John "Tiny" (210 pounds) Henderson earlier incurred a cut from a steel-plated shoe above his eye. "Blood, I should say so," unaware he "had so much to spare." French girls fainted when he came close to the side lines. Still wounded, he took the field, losing 0–12.[60]

Under Pershing's General Order No. 241 sixty teams participated in the second season—taking place on ground either frozen and covered in snow or partially thawed and suffused with mud. The number quickly dropped as too few recruits could be found. Only a handful who had not played in college broke into the lineups, but the 809th Pioneer Infantry (African American combat engineers) competed for a time. In January '19, near occupied Coblenz at Foch Field, on the top end of a 40-acre island in the Rhine River (an old soccer field, whitewashed lines, with no goal posts), a sanitary team from Ohio trained at Camp Sherman had a lot of German marks to bet but few takers as they overcame aviators.[61]

In February, the 36th Division, initially composed of elements of the Texas National Guard, created 52 teams, an infantry regiment having 17. One week brought thirteen contests. In one, 750 spectators bet over 7,000 francs, but little changed hands because the game ended scoreless. A company from a machine-gun battalion rolled to one title, while infantrymen carried another. A corps title remained up in the air in early February as the 6th Division played two ties, one with the 77th and the other with the 81st, before besting the former in a second encounter.

Billeted in woods on a pleasant day in August '18, a postal clerk for the 35th Division, pined for football in the fall. "It seems to be in my blood," Lloyd Staley mused. In February '19 he watched a "dandy game" which ended scoreless, finding it "rather peculiar" given the weather. Sounding like he might play in the next contest, he worked out and though tired, enjoyed "violent exercise." His 35th lost.[62]

A Princeton grad described 2nd Division victories over the First Division, 6–0, and the 32nd, 19–0, the latter before a "tremendous" and "noisy" crowd, Harry Le Gore (Yale), Billy Moore (Princeton) and another an All-Western Conference man starring. That almost all were officers was due to greater knowledge of the game among collegians. Tactics included an "a la Sam White" by the left end, a "Harvard delayed pass tackle play" and the "Princeton trick play with Bill Moore playing thirty yards out." Le Gore also pulled off one of his famed wide end-runs.[63]

The 4th Division eased by the 42nd, with the help of Captain Hamilton Fish of Harvard (a future Republican Congressman), a lieutenant tackle from Georgetown, a lieutenant end from Yale, three West Pointers, a captain from Michigan State and sergeants from Georgetown and Bethany (West Virginia). An All-American half back from Brown (a major), in another battle, kicked a winning field goal over those who "nosed out" the 3rd Division, endowed with a Washington quarterback and a couple of pros. The 4th also got by the 2nd Division, with a coach from Colgate, 10–7, before 20,000 to give the winners a shot at the title for the Army of Occupation. But the injured "Ivy" lost to the 89th before a huge gathering, including British and French officers.[64]

The 7th Division (2nd Army) won out after several scoreless matches and overtimes against the 28th, the winner finally determined by yardage gained during the final scoreless encounter. The losing eleven ended up undefeated. Experts figured the winner would be too worn out to contest for the championship.

The roster of the 88th Division, mostly Midwesterners trained at Camp Dodge, included five captains, six lieutenants, a sergeant, a corporal and three privates, all of whom had played in college. Of the three quarterbacks, one attended South Dakota University, another Illinois and the third was Sergeant F. Bender (Carlisle), brother of major league pitcher Chief Bender. They had a scoreless tie and a field-goal win with the 5th Division, a dominant victory over a 9th Corps club (38–0), a 13–0 over the 33rd Division, and a 9–13 loss to the 89th for the Third Army title.[65]

Tours of Service and Supply won all, including 20–0 over Bordeaux. An old Wisconsin man could still gain yardage, a couple of Yale linemen helping. St. Nazaire, the winners of the first round, had Mahan plus Oregon's Johnny Becket, who led the Mare Island Marines to the Pacific Coast title on 1 January '18. In early March 1919, Headquarters, based in Le Mans, with an All-Western and an All-American end from Minnesota plus a Cornell All-American end and punter, fell in old-fashioned football.[66]

The 36th Division re-enforced its personnel after losing to St. Nazaire in the first phase. Captain Wilmot Whitney (Harvard) took over as coach and quarterback. A former Longhorn from Texas coached the line. The 36th won the corps title by overcoming the 78th and 80th, winning the last at a racetrack near Paris. The 29th, led by Cedric Miller, a sergeant half back and once captain at Washington under Gil Dobie and coach of the frosh there in '16, overcame three battalions in securing the divisional championship and won another in a heavy snowstorm. The next week, playing in the same place in the mud, the Blue & Gray downed the 81st Division,

George "Potsy" Clark (running with the ball), who scored twice for the 89th Division to win the AEF title in 1919 in France, played for the University of Illinois before the war. *Courtesy University of Illinois Archives.*

20–0, as Miller, with a touchdown lead, ambled, with blocking, 75 yards. On Washington's birthday, the 29th fell to the 36th in a bruising battle in a natural amphitheater before 8,000, a fumble and a field goal critical. The 29th, consisting of a private, a corporal, four sergeants, a lieutenant and four captains, reached the 36th's 15-yard marker when time expired in the first half.[67]

Then the 36th faced the 7th in late March, King Albert and Queen Elizabeth of Belgium watched a "grueling" match before 25,000, many, including officers, standing six-deep entirely around the field and on surrounding hills. The queen looked for Native Americans, one of whom was supposedly Chief Bender. After the game, to please the queen, an avid photographer, both elevens be-splattered in mud, posed in front of her box. The 36th scored the only touchdown late in the contest.[68]

The 89th coached by Major Withington, a Haughton disciple, had verdicts over the 90th Division (6–0), the 88th, 13–0 and St. Nazaire, when they held Mahan and company for four downs within the one-foot marker on the Ides of March and bested Intermediate Sector S.O.S., after trailing at half. Composed mostly of little-known collegians, it relied on teamwork both on offense and defense, eight starters having played under Withington at Camp Funston in '17. Nine on the first eleven were officers, with a West Pointer and several Kansans, along with Lt. George "Potsy" Clark, from the University of Illinois.[69]

At the end of March, around 3,600 of the 36th came by train while 1,200 came from Germany to Paris to support the 89th. In an epic encounter, before Pershing and other dignitaries, among 15,000, the 36th led in the first half when the big Native American Carl Mahseet (Oklahoma A&M), who was not an officer, punted from his own end zone, the ball rolling nearly the entire length of the field. In the ensuing play, the 36th recovered a fumble in the end zone to take a 6–0 lead, Mahseet missing the point after. At half time, General Frank Winn "ordered" his 89th to win, so Clark scored two touchdowns, one via a dash of 65 yards. Pershing praised everyone for the spirited contest and for helping promote clean sports. The 89th, with money from bets, enjoyed a night in Paris.[70]

6

Track and Field

Colleges and amateur athletic clubs dominated track during this era, but only about 125 schools could carry out full dual meets (15 events). Several more had a few athletes that ran relays or cross country or picked up a few points at conference or state collegiate meets. Nationally, the war cut the number of dual meets by more than half in '17 and '18, rising in '19 but not attaining the '16 level.

In Maine in '17, with "stars in the service," Bates ended track until '19. Bowdoin, a close loss to MIT in '16 and suspended for two years, won the state meet in '19. In '16, the University of Maine captured the state (61, Bowdoin 39, Bates 13, Colby 13) and ran second at the N. England Intercollegiate, the next two years blanks. Bowdoin took first in '19, when, after humbling Holy Cross, the Black Bears ran second in the state, one of them winning the shot put at the National Intercollegiate. Lieutenant Charles Anthony Rice, a record holder in the 100 and 220 in '16, said to be going to the Millrose meet in '18, was on his way to France, where he died in Flanders.[1]

Dartmouth won the N. England Intercollegiate in '16, records abounding. MIT ran first for the next three years, with about half the schools represented in '17, a few more in '18, and a normal number in '19. Warren Hobbs, a record setter at Meadowbrook in the 50-yard hurdles, joined the Dartmouth ambulance corps, then became a lieutenant in the air service, anti-aircraft fire killing him in June '18. That year, Dartmouth cruised in a Connecticut Valley meet (88, Holy Cross 29, Springfield 6, RPI 3 and Trinity 1) and placed second at the Nationals.

New Hampshire State's Gordon Nightingale won the November '17 junior national AAU six-mile at Van Cortland Park in N.Y. Over the winter he won a three-mile and the Boston Athletic Association three-mile over a Bowdoin man. In July, he became a Marine, then went into naval aviation at MIT. In the winter of '19 he almost outran Joie Ray in two events and placed second in the 1,000-yard N. England AAU. N.H. won 2 of 3 duals in '16 and overwhelmed Tufts in '19.

The Eli, after dominating Princeton and Harvard outdoors in '16, saw

John Overton set a record in the mile (4:16) at the Meadowbrook in January and another in the 1,000 at the armory in N.Y. before war suspended track. Graduating in '17, Overton joined the Marines and set a "torrid pace" in the Soissons sector in June '18, posthumously receiving the Croix de Guerre. Yale ran second to Princeton in a triangle, Harvard trailing in '18. The postwar brought a loss to Princeton and a win over Harvard in duals.

Amherst, loser of two duals in '16, tied Williams in '18, losing to the same in '19. Boston College, bested by Trinity in '16 and loser in one in '17, won a dual and scored a few in the N.E. Intercollegiate in '19. Harvard, blanked for '17, lost to Princeton in '18 and Yale in '19, wining over Princeton in '19. The Mass Aggies, loser of a duo of duals in '16 and winner of 2 of 3 in '19 had nothing for '17 and '18. Williams won over Amherst and Wesleyan in '16, no meets reported for '17. A tie and a win ensued in '18, amid cancelations, followed by two wins in '19, along with a loss to Wesleyan.

Vermont, loser of 2 of 3 in '16, posted nothing for the war, while

University of Maine's Charles Anthony Rice, New England 100 and 220 record-holder, who was killed in action, 1918. *Courtesy University of Maine Fogler Library Special Collections.*

Middlebury, which won three in '16, narrowly lost to Trinity in '17, nothing for '18, splitting two in '19. Brown ran second in the '17 N. England's, Fritz Pollard winning two hurdles and placing third in the broad jump. R.I. State, suspended during the war, could only field a relay in '19, lacking funds.[2]

In cross-country '17, MIT won the N. England's, Williams (winner in '16) falling to third. New Hampshire prevailed in '19, no meets in '18. In '17, in one national meet, Penn had 38, Cornell 55, Columbia 74, MIT 90, Dartmouth 96 (low scores win) while the National Collegiate had Cornell 41, Penn 78 and Carnegie Tech 150. Several colleges could not contend, Yale pulling out at the last minute because its best runners went into the military. In October '18, the IC4A called off the intercollegiate championship scheduled for N.Y.'s Van Cortland Park because of flu.[3]

The Middle States (New Jersey, New York, Penn., and Del.), with 36 track programs through the era, dropped to 21 in '17 and rose to 26 in '18. In '16, N.Y. University took first in the Middle States meet over Lafayette's protest, ten other schools participating. Lafayette secured honors in '17, more easily in '18 with fewer participants. Rutgers, which reduced in '17 as many enlisted, ruled in '19.

Stevens Institute lost all four '16 duals and to Rutgers in '17 and '18, splitting two in '19. In '18, Princeton outscored Columbia, Yale and Harvard before placing third at the IC4As, with a hurdler setting a record (rare that year). Columbia lost to Navy and Brown in '16 but overcame the latter in '18, trailing Princeton. Union doubled the score on RPI, placing second to Colgate in the N.Y. Intercollegiate. Colgate's Michael Hayes (KIA) set a record in the Millrose in '17.

Cornell's Red & White dominated the war era, more than doubling Harvard and Penn in '16 and winning the IC4As. After having no meet in '17, for the first time since 1876, the IC4A had 19 schools in '18, 15 scoring. Even though fewer athletes than usual took part, no freshmen could compete. A reduced schedule of '18, with twenty schools, brought an easy win over MIT, plus dominance at the renewed IC4As at Franklin Field in Philadelphia. In '19, Cornell again controlled the IC4As, although Penn closed the gap. Cornell's record-setting miler, John Paul Jones, enlisted in the navy in '18, appropriately enough.[4]

Syracuse, whose coach made athletes out of less than ideal specimens, canceled at Ann Arbor, after tying Michigan indoors in '17. The coach, still a lieutenant at a Texas airfield, could not return when the '19 indoor got underway. Colgate lost to Syracuse in both '16 and '19 but dominated the N.Y. State Intercollegiate in '16 with over a 100 (Union 27; Rochester 10, St. Lawrence 5). In '19, Colgate edged Stevens in the Eastern Intercollegiate, six N. England schools trailing.[5]

In '17, "war lessened interest" at Bucknell, when seven entered the service. That year, a student at Dickinson, which dominated in four duals in '16, blamed the "Kaiser's unrestricted warfare" for the "destruction of the best, if not the very best, track team ever." Haverford, dealing with "varied sentiments" about the war in '17, ended athletics and coursework abruptly and trained men to drive and repair ambulances and tend to the wounded. Women learned nursing duties.[6]

Lafayette lost only to Navy in five duals in '16, winning three in '17, including over Carlisle. Lehigh, loser of 3 of 4 in '16 swatted Swarthmore but again lost to Lafayette in '17 amid "unsettled conditions." Freshmen did well. A brief '18 brought another loss to Lafayette. Muhlenberg, which sent competitors to the Middle States for the first time in years in '16, canceled '17, and split four in '18, the captain in the service. The Cardinal & Gray lost at least three in '19 because of SATC's earlier "disruption." Westminster College, with less than a hundred men, replaced scores in '17 with a cartoon, which read "THEY WARN'T NONE! 'COUNT O' TH' KAISER." In '18, they lost 50–76 to Carnegie Tech.[7]

J. Howard Berry, considered as great an athlete as Jim Thorpe, won the pentathlon at the Penn Relays with three firsts in '15 (9 points) as a freshman, ahead in all five events in '16 (5 points) and repeated again in '17 with 4 firsts (7 points). In the summer of '16, Pvt. Berry chased Mexicans as a Philadelphia national guardsmen. His future alma mater, after a loss to Navy, enlisted, "almost as a body" in '18. Penn got by Navy and captured a triangle with Dartmouth and Columbia in '19. Middle-distance runner Ted Meredith (gold medalist at Stockholm in 1912) set records at the substitute for the Olympics at the same place in '16, started aviation training in March '17 in case the country went to war. In '18, Penn freshman John Bartols captured the pentathlon.[8]

In '17, Penn State dominated the Western Collegiate over Pitt, Carnegie Tech and West Virginia. A win over Pitt pleased fans, but the "international situation" forced four schools to back out. Indoors, the Panthers won the 40-yard at Meadowbrook but shortened the season when sixteen, including the captain-elect, enlisted. Canceling classes in April ruined '18. In '19, Penn State lost to Pitt, the frosh eligibility rule waved. Second in the state meet and a win at the Penn relays summarizes '17. Indoors, in '18 the Panthers whipped two athletic clubs, won a triangle and outdueled Penn State and Lehigh in '19.[9]

Delaware lost to Muhlenberg and downed Drexel in '16, split two in '17, setting four school records. The Blue Hens mastered Muhlenberg in the only '18 dual, tying the same in '19, along with two wins.

In the S. Atlantic, Johns Hopkins put on its 14th annual indoor in '18, running seven events, with relays from Cornell and Pennsylvania and camps Meade and Dix before a big crowd of soldiers and sailors.

Maryland State ended indoor track because the government took over its only facility.[10]

In '18, Georgetown dominated the S. Atlantic outdoors: (46) Hopkins (21), Georgia Tech (20), several schools not coming. Georgetown had less than ten athletes, its captain planning to enter naval aviation after the Penn Relays. In '19, Georgetown's Robert LeGendre won the pentathlon at the Relays (14 points). His school and Hopkins tied at the South Atlantic as VMI and VPI tied for third.[11]

The Naval Academy won three meets in '16, yielding to University of Virginia. After winning indoors over St. John's (Annapolis) and Catholic in '17 and with Penn outdoors, the program abruptly ended. In '18, losing once, the Midshipmen overcame Lehigh and Penn. In '19, Navy eased by Hopkins but fell to Penn and Cornell, part of a hefty schedule.[12]

In '16, managing the Midshipmen, losing to Princeton and a disputed one to Penn State, University of Virginia amassed 79 points, more than the combined total for everyone else at the S. Atlantic Intercollegiate. Nothing surfaced about the Cavaliers for the next three years. VPI, which in '16, with 58½, outscored Richmond College 39½ and two others triumphed over Tennessee and VMI in '17, losing to VMI, overcoming Trinity (Duke) in '18 and edging VMI and taking Trinity and UNC in '19.

Trinity split with N.C. A&E (State) in '16, taking third in the state. The war years produced a loss to VPI, second in the state in '19, losing to VMI and VPI. N.C. A&E won the state meet in '17 over UNC and Wake Forest. It called off most of '17 and placed third in the state meet in '18. In '19, State set four records compared to three in '16 and two in '17. Davidson prevailed over Clemson in '16 and possibly '17 and South Carolina in '19. UNC whipped W & L in '16 and canceled '17, when half its squad headed to Fort Oglethorpe. UNC won the '18 and '19 state meets.

In Appalachia, four colleges in Kentucky, three in Tennessee and four in West Virginia fielded varsities. At Georgetown College (Kentucky) in '18, with about 200 in the service, coach Bobby Hinton, forged a fourth title from "mediocre material" at the state meet, the second spot going to Transylvania trailing by fifteen, followed by Centre and Berea. Kentucky State did not compete. Hinton then sailed to France to work with the Y, returning for another title in '19. West Virginia romped over Ohio University and West Virginia Wesleyan in '16, no scores surfacing for at least the next three years. Salem College split two with Fairmont Normal in '18, another Normal outscoring Fairmont in '16.[13]

In the '16 Southern Association (at Vanderbilt) LSU (43½) topped Mississippi A&M (42), Vanderbilt (15), Georgia Tech (13½), Kentucky (2) and Sewanee (1). Vanderbilt more than doubled Kentucky and missed by a point of tripling Auburn. The Southern called off the meet for May '17 because recognizing champions would somehow dishonor those in the services. Instead, a "preparedness" affair awarded ribbons, for which current students and those returning from the Mexican border could compete.[14]

Vanderbilt, third in the Southern Intercollegiate, dominated Kentucky and Auburn in '16 duals. The '18 Commodores complained about calling off the Southern meet "after much dilly-dallying." They yielded to Miss A&M in a triangle, swamping Sewanee, which, after dropping track in '16, returned in '17, scoring few at the substitute for the S.I.A.A. Georgia Tech trounced them, but the frosh made a better showing in a rematch. With more maturity in '19, Sewanee took the S.I.A.A. with 43 points, Georgia Tech (29½), Mississippi (17), Vanderbilt (13), Clemson (9), Alabama, (8) Georgia and Oglethorpe (5) and Auburn (2½). Tech, which dominated Auburn in '16, outscored three opponents in '18 and accused the Commodores of having "cold feet." Tulane, trailing Miss A&M and LSU in '16, reversed results in the first instance in '17. In '18, the war's havoc "estranged" all "athletic relations, thereby preventing the usual events in 19.[15]

In '16, Texas, which dominated the state's Athletic Association meet, piled up over sixty points in the Southwestern Intercollegiate Athletic Conf., with Texas A&M, Okla., Okla. A&M, Rice and Baylor in pursuit. In '17, after the Longhorns won over Rice and A&M, the war ended a "budding track season." In '18, they won a couple of duals but lost to the Sooners. Rice Institute, falling to Louisiana State, scored a fistful of firsts at the Texas Intercollegiate in '17. A high jumper made a record in the Southwest Conference at Stillwater in '18. After dropping track in '17, the Sooners romped in '18, winning the state and Southwestern titles. In '19 they scored more points than the next seven combined. Okla. A&M in '16 usually trailed the Sooners at the Southwestern and in the state, an even wider disparity in 18 and '19.[16]

The Western Conference meet in June '17 had 169 from 18 schools compared to 379 from 25 institutions the previous year. That season ('16) Wisconsin compiled 49 points, with Ill. at 33¾ in second. By June 1917, 52 stars from twelve colleges left for war service, including five captains. That year Chicago piled up 54½, pursued by Ill 42½, Simpson-led Missouri competing in the Western in track, with 24 and Oberlin in 4th with 10.

In '16, after defeating Notre Dame and Stanford in duals in the spring. Michigan canceled outdoors in '17. Competing for the first time since 1906, Michigan dominated the Western Conference indoors in '18, eight of the Big Ten competing, only Chicago competitive against Michigan. Outdoors in '18, the Maize & Blue doubled scores on Notre Dame and Chicago. Their 37½ gave them an ample margin over Illinois (26) and Missouri (24) at the Conference meet, with twelve others participating.

Minnesota, winner of two duals, loser to Wisconsin outdoors in

'16, fell to Nebraska narrowly in '17. Reliable Carl Wallace, captain of cross-country in '16, became a Marine captain, wounded at Chateau Thierry, decorated for heroism. Starting out with only five in the winter of '18, the Gophers negated Nebraska and edged Wisconsin, overcoming Iowa and Nebraska in '19.[17]

Wisconsin, with Olympic discus and shot putter Arlie Mucks, dominated Purdue and Minnesota in '16. Indoors, the Badgers lost to Notre Dame and tied Illinois in '17, third in the Conference. In '18, indoors, they took the Wisconsin state with 79 (Ripon 22, Lawrence 12 and Beloit 4). Outdoors in '18, they eased by Ripon, lost to Minnesota as well as Illinois, overwhelmed Chicago, overcoming "discouraging conditions." After a narrow loss to Notre Dame indoors in '19, they cruised past Chicago outdoors but lost to Illinois. The lack of a track (the SATC barracks still on the site) forced cancelation of a meet against arch-rival Minnesota. Two captains for '18 left for the military and the one elected to lead the '19 indoor joined the Navy.[18]

In '17, Carleton outpointed North Dakota and St. Olaf at the Dakota/Minnesota Association, with less than half the usual number. Carleton outpointed Hamline, with St. Olaf and St. Thomas trailing. That year, it was Beloit (44), Lawrence (40½), Ripon (28) and Carroll (13½). In '16, Beloit placed third in the Little 5 (Beloit and four Illinois colleges) and fourth in '19, nothing in between. Even though the commission in charge of college athletics rescinded its edict to stop sports, both '17 and '18 had many blanks. In '19, Ripon way outscored Milwaukee Normal and captured the state followed distantly by Carroll and Lawrence. Track ended at Macalester.[19]

Illinois started a Relay Carnival (indoors) in '17 and persisted with it through the war, coming in second all three years, giving way to Michigan in '18 and '19, when they only lost the Conference by two points. Chicago did well in duals in '17 and '18 indoors, taking three matches in '17 and outscoring everyone at the Illinois Relays. Chicago also won in '18, against Purdue, Ohio State and Nebraska. Northwestern, losing to Purdue and Chicago (winning over Indiana) in '16, scored few in the outdoor Conference. The Purple did better in the '17 winter, but the point total dropped off the following winter and the Evanston school had minimal impact on the Conference outdoor meets.

War made Bradley Institute suffer as did Monmouth, which won a couple in '16 but in '17 "practically abandoned" the sport, the war hurting in '19. The war still "hindered" Northwestern College, which was usually successful in the Little 5. The Cardinal & White lost to the YMCA college (Chicago) in '17 and '18, winning over the same in '19, when it ran second to Knox in the Little 5.[20]

DePauw ran strong among the smaller colleges in Indiana. It added indoor track for the first time in the '17 winter, losing to Indiana and Purdue (close), winning over two small colleges. No scores appeared the next winter but in the spring of '18 DePauw downed two small colleges, only losing to Indiana. The "war jinx" stuck around in '19, preventing anything indoors and injuries leading to a loss to Wabash outdoors. The war caused interest to drop at Indiana State Normal in Muncie in '19. In '17 (Indoors), Purdue nixed Northwestern and fell to Chicago. That spring a Conference record holder in the 880, plus the best high jumper, javelin thrower, shot putter and others took up farming, the team mid-range in the Conference. In '18, a former student won five events at Fort Harrison, the varsity again yielding to Chicago.[21]

In '16, Indiana trounced Earlham, Franklin and Wabash but lost to Northwestern and fell back in the state meet. In '17, the Hoosiers conquered Ohio State, and, when it looked like they might be improving, many enlisted before a match with Northwestern. In '18, they easily overcame DePauw, lost close to Ohio State and scored few in the Conference meet. In '19, they lost to Conference foes, narrowly to Ohio State.[22]

Notre Dame won the Indiana state meet in '16. Indoors '17, the Irish lost to Illinois and Michigan and bettered Wisconsin, losing narrowly to the Illinois and Michigan in '18. In '19, Michigan way outscored them, the Irish running close to Illinois and subduing Wisconsin. That spring, they ran first in Indiana and fourth in the Western Conference, winning duals over the Michigan Aggies in both '17 and '19.

Even with a possible tie with Northwestern in '17 and wins over Indiana in '18 and '19, Ohio State usually ran well back in the Conference but gave a good account in losing to Illinois in '18. State usually won the Big Six over small colleges, but on occasion Oberlin or Wesleyan came close. Case tripled Baldwin-Wallace in '16 but trailed Oberlin and Wooster. In '17, Case again lost to Oberlin, both a dual and a triangle but outran Wooster. Kenyon won 2 of 3 in '16, no other scores ensuing in subsequent years. Miami lost to Wesleyan and Cincinnati but overcame Denison in '16, losing to Wesleyan in '17, when the season ended. Miami conquered Cincinnati and took a triangle from Denison and Wesleyan in '18. In '19, Miami won four, including one over Kentucky. Oberlin took both Case and Wooster in a triangle in '18.

In Western Conference cross-country, Purdue won in '16, not scoring in '17, second in '18 and '19, when Iowa State, not usually part of the Western, dominated. In the '19 Missouri Valley, all five Iowa State runners crossed the finish line together for first. Michigan State outran Michigan and Albion in '17. Minnesota whipped Wisconsin in '16, the losers found revenge the next season, Minnesota reversing that result in '18. In '17, Wisconsin topped Minnesota, Chicago and Purdue. Illinois lost to Purdue and won over Michigan in '18. Cincinnati, second in the Ohio Conference in '17, lost to Miami. In '18, it took first in the Big 6, Ohio State second and Oberlin third. Ohio State won against Indiana but ran well back in the Western Conf. that fall. In '17, the Buckeyes led Indiana in a dual and Oberlin and Miami in the Big 6. The '19 scores show Ohio State winning (25), Oberlin (33), Wooster (42) and Case (43).

In Iowa, the Drake Relays featured Bob Simpson (Missouri) in the special 120-yard hurdles in '16. In duals, Iowa State overcame Nebraska, but lost to Drake by two and to Missouri by a lot more. At the state meet the Cyclones of Iowa State prevailed (57), Drake (41), Grinnell (19½), Iowa (18), Coe (8), Cornell (8), Highland Park (6), Morningside (3½), Des Moines (3), and Simpson College (2). Grinnell had a world-record holder in the sprints, Charles Hoyt, who would also compete in '17, after which he joined the navy.

Drake ran its '17 relays just about the time of the declaration of war. Northwestern won the university half-mile, Illinois the mile, Notre Dame the two-mile and Chicago the four-mile. Among smaller colleges, Wabash took the half-mile and mile, while Morningside retained its two-mile title. In '18, the same meet, in a snow-storm, brought wins for Illinois in the half-mile, Missouri in the mile, Chicago in the two-mile and Iowa State in the four-mile, while Grinnell carried the collegiate half-mile and mile. Those for '19 had Grinnell in the Valley half-mile and Michigan in the Big 10 half-mile. The university mile went to Nebraska, the two-mile to Notre Dame and the four-mile to Chicago. With Sol Butler, Dubuque overcame two other Iowa colleges and South Dakota in the half-mile while Morningside repeated in the two-mile. A Pioneer from Grinnell outran Butler in a special 100-yard dash.

In '16, Coe, which edged arch-rival Cornell College and ran second to Grinnell in Conference, easily outscored Cornell in '17 but lost to Grinnell, which again captured the Conference. The '18 ran the same though Simpson scored more than usual. Coe lost to Cornell in '18. In '17, Iowa State Teachers College's turnout "dwindled down" with the war declaration as athletes signed up for the army or went to farms.[23]

As a freshman in '16, Sol Butler scored 26 in one meet. Dubuque walloped two Wisconsin schools as well as Iowa's State Teachers. Butler set school records in the 100 (10 secs.), 220 (22 secs.), 120-yard-high hurdles (16.5), 220 low hurdles (25.6), broad jump (23' 5"). The school cut the program through '18. In '19, Butler, a "shining light" for all Iowa track, placed third in the pentathlon at the Penn Relays. A member of the SATC in '18, he went to the Inter-Allied Olympics in France in '19, the only black to participate for the U.S because Howard Drew, though qualified by military service, could not compete.[24]

Morningside's two-mile relay set a record in '18 but lost to Drake in '19, with some "still in the army." The Maroons lost to South Dakota University in '17 but overcame Nebraska Wesleyan in '17 and took 9 of 11 events against Yankton in '18. In '18, Penn College competed in the Little 7 meet despite many being drafted. Simpson Colleges' Red & Gold claimed first in the Little 7 outdoors in '18 and dominance in '17 and '19 in the so-called Little 5 (the number varying).[25]

Iowa State beat Nebraska, lost to Missouri and narrowly lost to Drake in duals in '16, surpassing Drake at the state meet. In the Missouri Valley meet, State fell way behind Missouri but came out ahead of the others. In '17, the Cyclones lost to Missouri but quadrupled the score on Drake and eased by Nebraska. They won an indoor quadrangle (42), Grinnell (35), Iowa (18), and Drake (14) in '18. In the post-war, with 50, they won a tri-Iowa (41), Drake (7). In April, with impending war and a lack of interest coinciding Iowa University canceled with Drake and Minnesota but sent seven to the state meet. In '18, they lost narrowly to Iowa State, crushing Coe.[26]

In '17, Uncle Sam employed most of Kansas State Normal's "famous" squad. Revived in '18, Normal lost to Kansas and Ottawa. In '17, like other conference schools, Kansas Wesleyan did not fully compete in any spring sport, except tennis, even though in February the students voted to emphasize track over baseball. The schedule had to be terminated just before a meet with Ft. Hays Normal. In '18, 103 from conference schools came to a state meet, the final pecking order being Southwestern 43, Baker 36½, Friends 29¾, Pittsburg Normal 17, Fairmount 14½, Ottawa 5½, Emporia Normal 5, College of Emporia 3 and Cooper 1. In '19, Haskell outpointed two schools in duals and ran second in the state meet after winning "an all-Indian" showdown with Chilocco (Okla.) in '18, many from both schools in the service.[27]

In '17, indoors, Kansas doubled the score on Normal (Emporia), more than quintupled Kansas State but lost to Missouri. The next year the Jayhawkers almost doubled Kansas State but Missouri almost tripled their score at Kansas City. In '19, the Wildcats of Kansas State turned the results in their favor, showing the volatility of the situation. Another loss to Missouri, this time by a slightly smaller margin, ensued. The '17 outdoor season at Kansas State ended abruptly as thirteen athletes went to Fort Riley.

The University of Missouri dominated the Missouri Valley Conference outdoor meet in both '17 and '18. In the "Show Me" state in '17, hurdler Simpson, "the Bosworth Flyer," took first in the 120 and 220 as the Tigers won duals over Kansas and Iowa State. In '18, another Tiger ran the 100 in 9.8 and high jumped over 6' at the Missouri Conference meet. William Jewell College triumphed over Tarkio in '16 and finished first in the Missouri Intercollegiate. Jewel ran ahead in the state meet again in '17. The

'18 season ended suddenly after a win over Drake, when the school closed early, thus ending the Cardinal six-year reign. Springfield Normal (Southwest Missouri State Teachers) started '17 with a loss to Pitt Normal, then had others cancel as athletes headed to farms or joined the navy. The Bears sent a few to the state meet but not in '18. With so many in military service, Drury canceled '17, finding the middle in a triangular meet with Rolla and Springfield in '18.

Nebraska more than tripled the score on Kansas Wesleyan in '16 but fell to Iowa State, Kansas, and Minnesota. In '17, the Cornhuskers turned the tables on the Jayhawkers. In '18, they placed second at the Missouri Valley Conference. In '19, they fell back at the same and lost duals to Grinnell and Minnesota, even though conditions were "fast returning" to pre-war status.[28]

Track activity fell off in the two war years in Arizona and New Mexico. The universities of Arizona and New Mexico, New Mexico's Aggies and the Texas School of Mines ranked in that order in a meet in '16. An Arizona team took both the mile and two-mile relays in '18 in Southern California. The '19 rankings had New Mexico Military Inst., Arizona and the Aggies. Drills replaced track at the University of New Mexico in '17.

Colorado College (Colorado Springs) scored more than all the others combined in the Rocky Mountain Conference in '16, when Colorado University won over Denver and the Aggies but lost to Colorado College. Nothing much transpired in '17. The '18 record ran (1) Aggies, (2) Colorado, (3) Mines, (4) Denver. In '19, Colorado crushed Colorado College and eked one out over the Aggies. The Rocky Mountain Conf. had the Aggies (49), Colorado (46), Colorado College (28), Denver (7) and Montana Agricultural (5).

In '17, Utah outdueled the Utah Aggies and Brigham Young University, the Aggies taking the state meet in '18. Brigham Young's Clinton Larsen, stationed at Waco for aviator training, jumped 6' 2" in '17 and soared to a world's record (over 6' 7") at the 22nd Regiment Armory in N.Y. in '18.

Idaho dominated Montana in '16 and overcame Washington State, setting three records. The Vandals took a hiatus in '17, resuming in '18 when they lost to State, though setting a shotput record. In '19, Idaho (42) led the Northwestern Conference with State (41), Oregon (35), and Montana 14, the results of a relay in dispute. A "spirit of unrest" in April '18 "discontinued" track in Montana. The Sage Brush Warriors (Nevada) overcame Cal Davis in '18, placing second in a quadrangular won by the Cal Frosh, with Cal Davis and St. Mary's posting points.

In the Dakota/Minnesota conference in '16 Carleton had (44), Hamline (39), South Dakota College (29), South Dakota University (21), North Dakota University (17), Macalester (8), three others not scoring at Huron.

The next year, only three schools competed at Carleton College, North Dakota second behind Carleton and ahead of St. Olaf. In '18, North Dakota only had intramurals.

In California in '16, Berkeley overcame the Olympic Club and USC, losing to Stanford, amassing 36 in a Pacific Coast Conference meet [Stanford (33), Oregon State (18), Oregon (12), Santa Clara (11), USC (6), Washington(5), Washington State (4), Idaho (2) and St. Ignatius (1)]. The Pacific Athletic Association meet widened the gap, Cal (89), Stanford (64), the Olympic A.C. (31), the Caledonian Club (10), and Visitacion Valley (5). Cal conquered Pomona in a dual in '17 succumbing to Stanford. In '18, the Bears overcame a combined Presidio-Aviation School as well as Camp Fremont and aviators, losing to the Olympic Club and Stanford. Track suffered "more than any sport."[29]

In '19, Cal won a Pacific Association meet over the Olympic Club and scored another first in the Pacific Coast Conference followed by Stanford, Washington State, Oregon State, Washington and Oregon. In duals, Stanford won over Cal every year between '16 and '19, the Cardinals tying Cal for third at the IC4As in '16. Duals in '17 included two over USC. Charley Paddock, an artillery officer with the Marines in France in '18 after graduating from Pasadena High, won several dashes for USC in the spring of '19.

In '16, Occidental almost tripled the score on USC, which also fell to the California Institute of Technology. Oxy lost to Pomona by a half dozen, and the latter outpointed Whittier, Redlands and Throop. Southern Cal, also loser to Cal in '16, lost duals to Stanford in '19, scoring more than Redlands and Pomona in a tri-meet, the years of the war coming up empty. Pomona overcame Occidental in '16 and in '17 by almost a double score, while also losing to Cal. That year, Pomona claimed 10 of 14 events at the meet for the state's smaller colleges, Oxy running a poor second.

The war prevented action in '17 for most everyone in the Northwest, including Washington State, which whipped Whitman and lost to Idaho in '16. State won two duals with Idaho in '18, overwhelming Idaho and Oregon Agricultural in duals but not winning the Northwest title in '19, when a relay runner dropped a baton. A German sniper killed a State letterman and Marine medic as he tended to a wounded Marine in France. Washington, which lost to Oregon and the Aggies in '16 and faced "unsettled" times in '18, but overcame Oregon's Aggies, which turned that outcome around in '19. Willamette, the best outside the conference in '16, dominated McMinnville and Pacific University, three others not participating as the war sharply reduced activity among the smaller schools.[30]

In the winter of '18 at the Boston Athletic Association, the Charlestown Navy Yard topped camps Devens and Dix in a relay, with the former captain of the Boston A.A. winning the last leg over an ex-Harvard. Devens sent one each from Princeton, Georgetown and Dartmouth and two from Harvard, along with one each from the Boston A.A. and the Providence Y to the Milrose in New York.[31]

The national half-mile champ, Mike Devaney, once with the Milrose A.A. but now representing the Boston Navy Yard, won the 600-yard Army-Navy handicap at Newark, N.J., over a former Dartmouth runner, now a lieutenant. He then bested Willie Gordon of the Pelham Naval Reserves in the 1,000-yard Metropolitan. A Camp Upton infantry regiment won in cross-country over two other military teams.

Joie Ray, from the Illinois A.C., surpassed Devaney in the mile in Boston. He also won the Meadowbrook in just under 4:18, a couple of seconds off the world indoor record set by Lieutenant Overton (Yale), a Western Conference champ now at Great Lakes coming in second, Devaney third. A week later Ray tied the record in the AAU meet, defeating Devaney in the 1,000 yards. Running his third major race, Ray set the record at Madison Square Garden for the three-quarter mile under 3:05, again over Devaney.[32]

N. Englanders training to be officers at Plattsburg in the spring of '17 fashioned a win over New Yorkers on Memorial Day. Crewmen from the U.S.R.S. *Granite State* took part in a meet put on by the New York A.C. In '17, naval airmen stationed near Pensacola outpointed soldiers from the fort that surrounded the airfield. At an air station in '18 on Memorial Day mechanics overcame aviators, the beach detail and those working with dirigibles.[33]

Among three hospital units at Fort McPherson, (1) Kansas City, (2) Chicago and (3) Minneapolis finished in that order. Hundreds of Atlanta civilians drove to the event. In the Southeastern Department meet held on the 4th of July 1918 at Columbia, South Carolina, Camp Jackson emerged with 25½ in ten events, McPherson (8½), followed by Miami, Arcadia and thirteen others.[34]

In the '17 outdoor AAU, the Chicago A.A. won the dashes, a Pittsburgh A.A., the 440, Mike Devaney, the 880 and Ray, the mile. Pores (Millrose A.C.) set a record in the five-mile. Another Millrose man won the 10-mile, a Meadowbrook A.C., the high hurdles, Loomis (Chicago A.C.), the 220 low hurdles and a Chicago A.A., the 440 hurdles. An Illinois A.C. member poled 12' 9". Mucks (Chicago A.A.) won the 16-lb. shot and discus while another Chicagoan took the broad and an Illinois A.C. the hop, step and jump. The Chicago A.A. amassed the most points. Larsen of Utah won the high jump. In the AAU in '18, 700 represented eighteen athletic clubs and a dozen colleges, Great Lakes figured to win, but several could not take part. The Chicago A.C. came out ahead again.[35]

Charles Pores and Willie Gordon ended up at Pelham Bay Naval Training Station. Before joining the navy, Pores won the AAU senior metropolitan in May '17 and a 2-mile in N.Y. in July '18, after going to the training station. Gordon won a 4:30 mile in a Knights of Columbus meet in September '18. Pores also won over Jim Henigan, the N. England 10-mile titlist. Mike Devaney, once with the Milrose A.A. but now representing the Boston Navy Yard as the national half-mile titlist, won the 600-yard Army-Navy handicap at Newark, N.J. over a former Dartmouth runner now a lieutenant at Camp Dix. Devaney also took the 1,000-yard Metropolitan title, besting Gordon.[36]

In '18 the Boston Athletic Association sponsored its famed marathon, inviting only military teams to run 25 miles, with ten men, each running two and a half miles. Fourteen military teams entered from three forts and an assortment of others, along with a divisional team from Devens. On good roads outside Boston, the Devens divisional team took an early lead and maintained it throughout, a former athletic club runner anchoring and bearing a message supporting the most recent Liberty Loan.[37]

On 1 January '18, one from a Camp Meade infantry regiment won a six-and-a-half-mile marathon in Philadelphia. The team title went to Dix, the Philadelphia Navy Yard and the Ambulance Corps also participating. In the spring at Meade, the same regiment won the most points in competition for the Second Liberty Fund. On the 4th of July '17 in Allentown, among those in training to drive ambulances, the University of Michigan won team honors.[38]

A multi-national military meet in Rome in the spring of '18 featured a Cornell miler and IC4A champ of '16 winning the 800-meter. In England, the 840th Aero Squadron won before a large crowd in late July, an ex-Olympian competing for the English. As some N.Y. machine gunners rested in woods after helping crack the Hindenburg Line, fifty competed within range of German shells on a field recently divested of its crop of wheat, a shell casing serving as the shot put.[39]

Fred Thomson's brother, also from Occidental College, won the high hurdles and broad jump while an aviator from a Southern college won the short races in a French championship. The French could not believe Fred, who had never thrown a grenade, beat the French record in that new event.[40]

In the 89th, infantry outscored field artillerists and others. In a tri-corner, the 77th more than doubled the 35th Division. The universities for American military at four sites competed. The 33d Division amassed 75 against 52 for the 5th Division in Luxembourg in May. Also, the 33rd Division ran intramurals before 10,000, with an ammo unit taking the title over an infantry regiment and artillerists.

In May '19 at the University Sporting Club, Lt. Earl Eby (Pennsylvania), volunteering after his freshman year, set a record in the 800-meter, far ahead of a fleet of Frenchmen. He later returned to Penn and set more records and won silver at the 1920 Olympics. Lt. Harry B. Liversedge (University Cal), putting the shot over 46', later commanded Marines on Iwo Jima. Lt. Alma Richards (Cornell), Utah farm boy and gold medalist at Stockholm in 1912, set a record in the discus. Paddy Ryan, the old Irish-born New Yorker and AAU champ, tossed the 16 lb. hammer over 172 feet, a small distance for him. A Missourian poled 12' 6". At Colombes, Section SOS amassed 59 (Richards two firsts, Lt Edward Teschner [Harvard] two dashes and a Boston A.A. a half-marathon). AEF championships brought the 77th Division way ahead of Le Mans, which far exceeded the 35th Division.[41]

7

Basketball and Volleyball

Several hundred intercollegiate programs existed between 1917 and 1919 but roundball exhibited weakness in Maine, Florida and Arkansas. The war had less impact, given the smaller number needed to compete, but enlistments took away players and a lack of coal occasionally prevented games. An online site, with records for about 125 institutions, shows about a 10 percent reduction in scores between '17 and '18, a downward trend that continued, though moderating, in '19. My analysis, with thinner coverage, of 400 schools, showed the same trend. The post-war year did not bring full recovery because many athletes did not return for some time and rebuilding gyms the SATC used took time. And flu kept disrupting life.

Maine was the only college in the Pine Tree State that had a team during the war and only for four games in '18, losing to New Hampshire State. The latter, 6–3 in '18 plus two dominant wins over naval reservists at Portland, won ten straight in '19, losing the last three. Dartmouth, a bit below .500 in the Eastern Intercollegiate in '17, went 0–26 in '18, the coach dismissed half-way through the season. Shutting down the SATC and probably the previous year's record ended chances for any team in '19. In '18, Middlebury won all six against Vermont, Norwich and St. Michael's. In '19, with a green team and no league, Middlebury numbed Norwich twice and lost to two upstate N.Y. colleges.

Boston College, with no program for a while, had a brief '19. The Mass Aggies re-activated in '17 after a 9-year lapse but rarely played. Amherst canceled against NYU, lacking coal to heat the gym in '18. Holy Cross and MIT had no varsities. Boston University had one, but a student death in an unofficial match with Tufts discouraged continuing. Williams lost most in both '17 and in '18, when three starters enlisted before the end of the season. Springfield downed Yale, posting 9–3 in '18.[1]

Brown had scores only for '19, losing to the Second Naval District (Newport) and Yale. Rhode Island State, 2–5 in '17 and 2–3 in '18, including over Fort Kearny and a loss to the respected Newport Naval Reserves, improved in '19, with two over Brown and one each against Connecticut and Reservists.

The Eli won 9 of 10 in the Eastern Intercollegiate plus four out of conference in '17, losing to CCNY and Navy, not as successful in '18, and '19. Trinity only had a frosh five in '18. Both a coach and a player left for military aviation at Wesleyan, which struggled for .500 in '17 and '18.

City College of N.Y., the city champion, overall 14–3 in '17, did well all three seasons, while NYU won most of its games in '17, not so many in '18, when the returning five all enlisted. In '19, four were kicked off the team when they refused to pay an activity fee. Pratt Institute rolled to at least thirteen straight in '18, including wins over the Newport Naval Reserves, a naval battalion and Pelham Bay. Union won 15 of 16 in '18. Syracuse fell to Penn by a point for its only loss (17 wins) and one of two ever lost in the gym built seven years earlier. The Helms Foundation retroactively made Syracuse the national champion for '18. The Orange, which tried to join the Eastern Intercollegiate, stood first in the N.Y. Intercollegiate League, ahead of 6–2 Buffalo.[2]

Princeton lost only a couple each season in '17 and '18 in the Eastern Intercollegiate, falling back in '19. In '17, Seton Hall registered its 61st straight wins at home. Stevens won at least fifteen in a row in '18. The Delaware Blue Hens, so-so in '17, about breaking even in fifteen in '18, were quite a bit better in '19, including a lopsided win over an aero squadron.

In '18, Pennsylvania caught a break when its entire freshmen five returned, so even with all the previous varsity in the service, the Big Quakers won the Eastern Intercollegiate title. They were also the best in '19 (overall 15–1), when no titles or trophies were handed out because Dartmouth withdrew and not everyone played each other twice. Penn State, 9–1 in '18, went 11–2 in '19, defeating Geneva (Beaver Falls), which Nittany folk thought led a western Pennsylvania conference (un-named) in '18 (13–2).[3]

Bucknell ran well above .500 for the three years. Lehigh, dominant in '17, lost 11 or 12 of 20 in '18, doing better in '19. Swarthmore, 4–7 in '17, recovered from several close losses to start the '18 season, including to Army Ambulance. The women of Swarthmore, after taking Temple in '17 and '18, split with them in '19, part of 8–1. In '19, faculty at Haverford, acquiescing to demands of returning soldiers, made basketball a major sport. Temple lost twice to Franklin & Marshall in '17 and split two with the Blue & White in '18. Lebanon Valley dominated Drexel in '17 and '18, about .500 overall. "Abnormal conditions" prevented play for both men and women in '19. The Presidents of Washington & Jefferson won 9 of 12 in '18. When Pitt won less than half the time in '18, partisans complained about "war conditions." Pitt's women were undefeated in every winter except '18 when they won 9 of 10.[4]

Bloomsburg Normal lost 2 of 3 versus Shippensburg Normal in '17 and

7. Basketball and Volleyball 121

split with the same in '18. In '19, the campus YMCA represented the men, the women considered "exceptionally strong." Someone at Mansfield Normal (6–0) thought a blowout against Bloomsburg gave them the Pennsylvania Normal School title in '18, the third in ten years. In '17, Kutztown claimed the title, 18–0 overall, downing Bloomsburg, Millersville and Shippensburg twice each and mangling Mansfield. A one-point loss to Mansfield in '19 (the only loss that year) probably prevented Kutztown from remaining enthroned.[5]

Catholic, 5–1 in the D.C. League in '17 (G. Washington, Gallaudet and Maryland St), lost a playoff to G.W. in '18, the league then ceasing to exist. None of the D.C. quintets had much success against Georgetown (not in the league), which in '18 lost to ambulance corpsmen, infantrymen from Camp Meade and three colleges (one in the South Atlantic). They also routinely lost to Navy, which had no known losses in '17. A full '18 shows only a loss or two—one against CCNY—improving to 16–0 in '19.

In 1917, Eastern Virginia Intercollegiate had Richmond 5–1, Randolph-Macon, Hampden-Sydney, W&M 1–5. The Indians moved into second in '18, Hampden-Sydney at the front. Randy-Mac won all six in '19, trouncing Richmond twice, the Spiders having no court for practice. A 13–0 gave Washington & Lee the S. Atlantic title for '17. University of Virginia, winning two-thirds in '17 faced fewer opponents in '18 (7–2), a strong 11–4 in '19. VPI went 17–2 in '17, posted more losses out of a smaller number in '18. In '19, reporters considered Tech, at 18–4, the best in the S. Atlantic, even though Georgetown and Gallaudet inflicted defeats in D.C., when Tech's captain could not play. VMI, 9–5 in '17, split about even in '18. In '19, a possible 10–6, including a loss to Roanoke College, a traditional small college power, encouraged a cadet to think that VMI should be rated runner-up in the South Atlantic.[6]

North Carolina A&E's refusal to accept a referee for a playoff in '17 gave Trinity (Duke), 20–4, the state title. State won 13 of 15 in '18, 8 of 9 against North Carolina colleges, subduing Trinity in a playoff where rooters snake danced around West Raleigh. State retained that title in '19, when it dominated a playoff over UNC, when the schools renewed athletic relations after a long lapse. Among the state's small colleges, Elon, Guilford and Lenoir usually were below .500, although Elon may have more than broken even in '18. Guilford probably went 3–7 in '18, the year their captain for '16 was killed in action.

In '19, Alabama Poly (Auburn) downed Camp Benning and Georgia twice after humbling losses in '17 and '18 to athletic clubs of Atlanta and Birmingham. Georgia, in '17, romped over Auburn and vanquished Vanderbilt in Nashville, splitting with the Atlanta A.C., thereby sharing the Southern title. In '18, Georgia, with a close win over W & Lee and a loss due to injuries to UNC, with a couple of verdicts over the Atlanta A.C., ranked the best in the Deep South. Losses to Auburn ruined '19.

In '17, Newberry gored the Gamecocks twice (once 71–19) for their third straight state title (two losses over two years). Spinal meningitis, originating in Camp Jackson, closed down the campus and prevented any chance for the Indians to repeat in '18, when South Carolina won its four against state colleges and claimed the title. Although splitting with Newberry in '17, a loss to South Carolina prevented Clemson from sharing the title. With only one loss in '18 (to Presbyterian), Clemson, after halting in February because of meningitis, tried unsuccessfully to arrange contests with South Carolina to determine the title. The Tigers, the only college in South Carolina to play out of state, fell by a lot to Georgia in '19. In '17, the Citadel won the Charleston city title. The next year, meningitis moving into the Naval Training Camp near the Charleston Navy Yard dissuaded Florida's Alligators from playing the Bulldogs, who downed the Gamecocks twice and Newberry in '19.[7]

In '17, Stetson's women went 8–8 on a 17-day trip, playing YWCAs in the Carolinas. Male Hatters, who manhandled competition in Florida, on their trip, lost to Davidson, North Carolina A&E and Wake Forest but stunned Trinity, then collapsed and lost to a high school. Nothing shows up in '18 for the men, the women winning 6 of 7 against locals.

Miss. A&M, 5–3 in '17, downed Ole Miss 3 of 4 and split with Miss. College, which took 3 of 4 from Ole Miss, suggesting A&M and Miss. College tied for state honors. Neither A&M nor Ole Miss ran in '18, when the Gold & Blue of Miss. College, 11–3, griped about losing twice to Millsaps in "their barn." Ole Miss had a promising quint for '19 before several SATC failed to return for the next semester.[8]

On 20 December 1916, Louisiana State Normal (Natchitoches) celebrated when the Panthers surprised LSU, part of a 13–0 that '17 season, while their women were also undefeated in fewer encounters. Only two losses against LSU marred '18, while in '19, they rolled over several small colleges. In '17, LSU lost to State Normal but dominated a mixed schedule of colleges, Ys and athletic clubs (losing one), making them Southern champs in some minds in '17 as well as in '18, when they lambasted State Normal and other small Louisiana colleges and also whipped Auburn twice, only Arkansas coming close. Tulane's '17 split with a Catholic prep school, won over Alabama and Texas A&M twice, losing twice to LSU. The '18 Greenbacks split four with Auburn, beat Alabama, won over some Y's and overcame the Crescents, the local AAU champ. The '19 rendition, "handicapped" by war and the loss of captain "Cajin" due to a heart condition, romped over several small colleges. LSU was unable to "stand the pace," they claimed.[9]

7. Basketball and Volleyball   123

Centre College likely won the Kentucky title three years (probably 11–0 in '17), though Bo McMillin was ejected from one contest for rough play. Some considered the Praying Colonels the "premier" quintet in the South in '19. Kentucky State lost four to Tennessee in '17. Its women kayoed Wesleyan and the Kentucky College for Women each twice plus the University of Louisville. In the war year, the Colonels took 3 of 4 over Tennessee, the women losing to Wesleyan and to Cincinnati twice (the same score), a Kentuckian hospitalized. In '19, after the women whipped Wesleyan twice, they couldn't find anyone to play.

Tennessee, in '19, kayoed Kentucky, but after losses, the Volunteers canceled the season. Sewanee, mediocre in '17, was moribund in '18 and '19. Vanderbilt, after a brief '18, beat Kentucky and lost to Centre, downed Park Field's Aviators and routed semi-pro Ramblers in '19. In '17, Maryville lost 2 of 3 to Tennessee, taking two over Tusculum. Its women cut down Cumberland, lost twice a women's college and overcame E. Tennessee Normal. In '18, Maryville men split with Tennessee, 7–1 overall, the women losing only to Normal. In '19, the men, 2–2 versus colleges, overcoming Tennessee, stalked off the floor after not getting a "square deal" against Cumberland. The women conquered Cumberland but lost again to Normal, which in '19 went, 6–2; the SATC's occupation of the gym delayed preparing for the season.[10]

West Virginia University played full schedules, roaming into Ohio, Virginia and the Northeast. The '17 season (8–8) brought losses to University of Virginia, W & L and VMI. The Mountaineers in '18 went 3–4 at home, 0–9 on the road, falling to some of the best in upstate N.Y. They tried the same again in '18, with about the same outcome, a loss to Washington and Jefferson in dispute.

In the Midwest, a bastion for basketball, Michigan lost all in the Big 10 in '18, improving markedly in '19 both in conference and overall. In '17, Michigan State downed the Illinois A.C. as well as the University of Buffalo, whose players had a hard time with state's low ceiling but committed no fouls. An Aggie cracked a rib, another broke a thumb, several losses ensuing. In '18, they lost to Camp Custer's enlisted but beat its officers, 7–6 overall. In '19, they overcame Custer's officers and split with Notre Dame, DePauw, Michigan and Wabash.[11]

Michigan State Normal at Ypsilanti, 18–0 in '17 against a mixed schedule even though three of their top players had not yet made it back from the Mexican border at the start, lost but once in '18, in a shorter schedule. The next winter, the Green & White, 11–3, won over Camp Custer's officers. Hope College, playing a mix of Ys, businesses and colleges, almost broke .500 in 15 in '17, losing to the pro Whiting Owls and taking Kalamazoo Normal twice. The Orange and Blue held at .500 in a lighter '18, losing four to enlistments. An 8–4 in '19 included a win over Camp Custer's officers.[12]

Kalamazoo College, 7–0 in the Michigan Intercollegiate Athletic Association in '17, edged Notre Dame, losing in the second round of the National AAU to Montana State. In the war year, the Orange & Black tied with Alma and Adrian for the title, the loss to Alma the first on their home court in five years, defeats to Michigan and Adrian attributed to the loss of "Fiend" for academic reasons. In January '18, students voted down closing the gym to save coal. In '19, Old Kazoo returned to the top alone, 6–2 in the conference. Alma in '17 posted 5–2 in conference when Kazoo missed a train. Even though Alma lost half its men to the service in '18 and the first Kalamazoo game at home, the Maroon & Cream turned on those Celery Eaters in the second encounter, "sweet music to our ears."[13]

Minnesota slew six small colleges in '17 and tied Illinois for tops in the Western. One of the Gopher guards (also team captain), Addison Douglass, the best defender and foul shooter, received the Croix de Guerre for gallantry as a captain of artillery. The Gophers fell to second in conference in '18 after winning eight prelims. The Helms Foundation later gave them a national title for '19. That year, Hamline, bested the "Swedes" (Gustavus-Adolphus), "Tommies" (St. Thomas), and "Farmers" (Minnesota Aggies) and split with the "Norkies" (St. Olaf), also losing twice to Carleton. The year before, St. Thomas and Carleton tied for small-college conference honors.[14]

Among Wisconsin's ten normal schools, Stevens Point won the northern title and overcame La Crosse, the southern champ in '18. In '17, Ripon won 12, 5–0 in the state's small college conference (Carroll, Lawrence, Beloit). The "exigencies of war" in '18 forced Beloit to forfeit a title game to Ripon. The university at Madison fell from first in '17 and '18 (9–3 each) to last in '19 (3–9) in the Western Conference after winning four over small colleges. About two hundred women played intramurals, their lives complicated by the SATC occupation of their gym.[15]

The Illinois Little 5, in '18, had Beloit (Wisconsin), which played in two conferences, 6–0, Knox 5–3, Lake Forest 4–4, Northwestern 2–4 and Monmouth 1–7. In '17, Augustana, 8–2, reeled off three more in the tournament for the Major Division title. Eureka took the Major in '18, after which 4 of 5 starters signed up for the military. Wesleyan slipped by arch-rival Millikin for first in '19.[16]

Chicago and Northwestern improved in the Big 10 in '19, while Illinois tended to go in the other direction, dominating in '17. In '18, George Halas, the captain of the Illini, went to Great Lakes after the season started, another starter suffering from a heart ailment, after which the "Indians" lost 4 of 5 on the road, finishing at 6–6. Northwestern, in the second division in the Western Conference in '17, rose in '18 and '19. Franklin Bellows ('17) was killed in action.[17]

Franklin College claimed the '18 title of the Indiana Conference Athletic League, splitting with Earlham and bouncing Butler and four others each twice as well as some infantrymen, losing to Purdue. The best in the Midwest in '17 was Wabash, 19–2, whipping Purdue, Notre Dame, Illinois, Missouri, losing to Michigan State and the Illinois A.C., the AAU champ. With Homer Stonebraker graduated and in the service, the Little Giants about broke even in '18 in fewer games, recovering in '19. Indiana opened a new gym just before the war, but the conference record remained at or below .500. Purdue overcame Notre Dame in '17, losing to Franklin and Wabash, 7–9 in the Western. The record dipped in '18, unable to use the gym because of a lack of coal. Notre Dame, which contributed many former players to the service, won more than half in '17. The next year brought few scores and another loss to Wabash, the Irish not much better in '19 under Gus Dorias just out of the service.[18]

Ohio State, below .500 in the Conference in '17 and '19, broke even in '18, though the leading scorer and another starter enlisted in mid-season. The tardy departure of the military from the gym in late '18 contributed to weakness in '19. Case, winning all but one with Ohio small colleges in '17, the same in '18, second in the Conference to undefeated Miami, fell below .500 in '19. Mt. Union, 3–5 in conference in '17 and 5–2 in '18 and '19, yielding by one point to Akron, the best in the conference that year. Ohio Northern considered '18 a "success," given the lack of a place to practice. Smallpox cut one Ohio small college program in '18, while Bowling Green won about half the time but could not practice and canceled some home games because coal could "could not be found anywhere in this part of the state."[19]

The University of Iowa fell into the Western cellar in '17 and leaned that way in '18 and '19. Old Gold lost only one in state in '17 (to Iowa St), winning both against the same in '18 and '19, edging Coe the latter year. Coe, 1–11 in '17 and 3–7 in '18, conquered Cornell twice in '19, stunning Iowa State and holding Sol Butler of Dubuque without a field goal, ranking second in the Iowa small-college ranks, the improvement attributed to having 60 percent of former SATC returning for another semester.[20]

Cornell College (Mt. Vernon) was the best small college in the state in '17. Wesleyan, passable in '17 and '18, won the Iowa conference in '19. St. Ambrose (Davenport), 6–5 in '17, lost twice in both '17 and '18 to Dubuque College, which split with Creighton in '17 and bested St. Louis University, 8–4 overall. Playing its first round-ball in '18, Morningside in '19, with a captain back from the army had more wins, though somehow the SATC prevented cheering practice. Grinnell joined the Missouri Valley in '19, splitting four with Iowa State, which went 12–6 in '17 (6–4 in conference), lost to Camp Dodge Officers in '18. Wins over a small college, Camp Dodge, Drake and Iowa sums up the positives in '19.[21]

Someone at Kansas State Normal thought it was time to pass around the winning of the state title (11–1 in '17; 6–6 in '18). A guard for Ft. Hays Normal served in France in '18, the '17 quintet, 10–7. The leader at Ottawa University (13–3 in Conference in '17) was center Ken Cassidy (All-Conference football), praised for heroism against the Germans. In '18, the Baptists, with double wins over nearly all conference foes, also eclipsed Camp Funston and pros in winning the Southwest Patriotic Tournament in Kansas City. Washburn (Topeka) fell to 2–9 in conference in '18, when a dispute forced the frosh to replace the varsity. The faculty stopped play when revenues lagged, each game costing $25, a voluntary assessment resuming the season. The Sons of Ichabod recovered, at 9–5 in '19, when Baker University breezed to the Kansas small college title, 14–0, the best up to that time.[22]

Kansas State (Manhattan) came in first in the Missouri Valley in '17 and '19 and second in '18, when the Wildcats overcame Fort Riley, Camp Funston and small colleges, losing to Missouri. The Jayhawkers of Kansas, a bit above .500 in '17 in conference, started '18 downing Funston and breaking even in conference. They fell back in '19. Missouri finished second in '17, the Columbians using frosh while complaining about the "unsportsmanlike" behavior of the Pikers of Washington University (St. Louis), which lost all four to the Gold & Black. The Tigers lost only once in '18, first in the conference. They were not quite as robust in '19, with three losses.[23]

Central Wesleyan (Warrenton) went 9–1 in '18, after which eight went into the service, four returning for '19, a 10–1. Drury, 9–4 in '17, overcame poor heating in '18 (8–4). Panther women undefeated claimed a state title, repeating in '19. Springfield Normal (Southwest Missouri State Teachers College), 11–1, first in Missouri intercollegiate in '17 (the top player a chaplain in the army), lost three of 13 in '18. That year, the Cardinals of William Jewell earned first in the state, 7–1 (a loss to Springfield) and overtime wins in the last two. In '19, Jewell outshone Springfield, which had an off season, missing the Bernard twins, Chester and Lester, still serving in Uncle Sam's navy. Warrensburg Normal (Central Missouri State Teachers College), with only a handful of scores in '17 and '18 won most of about twenty in '19, routing Rolla (the engineering school) four times, even "scaring" the quintet from Great Lakes.[24]

The University of Nebraska won eight warm-ups against small colleges in '17 and ran about even in the Missouri Valley Conference. The '18 Cornhuskers split with Camp Dodge, defeated Drake twice, losing to Missouri twice, splitting pairs with Kansas and Kansas State and losing the only one against Washington University. The '19 version shot down the Omaha Balloon School twice in '19, losing to Camp Dodge Officers, with an improved 10–6 for third in the conference. Omaha got its program running for '19, even though it "looked impossible," given the flu. The Scarlet & Black lost many in '19 but went 13–1 the next season. Creighton, with its new $100,000 gym, won at least 16 in '17, losing to a couple of colleges and an Omaha department store. They fared even better in '18, a student from Santa Clara stationed at Fort Omaha reporting that undefeated Creighton had "some team." In '19, Creighton overcame Great Lakes.[25]

Bellevue College, located in a suburb of Omaha, won a few of its dozen or so contests in '17, the '18 record with even fewer wins amid a briefer schedule, a close loss to nearby Fort Crook. Three former players from one squad died in Europe (2 KIA) and one severely wounded, despite which the school put a five on the court in '19, which again earned only a few wins. The school closed for good after the '19 spring semester ended.[26]

Henderson-Brown College in Arkansas did not have much of a college schedule until 1920, when at 3–1 it placed second in a league for small colleges to Little Rock (4–1), trailed by Hendrix and Arkansas College. In '17, Hendrix played outdoors; the school built a gym but couldn't use it until the SATC left late in '18. Most Arkansas schools had not yet adopted the sport.

In '17, A&M may have had the best record in Okla. with Kendall (Tulsa), Okla. and Southwestern Normal a few games above .500. The '18 Aggies had trouble breaking .500. The '18 Sooners split with Chilocco but could not play the Indians for the state title when that school went under quarantine. In '17, the Rangers of Northwest Oklahoma Normal (Alva) went to the National AAU invitational in Chicago, after an impressive lengthy road trip. Few scores surfaced the next two years. In '19, Southwest Okla. Normal won four each over Okla. Baptist and Northwest Normal, two against Central Normal and Kingfisher (114–9). In '19, Phillips University, 10–2, had the best record. The Orange & Black of Kendall College (Tulsa) won over half of 19 in '17, led by 6' 4" William Pappan, a Kaw. In '18, without Pappan who drove ambulances in France, Kendall collapsed, the coach and players quitting over scholarship rules.[27]

North Texas, so-so in '17, upset Texas in '18. Rice Institute, running off nine in a row, claimed the Texas title in '17 but the Longhorns prevailed that year in their new gym that held 2,500, taking 3 of 4 from A&M. The Owls reigned, 10–4 overall in '18. In "transitional" '19, Rice fell back as Texas took four over the Owls and split four with A&M. for another Texas title, another loss to N. Texas notwithstanding.[28]

In '17, Southern Methodist "unaccustomed to indoor courts," played Okla. at a Y, where, unfamiliar with dribbling, they lost; the next day on a field in a light rain before a large crowd, they more than doubled the Sooner point total. The Mustangs, losing only once in the Texas Intercollegiate, claimed to be as good as Texas and A&M, whom they did not play. In '18, when the Mustang men lost more than they won, SMU women ran eleven straight for the state championship. In '19 the ladies lost 4 of 5 before running the table. The men almost broke even, playing at a Y and practicing on any available court. Outdoors, they lost to Southwestern by a point, overwhelming the same in the next encounter—indoors.[29]

Arizona surpassed the Phoenix Y, two high schools, an athletic club and an academy twice, plus the University of New Mexico (a split) and the New Mexico Aggies in '17. In '18, wins came over the Y's of Bisbee (twice), Tucson and El Paso plus army officers at Nogales. The '19 edition downed the 25th Infantry (Nogales), a Y, Tempe Normal twice, and the New Mexico Aggies. The women of Northern Arizona Normal, who normally played high schools, had "severe" flu wipe out the '19 season.

In 1917, New Mexico, which shut out an Indian school and overcame a Y and a high school, won one over Arizona and lost to the Aggies. The state Farmers rang up four over the Hill Dwellers in '19, when the former split four with Arizona and overcame ambulance drivers and the 7th Cavalry. The '18 Aggies lost to a military institute.

Brigham Young University claimed the Utah title in '17, their sixth in eight years. In the AAU tournament the White & Blue ran second, winning over Alva Normal (Oklahoma) and losing to the Illinois A.C. In '18, losses to Utah (rough tactics) and flu ruined the season. The Utah Aggies (Logan), after losing to the Montana Aggies in an AAU invitational in '17, claimed the state in '18 and almost secured the Rocky Mountain title, losing to Colorado University at Boulder, 2 of 3. Utah, which won the AAU in '16, twice overcame BYU and the Aggies to take the '19 state title (also winning in '13 and '16) before they lost a tournament in Los Angeles, where their "aggressive Eastern style" led to a lot of fouls.[30]

Colorado College, at 7–1, claimed a conference title in '17, Colorado University (at Boulder) contending that the Tiger record was really 6–2, the same as theirs. In '18, the Tigers, grumbling about the "attitude of faculty and student body," quit after two conference wins. In '19, they secured second. In the absence of Tigers in '18, Boulder won the state and the Rocky Mountain playoff, only a loss to Denver's Ministers marring their record. The Silver& Gold also absorbed only one loss in '19 to take another title.[31]

After a so-so '17, the Idaho Gem Staters in '18 took the western division of the Northwest Conference. They lost one to Montana, when a player failed to report to two officials on coming into the game, his half-court shot thereby not counting. Idaho retained first in '19 with a 10–2.

In '17, the Montana Aggies (a.k.a. Bobcats) reaped sixteen until a loss in the AAU championships after overcoming Kalamazoo College in a preliminary. In the regular season, they won at least five on their trip through the Inland Empire (Idaho and Eastern Washington). After the start of '18, the coach left, causing a downturn, which spilled over into '19 when they recorded only two lopsided losses to the Utah Aggies.

In '17, Montana started 4–1 (splitting with Okla. Normal), but when Christian Benz, the football captain, went into the Navy, nine straight losses ensued. The next year they ousted the Oregon Aggies 3 of 4, yet still ran below .500 in the Northwest Conference. Nothing was recorded for '19, possibly the campus closing, with the flu.

South Dakota split with Yankton and North Dakota State, winning over most small colleges in '17. North Dakota State took South Dakota State twice in '17, losing to Fargo, which lost to North Dakota. In '17, North Dakota took down South Dakota State and jettisoned Jamestown College as well as Fargo. In '18 (15–0), 1,000 packed the Flickertail gym to watch the Aggies routed. With a former service man leading, North Dakota lost only once, when they put in a returning serviceman who had not had time to adjust. At Jamestown in '17, "small in stature" Kennedy Wanner, who perished in the Argonne, had a sixth sense of foe weaknesses, his team collapsing when injuries took him out of games.[32]

In '17, Y's, athletic clubs, even a high school gave Cal Berkeley 9 of its 17 wins. In '18, Cal took two from the 63rd Infantry and 2 of 3 from Stanford and in '19, claimed part of the California/Nevada League title. Nevada claimed a tie for first with Santa Clara in '17. In '19, the Sagebrush Warriors fell to 1–6 in conference, weak in '18 as well. Yet, in 1920, fully recovered, Nevada went undefeated and not only claimed the Cal-Nevada title but also that of the Pacific Coast Intercollegiate. In '18, Santa Clara won by a point over St. Ignatius (University of S. Francisco) in the only game that counted out of four played all winter. Stanford would not play them even though they promised not to use frosh. In '18, Ignatius sent one of its best to a be a quartermaster on the eve of a game with Cal, after which all athletics ended "for the present semester at least." In '19, the Santa Clara score keeper recorded a foul rather than a basket for an Ignatian and the referee took away a made basket from one fouled while shooting. Although admitting refereeing left something to be desired, a Missionite thought the ref and scorekeeping did not determine the outcome. Cal and Santa Clara, therefore, tied for first. Standings in at least one yearbook do not concur.[33]

In '17, Stanford, winless in the Pacific Coast Conference, sustained double losses to Cal, Washington State and Oregon State. In '18, the Cardinals only won 1 of 3 against Cal in the only contests against conference foes but for some reason those losses did not count in the Pacific or the Cal/Nevada Conference, so Stanford ran second in that league to St. Mary's. They also overcame Camp Fremont's infantry twice and another infantry regiment once along with the base hospital. Two losses to Cal doomed Stanford in '19.

The Helms Foundation later put Washington State, under Fred "Doc" Bohler, first nationally in '17, based on its 11–0 in the Northwest Conference and 8–1 in the Pacific Coast. Ivan Price, considered an All-Star in the Northwest and on the Pacific Coast, went to Mare Island at the start of the '18 season and died fighting in France about a week before the Armistice, one of at least 43 former students who gave their lives out of over a thousand who joined the military from State. The Crimson & Gray lost all but their captain to the service, and, with three frosh, lost more than they won (two to the 91st Division from Camp Lewis), taking pride in winning 1 of 4 from Inland Empire champ Idaho in '18. The '19, with frosh no longer eligible, lost thrice to Idaho, 10–11 overall.

The '18 Washington overcame the 361st Infantry (Camp Lewis), before losing several to the Oregon Aggies and Oregon. Maybe a few more wins showed up in '19 but they also fell to Idaho twice. In '17, students at Washington State Normal (Bellingham), which overwhelmed the College of Puget Sound and a few less prestigious, griped about wimpy Whitman and Washington not responding to their challenge.[34]

Hugo Bezdeck's Yellow-Lemon at Oregon lost all 11 in '17. They ran second in the Western Division of the Northwest Conference in '18, 3–5 (3–8 overall), rose to first in the Pacific Coast Conference, 11–3 (13–4 overall) in '19, taking Cal in two close ones, earlier edging the winner of the Northwest title, Idaho, in the only game between the two. Oregon State (the Aggies) topped the Pacific Coast at 15–0 in '18, with four of their five All-Conference, no championship game played against Californians. In '19, they lost to Washington State twice and then lost most on an extended trip through the Northwest, including Idaho. Flu ruined the '19 season for the women after winning over Reed College.[35]

Among Eastern League pros the second half '17 Greystock Churchmen, 14–6, stood first in the standings. New rules for amateurs cut back on rough play, but pros preferred a vigorous form, putting players in cages to separate them from fans, who were told not to throw "missiles" at them. The playoffs in '17 at Camden, New Jersey, whose armory held 4,000, drew successively larger crowds. The Jasper Jewels surprised Greystock when a designated foul shooter hit 22 of 27 compared to 14 of 25 for his counterpart, the losers administering an "artistic lacing" in the second. The Churchman took the finale, 23–21, as foul shooters each hit 15. The Philadelphia press praised Marty Friedman for the Jewels.[36]

In '18, the Eastern, the New York and Pennsylvania leagues disappeared. The American Basketball League, which operated in the Philadelphia area in '17 as a minor league, acquired some Eastern Leaguers in '18, St. Columba prevailing. In '19, the Saints led the eight-team league early on.[37]

In January '18, Raycroft, the Princeton prof overseeing athletics at

7. Basketball and Volleyball 131

all the army camps, calculated that 118,000 were in organized games. Fort Oglethorpe had 200 teams playing 650 games. Camp Devens in '18, had 160 teams in 25 leagues, based on regiments and companies. After about a thousand games an infantry company won out. Devens had well-known collegians, including an Eli All-American and at least one each from Colgate and Dartmouth plus "well known" pros.[38]

In '18, naval reservists at Newport, coached by Clinton Black and consisting of a former Princeton player, a Penn State Leaguer, another pro from a Buffalo league and a Michigan Aggie, lost to two colleges and the Crescent A.C. on a trip to Gotham. In '19, the Torpedo Station (Newport) overcame a local five before 1,200, while the Reservists won a close one over some blue-jacketed guards. The year before, after an explosion killed several at the torpedo station, several games raised money for afflicted families.

In '18, naval reservists from Pelham Bay fell to Naval militia. Their headquarters sank a section base. Pelham Bay overwhelmed Fort Slocum, despite the efforts of a Yankee pitcher as a sub for the losers. CCNY almost doubled the fort's score, while Princeton downed an aeronautics school.[39]

In '18, the Crescent A.C. (New Moon of Brooklyn) toward the end of February more than doubled up on Naval militia, followed a few days later with a verdict over Pelham Bay. In early March, Crescent struggled to beat some naval reservists. The next year, Crescent split with a naval auxiliary club, the loss the only one to the military in two years, and downed officers of the Rockaway Naval Air Station, 34–25.

The U.S. Ambulance Corps (Allentown) lost narrowly to Lafayette, by a wider margin to Penn State and Cape May Naval by three, winning the last 14, mostly against top colleges (Georgetown, Lehigh, Pitt and Princeton). Despite this record, military fives fell short of winning half their games against colleges in '18 in about seventy-five known encounters and dropped to less than a third of almost fifty in '19.

At Camp Dix, an infantry regiment outscored everyone 671–143, as the leagues totaled over 1,000 contests divided into 16 majors and 8 minors, with playoffs. Within a few weeks of arriving at Camp Meade, Co. B copped the 315th Infantry (outdoors) title, "rough and tumble" describing the action. Two teams at the Y (Officers and Enlisted) were both coached by a star at Allegheny College who also captained the officers that reeled off four in a row while enlisted took five, losing one, and then beating Catholic University, 22–21, with a shot from center court at game's end. Enlisted fell to St. Columba pros twice and Mt. St. Joseph College after winning 5 or 6.[40]

Camp Greene played at the Y in Charlotte, two infantry regiments the most impressive in a 10-team league that also included three Massachusetts units, Vermont officers and the camp hospital. So much interest ensued that the athletic director started another eight-team league. Gordon's camp divisions, one a variant of basketball, the other volleyball, mostly for businessmen. "Invented" at the Holyoke, Massachusetts, Y in 1895 by stretching a tennis net and inflating the rubber bladder of a basketball, the game first appeared in Charleston in 1900 (possibly the first with outside electric-lit courts) and spread across North America to China and the Philippines. Courts materialized at parks and playgrounds, allowing both sexes the opportunity for "wholesome exercise." Over 200,000 Americans played regularly, including 10,000 collegians (intramurals), plus 50,000 children at playgrounds and another 85,000 at either Y.W.C.A.s or Y.M.C.A.s. In Charleston, the league consisted of Lobsters, Clams, Shrimps and Blackfish. They all attended a banquet—to eat seafood, one presumes. In '18, although the "second annual Oyster League" got off to a good start, participants relied on a form of basketball, not volleyball. Winter weather ended using outside courts. The Y also lacked heat and warm water due to the coal shortage.[52]

At Keokuk, Iowa, volleyball aroused interest in the winter of '17, vying for as much attention as high school basketball. The Y league consisted of Cannibals, Explorers, Kangaroos and Crabbers. Keokuk hosted a "second annual" meet around the Ides of March, an Illinois team taking honors. Many in the Y balcony had never seen the sport before. The press assumed such interest would be sustained the next year, but '18 brought only basketball.

In army camps, the sport prevailed, but, unlike basketball, not extramurally. In 28 camps in the Southeast in August '18, it ranked third, behind baseball and swimming. A league at one included only teams from management. In October, the net game rose to first, more popular than either baseball or football, with almost 95,000 participating, despite the flu. Overseas, between 1 August and the end of 1918, 396,334 played as 352,496 watched. Between January and May 1919, 1,625,708 turned out, about as much as for baseball and basketball.[53]

8

Golf and Tennis

In intercollegiate golf, Dartmouth defeated Amherst in '16, and lost to a country club in '17. Harvard lost to Yale and overcame Columbia in '16. Williams, which lost to Cornell, Yale and a country club in '16 and faced "unusual conditions" in '17, played a full slate in '18, losing to Dartmouth, Columbia, Harvard and the Newport Naval Reservists. Cornell won over Yale and Williams in '16 and lost to Harvard. Princeton, way ahead of Yale in '16, lost to Columbia in '18, but participated in an elaborate Intercollegiate Golf Association match in '19, outscoring Harvard, Yale, Penn, Columbia and Williams. Penn lost to Columbia twice in '18 and once to Yale in '19. Princeton won the intercollegiate title in '16 and '19, no champions announced for '17 or '18. Columbia surprised everyone in '18, taking matches against Penn twice as well as one versus Princeton.

Activity dropped just after the declaration of war in April '17, some recovery occurring in '18. Perry Adair, who pitched over a stymie to win the individual championship over A.L. Walker of Columbia, led Georgia Tech, which in '18 came north, despite the war, to pass Columbia, Penn and Yale, three of the top Northeastern clubs. Adair bested Walker, 81 to 86 in the afternoon after a 76 in the morning. Bobby Jones joined Tech in '19, as the school planned to invade the north once again, but Princeton won the championship, besting Harvard by 31 strokes and Yale by 32, Walker the individual titlist. The only other intercollegiate golf took place in the Midwest, where Illinois overcame Chicago and Northwestern. Illinois lost to Cornell in '16, and repeated the win over Northwestern in '17, when the season abruptly ended as everyone went into the service.

During '17 and '18, the U.S. Golf Association cancelled its amateurs for men and women and opens for men. The Professional Golf Association that had its first championship in '16 also canceled. Eastern associations followed suit. With the British Open not resuming until 1920, it looked like competitive golf would disappear. But the Western Golf Association and Southern Golf Association held tournaments, young Jones capturing the latter.

With the declaration of war, clubs held "Red Cross" tournaments, pro Jock Hutchinson ahead in one. Pros raised $4,000 at one benefit after calling off its championship. In June, women at the Los Angeles Country Club paid a $1 entry fee, all of which went to the Red Cross. The New Jersey Golf Association replaced its championship in April with events to raise funds for the Red Cross, one collecting over $1,000. Howard F. Whitney, secretary of the U.S. Golf Association, praised tournaments on the 4th of July '17 at over 400 courses in 44 states, yielding $80,000 for the Red Cross. An association Patriotic Tournament in Pennsylvania for both amateurs and pros, raised $72,375.[1]

Robert Gardner, Chick Evans, Perry Adair and Bobby Jones played at a country club near Chicago for the Red Cross. Gardner, the national amateur golf titlist in '15 and a pole vault champ at Yale, joined a officers training camp in Texas. At age 15 in April '17, Jones broke the record at the East Lake Country Club, with a 68. He and Perry Adair played pros to earn money for the women of Atlanta to buy wool to make clothing for soldiers. In August '18, Jones and Adair won a tournament sponsored by the Western Golf Association at White Sulphur Springs, raising $37,000 for the YMCA.[2]

At the end of '17, a critic claimed the season in New York "the deadest" since the infancy of golf. Another argued that even with cancellations, those that were held were "brilliant." The Metropolitan Golf Association (N.Y.) cancelled championships but sponsored a Memorial Day event that raised over $100,000 for the Red Cross. That may have left only two events in the New York area, both for women. In early July, Jesse Guilford won a "Liberty Tournament" in Vermont, named for a federal bond drive. Chick Evans defended his title as the best amateur as the association raised thousands for the Red Cross.[3]

In July '17 near New York, American born golfers took on those born in Britain to fund the Red Cross. Pros Walter Hagen and Jerome Travers and several American amateurs faced Brits led by Hutchinson, who, with long drives, mastered Travers, who the day before overcame a British pro. Of eight prizes, Americans secured five, the English two and a Scot one.[4]

Denver golfers had a great '17 "in spite of war," with two new courses under construction. A local commentator believed nothing could be better than "good, honest sports," to sustain "the spirit of the nation" at a "high standard." More members were playing at the Denver Country Club (the state champion) than ever before. On the 4th of July, way over a hundred competed for a Red Cross medal.[5]

Pinehurst in North Carolina had many scores recorded in November and December '17 over five different courses, under the supervision of a famous landscape architect. In the cold winter of '18, Valentine's Day still brought a lot of action for men and women, amateurs and pros, the season not ending until late April. Pinehurst produced fewer matches in the fall of '18 than it had in '17, possibly disrupted by the flu, but golf did well weathering war and flu.

Commenting on '18, a columnist argued that although championships were called off, golfers did more in raising funds for war-related charities than any other sport. Whatever the amount donated in '17, the U.S. Golf Association hoped to raise a million in '18. Dozens of Red Cross benefits took place, among them Francis Ouimet and Jesse Guilford winning one in August. Later, the two teamed up to raise money for the athletic fund at Camp Devens. The Western Association raised $200,000 by one estimate, $313,000 by another. Over $30,000 came from one Lake Shore County Club near Chicago. Scattered returns produced $5, $10 or $15,000 in the fall for the United War Work drive to entertain soldiers and sailors. The ex-President of the Mass Golf Association ran the N. England part of the program.[6]

The price of golf balls and clubs rose, hickory shafts going from 25 cents a few years earlier to 90 cents after the first of January '18 at one Manhattan supplier, but no major reduction in sales took place, receipts in '17 being about half a million over those for '16, while the first nine months of '18 reached $10,500,000, compared to $8,200,000 for all of '17. Golfers could expect to "get badly bunkered" by an increase in links fees in effect on 19 November, as the federal government levied a 10 percent duty on club dues over $12 annually, country clubs collecting the money.[7]

At the war declaration, the U.S. Golf Association seemed to endorse the idea of plowing up courses. Evans praised a plan at a N.Y. country club to plow part of its property not in use, sell the crops and buy ambulances and other necessities for the military, a far cry from plowing up an entire course. Even the British, with much less land and heavier losses from the war, kept courses, but one losing out to the plow. So far as is known, none were plowed up in the U.S. Nearly every Canadian club produced crops to use in clubhouses, a Toronto club cultivating 25 acres.[8]

A country club in N.Y. stopped construction of a new course in May '17 "because of war." Yet another club bought 140 acres for $500,000 to build a new course in November. In '18, when the U.S. had 2,002 courses (1,618 clubs, 297 public and 87 families), 150 more courses were being constructed. The summer of '17 brought less "feverish anxiety" about new courses in the "American Riviera." But capitalists in Florida planned to add twelve including two 18-hole "where croquet and quoit pitching" had previously prevailed. Near Tampa Bay, another new course would have water hazards to go along with 4,000 yards of green and a big new hotel.[9]

During the cold '18 winter country clubs cut down trees and burned firewood in the clubhouses. Possibly two fires in New Jersey and one on

Long Island started because of the practice, but these started in cellars, one in a defective flue next to a furnace. After a third fire, golfers suspected someone who believed such sports might be "detrimental" to the war effort could be committing arson.[10]

The U.S. Golf Association considered cutting caddies and turning over fees to the Red Cross. Some clubs thought about having girls caddy. In '19, forty caddies went on strike at one country club, demanding pay per round be increased from 75 cents to $1. Police arrested four boys who went to the home of the club manager. The boys behaved much like millions of other American workers in a year loaded with strikes.[11]

Francis Ouimet, the '13 U.S. Open winner, banned from the U.S. Golf

Francis Ouimet, prominent golfer, rose from the rank of private to lieutenant at Camp Devens. *Library of Congress: LC-DIG-ggbain-14156.*

Association Amateur because he sold sporting goods, carried the Western Amateur in Chicago in '17. He became a private at Devens, playing in Red Cross exhibitions and continuing his weekly column as he rose to a lieutenancy. In January '18, the national association returned Ouimet to amateur status, to public applause.[12]

By the end of '17, seven other prominent amateurs, including an Eli of '04, joined Ouimet and Gardner in the service. Few pro golfers served, being either Scots or English and "a mature lot" (42 of 44 ex-champs still played). Pro Tom Kerrigan, age 22, enlisted in the Naval Reserves at Pelham Bay, hoping he could fulfill his duty while pursuing golf. He won a match at the Brookline club.[13]

In July '18, in Minneapolis, federal agents detained Chic Evans, the top amateur (some wanted to classify him a pro for writing about golf for pay) for not having a certificate showing his draft status. With proof of his class 3 rating, the agents released him, but he had a lousy day on the links.[14]

Ouimet and athletic directors in the fall of '18 urged the War Department to build courses near Army Camps and naval installations. The government agreed to create courses if the U.S. Golf Association donated equipment. The Commission on Training Camp Activities chimed in with "evidence that golf as recreational activity played an important part in counteracting the tension of intensive training."[15]

The athletic director at Camp Funston in Kansas thought it would be difficult to put links in hills that served as drill grounds. Camp Beauregard in Louisiana had two courses, one nine holes, the other six. At Camp Las Casas in Puerto Rico a nine-hole course met the needs of officers. Fort Bliss, near El Paso, had links, with others located three miles away for both enlisted and officers, who needed red or yellow balls, white ones hard to find in the desert. The Devens' director did not think it feasible to build a course in the camp, but officers played near Boston, Fitchburg and Worcester. Near San Diego, Kearny officers and enlisted played at Del Mar, for free, winning prizes (the Red Cross supplying balls) and at La Jolla. Camp Upton opened a nine-hole in the spring of '19 for officers and men, which started almost dead center in the camp right next to the home of its commandant and meandered throughout the place. A well-known left-handed golfer now in charge of baking pies helped supervise construction.[16]

In '19, at Nice, France, Sgt. William Rautenbush (7th Corps and Chicago titlist in '16) won the AEF title. Coming to the 18th hole with a 67 in a qualifying round and closing in on a course record, his first shot came within two feet of the hole, but he way overshot and took two more to finish.[17]

In tennis, a reduction took place in the spring of '17 followed by a modest recovery in '18, and a return to more normal conditions in '19.

College championships were canceled in both '17 and '18. Harvard, as usual, won both the singles and doubles national championship in '16 plus at least 8 of 10 duals, halting Stanford's until then successful invasion of the Midwest and Northeast. The next year, with war looming, Harvard lost to Dartmouth, then canceled the schedule. Although winning over Tufts in '18, it lost several nor did it fully recover in '19, when Yale prevailed as the national singles and doubles champion.

Bates won the Maine state in '17 and placed second in the N. England Intercollegiate held despite the war. Amherst had "unsettled conditions" in '17 when military drilling interrupted activity at Williams. MIT, cancelling several '17, won 5 of 6 in '18 and placed first in the regional championship. Trinity was "not altogether unsuccessful" (1–3), with one entering a tank corps in '17.[18]

Columbia, at 5–0–1, in '16, recorded little in '17; in '18 it won seven before losing to Yale. Bucknell, 4–0 in '16, had nothing for '17 or '18, "injured by war." Claiming most colleges stopped play in '18, Westminster downed Hiram. Washington & Jefferson, having restarted tennis in '16 after a three-year lapse, was "somewhat hindered by the war in '17. Moravian, with over a dozen matches (none of them colleges) in '17, produced one score for '18.[19]

Save for Georgetown, tennis must not have been sustained in D.C. In '17, Randolph-Macon, winning 2 of 3 from Richmond, carried the Virginia state tournament. In '19, it took both singles and doubles over three others for the Eastern Virginia title. The Virginia Cavaliers in '19 won over Washington & Lee, which gave up the sport the next year after a one-year experiment.

In '18, Georgia Tech captured the Southern Intercollegiate at East Lake, winning both singles and doubles, taken by Tulane the previous year ('17). Doug Watters (Tulane), who did well in the Gulf States Tournament, after the collegiate season ended in '17, went to war in '18. In the Southwestern Conference in '18, after a verdict over Okla., the Longhorns won the singles and doubles as they did in '19, although the war "seriously interfered."[20]

At Iowa State, the war afflicted tennis "more than other sports," bringing it to a "standstill" which turned into "convalescent" in '19. Missouri took the Western Conference doubles in '18, but '19 produced a blank, a revival detected the next year.[21]

Michigan State overcame Ypsilanti combining men and women in '16, nothing reported in '17 or '18, a modest recovery in '19. Ann Arbor took the Western Conference singles in '18. With only two on the team in '17 and '18, they returned to the four-man model in '19. Minnesota doubles combo overcame Michigan and Wisconsin in '18. The war was still playing "havoc" at Wisconsin in '19.[22]

Chicago, which lost but 1 of 10 in '16 and carried the Western Conference singles and doubles, had a weak '17 and '18 and went 3–2 in conference, 3–0 against small colleges in '19. Illinois claimed conference singles and doubles in '17. Ohio State usually dominated in the state and competed well in the Western, but retaining the state, it fell back in the Big 9 in '17 in fewer matches, a pattern repeated in '18 but not in '19 when Oberlin took the state singles, while State split four matches in the Big 10.[23]

California, which won 19 of 24 matches in one batch and tied USC and overcame Stanford in '16, won 73 of 98 and swept through Pomona and USC, Stanford, and USC in '17, only one score appearing for '18. In '19, Cal won five cups and three championships in various tournaments, also shutting out Stanford. Pomona claimed a championship involving Occidental, Throop and USC, its women winning 2 of 6. Southern Cal women tied Cal in '16. Stanford, after losing to Cal in '16, won a bunch, finally losing to Harvard. No victories surfaced for '17 or '18.

The Davis Cup did not take place between '14 and '19 nor did matches at Wimbledon or in France for any championships. In '17, Robert L. Murray won the unofficial "patriotic" U.S. men's singles national championship at Forest Hills. Officers at Plattsburg allowed Richard Norris Williams, Clarence "Peck" Griffin, Watson M. Washburn and Dean Mathey to participate, but lack of practice hindered them. In '17, with almost all the top players in the military, Fred Alexander and Harold Throckmorton (both older) won the doubles. In '18, a lack of coal at an armory delayed the national indoor tennis championships. On a tour of the Northeast in late summer and fall in '17, Californian Mary Browne went 14–9–1 over Norwegian Molla Bjurstedt, rated the best women tennis player in the U.S. The tour grossed almost $59,000, about $32,000 going to the Red Cross to fund an ambulance corps at Allentown. Several stars helped, including Fred Alexander (55 matches), S. Howard Voshell (24) and Bill Tilden (8).[24]

Most categories produced at least seventeen unofficial champions in '17. In '18, two obscure players took the men's indoor doubles while Ben Tilden paired with 15-year-old Vincent Richards to win outdoors. With War Department approval, the U.S. National Lawn Tennis Association played out its regular schedule but with no prizes, challenge cups or national rankings. Gate receipts would in most cases be turned over to the American Red Cross. "Patriotic" tournaments replaced championship matches.

The Pelham Country Club had few skilled players, several in the service and the absence of prizes reducing interest. Despite setbacks, the national association planned for the doubles-championship in Massachusetts and for the singles at Forest Hills in August in hopes of raising $100,000 for three ambulance companies. Women made up for the loss of the most talented male players.[25]

By August '17, 8 of the top 10 in '16 had joined the service. No. 1, Williams, Harvard's intercollegiate singles champ in '13 and '15 and doubles in '14 and '15, U.S. Lawn tennis outdoor titlist in '16 volunteered for officer training at Plattsburg. He failed his first physical with a foot defect, which did not impair him earlier in a five-set match nor later firing shells at Germans. Two other top 10 won the doubles for Harvard ('13) along with two Princeton doubles champs, one doing it twice. Only 2 of the 10 had no known college experience. The only two not in the service were Ichiya Kumagae (No. 5), a collegian in his native Japan and Murray (No. 4), a Pacific Coast titlist in '13, with degrees in chemistry from Stanford, now occupied producing war materials.

Of those not in top ten, another Princetonian became an artillerist in '18. Two well-known Californians missed a tourney because one joined the Quartermasters Corps and the other Naval Coast Defense Reserves. Red-haired Maurice "California Comet" McLaughlin (thrice national champion) also went into the reserves. A titlist at Princeton in '12 joined the Coast Artillery. Fred Alexander (Princeton, collegiate doubles in '00 and singles in '01), who raised $50,000 for the Red Cross, went into Coast Artillery, William A. Larned (Harvard's collegiate singles champ in '92 and the Outdoor Singles in '01 and '02) became a major in the Signal Corps and Robert D. Wrenn (Harvard, doubles in '92, outdoor singles in '93 and '94) served as a major in the regular army.

The D.C. area endured an estimated 40 percent loss in activity, less than amateur baseball but greater than golf. Equipment sales seemed especially hard hit. Despite these losses, the D.C. bureaucracy (War, Navy, Treasury, Justice, Trade, Agriculture and at least a half dozen others), kept playing. On Labor Day, '18, the Dunbarton Club hosted the D.C. championship, a lieutenant besting a captain.[26]

In '18, the U.S. National Lawn Tennis Association restored championships, Murray ending up with the #1 ranking. The "Yellow Peril" (Kumagae), winner of the N.Y. state title for the second year, fell in straight sets to Bill Tilden, who showed "no mercy." Then Murray buried the tall Philadelphian in an "avalanche" of "burning drives" at Forest Hills, the receipts donated to a fund for soldiers and sailors. Tilden won the clay court singles in Chicago in early July. He and Vince Richards secured the doubles.[27]

In July '18, Major Larned coordinated with an English counterpart to put on grass matches near London to benefit the Red Cross. When stars could not be released, less known took their places. Naval officers from South African, Australia, Canada and the U.S. came to the Queen's Club to go against army officers from the same nations, Navy winning, 5–4. Two young American ensigns performed well.[28]

Col. Wait C. Johnson, one-time N. England champ and Philippine titlist, brought 188 officers to "The Pearl of the Riviera" in February '19, at a 338-room hotel, with 13 courts (five rented by the Red Cross and the YMCA, Albert Spalding also covering some costs). After two days of rain, 47 matches took place in one day. Col. Dwight Davis (Harvard singles titlist in '99), weak in the backcourt, lost. Lt. H.C. Breck, who had won the Pacific Northwest Tournament (Tacoma) the previous summer while stationed at Camp Lewis, bested Southern champ Captain Doug Watters (Tulane). In the finals, Williams prevailed over Washburn. The two captains then carried the doubles.[29]

The AEF championships, team and individual, took place in May at the Racing Club de France in the Bois de Boulogne. A major, a sergeant and three privates for Base Section No. 2 took 6 of 7 from General Headquarters, edging the Embarkation Corps and Intermediate Section. Washburn won the singles. Base Section carried the doubles. In June, a major, several officers, including Washburn and Dean Mathey (Princeton), went to the first tournament at Wimbledon since '14. None made the finals in either singles or doubles, even though "in fine fettle." Australian Pat Wood whipped Washburn. An American doubles team lost to French champions in an exhibition after the AEF matches.[30]

The Lawn Tennis Association, which had about 10,000 members serving in the military, received reports from eighty clubs of 168 war-related deaths, the Haverford Cricket Club leading with 16, the Germantown Cricket Club with 7. Why these Philadelphia area country clubs sustained such a high number is unknown. Germantown's list had five lieutenants, a captain and a major. At least three were aviators, one dying in combat over the English Channel. Likely, all had gone to college with at least two each from Harvard and Penn, plus one Princeton ('15). One was the son of a prominent Philadelphia banker; another's father was a former president of the Pennsylvania Railroad. A star football player at Princeton in '12 died falling off a horse at Fort Oglethorpe in '17. His mother paid for an auditorium and barracks at the fort named Camp Warden McClean, later absorbed by Camp Greenleaf. Clearly, the Philadelphia elite (country club set) answered the call for sacrifice during the Great War.

9

Rowing, Swimming, Yachting and Motorboat Racing

Only a few colleges had crew in '16. The Big Three plus Cornell, Penn and Syracuse indulged, with Harvard's eight-oar varsity losing to Princeton in '16, winning over Princeton and Yale at New London in '18, the '17 season lost. Preparatory to the Yale and Harvard race in '18, officials cut the distance to two miles, the first time in over forty years for such a short run, attributed to injuries and a "slump of collegiate sports." The Crimson won on the Housatonic River.[1]

Yale defeated Penn in '17 just after the country went to war but lost in '18. A regatta in '19 gave Penn a win over Yale, the Eli prevailing over Princeton in May and over Harvard in June in the two-mile, eight-oar, plus a second in the American Henley at Philadelphia, the end of the war bringing a fuller schedule. After an active '16, Cornell could not compete the next year. After a busy '16, "sorrow" reigned as Syracuse cut its '17 season; in '18, only frosh went to Poughkeepsie though a team out oared Navy on the Severn. The '17 Penn lost to Yale on the Schuylkill before cancelling the rest. In 1918, Penn surpassed Annapolis and did well enough at Poughkeepsie, given the absence of two in the service at season's start and two more to aviation later, after which Penn lost to Navy and Yale. Although Columbia had some achievements before the war, the program weakened during the war, even though some Chinese students tried to keep it alive. Of 19 on the varsity from '14 through '16, 16 joined the army, one dying in combat.[2]

The Naval Academy raced on the Severn against boat clubs as well as colleges. Navy posted a third against Harvard and Yale in the American Henley in '16, a second against Princeton, Columbia and Penn. In '17, only the "Plebe Crew" took on collegians because an early graduation lost several starters, the replacements still able to sink the Potomac Boat Club just before all varsity athletic activity ceased. The '18 varsity lost to Penn on the Severn but later beat the Quakers and Columbia in an American Rowing

Association regatta. Midshipmen aboard the U.S.S. *Wisconsin* in '18 (eight plus stroke and coxswain) won a cup at an undisclosed site.³

The Annual Regatta gave Stanford an eight-length win over Cal in '16, when Washington won the Pacific Coast title over Cal and Stanford. No Annual Regatta took place in '17, Washington overcoming Stanford and Cal in a match. The American Henley Regatta (Philadelphia) was cancelled only a day or two after the war declaration, Princeton, Colgate, Yale and Harvard withdrawing. The Intercollegiate Regatta, scheduled for the Hudson River near Poughkeepsie, suffered the same fate and for the same reason. No noteworthy races took place in '18. Washington prevailed in '19 over Cal and Stanford, which lost the eight-oared Pacific Coast Conference race to Washington, its second team and frosh winning. Washington, which had 8 of its top 9 enter the service in '17, sustained interclass competition in '18 even though construction of a naval training station on a Seattle golf course cut off access to the boat house.⁴

The U.S. Navy carried out customary competition during the war, the press keeping quiet about the location. The U.S.S. *Arizona* overcame the U.S.S. *Nevada* in '18 to take the Battenberg Cup, donated earlier by an English lord who changed his German title. Being new and oil-fired, neither ship went into European waters. In 1919, *Arizona* retained the cup in "Southern waters" over the U.S.S. *Arkansas*, the *Nevada* running third. The U.S.S. *Oklahoma* won three other cups, with a victory over the U.S.S. *New York* for the Colonial Dames trophy and two wins over the U.S.S. *Pennsylvania*. One of the latter's two crews secured the San Pedro Cup.⁵

In June 1916, the Virginia Boat Club (Richmond) replaced three junior scullers chasing Villa and won over two Baltimore clubs in the first Southern Rowing Association regatta a D.C. eight winning the seniors, when a steamboat got in the way. At the Middle States Regatta, with seventeen clubs from seven cities represented on the Potomac on Labor Day, Richmond gave the Potomac Club all it could handle in the juniors, Philadelphians pushing past Potomac in the seniors. Little took place in '17. In '18, with most members in the service and other clubs sending no crews with the loss of manpower, Richmond activated thirteen retired scullers to have enough to carry on intramurals. In 1919, it won the junior-eight at the Southern Rowing Association's second regatta (near Baltimore), overtaking the Arundels, who triumphed in other races. Richmond sent no one to the 58th Annual Middle States Regatta, on the Schuylkill on Labor Day, where Philadelphians took 12 of 17 races.⁶

In collegiate swimming in '17, Yale split with Columbia but took a playoff despite three firsts by Herbert Vollmer, who would become an ensign and later receive a bronze medal at the 1920 Olympics in water polo. After an 8–1 to win the '17 title, Yale was 8–0 in '18 to retain the Eastern

Intercollegiate title. Standings for water polo in '17—Princeton 8-0; Penn 5-3; Columbia 4-4; Yale 2-6; CCNY 1-7 and '18—Yale 7-1; Columbia 6-2; Penn 4-4; Princeton 3-5; CCNY 0-8, the last trailing in both swimming and water polo. In 1919, the league did not continue, but several schools competed.

MIT went three years with no defeats until Navy dunked them in '18. That year, Yale canceled a meet with MIT because it lacked coal to heat the pool. Failure to re-schedule left the impression the Eli were afraid of MIT. Williams canceled '18, not using any coal. The school's president, Harry A. Garfield (son of an assassinated U.S. President), was currently on leave, running the Fuel Administration.[7]

Navy won over Hopkins, Princeton and two others in '17, but only Plebes participated in '18. The '19 edition easily outswam Columbia and Hopkins but lost to Pitt and MIT, the only winter sport at the Academy to lose any contests. Georgia Tech had its first intercollegiate meet in '19, swamping Clemson, neither college familiar with such competition. No competitive swimming showed up in the rest of the South, the Southwest, the Border States or the Mountains States.

Everyone conceded the Western Conference meet to Northwestern in '17 and '18 (Chicago in '19), while Illinois won water basketball over Chicago in '17 (nothing in '18 or '19). In '17, Chicago sank Cincinnati and three conference foes. Illinois lost twice to Northwestern and once to Wisconsin, occasionally prevailing in water basketball. In '18, Wisconsin lost any chance of winning the Western Conference indoor meet at Evanston when four stars enlisted to become officers. Northwestern overwhelmed Cincinnati in '17, washed away Wisconsin and Illinois but lost to Chicago. Its water basketball whipped Wisconsin, losing to Chicago and Illinois.

Shunning the conference, Minnesota, losing to a local Y twice and the Michigan Aggies in '17, joined the Northwestern Swimming League in '18. The war still creating havoc, the Gophers did not compete in '19. Ohio State had its first swimming team in '17, yielding to Ohio Wesleyan. It did not compete in the Western Conference and probably eliminated the sport in '18. Iowa State, winner over Iowa in '17, stopped swimming in '18, when "other schools gave up."[8]

California, losers to Stanford in water polo by a point in '17, doubled the Cardinals in '18. In 1919, Berkeley overcame two athletic clubs and Stanford, which started a "minor sport" in '16, when Norman Ross set a record. Stanford outswam Cal in '17. Without Ross, who became a lieutenant in the army air corps, the Cardinals lost to a high school, Cal and the Olympic Club by 50. In '19, Stanford nearly doubled up on another athletic club and overcame the Olympic Club Juniors, again losing to California as well as St. Mary's. Ross set a world record in the 220 at the National AAU

9. Rowing, Swimming, Yachting and Motorboat Racing 147

championships in March '17 at the N.Y.A.C. and later captured the 440 and one-mile free styles. Off Travers Island in '18, in a meet sponsored by the N.Y. Athletic Club, Ross, representing the Illinois A.C., outswam Vollmer. He represented the Olympic Club of San Francisco in the National AAU '18 indoor championships in Chicago, where he set four world records (200, 220, 250 and 330).

In the AAU, the Hamilton Club (Chicago) sent seven "speed merchants" into the service. In January 1918, Apprentice Herman Laubis and Chief Yeoman Perry McGillivray, the world's sprint record holder, represented Great Lakes Naval Training. They worked morning to night six days a week instructing sailors how to swim. Honolulu's George Cunnha, who on occasion beat Duke Kahanamoku, supervised the program at Camp Lewis.[9]

The AAU held outdoor championships in '17 and '18, Kahanamoku and McGillivray trading the 100-yard free-style title. At the '18 indoor National A.A.U., the Illinois A.C. amassed forty points followed by Great Lakes (37), and four other clubs, as Chicago refused to replay a disputed water polo component, allegedly won by Illinois. The AAU sustained women's competition, started in '16.[10]

No America's Cup yacht races took place after 1903. Sir Thomas Lipton considered re-issuing a challenge in '19, but it took another year to carry out the race. Trans-Atlantic and Trans-Pacific races were rare, so the war had no impact. The Chicago Yacht Club run to Mackinac Island, held continuously from 1905 through 1916, had to be given up and did not resume until 1920.

In California, the South Coast Yacht Club predicted a busy season in May '17 even with depleted ranks. One member left two years earlier for the English navy—Egypt his location. Two others commanded naval ships while a fourth ran recruiting for the Naval Coast Defense Reserve in Los Angeles. A fifth became a captain in the Ambulance Corps in France. Club officials expected to keep close ties with the U.S. Navy. By the middle of September, 25 members served the Allies, one still with the British. Eighteen were now at the U.S. Naval Reserve training station at San Pedro, the others in a variety of jobs, including as a doctor on a torpedo boat in Panama.[11]

On Long Island Sound, the Corinthian Club raced six events on Memorial Day, '17 but had no plans for open regattas. It would teach youngsters, assuming they would help with coast patrolling. Most clubs on Gravesend and Jamaica bays opened, but little racing could be permitted near a fort. Although war cancelled traditional races of the N.Y. Yacht and Manhasset Bay clubs, the Larchmont Club carried out its annual run, the *Nimbus* taking honors off Long Island. On the 4th of July, the Bensonhurst Yacht Club, even though many were serving with the Naval Reserves, ran a regatta on Gravesend Bay with only two craft competing, the Oriole out sailing the *Sea Bird*. A Manhasset Bay club ran a six-mile course off Port Washington, with 11 entrants near the end of July.[12]

The annual Sea Island Regatta (South Carolina), went off without a hitch in early August '17, using a complicated set of rules. Folks came by rail, auto or boat to watch the same five craft that had been vying since 1914. A Sullivan Island craft failed to defend its title, coming in last. The winner, *Nell*, not being eligible for the Sea Island Cup, received a special trophy while the *Undine* copped the cup. A "free-for-all" race went to the *Pirate* of Charleston.[13]

In Seattle, where there was even less concern about German subs, the Queen City Yacht Club ran its usual events on Memorial Day, with a mosquito fleet temporarily anchoring near the University Training Station to honor those who perished serving their country. Almost all the pre-war yacht clubs resumed normal racing in '19, including the Interlake Yachting Association, based at Lake Erie's Put-In-Bay, which held an annual regatta in July '19 with five clubs represented.

The government registered about 1,200 motorboats for government service in the 3rd Naval District, extending from N. London into New Jersey. The Yacht Racing Association of Jamaica Bay had its annual race in August 1917. In September, Hudson River Yacht had nineteen under a handicap system, starting near the clubhouse to a spot opposite Fort Lee, down river to near the Jersey shore, westward to warships at anchor and back to the starting point. Thousands lined Riverside Park to watch. It took time, using something that looked like logarithms, to determine that Kathryn III was the winner.

No Harmsworth Trophy races occurred from 1914 through 1919, but Gold Cup races did. Gar Wood's revamped Miss Detroit III triumphed in '17, '18 and '19 on the Detroit River. In early August 1917, it came in first in the gold challenge cup at Alexandria Bay sponsored by the Thousand Island Yacht Club, most boats succumbing to engine trouble. A couple of weeks later, Wood averaged over 56 mph in several heats to win in Minneapolis. The previous year's winner, *Miss Minneapolis* (the only boat to finish), averaged 49 mph. *Miss Detroit II* lost to *Whip Po Will* at Toronto in '18.

During the war preparation phase, government officials asked the American Power Boat Association (160 clubs) to remain active. Serving as an auxiliary of the U.S. Navy, the association planned to sponsor events such as the Thousand Island and the Long Island Sound regattas. The war did not prevent a 270-mi. race up the Hudson from N.Y. City to Albany and back.[14]

10

Boxing and Wrestling

With the camp training programs under way in the late summer of '17, pugilism became part of the daily routine in nearly every army or marine camp, feints and thrusts resembling fighting with bayonets. The sport, also popular among navy personnel, now had ever larger audiences. Some 11,000 watched matches at the Great Lakes Naval Training Station's ravine.[1]

At Camp Lee, a Virginia regiment took on engineers from Pennsylvania. "The boys" enjoyed matches nearly every day, some designed to settle issues. In April '18, the Liberty Theater had the "largest boxing tournament ever held" in the state. Rounds lasted three minutes supervised by a former athletic director at Penn State. A "battle royal" of seven African Americans finished the program, receipts from the .25 admission going to the camp athletic fund. Winners won gold medals.[2]

Most pro titlists at the various weight levels helped the war effort, the press regarding Jess Willard a no show in the ring and for the country. Just before America entered the war, he defended his title against Frank Moran at Madison Square Garden where reporters agreed he won. He didn't fight again until the Fourth of July '19. A proposed bout with Fred Fulton, never came off. Politicians sometimes prevented these matches but even Willard's manager argued that such matches should not take place while American troops were dying in France. The governor of Nevada, where prize fighting was legal, in turning down the idea of a Willard-Fulton match in Reno on the 4th of July '18, told them that they had "my unqualified permission" to fight the Huns in France. The governor of New Mexico concurred.[3]

Pros scattered about the military camps. Middleweight Mike Gibbons from St. Paul (Dodge), featherweight titlist Lt. Johnny Kilbane (Sherman), lightweight champ Benny Lenard (Upton), "Battling" Levinsky (Devens), Packey McFarland (MacArthur) and Willie Ritchie (Lewis). Raycroft exonerated Levinsky of rigging a match in Boston. Eddie McGoorty and Mike O'Dowd, the two top middleweights and two well-known heavies, plus a feather went to Camp Grant. In '18, Bantam champ Pete Herman, who preferred sharing earnings with the government to being drafted, represented a naval training station near New Orleans, and, through an arrangement with the commandant, shared receipts with the station from matches in Atlanta and elsewhere.[4]

"The Hosier Giant Killer" chose the navy over the army because serving in trenches might give him rheumatism. A scrappy welterweight headed to San Francisco to rejoin the Navy. A lightweight from the Pacific Coast tracked subs in the naval militia.[5]

In May, the Denver press reported "boxing conditions in a cloudy mood," as a local signed up for the Colorado cavalry and another who had fought on occasions at an athletic club planned to farm. A Denver boxer with nineteen matches in N.Y. came home to sign up with the local military.[6]

In Utah, one of the few states that allowed matches where the referee decided the winner, Jack Dempsey, representing Salt Lake City, bested an Ogden fighter in a 10-round decision before about 2,000 at the Alhambra in Ogden in May '16. Fewer fights took place in '18. In an Arizona mining town in '16, 1,500 yelled themselves "hoarse" on the 4th of July at the Airdrome, exceeding "anything ever seen." A pug from Goldfield kayoed a "Flying Dutchman," prompting the reporter to compare the loser to Germans at Verdun. The next year, a match of 120-pounders produced 'bales" of bets (someone lost $1,000) for a 10-rounder which featured a lot of dancing. Never had "such a crowd been packed away at the Airdrome." The 4th of July in '18 yielded less interest, a sober affair, amid concern about overspending.[7]

Among the enlisted at Camp Meade, "Young Johnny Dundee" (not the real one) never lost in thirty bouts. In March '18, an exhibition at Fort Myer's Liberty Theater included individual and team titles covering several weight levels. Regimental bouts ran four rounds, three minutes each. A Baltimore bantam planned to donate his services in a fight against an aspiring youngster while a New Yorker and another Baltimore pro would fight at a slightly higher weight. A "fighting policeman" from D.C. would take on an army ex-middleweight champion in the 150-pound class. Receipts from these matches went into athletic funds for army camps in the D.C. area.[8]

A smoker in a Tacoma club in the fall '17 for one regiment attracted about 1,000, a train bringing soldiers. After a smoker in a "sawmill" town, officers banned off base bouts. Those in January '18 featured "Young Jack Johnson" and "Young Joe Gans." Pvt. Willie Ritchie (a.k.a. Gerhardt Steffens), world lightweight champ in 1914 and winner of almost fifty in his career, arranged championships. This honorary lieutenant organized a tournament in February '18, attracting 3,000, eight matches producing five knock outs. Another, with the help of an old boxer and manager of an athletic club, took six evenings, the packed arena holding 20,000 to watch 150

10. Boxing and Wrestling 151

"The Punch," 4 July 1918—Ripley, like many commentators, compares boxing and bayoneting. *Norfolk Ledger Dispatch.*

(pro and amateur, seven weight levels each). Only two of the pros had, or would ever have, much fame.[9]

At Camp Upton, in one "hot" bout, an infantryman held off one "Machine Gun Joe." Field artillerists, motor truck drivers, infantry and machine gunners carried the feather, light, welter weight and light heavy respectively, while another truck driver took the middleweight. In the finals, with Benny Leonard refereeing, they "fought like wildcats and spread American blood over half of Long Island."[10]

In late '17, at Camp Gordon, one of the reigning army boxing champions (lightweight) hoped to take on Pennsylvania pros training at the camp. "Crack fighters" fought at Atlanta's Auditorium before the main attraction, a brigadier general from Gordon and a colonel and commander at Fort McPherson lending "an official and military touch to the occasion." The referee stopped the main event in the 6th round when the loser stalled. Neither received any money, all going to the Red Cross. Gordon soldiers cheered wildly when the 82nd division heavyweight champ outpointed the Camp Wheeler titlist in ten rounds, giving their camp the Southeast boxing title and its soldiers many winning bets. In October '18, many current and former champs came to a school at Gordon run by Mike Gibbons, the "St. Paul Phantom." The one-time middleweight champ occasionally exhibited at the camp and at Atlanta's Auditorium, benefiting the nearby army and navy Ys.[11]

Although athletics were somewhat limited on the ships loaded with newly trained soldiers, under Y supervision, members of the 32nd Division watched several matches (three rounds, two minutes each) aboard the *George Washington*. Sailors fought only sailors and blacks only others of the same color. Matches were routine on decks in the afternoon on many troop ships. Even comparatively small outfits held "lively bouts" with companies competing to help pass the idle hours aboard the *Mauretania*. Chaplains aboard the U.S.S. *North Carolina* expressed concern about a battle royal carried out by blacks. As the ship zigzagged, members of the 29th Division watched four "husky" blacks fight for coins. Each had a glove on one hand and tried to grab coins from their opponents. On another ship, others from the same regiment cheered as their men fought against ship crewmen, most ending in draws. Members of the 88th Division (Iowa and Nebraska) often watched bouts as officers played quoits aboard a British ship.[12]

Aviators took up boxing, although their need to learn bayoneting seemed minimal. Various squadrons fought each other in England in May '18. One lost to a more experienced Canadian even though the loser wore blue knickers with a red band and white stripe attached. That match received coverage in the London press as did those between the only pro of the 840th squadron and two Brits. The American knocked down the first opponent in the second round and won on points, but in the second match he lost a split decision even though he knocked down the winner twice in three rounds.[13]

Stationed near the British sector around the 4th of July '18, members of the 35th Division put on several bouts. The third one, matching two middleweights, had many "vicious" blows that would have kayoed an ordinary person. A French chaplain said he had been worried until he realized they were wearing "nice soft gloves." In June, the press carried a picture of a military engineer battling one from the cavalry before a crowd that included French officers all within earshot of Hun guns.[14]

At their first two locations in France, a corporal from headquarters in an infantry company whose name did not appear at Meade, became the top man until he fractured his hand knocking out an opponent. Before then, he fought a draw against a black fighter, a former Battling Nelson sparring mate. Flu floored another combatant, but he recovered. Matches among companies soon gave way to regimental and divisional bouts. Some field artillerists had matches two or three times a week, sometimes taking place in the public square of the village.[15]

The 29th Division, with personnel almost as interested in boxing as football, produced about a dozen contenders, under Sgt. H.M. "Spike" Webb, who escorted them to Paris, where they won all nine against Frenchmen, five by knock outs. Webb sent the welcome news back to the Division by telegram. The 29th also trounced an entire corps, only the heavyweight taking a loss. They then swept the 81st Division. Webb would later coach the 1st Army and help with the Inter-allied affair.[16]

In a survey of 6,835 soldiers for a week in October not far from the trenches, boxing, with 1,027 participating, had the best ratio of performers to spectators. From 1 August to the end of '18, over 180,000 boxed, 1,700,000 watching. Wrestling was less popular, with about 54,000 grappling, attracting 400,000 viewers. Between 1 January and May '19, 542,779 either watched others box or fought among the American military in Europe. Obviously, many were involved in multiple matches.[17]

Harry Truman, writing to Bess from near Verdun where he captained an artillery company for the 35th Division, grumbled that on New Year's Day '19, his sergeant lost to "a gorilla." The verdict cost Truman 1,000 francs (his company 7,000). He thought the decision faulty, given his man walked away and returned to work the next day, the winner carried out and not reporting for several days.[18]

After the armistice, engineers erected a ring which had electric lighting. At least three from one company won for a battalion over another that sent truckloads of spectators from the neighboring village. A battery of field artillerists waited in vain for a match. The "Iowa Cyclone and the "Buffalo Whirlwind" had imbibed so much at a nearby pub they were in no condition to fight.[19]

Having grounded Germans, could "Uncle Sam Whip John Bull"? In early December '18 at Albert Hall, London. "Oshkosh Eddie" McGoorty and Mike "the Fighting Harp" O'Dowd, among others, took on the British Empire. Combat engineer O'Dowd, the only American titlist who saw "plenty of action before the Germans threw up the sponge," toured France (fighting in Rome), hoping to arrange a match with the French hero Georges Carpentier.[20]

The initial matches in early December '18, favored the Brits, as only Harry Greb, "the Human Windmill" and '18 U.S. Army champ, bested a South African in the light-heavy and Pal Moore, Navy, won the bantam. As royalty watched, a British soldier overcame an American sailor in the heavyweight and an American soldier lost to Jimmy Wilde, a British flyweight titlist. Although unaccustomed to surroundings with a ring on one side of the hall and royal boxes and a pipe organ on the other, Moore of Memphis upset Wilde, but "Bombardier" Billy Wells of the British army, with more weight and a longer reach, overcame McGoorty, preventing an American sweep. O'Dowd won three, defeating a Canadian and two Brits and other Doughboys ran off five welter wins. Final tabulations had the British Army (50), the American Army (39), Royal Air Force (32½), Royal Navy (32½), American Navy (32), Australia (26), Canada (18), New Zealand (14½) and South Africa (10½). The Knights of Columbus arranged the affair, receipts helping wounded British soldiers.[21]

Americans thought British referees had an odd way of figuring out winners. Americans admired close-in fighting, back-pedaling a negative, while Brits applauded hitting at a distance. Americans praised the English as good sportsmen but thought British rules hampered them, especially the brevity (3 rounds). A Navy reporter later excused the poor showing on improper registration or late arrivals, residences having no running water or heat and the food not appropriate for training. Four fighters had flu-like symptoms. All rejected the idea of going to Paris for another benefit.[22]

The Navy press thought Willie Meehan's reputed win over Jack Dempsey "no joke." But the crew on the U.S.S. *Illinois* would not accept Meehan as the naval heavyweight until he fought Andy Schmader, who after transferring to the U.S.S. *Pennsylvania*, secured the navy title.[23]

In January '19, a reporter worked his way through a wall of khaki in Paris on a Thursday night to watch four-round bouts sponsored by the Knights of Columbus. Over a thousand sat in chairs on the main floor, but many more in American army uniforms, along with patches of French military blue, stood in the rear, amid cigarette and cigar smoke. A French fighter had the only knockout that evening.[24]

In a forgotten theater after the Armistice, American troops fought the Bolsheviks near Archangel. There, a sergeant from headquarters fought a three-round draw with a ranked welterweight from the French Army in one of several matches in the Y hut.[25]

In April '19, the Army held championships, with seven titles at stake. The 88th Division, through a process of elimination in March, sent five to

Paris. The AEF rewrote rules, cutting rounds to two minutes but allowing a greater number of rounds. The championships, following a slew of exhibitions in five different nations, boiled down to 39 matches, 22 of which went ten rounds, only five knockouts recorded. Crowds packed the Cirque de Paris (near Napoleon's Tomb), Carpentier's home ring. Observers thought such interest would translate into increased popularity of the sport in America.[26]

The championships came down to seven matches, one for each weight level. O'Dowd exhibited before a crowd that included Pershing and Foch but had to be goaded into moving more. Marine Pvt. Gene Tunney, with powerful uppercuts, took the light heavy. Tunney, from N.Y. City, started his career at age 18 in 1915. In France, he lost one, then ran an eight-match streak, finally besting Bob Martin, a pro heavyweight titlist from N.Y.

Leo Patterson, a black from Pioneer Infantry (combat engineers), won the lightweight over "Bushy" Graham, whose identify remains allusive. Although not his usually clever self, Patterson, seeking revenge for an earlier loss, cut his rival's face and bloodied his nose, winning, though with a split lip. The press praised him as a model for his race, reminiscent of Joe Gans, a "peerless colored scrapper and sportsman." Patterson contrasted with those who were too interested in money, an obvious reference to Willard, who since winning the world title seemed more interested in his circus and oil wells than in defending his title. Fans looked forward to a Memorial Day 10-round re-match, but Patterson received orders to sail home, where he resumed his pro career, winning a string of fights.[27]

Le Mans, the main embarkation center, had an arena that held 25,000. Many matches entertained the men as they prepared to re-cross the Atlantic. On one ship, over a dozen boxers put on an exhibition for the wounded. An infantry regiment gave Boatswain Joe Fisher, the Atlantic Fleet champ, a hard time when ship after ship passed their ship. When Fisher bragged that they passed another ship during the night, the soldiers replied that the other ship must have been going in the opposite direction, but they knew not to push Fisher too far because of his prowess as a pugilist.[28]

Even though the number of Americans in the military fell quickly in '19, the Charleston newspaper reported matches on the 4th of July, including a crewman from a cruiser. Four other matches paired two machinists, two colored stevedores from another ship, a machinist mate, plus two others from naval craft in the harbor.[29]

The Commission on Training Camp Activities in May '19, claimed that the armed services taught some 3,000,000 to box. In some regiments no one ever indulged before. The "Boxing Moses of the U.S. Army" (Raycroft), taking a cue from Canadians, urged its instruction.[30]

Even though many pros served in the military during the war, the number of fights in normal venues seems not to have diminished noticeably. Way over 1,000 bouts took place in Eastern cities in '17, reporters deciding the winners. But flu posed problems. New Jersey, a hot bed of boxing, held off opening its indoor season in October '18. At the same time the state legislature considered cracking down on abuses. Commissioners ended the ban on blacks fighting whites, which N.Y. retained.[31]

The Knights of Columbus encountered problems with a carnival for 20,000 at Ebbet's Field in August '18. An exhibition involving the real Dundee (a.k.a. "the Scotch Wop") became "bubbling cauldron of excitement." With the crowd yelling, Dempsey finally agreed to box "Battling" Levinsky, but management matched him against someone else.[32]

On the 4th of July '19, Dempsey walloped Willard at Toledo to earn the world heavyweight title. Based on rumors that the new champion evaded the draft, the New Jersey boxing commission banned a possible fight between Carpentier and Dempsey. An American Legion post accused him of being a draft dodger and a military newspaper pointed out that "our greatest fighter sidestepped America's greatest war."[33]

Sixteen boxers and wrestlers wrote a public letter complaining about the bout on the 4th of July, arguing that neither Dempsey nor Willard showed "a proper spirit toward the war or war activities in general." While they served for an "average wage of only a few francs a month," the two took in thousands. The men had no desire to take up promoter Rickard's offer of $1,000 to fight in a prelim, which would supplement their income and get them home early.[34]

As public opinion leaned toward taking Dempsey's title (appeals to the American Legion and the Board of Boxing Control of no avail), no one would challenge him except Jack Johnson, about to serve a sentence at Leavenworth. More ominously, a federal grand jury in San Francisco indicted Dempsey and manager, Jack Kearns, the former for evading the draft and conspiring in the same and the latter for conspiring. Facing two years in prison and a $2,000 fine, Dempsey went to trial, during which his divorced wife reluctantly acknowledged she had received support as had her parents and admitted making up stories after seeing a picture of Jack in the guise of a shipyard worker. She said Jack hit her and she did not need money because of her "underworld" connections.[35]

Taking the stand, Dempsey described himself as the principal support for his family (starting at age 14) as a farmhand, miner, carpenter and boxer. He paid his wife until she officially left him even though she started a rumor that he had thrown a bout. In 1917, he earned $4,000 but made much less the next year because almost all went to charities. He worked for the government in Philadelphia as a recruiter, the source of an infamous photo of him in workman's attire. The director of athletics at Great Lakes testified that Dempsey helped with boxing and asked him to end his exemption so he could join the Navy in September '18, but red tape and the Armistice prevented his enlisting. The jury took ten minutes to acquit Dempsey, the prosecutor quashing the conspiracy charge.[36]

Long part of intramurals, boxing went intercollegiate due to the war. Penn State hired a coach and Pennsylvania adopted it as a minor sport. Harvard had started to do so in the winter before America entered the war and affirmed that decision once the war was over. In 1917, Stanford supposedly had a 3–3 draw with California in one of the few intercollegiate matches, but, as in wrestling, problems with defaulting occurred. The Cardinals won over Cal in '19. South Dakota State (Brookings) upgraded boxing just after the war because of the "keen interest in manly arts" brought on by "ex-service men" on campus who were also "the best of the fistic artists" in four military companies.[37]

In Western Conference wrestling, undefeated Illinois outmatched Wisconsin and took the conference in '17. In '19, Minnesota lost to Iowa and Nebraska and whipped Wisconsin. It proved impossible at Northwestern in '19, perhaps related to the changes due to the war's ending. Indiana, losing a competitor to Great Lakes, canceled with Illinois and Purdue. In '18, the war hit wrestling harder than any sport, but Purdue still subdued Chicago.[38]

The war did not stop Iowa State in '18, even though no one returned from the previous year. The Cyclones dominated Nebraska and Indiana, which reputedly tied for second in the Western championships in '17, when Iowa State owned Iowa University, which in '18, got by Indiana by a point, giving the Hawkeyes thoughts about a title, but no conference meet seems to have taken place. After not competing against the Hawkeyes in '18, the Cyclones pinned them in '19, taking Wisconsin and Nebraska as well, leading to their claim as best in the Midwest.

In N. England, with at least eight programs, Harvard won three matches, only MIT proving troublesome in '17. Nothing showed up for the Crimson '18; a loss to Yale and a win over Brown featured '19. Yale had the most success in '17, shutting out Columbia in seven weight levels and outscoring Princeton, Penn and Navy, the last one close. The Eli also captured the N.E. championships over five others. No such matches took place in '18, when Yale downed Columbia, nor apparently in '19, when Yale prevailed over Princeton and Harvard, losing to Navy.

In the Middle States, also with but a few programs, Princeton downed Columbia before succumbing to four major programs in '17 when the Intercollegiate finals came up with Cornell, Penn, Lehigh, Columbia and Princeton. In '18, Princeton lost to Penn and Yale in a shutout, before rebounding against Columbia, which (collegiately) went 1–4 in '17 and 0–3 in '18, possibly splitting six in '19.

Lehigh, falling to the top programs in the East in '18, outdueled Penn State in a hard-fought affair in '19 but lost to the same in the Intercollegiate. Cornell, Penn and Columbia followed the two leaders. In '17 Penn State punished at least six in duals and dominated a championship, going undefeated for the second year. In '19, State lost to Navy but came in first in the Intercollegiate. Pittsburgh started up in '17 (nothing for '18) and in '19 fell to Penn State. In '17, Navy lost twice, winning several in '18, at least five duals in '19. While a couple of small colleges and Harvard ceased during the war, most sustained their programs—contrasting with the Midwest, where more programs shut down in '18.

Although Okla. State downed Kansas State Normal, possibly tied Arkansas and triumphed over Texas, 20–5, insufficient returns make it impossible to know how the war affected wrestling in the Southwest. On the Pacific Coast, California which overcame Stanford in '17 tied the same in '18, but a dispute arose over two matches. Oregon State (the Aggies) in '17 claimed the Conference for the 6th time out of the past 7 years, with wins over Oregon, Washington and Washington State. The '18 Aggies beat Washington but lost to Oregon, the Northwest Association disbanding. Oregon dropped intramural wrestling due to the war. In '19, it lost to the state's Aggies and Washington, having trouble recovering from the war. In '17, Washington lost to the Aggies by three and to Washington State by a good deal more. In '18, Washington ousted Oregon only to lose to the Aggies. In '19, Washington finally pinned the Aggies, also bettering Bremerton Sailors, while Washington State manhandled Montana.

Among pro heavies in '18, Wladek Zbyszko, "the Polish Hercules" born in Austria-Hungary, threw an opponent twice within half an hour in January before a crowd that included several hundred "fashionably dressed" women at Madison Square Garden in early March. A couple of weeks later the crowd screamed "kill him" after he head butted "Strangler" Lewis through the ropes and lost on a foul. Earl Caddock, at Camp Dodge represented the army when he won the world title. When he headed overseas, title matches ceased until he mustered out. Zbyszko and Joe Stetcher had a draw in N.Y., to help the United War Work campaign in November, a couple of weeks after the armistice.[39]

A Georgian thought a "good sporting town" like Atlanta should be rid of "this flimflam, gold brick frame-up stuff," used by "the highly organized wrestling wrecking crew that hits here and there, wherever the suckers are the thickest." Another writer recalled one well known wrestler throwing an opponent in a matter of seconds in one match but somehow losing to him the next time. Should newspapers follow the lead of the Atlanta Constitution and not publicize such matches, fraud would cease.[40]

With no fear of being accused of fake fighting, the AAU went ahead in '18 with its national free-style championships in Chicago, with winners determined in seven levels, plus heavy, which Caddock had won in 1915. N.Y. also proceeded with the Metropolitan District contests in April.[41]

At the Naval Y in downtown Norfolk, a thousand sailors made their way into the "rotunda" room. "Roars of approval" accompanied a speedy match. A Central Y member carried a marine in the 150-pound range to a draw, both demonstrating "skill and knowledge." In a lightweight match, naval training sailors evidenced a lot of spirit. A naval station band played "martial airs" followed by a saxophone quartette, all to honor visiting British sailors.[42]

The AEF championships had a corporal in the engineers as bantam. Another corporal captured the featherweight. The lightweight went to a sergeant in the 33rd Division. A private in the 6th Division took the welter, a sergeant in the 3rd. Army the middleweight. Two privates, one a marine and the other a soldier the light heavy and the heavyweight respectively, amid praises for a private for not demanding a forfeit when his opponent, the final middleweight winner, fell ill.[43]

An infantry regiment was especially proud of Sgt. James B. McIntosh, who reeled off 34 pins for the 81st Division. His biggest triumph came at the expense of "The Russian Lion" at the Monte Carlo Casino before 7,000. A full-page photo shows "Big Mac" flexing his muscles. McIntosh lost his bid for the AEF heavy title in the finals.[44]

Walter Camp ordered standardized matches. A pro champ middleweight, an AAU welterweight titlist at Great Lakes and a one-time football coach and athletic director at Kansas drew up guidelines for both boxing and wrestling for naval training stations.[45]

11

Auto, Motorbike and Bicycle Racing

In auto racing, frequented largely by pros as drivers and mechanics, the Indianapolis Speedway canceled in both '17 and '18. The Kansas City Speedway canceled all events for '17 but only because the wooden stands burned up. Those who ran the Chicago and Cincinnati speedways decided against closing after they said they would.

Few drivers or mechanics volunteered for service. Californian Billy Taylor, who won at least one major race in the East, volunteered for a Canadian squadron. When Eddie Rickenbacker first came to France, he chauffeured General Pershing, after which he gained more fame shooting down Huns.

In '17, Ralph De Palma, an Italian, occasionally gave advice to the military on aviation motors, one of which was in his Packard. He overcame some sort of jinx taking two in Chicago in September and three (25-, 30-, and 50-mile) at Sheepshead Bay in July before some 40,000. Piloting his Packard with its Liberty motor, he broke a world's record for a 10-miler in early November, then set another in driving over 633 miles in six hours, establishing a new world's record, a cold wind making the skin on his face bleed. Louis Chevrolet, with no pit stops, captured the 250-mile International Sweepstakes at Cincinnati on Memorial Day and in late September, broke a world record for 100 miles in the Harkness Gold Trophy race. Barney Oldfield bested De Palma in match races in Indianapolis in '17 and in early August in three races on a one-mile dirt track at the Indiana state fair grounds. In one, a racer, losing control in the dust, crashed through a fence, came back on the track and drive into the pits with parts of the fence dangling from his car. A week later Oldfield again overcame De Palma on a dirt track outside St. Louis, setting records in two races.[1]

In the late fall of '17, in a move that pleased the Fuel Administration, the American Automobile Association stopped sanctioning races. The chair of its Military Preparedness Committee thought the action would free

11. Auto, Motorbike and Bicycle Racing 161

up a thousand skilled mechanics for government motor work. President Wilson praised the decision, adding that it would cut gas consumption. In March '18, the association decided to sanction some races, but in late September, it again reversed itself.[2]

In '18, recalculations gave the Memorial Day Harkness Handicap on the pine-boarded Sheepshead Speedway to De Palma, who also took the 100-mile Liberty Handicap at Cincinnati on the 4th of July. The Italian broke the world's record for 10 and 20 miles at Chicago later that month. In August, he set four more world records at Sheepshead Bay, as 30,000 perused his "big yellow hornet." In September, the AAA suspended Oldfield and three others for taking part in outlawed events just before it announced an end to its sanctioning any races. Fall races at Sheepshead Bay were canceled.[3]

Before the war, about fifteen drivers and mechanics died in crashes each year, a number maintained in '17. Fewer races in '18 diminished deaths but at Stockton, California, in February '18, Italian-born Nina Vitagliano perished in a crash in a race for women before a big crowd. On the last day of the Arizona State Fair in '17 before some 25,000, a piece of wood, dislodged by another car crashing through a fence, struck a mechanic's head.[4]

When the International Motor Contest Association (the I.M.C.A.) would not allow Arizonans in a race for failing to sign up in time, the banned ones and their supporters blocked the track. As the crowd watched an impromptu rodeo, negotiators authorized four Arizonans to race against four others, all under the aegis of the fair commission, not the I.M.C.A. Glenn Breed, a veteran of three Indy runs, won and, after participating in over twenty races in '17, cut back to five in '18, likely due to the canceling of fairs in Texas and Kansas. Fred Horey won three in '16, about the same number in '17 and '18 (a 10-mile free-for-all at the Michigan State Fair in August and near Atlanta earlier). The I.M.C.A., organized in 1915, sponsored these races. Unlike the AAA, it did not stop races during the war.[5]

In addition to a track for top tier racing, Omaha featured the Benson Oval for dirt events, one in '18, when another "King of the Dirt Track" (a Brit) won the half-mile, the three-mile as well as the 10-mile free-for-all in front of 5,000 in early August. The 5-mile victor drove Rickenbacker's old Maxwell. The event spotlighted Omaha, with ten of the best "dirt track pilots." The 1914 record-holder at Omaha enlisted in the Navy, one of a handful of auto racers to join the service.[6]

The dirt Bennington Track (initially for horses), within sight of the capitol in D.C, received the AAA's blessing for car racing on Labor Day, '18, as some 10,000 came compared to 7,000 the previous year. In one of the ten races, about half for motorcycles, after an ambulance carried away a fallen rider, he returned to win another race. Labor Days for both '16 and '19 had no such races.[7]

At the Virginia State Fair (Richmond), auto racing gaining popularity, with one day devoted to the sport in '16 (mostly local competitors) and two in '17, when Eddie Hearne won the time trials and three races (all the ones he entered) in his Duesenberg. In October 1918, Fred Horey, Arthur Chevrolet, the Canadian national titlist and at least one other well-known racer were scheduled to compete for at least two days. Initially, the State Board of Health okayed the fair's opening even though the flu prevailed in the area. Church services, theater and other indoor activities had been banned. That thousands would be packed in trolley cars to reach the fairgrounds likely factored into the decision to call off the entire fair. Promoters absorbed a lot of red ink and no such races took place in '19.[8]

Motorcycle racing continued during the war. At Richmond in '18 four companies from West Virginia were stationed at the fairgrounds, some undergoing training as dispatch riders. On the 4th of July, with about 800 soldiers on hand, some participating in a track meet, military motorcycle riders raced before a large crowd of civilians. That year, Phoenix resurrected a club with a potential two hundred members who raced in the nearby hills. A cyclist crashed through a barrier at the Indianapolis fair grounds and died when a splinter penetrated his chest.[9]

On Memorial Day '17, in Pennsylvania, even with war declared, some 5,000 came to see local William "Butch" Lineaweaver, on an Indian, win the feature. On Labor Day, he won the 10- and 15-milers as a rider broke his collar bone. Memorial Day '18 attracted about half the usual crowd, Lineaweaver, breaking a record, won the 10- and 15-mile runs for a $60 prize. The Keystone Club ran the affair at the fairgrounds. No reports appear for the rest of '18 and all of '19. On the 4th of July '17, a biker fell at Pottstown before 10,000 on the same turn where another crashed through a fence and perished on Memorial Day. Four were seriously hurt at Pottstown on the 4th in '18, at a run sponsored by the Reading Motorcycle Club, excessive dust the cause.[10]

Tests in war-torn Europe improved construction. New machines were tested at the Uniontown Oval in Pennsylvania in July. In October '19, a third-place finisher at Dodge City in '16, broke the world's 50-mile at Sheepshead on a Harley-Davidson. A third racer, riding an Indian, took the 10-mile. Other national titles that day were the 10-mile (Sidecar) won on an Indian, the 10-mile Metropolitan on a Harley, the 250-mile (Sidecar) on an Indian-Flexible.[11]

A first-class machinist's mate on furlough from the navy air corps recovering from a broken collar bone won a 50-mile at the Port Breeze Velodrome (Philadelphia) on Labor Day, '18. After losing at Pottstown

11. Auto, Motorbike and Bicycle Racing

before 6,000 in the summer of '19, Clarence Carman returned to Point Breeze for a 40-mile Labor Day run. Near the start, his front tire blowing, Carman fell, his bike trailing as he bounced and tumbled down the wooden incline at a diagonal sixty feet, considered a record. The bruised biker whose collar bone still hurt soon went to another race.[12]

International competition among amateur bicycle riders dated from the early 1890s but the war canceled most events from 1914 through 1919. Undeterred by war and construction, 103 bicyclists, under a system of handicapping, took part in a sponsored race on Pelham Parkway on Memorial Day. Frank Kramer, one of the two or three best bicyclists raced at Point Breeze, but almost no one came because he refused to trail a motorbike whose draft would allow him to reach faster speeds. In '17, Arthur Spencer (age 20) captured the national pro cycling two miles before 12,000 at Newark's Velodrome on a Sunday afternoon in early July, taking the title from Kramer, who had it for 16 years. A week later Alfred Goulet took the 5-mile at the same location. In June, Goulet came in ahead in the one-mile national race, but Spencer won three shorter races over Kramer. All these title runs took place in Newark, a busy place, war or no war. African American Major Taylor, champ in 1900, received plaudits as he took an Old Timers' race. Kramer outraced two while the blond Goulet took a half-mile handicap and a five-mile open. In the annual six-day race before a packed Madison Square Garden, Goulet and his partner won. These near week-long events also took place in other American cities.[13]

12

Ice Hockey and Other Winter Sports

Ice yachting had an excellent season in '17 before the war, an even better one in '18, due to the cold winter in New Jersey. Long Branch had at least eleven days of racing in January along with a championship cup race for two days in February. Red Bank came in with nine days, including a race for the state title, followed by about a dozen more, through February, including the North American championships.[1]

Bobby McLean, the American amateur champion in '16 turned pro in '17 but was unable to make a deal with the best European pro (a Norwegian) that season. He set a world's half mile record in ice skating at Lake Placid in February '18 after winning on Saranac Lake. At an arena in Chicago, McClean won the '18 world speed title over the Norwegian in 5 of 6 races carried out over two days. Many spectators from the upper Midwest of Scandinavian origins lost their bets. McLean did not race in '19, finishing up his requirements to become a reserve naval officer. He lost his world title upon his return to competition. Later that year the government banned the use of ammonia for making ice, thus potentially closing arenas, including one in N.Y., the site of a Metropolitan championship and home of hockey's Wanderers. Ammonia is sometimes an ingredient in making explosives, more vital for Germany's war machine than for the American military. Fortunately, the European war ended before ice hockey and skating (both considered non-essentials) started up late in the fall of '18.[2]

In '18, curlers in the Northeast dropped an international match because of war, but otherwise Boston bested Utica, the Caledonian Club overcame the Thistle Club at Yonkers in February (plenty of ice) and doubled the score on another club. Teams representing Northern and Southern Scotland battled for supremacy at a N.Y. park. Abundant ice helped the Caledonian and Duluth Curling clubs, which planned for 600 matches in less than a week, with the help of another club. The bonspiel would include women, apparently participating for the first time. That gender would not compete for either the Canadians or the Americans in the international showdown, half the proceeds of which would be turned over to the Red Cross. Other international competition ceased in '16, a year after the U.S. overcame Canada at Utica in and did not resume until '19, Canada winning.[3]

All four colleges in Maine had an ice hockey score or two but not enough to indicate such were routine. Class competition replaced collegiate in '18 at Bates. Boston College overcame Boston University in '18 in the only known match for either. In '19, the former lost to Harvard and beat Army. Dartmouth played at least seven in '17, splitting with Princeton, beating Army, Mass twice, and Yale, losing to Harvard. The next year, the Green beat Tufts, lost to the Pitt A.A. twice, split with the Mass Aggies, Camp Upton canceling. The post-war year drew a blank, a depleted treasury canceling basketball and hockey. The Mass Aggies, under .500 in over ten matches in '17, won more than half in '18 in fewer contests. Williams, loser to Dartmouth, Princeton and Yale (2–4–1 overall) in '17, at 2–1 with bright prospects lost two weeks in February because of snow. A delay in re-instating academic programs in '19 caused an "impromptu" abbreviated season consisting of a loss to the Mass Aggies.[4]

Among the Big Three in '17, Yale beat Harvard 2 of 3, losing 2 of 3 to Princeton, probably victorious in 5 of the other 6 (two athletic clubs). In '18, the Eli "Informal" speared Springfield's seven. In '19 they lost to Harvard but beat Princeton. In '17, Harvard polished off Princeton twice, meaning the three triple-tied for the title, all at .500. Colgate, with Michael Hayes (KIA), ambushed Army in '17. After officer training, Hayes coached at Camp Upton. West Point in '17 slid by the 27th Regiment, overcame MIT, then lost at least two. In '18, West Point edged Princeton, Oliphant starring. The cadets also got by the Mass Aggies before falling to Camp Upton. In '19, a mild winter reduced ice on two rinks at West Point forcing cancellation of over half the schedule. Albany Teachers College, possibly playing for the first time, split eight, losing twice to RPI and once to Army in '17, but nothing shows up for '18, possibly because too much snow fell on the ice. In '17, Pittsburgh bested McGill (Canada), no other scores appearing. Outside of the Northeast, Wisconsin tied a military academy and lost to an athletic club in '18, vying with Northwestern University in another season. A small college created a team but could find only a nearby high school to play. On the Pacific Coast in '17, California secured two wins and a tie against Stanford.[5]

In supposed amateur hockey, favored Charlestown Navy Yard, winner of the Amateur Hockey League in '17, opened its next season with the Arena Hockey Club in Boston in late December '17. The AAU allowed three members of the presumed pro Pitt Athletic Association to play, turning to the International Skating Union to determine the current standing of previous pros. The union returned one to amateur status despite charges that he received pay in Canada. Two others for the First Naval District would be considered amateurs. The AAU worked with the International Union against the American Amateur Hockey League and its Canadian counterparts, the war confusing the issue of amateurism. The Pitt club stayed undefeated, late in the winter of '18.[6]

Pro hockey flourished in the Pacific Coast Hockey League, organized two years earlier. In '17, the Seattle Mets won the title, 16–8 (Vancouver Millionaires, 14–9; Portland "Rose City" Buds, 9–15 and the Spokane Canaries 8–15), then defeating the Montreal Canadiens for the Stanley Cup. In '18, fan enthusiasm peaking, the Millionaires, after a tie in Vancouver before 8,000 and a 1–0 before 3,500 at the Seattle arena, took the title. In '19, Seattle reigned, when, tied with Vancouver (Victoria a distant third), they scored 6–1, forcing the Millionaires to win by over five goals in the finale before 10,000 at Vancouver. In the Stanley Cup, Les Canadiens scored a late goal to knot the series with Seattle, players falling to the flu and federal agents who hauled off a Met for draft evasion. No one claimed the cup.[7]

Norwegians succeeded in winter sports, as their homeland remained neutral in the Great War. The winners at the Mid-Winter Sports carnival at Steamboat Springs, Colorado at the end of February '18 mostly had Scandinavian names. Norwegian Lars Haugen, who had come to America a few years earlier, held several records for distance jumps. Weather conditions prevented any new world record the next year in Colorado. Henry Hall, the only one of the prominent pros born in the U.S., set the record at 203' in '17. Lars did amass the most points (a record). Anders Haugen outpointed his brother at Steamboat Springs in '19, when the amateur winner represented Great Lakes Naval Training.[8]

Haugen also ran first in the annual national championship held in a Chicago suburb in January '18, brother Anders second. The event in '18 took place in less than ideal conditions, five thousand fans standing knee deep in snow, the participants facing a 60-m.p.h. wind. Norwegian Ragnar Omvedt, the previous year's winner, did not do well but retained his distance record for the time being. He applied to fly for Uncle Sam in the reserves, though another source claimed he was in the merchant marine in '19.[9]

Cross country skiing and tobogganing were popular activities in most northern states but sport sections in daily papers rarely mention any organized competition, which had become commonplace in Norway and Sweden. Many American colleges had winter carnivals, but intercollegiate competition seems not to have existed on any noticeable scale.

In January '18, near Montpelier Vermont, a driving club (horses), divided into classes, raced on the frozen Winooski River, apparently using sleds drawn by horses using grooved shoes. The race for one class required five heats to determine a winner. A couple of weeks later they raced again before a "small crowd" in the face of a "sharp gale." Although the mean average temperature at that time of the year was usually around fifteen degrees Fahrenheit, it registered ten degrees less than the average.[10]

13

Equestrian Sports

The region around the nation's capital had long had a love affair with thoroughbred racing. In '17, Laurel Park, working with the Maryland State Fair, had its cars stuck on a siding in October, which delayed the arrival of the animals and cut the number in a seven-race program. This track had a Camp Meade Handicap and raised money for a Liberty Bond drive. A horse named Soldier won a race. Some 15,000 showed up for the Preakness at Pimlico, Maryland in the spring of '18.[1]

Occasionally difficulties arose with Grant Circuit trotting, as when the police commissioner in Detroit would not allow organized betting. One assessor thought trotting did well despite the war, but pacing, inexplicably, fell off. The earnings of the top money-winning trotter in '18 fell to levels not seen in a decade. Among pacers, '17 proved worse than '18.[2]

In '17, a Labor Day crowd of 50,000 came to the fair and races at Hartford, indicating that the war had only a limited impact on the Grand Circuit. The last of these races—in Atlanta in '18—featured the best "trotters in the world," and ended "one of the greatest seasons the "sulk-driven 'dogs'" ever experienced, with numerous records and close races. But the first day's attendance, even though it "comfortably" filled the stands, fell off the norm, because of "the briskness of the air, the Spanish 'flu' or some other combination of causes." Numbers rose over the rest of the week.[3]

At Watertown, Wisconsin, a fair came off in September of '17 and '18, a big crowd for the opening day in the first instance and the "Biggest Racing Card Ever" in the second. The word "patriotic" appeared in '18, when the agenda had three races each of the four days, mixing trotting and pacing. The crowd (25,000) in Danbury, Conn. was as big in October '17 as in '16, with even more races. In 1918, the lack of reports suggests cancelation.[4]

The Winchester, Virginia, fair took place as usual in September '18, but the war reduced attendance and gambling on trotters lessened because everyone faced a lot of sacrifice in the immediate future—a "real war tax." The state fair in Richmond, scheduled for October, had to be canceled at the last minute because of flu. Normally that fair lasted six days, with up to

13. Equestrian Sports

six harness and/or running races nearly every day, along with a few steeplechases. Crowds coming by trolley averaged about 15,000 daily in '16, falling to around 11,000 in '17, because of a couple of rainy days. In resuming in '19, two captains and four lieutenants, likely out of the remount station at Camp Lee, vied in a military race. The number of horses brought to the daily races rose well above two hundred, roughly the same number as in '17.[5]

Thoroughbred racing remained active in '18, except in the fall. The U.S. and Canada had an estimated 200 courses running 1,915 meets. Three major races—the Kentucky Derby (Omar Khayyam winner in '17 and Exterminator in '18), the Preakness, and the Belmont—were sustained. Those running Churchill Downs, after the Kentucky Derby in the spring, announced they would grow potatoes in their infield but that they really did is unknown. As the war heated up in '18, Kentucky officials cancelled some thoroughbred contests as horse owners began to withdraw, the flu playing a role. Grand Circuit harness races had to be canceled at Lexington because of flu in late October. The usual crowds showed up at the hotels and at the track in August near Saratoga, N.Y. in '18, but an eerie silence pervaded. A month or so later, Maryland's Board of Health notified the track managers at Laurel to close gates because of the flu. They re-opened near the end of the next month.[6]

A N.Y. jockey club, at Jamaica, opened up the fall '18, without a hitch, in conjunction with the launching of the Fourth LIBERTY Loan. Two sons of a prominent turf man (both in the service) sent telegrams telling their dad to subscribe for them. That family invested $15,000.[7]

In November '18, riders in khaki were expected to take part in the National Horse Show in Madison Square Garden, hunting costumes in the Corinthian classes no longer required because army officers had to wear military uniforms. Expected to participate were Major Thomas Hitchcock and his son. Among the other nine prospective participants—all officers— was Captain Alan Thurman (University of Virginia), although one wonders how he made it back from France so fast. Officers from France, Britain, Russia, Belgium, and Italy took part in such shows before, but this would be the first time for Americans. Occasionally the army allowed officers to ride in horseraces, as in February '19, when two lieutenants, one from Shelby, the other from Beauregard, took part in a New Orleans handicap.[8]

Even though technology ruled out a heavy reliance on horses in combat, a battery of field artillerists that started out at Camp Meade competed against a battalion. At least six units competed in the 79th, when it faced off against the 88th Division.[9]

The 80th Division (Camp Lee) put on shows that included horses and mules moving equipment. In one event, a machine gun company won first for guiding an animal moving a gun in a cart. Based on the results of this competition, the 318th entered the divisional horse show where the regiment amassed 15 points, second place going to field artillerists, with 14. Then in February '19, the 80th Division took first in 14 of 33 events with 102 points out of a possible 201, the 78th coming in second.[10]

Fox hunting had a following in the N.Y. area in the year before the country went to war. Four hunt clubs ran in October or November '16. All these clubs canceled for '17, two resuming for '18, '19 also somewhat inactive. The Keswick Club in Virginia ran in '16 but no accounts surfaced during the war. In '19, Brunswick, Mass resumed foxhound trials, last held in the fall of '16 on Cape Cod (moved from Worcester County where too many deer got in the way). So many members joined the service that the organization shut down and when reopened, with the same officers, everyone had a "clean slate."[11]

Only one account of fox hunting among the military overseas surfaced—fictional. Artillerists with the 77th Division, reported their N. England–led "troubadours of the turf" yielded "nothing to the blue-blooded gentry of Bar Harbor or Palm Beach," as they sojourned "over field and stream" some distance from where they were billeted in early April for "a Bacchanalian siesta."[12]

Polo had elite riders and for the most part took place near country clubs or military reservations. Some 10,000 supposedly played polo while about 30,000 polo ponies resided in the country. The president of the American Polo Association wanted to continue, but, learning that the British had pretty much suspended play in August 1914, he urged Americans to do the same. June photos showed about a dozen players all in army uniforms practicing at Morristown, New Jersey.[13]

The N.Y. area, in '17, had the "quietest year" since the start of the association, the usual major matches in Newport called off because so many enlisted. In N.Y., where volunteers for the army could still play, most activity was of the "scrub" variety, an exception being at a hunting club in July, which collected $7,000 for Red Cross ambulances. Foxhall Keene (about 50 years old) led one quartet. One country club team had a brisk season as officers on furlough played. At the Meadowbrook on Long Island, almost all the best-known players alternated military drilling and playing. Several army teams had to be broken up as the men transferred to active duty. In December, the Polo Association, after the initial "flurry" patriotism, continued matches "as a diversion from the routine of military life." Reports that matches were being arranged for the next season near military camps in the Midwest encouraged polo enthusiasts. The next year, "crack cavalry units" were broken up and its members dispersed among regiments of infantry and artillery, negatively affecting hundreds of famous players, many with world-wide "reputations." No national tournament took place in '18.[14]

13. Equestrian Sports

Near San Diego at Coronado, polo made a comeback, promoted by an artillery colonel who played for the first Coronado club in 1906, now serving at Camp Kearny. Several other officers from the same artillery unit as well as another captain and a major signed on. Horses came from a government remount station. Cavalry at Fort Ethan Allan in Vermont played polo, as well as football, before heading overseas.[15]

In the summer, '18, Camp Wheeler's athletic director near Macon put in a regulation field, including goal posts. Officers played before large audiences, including civilians. Two hundred officers, ranging from lieutenants to a general, at Camp Hancock (Augusta), organized a Machine Gun Polo Association. They found ponies and used a field owned by a corporation, playing nearby army clubs and civilians, encouraged by Secretary of War Baker and the Commission on Training Camp Activities. Members of a battery of field artillerists from Ohio, tried polo in Texas but, being inexperienced, tended to trip ponies with their sticks. When they moved to Camp Sheridan, only majors or above could play.[16]

Devereux Milburn, who had participated in at least three international contests, signed up for the second Plattsburg camp for reserve officers starting late in August '17, leading a parade of polo players into the service. Future great, Tommy Hitchcock, Jr., became a pilot. When shot down and captured by the Germans, he jumped off a train and walked for eight days to reach Allied trenches. He would die in the army air service in World War II in a test dive. Thomas Hitchcock, Sr., one of the greatest American polo players ever, supervised aviation fields near N.Y. City. A colonel polo player moved from Camp Greene to take command at Mitchell Field at Hempstead. A lieutenant served as the adjutant at another N.Y. area field. A major and a former star for Meadow Brook ran one flying wing. Another major and polo competitor, also known in tennis, took charge of Mineola Field.[17]

After the fighting ended, the Polo Association figured that of 1,440 registered members, 1,005 served during the war. Optimism prevailed about the future of the sport. Cornell University considered starting intercollegiate polo. The idea originated during the war in the reserve officer training camp. School officials would run the program, but army officers would coach. West Point had polo intramurals, but it is unlikely that any college played inter-collegiately. While admitting practical problems, a New York columnist thought no other sport was better calculated to develop qualities needed in a good soldier like "skill and endurance" and "strategic thinking. Polo, "as exciting as football, as wide open to the spectator as baseball and as full off action as hockey" ought to have a strong appeal among colleges. L. Islanders were enjoying the best polo ever in the middle of June '19, as dozens of the nation's top players representing several clubs vied every

Wednesday and Saturday. A team from Santa Barbara, California, outscored Cooperstown, as extensive travel resumed.[18]

Rodeos came through the war in good shape, at least in '17, if coverage of one in Cheyenne is accurate. Some 75,000 watched the last day of rough riding, steer bulldogging, steer roping, relays, some events for both men and women. "Howling equestrians" set all sorts of records in this 21st Wild West competition. Director Fairbanks came to Wyoming, with an entourage that year, to find the world's best bronco buster for his latest western film. Fairbanks also financed a rodeo (more like a Wild West show with a stagecoach robbery) in Los Angeles that raised $18,000 for the Red Cross. He moved to San Francisco for another "rodeo" to raise money for the military camp recreation fund. An Arizona rider serving in the Navy was able to stay on a bronco named "Billy Sunday" for a minute and thus captured the $100 prize.[19]

An artillery regiment at Camp Lewis whose members came from four western states planned for a roundup they hoped would rival one held every year in eastern Oregon, which featured a typical rodeo selection. Several so-called "rodeos" focused more on auto and motorcycle racing, with a few equestrian activities. In '18, two Native Americans ("chiefs" in the press) who had enlisted in Bismarck and were frequent winners in Montana rodeos, had the job of taming animals no one else in the cavalry could control at Camp Lewis.[20]

14

Gymnastics, Lacrosse and Soccer

The Intercollegiate championship for gymnastics in '17 in N. Haven came up with Chicago 14½, Haverford 10, Princeton 13, NYU 9, Penn 8, Harvard 5, Rutgers 5, Yale 2, and Amherst ½. At least four other schools, including Navy, competed but not at this tournament. The war supposedly "crippled" gymnastics at the Naval Academy, yet the Midshipmen outperformed Penn and nearly doubled the NYU score in '18. In '19, Navy outscored Haverford and Princeton, losing an exhibition to the Philadelphia Turners. Haverford lost to Navy but overcame Penn and Princeton. In '17, the Western Conference order of finish was Wisconsin, Chicago, Nebraska, Illinois, Minnesota and Luther College. Illinois fell to Chicago in a dual. Wisconsin canceled gymnastics in '18 and '19. Indiana sent only two to Conference (10 allowed from each) in '18, but still scored a lot of points. The Big 10 continued gymnastics during the war with fewer teams.

Unlike in colleges, the AAU retained title competition in rings, horizontal bar, Indian clubs, vault, parallel bars, vault, Pommel horse, tumbling, rope climb, all-round, and team right through the war. One wonders about the role of the German roots of the sport (a product of liberal reforms of the early 19th century) and its popularity among European countries that remained neutral during the Great War. The French dominated gymnastics in 1900 when the Olympics were in Paris while Americans perched on top in 1904 when they took place in St. Louis.

Lacrosse was making a comeback, having been played little during the war and for a time before the war. In Canada, many amateurs who responded "to the call of service" perished. A decade earlier Canadians had considerable interest in pros but amateurs, mostly ex-servicemen, now took up the sport.[1]

Collegiate competition could only be found at a baker's dozen schools in two states in N. England plus several in New York and Pennsylvania and three in Maryland. All league members were also SATC participants in 1918.

In the Northern Division of the U.S. Intercollegiate Lacrosse League, Harvard, which won half of six in '16, gave up for the duration. Yale had only one recorded collegiate win from '16 through '19. In '17, Stevens Institute, which in 1913 moved to the Northern Division after playing in the Southern for 24 years, edged Swarthmore. They more than doubled matches in '18, besting an athletic club and defeating Yale (the only Northern rival) and Penn. Cornell, the best in the Northern Division in '16, lanced lacrosse in April '17. Syracuse, 2–4–1 in '16, canceled its newest sport in '17, reviving the next year, with a losing season. Hobart, which upset Yale and Stevens but fell to Harvard and Cornell in its first year in '16, suspended in '17, re-instating in '19, winning the North Division, with but one loss.

Lehigh, Southern Division claimant in '16, started '17 with three wins but could not repeat because of cancelations. The Brown & White dominated Penn, Swarthmore and Yale in '18, but Johns Hopkins derailed their title quest. Penn, loser to Harvard in '16 and winner over Swarthmore, fashioned a more complete schedule in '17, its captain enlisting. The '18 Penn narrowly lost to Hopkins and Stevens. Swarthmore, 1–6–1 in '16 got through '17, 2–2 against colleges (2–3–1 overall), 3–4 against a mix of colleges and clubs in '18. Penn State, which in '16 split with Maryland State and lost to Hopkins by a lot, yielded to Swarthmore and Lafayette in '17, "unsettled conditions prevailing." The Blue and White had few, if any, contests in '18. In '19 Navy swamped Penn State amid problems with minor sports due to the SATC on campus. Hopkins carried the Southern Division in '18; they retained the title in '19 (7–1).[2]

Navy, not a league member nor a participant in the SATC, won over Cornell, Penn, Harvard, Swarthmore (two overtimes), losing to Hopkins in '16. Navy practiced against Baltimore City College in '17, losing to Penn, canceling the rest. In '18, the academy outscored Hopkins and two others 25–1, extending domination into '19. Carlisle Institute, also not in the league, had a successful spring in '18, at 6–1–1, falling in a close one to Navy but downing Syracuse, Hopkins and Penn as well as the Onondagas. The winning season was sort of a "Last Hurrah" as the institute ceased to exist that summer.

A handful of colleges had soccer, with Pennsylvania the leading state with eight programs. The schedule often ran well into December and sometimes they tried to play in the winter, sensible behavior in California but not in the Middle States.

In the Intercollegiate Soccer Football League in '16, Princeton (4–2) prevailed against everyone except Penn (5–1), Haverford (3–1–1), Harvard (2–2–1), Yale (1–4) and Cornell (0–5). Penn won the playoff after tying with Princeton in the regular season. Haverford, with its captain-elect in the service in '17, secured a 2-overtime win over Cornell and at least two

14. Gymnastics, Lacrosse and Soccer   175

(possibly three) over Penn, one in October supposedly winning a league title. Running 6–1 against athletic clubs, the real Quakers also secured the title for the Cricket League, with a playoff win over Penn the next April ('18). In '17 Lehigh claimed its first win in the Pennsylvania Intercollegiate League—over Haverford—a result not mentioned in the latter's sources. In the '18 fall, Haverford stood 8–2 in the Cricket League. In '19, the Soccer Football League standings had Penn (5–0–0) in first, followed by Princeton (4–1–0), Cornell (1–2–2), Harvard (1–2–2), Haverford (1–3–1), Yale (0–4–1), respectively. No standings for this association appeared in either '17 or '18.[3]

CCNY, shifting from rugby to soccer, edged Yale and Princeton, losing to the Crescent A.C. and another club in '17. With Nat Holman (famous for basketball) coaching, the Lavender bested one from the N.Y. State League, Yale and Naval Reservists. The next year, demobilizing the SATC forced a canceling of a December showdown with Pelham Naval Training. After a poor performance against Crescent A.C. (Brooklyn) early on, they later tied the New Moon and shut out Columbia, also overcoming flu.[4]

At Franklin & Marshall, the war killed the idea of joining the new Pennsylvania State Intercollegiate League. After nothing transpired in '17 or '18, the '19 season featured dominance over an academy and a YMCA, no collegiate competition whatsoever. Lehigh, in '17, claimed a victory over Haverford, a result not mentioned in the latter's sources. The war put the sport "in a precarious position in a great many institutions," a Lehigh student reported. Swarthmore fielded its first official soccer club in '16, absorbing a drubbing at the hands of Penn State. The war prevented joining the Pennsylvania State league in '17, a much closer loss to Penn State that season. The '18 schedule was shortened by seven winter matches due to the weather. The program claimed the State League title in '19, with wins over Haverford, Lehigh and Penn.[5]

The University of Penn claimed championships in the Intercollegiate Soccer League in '16 and '19, In '17, Penn edged Yale and won over several cricket clubs, losing to a rubber company and at least twice to Haverford. Penn State, with dominant wins over Lafayette and Swarthmore in '16 slipped by Swarthmore before winter froze them out the next season. In '18 the "demobilization of the SATC" and "unsettled conditions in minor sports" ruined plans for a Christmas trip after one of the two coaches who entered military service returned. Icy conditions in '19 prevented playing University of Penn on a Christmas trip after Lehigh succumbed twice and Swarthmore once."[6]

Baylor in the North Texas Soccer League in '17 lost to Sears-Roebuck and the Dallas Athletics twice if not thrice. In '18, Camp MacArthur shut out Baylor, as did Scotsmen from Dallas and the Royal Flying Corps from Ft. Worth; Baylor tied Sears and, in the only recorded intercollegiate, took Texas A&M, 3–0.

On the Pacific Coast in the spring of '16 Cal warmed up with Marines and split with the Olympic Club, absorbing two losses with Stanford. That fall, Berkeley lost to a combination of Olympians and Barbarians and split with Stanford. In the fall, '17, after downing the Olympics, Cal won two over Stanford, which in the spring '16 tamed the Barbarians and lost to some All-Stars. That fall the Cardinals beat Barbarians, split with All-Stars and overcame Olympians before splitting with Cal, giving them three legs on the Lathrop Cup. In '17, Stanford took Camp Fremont twice and two tight ones with the Olympic club but lost to Cal twice. No scores surfaced for either Cal or Stanford in '18, but the cup in '19 listed five wins for each, suggesting play continued in '18. In '17, Oregon ousted the Oregon Aggies twice, but in '18, the latter returned the favor.

The Upper Midwest only had a few programs, among them the University of Minnesota and the University of Wisconsin, plus Eastern Michigan at Ypsilanti. St. Olaf vied with St. Thomas as Ohio Wesleyan did the same with Ohio State. In Illinois, only Bradley recorded any action, along with an obscure small college that played an even less well-known seminary.

In '18, among non-collegians, a Chicago club lost all its 18 members to enlistments. The Southern N.E. League ceased with the war. The U.S. Football Association, existing for six years, lost 27 of 81 teams, the Blue Mountain League 4 of 6. Copies of the English new rule book went to the bottom of the ocean thanks to a German torpedo, but reporters found cause to be optimistic. American junior high schools continued play and many army cantonments took up the game among young men who had never seen it played. Maybe the end of the fighting would bring greater growth.

The Football Association carried through the winter and into the spring to determine the National Cup champion, which turned out to be Bethlehem Steel, winner in '16 but loser to the Fall River Rovers in May '17 at Pawtucket 1–0. In the finals in May '18, the two fought 2–2 before 10,000 at Pawtucket, forcing a repeat at Harrison, New Jersey, at the old Federal League Park, which had ample seating but not a large crowd, a 3–0 for the men of steel. Charles Schwab donated to the cause. In the American (National) Football Association (restarted in 1906, membership dropping slightly during the war), Bethlehem beat Babcock and Wilcox (Bayonne, New Jersey) at Pawtucket in two matches. The N.Y. Footballers Protective Association raised $25,000 to equip army camps, using a chain letter. Other associations also employed the same device, with similar results.

Camp Lewis fielded soccer clubs, mostly playing each other in an 8-team league. In January '18, one squad tied the Victoria "Fragments" composed of convalescing Canadians. Between January and May '19 soccer attracted thousands of participants and spectators at the AEF championships. The winner (Le Mans), 80th Division, downed Intermediate,

14. Gymnastics, Lacrosse and Soccer

General Headquarters and the 3rd Army, 6th Division. Almost all the players were British by birth. Le Mans had five privates, four corporals and two sergeants. The 3rd Army consisted of nine privates, one corporal and one sergeant, not one officer in the entire lot, which contrasts with officer-dominated American football.[7]

15

Potpourri: Archery—Trapshooting

Organizations promoting archery by determining national champions started in the U.S. in 1879 for men and women. The male winner of '16 repeated in '19, the event canceled in the war years. Among the women, the '16 champ did not repeat in '19, waiting until 1920 to regain the title. In both instances, the National Archery Association canceled the tourney during the war.

Women were also quite active in aviation. In 1916, Ruth Law Oliver set a cross-country (distance) record of nearly 590 miles, from Chicago to central N.Y. flying onto N.Y. City (Governor's Island) the next day. She also broke the women's record for altitude. Katherine Stinson broke the distance record the next year (1917) in a run between San Francisco and San Diego and then topped that with one from Chicago to Binghamton N.Y. (over 700 miles). The year before in October, the nineteen year old entertained the crowd at the Virginia state fair for several days, ascending to a high altitude, when her engine stalled. She was able to land safely. Both Law and Stinson wanted to fly for the military but reluctantly accepted the role of raising money for the Red Cross via exhibitions.[1]

Congress imposed a federal tax of $5 on every bowling alley and billiard table in the country, including those in private clubs (at first Internal Revenue only collected from businesses open to the public). It is unlikely that these taxes seriously impaired either sport. Because of limited physical exertion, billiards and/or pocket pool was a sport but not an athletic activity. William Hoppe won titles so often (Alfredo de Oro won the three-cushion at some point) that reporters tired of writing about it. "War duties" prevented a few from competing. Several, including Hoppe, gave exhibitions, raising money for ambulances. Early in the fall of '18, he and others agreed to continue to circulate, with all receipts above traveling expenses going to war-related charities. Hoppe helped the National Association of American Billiard Players in its United War Work campaign.[2]

N.Y. City still had 900 pool parlors in '18, when the state toughened licensing to reduce the number. Almost every city had parlors where the elite played. But the activity also appealed to elements of the lower classes. Chiefs of police often branded young players "slackers." Just after the Declaration of War, Governor James Cox told Ohio mayors to send idle men to farms to help end the food shortage. A report labeled "POOL ROOM" figured the governor meant to end the easy lives of "street corner loafers."[3]

Every city, most towns, villages and even a few hamlets had bowling leagues with teams sponsored by businesses, fraternal associations and churches. The sport attracted a great many of both genders with a wide range of ages. The lack of fuel in the winter '18 closed down alleys and government directives discouraged amusements. Yet, the Bowling Congress annual tournament in Cincinnati in '18, had a record-high 700 teams. The affiliated women's organization, started in '16, competed at Cincinnati. In El Paso, the '17 winter had 16 quintets at the Cactus Alley vying in four leagues. A Real Estate five led an Industrial League. The '18 winter produced the same, including one for women. Around September "a large percent" of the Cactus Club went "overseas to stop the Hun." In Brattleboro, Vermont, on a Monday in January '18, when no one could use coal, scores fell off a bit. Given the average daily temperature was about five degrees, we should excuse the poor candle-pin count.[4]

In '19, a Rock Islander (Illinois) made 727 in the Central States Bowling Tournament in Peoria. A year earlier he had, with a partner, won the doubles in a tournament put on by the Tri-State League. The press reported the doings of the International Bowling Association as well as a Ten Pin club in Detroit, where a woman made eight straight strikes—her prize—a ton of coal.[5]

South Bend, Indiana, in '18 adjusted to days without heat, not "severely disturbing" their bowling. In '19, a reporter, noting the "lethargy that had been hanging over the institution" expected the boom in bowling that began just before the war to resume. One navy vet pointed out that nearly every young man he talked with when stationed near Cleveland was an experienced bowler. Every Saturday evening about forty of his mates headed downtown to bowl. He had letters from two buddies in France, who could not wait to get back to South Bend to knock down pins.[6]

The sponsors of teams in Denver reflected the local economic base, divided into major and minor leagues in '17. The fall of '18 brought out the usual leagues, but in October, a city-wide quarantine against flu forced all alleys to shut down. The press thought the closures would only last a week or so, but they did not re-open for closer to a month.

Missoula, Montana's eight-team City Bowling League had its first season in '17. The second year ('18) United led with a 59–25, Foresters in the cellar both years, 23 different individuals representing their five-man team. The Montana tournament in Lewistown in February had 110 as individuals and about the same number on two-man teams from ten communities vying for $1,000 in prizes, the top one $72.50. An April tournament of the Pacific International Northwest Bowling Congress in Spokane drew 25 entries from major cities, including Vancouver.[7]

A tournament, at Jamestown, North Dakota, in January '19 brought out eighty quintets, with one from Valley City, the location of the tournament the previous year, leading in the early going. Grand Forks had an active eight-team league at the Grand Alleys even during the war. In '18, one of the city's own was champion at a fort in Washington state.[8]

As in billiards, someone winning the roque or croquet titles bored reporters. The reigning roque monarch won his 11th time in a row during the war. A new champion emerged in croquet at Norwich, Connecticut, in '18, but it reverted to the previous winner the next year for his 11th title in 12 years, the event having more participating than usual.

Squash clubs raised money for the Red Cross, with a "patriotic tourney" in Massachusetts in February '18 and matches involving Harvard (alumni) in New York and the Crescent A.C. that winter. Yale alumni withdrew from the N.Y. Metropolitan League tournament, Harvard winning. The New York A.C. had at least one match for the Red Cross.[9]

World contests for racquets, also with elitist tendencies, stopped from 1914 well into the 1920s, the American championships canceled only in '18 when Clarence Pell, winner of '17 and '19, flew planes in France. A new form of handball showed up on beaches near N.Y. City just before the war, the war impacting the sport little. The A.A.U. started championships for another form just after the war.

Americans had been competing for titles for fishing (Angling) since the 1870s, with only an occasional hiccup, but in '17, none of the nine existing events took place, while all were carried out in '18. That suggests that those who ran fly and bait casting championships responded dramatically to the coming of war and then calmed down. Although young men participated in such competition, the sport was far from age related. Women started competing in the early 1920s.

In fencing in '17, Colgate lost to Army, which also overcame Columbia. The intercollegiate championship tournament, held at New York's Hotel Astoria, was won by the undefeated Naval Academy, followed by Harvard, Columbia, Yale, and Penn, in that order. In '18, eastern universities supposedly dropped fencing as a sport "in spite of its military value." No matter, Penn lost to Columbia again and to Navy in foils but tied the Midshipmen in sabers. A championship match for '18 did take place with Columbia (13), Yale (8) and Penn (5) contending. Early graduation hurt the Naval Academy in '18, but a 5–4 over Columbia late in the season suggests another national title. In '19, fencing resumed in earnest with wins over Harvard, Penn, Columbia, and Yale, giving the Academy a possible 10th national title.[10]

The Amateur Fencers League, regulating the non-collegiate side, finished up its championships in '17 before the war, calling off all championships in '18—men's individual foil, epee, saber, three-weapon and team titles for all four categories. All but the team saber and three-weapon resumed in '19. No world championship matches occurred in any category for several years both before and after the war. The same league gave out a gold medal in saber competition in February '18 while the N.Y.A.C. won a three-weapon match in early January—a special medal for Sherman Hall, with several fencing titles over the years, winning foils, another competitor taking the three-weapon.[11]

Officers aboard troop ships sometimes played quoits, but whether this game was like the ones on later cruise ships is not known. Tossing horseshoes, a sort of poor man's quoits, had become organized just a few years before the war. Popular in rural America and in California, it had a major tournament at Kansas State about ten years before the war. With a national code in place a few years later, the first world tournament took place in Kansas City in 1915, not renewed until '19. Whether the gap was due to the war or to the dominance of one star remains unclear.

The war did little to or for roller polo (roller skates), introduced in the 1880s. Among pros in '18, the American League had Lowell leading, 55–41, the Providence Gold Bugs, 51–40, followed by Lewiston, 47–38; Lawrence, 49–41; Worcester, 36–50 and Portland, 27–46. The year after the war the standings registered Lowell, 54–40; Salem Witches 51–42; Providence, 49–44; Worcester. 41–46; New Bedford Whalers, 40–48 and Lawrence 17–52.

Trapshooting, which mixed gun salesmen, doctors, lawyers and such, experienced a boom during the war. Public interest in the sport had never enjoyed such interest. The top Denver marksman described gains with the war as skeet was becoming "America's Favorite Pastime." Almost every community clamored for instruction. Although the war "stopped other athletics, at least temporarily," trapshooting experienced "the biggest boom it ever knew." Four hundred were shooting at Greeley, similar numbers at the Lakewood Gun Club at Denver, even though many members enlisted in the service. Denver also had an active revolver club, including the president of the national association who taught about rifles and pistols at army camps.[12]

The secretary of the national association agreed the long-term trend showed an increase, but '17 had less members than '16 because of enlistments. Thirty-eight state championships were held in '13, 39 in '14, 42 in '15, and 46 in '16, the same number in '17 (Arizona and New Mexico absent). The number of clubs increased to 4,610. Sixteen states had championships for women. A sailor won the Atlantic Fleet and Princeton the individual and team intercollegiate. Yes, there was a national collegiate champion even though skeet fails to show up in yearbooks.

Unlike golf and tennis, the national association distributed trophies to winners of state titles in '17, Oklahoma having the most participants in its championship, Pennsylvanians recording the highest number of targets thrown and Illinois receiving the most prize money, while N. Carolinians averaged the best scores (93 amateurs and seven pros). Members were concerned about the increased cost for guns, ammunition and clay pigeons. In '17, an amateur trapshooting association put an entry fee of two cents a target to raise $30,000 in the U.S. and Canada to purchase ambulances. Silk ribbons replaced trophies.[13]

Several colleges and universities recorded rifle scores for '16. Another league, sponsored by the NRA had quintets wield .22 calibers, shooting a hundred times from fifty feet. Presumably, traveling not taking place, observers made sure targets, weapons and distances met standards. The '16 results seem to have been in dispute. Few results surfaced for the war years, although Washington State came up with the collegiate rifle championship at some point.

The National Rifle Association (NRA), with several hundred thousand members in 1,845 clubs, encouraged rifle shooting, especially among youngsters. In '18 Washington State's coach showed up as an instructor at Camp Perry on Lake Erie, where the war department and the NRA cooperated in running target shooting contests in September '18 at the reputed largest rifle range ever created. Instructors at Perry had the team lead at one point. National guardsmen from Arkansas took first in state competition. A marine corporal won gold in one category. A civilian from Kansas led pistol shooting out of over 1,100 contestants, a marine sergeant earning silver.

AEF competition involving 400,000, starting in February and not ending in Belgium until April, produced 2,000 contestants. After a long process and daily competition, on June 20, '19, officials picked twelve with rifles, ten with handguns and backups to compete in the Inter-Allied Olympics.

16

The Inter-Allied Military Olympics

General Pershing, embracing the desire to bring the world back to peaceful competition as in the International Olympics (canceled in '16), called for athletic competition among the Allies in May and June '19. With the number of troops in Europe dwindling, Pershing made anyone who had served in the army or Marines at home or overseas, including 150,000 SATC, eligible, the total number qualifying about 4,000,000. Naval personnel, not under his jurisdiction, were excluded. On the day Pershing issued General Order #241 for the AEF championships, he invited 29 nations, including colonies, to the Inter-Allied Olympics. Eighteen returned positive responses. A committee under Col. Wait C. Johnson, composed of American officers and Y officials, selected 26 sports (a number later reduced), only one of which was strictly military (hand-grenade throwing, bayoneting not accepted). Most were traditional events of the pre-war Olympics. Except for boxing, most of the rules for each sport were the ones prevailing in the private sector.[1]

In February, workers broke ground for Pershing Stadium, accessible with good roads to the city. The committee also picked another site outside Paris near the barracks of the French gymnastics school then covered with trenches and wire. Colombes Field became a training site for some athletes, but many Americans also worked out on the Rhine, marksmen being based near Le Mans, in Belgium, the location of the AEF championships.

The Y raised money for the structure built by a private contractor. French military engineers graded the field and created a track. Americans took care of plumbing and wiring in the stands made of re-enforced concrete. Construction commenced on 11 April, with ninety working days for completion. Over 3,000 worked three shifts of eight hours each. When a labor dispute arose, Pershing sent in Pioneers (African American) to complete the structure. The stadium covered nine acres with a periphery of almost half a mile, the grandstand for 2,500 spectators ran for one hundred yards, bleachers holding 22,500, nowhere near enough for opening-day crowds. These girded a field with a 200-meter straight track and a 500-meter oval one. French soldiers finished the track, the base four layers of cinders. The field for track and soccer and rugby ran 144 by 70 meters.

Decorations covered the Stadium, with poles around the inner line of the oval track bearing streamers representing participating nations. Some nations were so new that Paris seamstresses sewed flags from sketches. A bronze plate informed everyone that the YMCA paid for Pershing Stadium for the Inter-Allied Games, June–July 1919. Participants occupied various camps nearby and consumed "doughboy" fare. Everyone slept in American tents.

All participants had to have worn the uniform of the nation they represented, but each country adopted its own selection process. Some 600 athletics, most of them competitors in the AEF games, assembled in Paris at the end of May, from which officials picked 80, and then added those from the homeland on an AAU list. In track, 32 collegians appeared on the recommend roster, along with 18 from athletic clubs, several of whom had competed in college.

In late April, the Navy had a meet on Travers Island for some 30,000 members of the "Victory Fleet," perhaps with the intention to pick their best athletes to participate in France. Had they not learned about the exclusion of the navy? The Navy even used Olympic or European measurements, but no results of that meet made its way into the press and the AAU listed no one, except Marines, from naval installations.

General Pershing (second from left in front group) leads Opening Ceremonies of the Inter-Allied Military Olympics, 1919. *Library of Congress: LC-DIG-anrc-01582.*

16. The Inter-Allied Military Olympics

In June, 48 athletes, including Sol Butler (Dubuque) and Lt. Charles Paddock, left Hoboken aboard the *Great Northern*. The colonel in charge, thanking the AAU, described an "ideal crowd," all in "dead earnest." Butler recovered from sea sickness. In France, in tryouts William Sylvester equaled a world record in the hurdles; Teschner, the AEF champion, upset Butler in the 100-meter but the latter outdistanced the broad jump champ from Dartmouth.[2]

Americans amassed 92 points in track, with France a distant second, with 12 of the remaining 28 points, six nations participating. France won

Pvt. Solomon Butler, winner of broad jump, receives award from General Pershing at the Military Olympics. *The Inter-Allied Games, Paris, 22nd June to 6th July 1919*, p. 487.

most of the longer runs. Had Britain taken part, the results would likely have been far less one-sided. Doughboys packed the stadium cheering on the American athletes adorned in red-edged white shirts and navy-blue trousers.

In an exhibition, future movie actor Fred Thomson and a chaplain in the Army, having recovered from a broken leg playing football, tossed a grenade 254' 11", a world record, his brother placing second, part of an American sweep. They may have twirled the two-pound object more like a discus, a method first used by an army officer on Governor's Island in '17.

"PADDOCK WINS FURLONG," the headline blared as the USC freshman captured the 200 (21.6) meter, Teschner a close second. Even before the relay finals, the Canadian and American teams set world records for the 800-meter relay. With Paddock leading off and Teschner anchoring, the U.S. won over Canada. Tom Campbell (University of Chicago) led the 1,600-meter, with Teschner again at anchor, overcoming Australia and France. Four others carried the medley relay, over Australia and France.[3]

Lt. Bob Simpson established a new French record in both the 110-meter high hurdles and 200-meter lows. His cousin, William Sylvester, also from Bosworth and Missouri University, came in second in the longer race. A New Zealander upset Earl Eby in the 800-meter after the latter won the 400. Robert Legendre (Georgetown) pulled first in the Pentathlon (five events) followed by Lt. Eugene Vidal (South Dakota and West Point). A Stanford athlete tossed the shot over 45'. Americans also swept the discus, a world record holder staggering from a sickbed, taking third. Pat Ryan failed to break his own world record in the hammer in an unofficial event. Except for a technicality, the U.S. would have swept all top three places in every field event. Sol Butler, of Dubuque College, the only black American participating because sprinter Sgt. Howard Drew injured his leg, won the broad jump at over 24 feet, 9 inches. Cheers resounded as the king of Montenegro handed him a medal and patted him on the back.

As might be expected, the U.S. triumphed in baseball, winning 3 of 4 against the only competition, the Canadians. Americans won the third, 10–0, on the 4th of July. With some changes in the AEF championship lineup, but with Friedman leading the way, the Americans struck down the Italians in basketball 55–17, on 28 June on the outdoor court inside the stadium. The losers then edged the French. In the final, Americans romped, 93–8, over France, no surprise given the inexperience of the Italians and French. Americans also dominated the Tug of War.[4]

The U.S. did the same in rifle and pistol shooting, the British not competing. Using Stockholm Olympics rules on the range near Le Mans in late June (not on Sunday), a first sergeant took the individual rifle title with 275 points out of a possible 300 over several distances. Twenty-five American

16. The Inter-Allied Military Olympics

U.S. basketball team, winner of Military Olympic title, in action in the middle of the field inside Pershing Stadium. *Inter-Allied Games*, p. 165.

entrants won the first 18 places, riflemen 2,651 out of a possible 3,000 and hand-gunners 4,080 out of 5,000. A Frenchman tied two Americans for third place as an individual in the team competition. An American engineer took first place in the individual pistol, a captain placing above him in the team event.

Nine countries sent swimmers to Lake St. James, next to the Stadium, but all eyes were on 2nd Lieutenant Norman Ross, who won the 100-meter free style, 100-meter back stroke, 400-meter free style, 800-meter free style and 1,500-meter free style. Only in the 100-meter did anyone even come close. Thanks largely to Ross, the U.S. amassed 21 points to 14 earned by Australians. Even though Ross gave the Americans a lead, Australia won the 800-meter relay. Belgium won water polo, the U.S. losing to France, 4–3.

It did not go so well with crew, not a surprise given no sailors were involved and the British and commonwealth countries competed. With a lot of turnover, Americans lost an exhibition on the Seine to a New Zealander before going to the Henley Regatta. Ten competed on the Seine in July '19 in the Olympics, a few days after the main events. In the first heat for single sculls, Major Paul Withington, coach of the AEF football champions, placed second. In a four-oared shell second heat, Americans overcame New Zealanders. In the eight-oared third heat, Cambridge led Americans by half a length. In the finals, Withington lost to a New Zealander. France secured a half-length win over Americans in the four-oared finals and England, Australia and New Zealand placed in that order in the eight-oar finale.

Boxing proved competitive, even though Britain did not take part. In the finals, an Australian and fan favorite, outpointed an AEF champ, in ten rounds (2 minutes each). A Frenchman overcame an Australian in the lightweight, also in ten. In the welter a Canadian decisioned a Frenchman. Lt. Edward Eagan, who had not fought in the AEF championships, won a defaulted match over a Frenchman in the middle weight. An Italian got by an Australian in the light heavy and Bob Martin carried the heavy over an Australian. Overall, Americans went 8–4.

Lt. Norman Ross, Stanford record setting-swimmer, won five first-place medals at the Military Olympics and three gold at the 1920 Summer Olympics at Antwerp. *Inter-Allied Games*, p. 401.

That AAU list for these Olympics included wrestler "Strangler" Lewis because he served at Camp Grant, promoted to sergeant when he simultaneously head-locked two privates who harassed him, not knowing who he was. Pershing decreed he did not need any more wrestlers. Americans won only 1 of 6 in Greco-Roman wrestling, a style rarely practiced among the AEF. Czechoslovakia tied Belgium for the most points in that style. The U.S. won 6 of 7 of the catch-as-catch-can, losing only the heavyweight to a Frenchman, accumulating 15 of the 23 points available in that category.

In early July '19 near the Palace at Versailles, where peace had recently been negotiated, the British and French sent eight golf pros each, the Americans amateurs. Playoffs (10 doughboys and 10 officers) came up with Rautenbush, plus a former Panama-Pacific champion and a Kansas state champ. The French receiving a bye, the Americans beat the Brits 7–5. In the Foursomes (18 holes) Rautenbush and his partner defeated Frenchmen, but the latter secured an 8–4 verdict. The 4th of July and the two days surrounding were for leisurely play, the tourney resuming on the 6th with qualifying rounds for singles competition hindered by rain-soaked greens. The English, except for one, withdrew. Four Americans played off against each other, leaving six French against two Americans, both of whom lost. The French then contested for the title.

At the Racing Club close to the stadium in early June, with several celebrities present, tennis matches had representatives from Australia, Belgium, Canada, Czechoslovakia (an emerging country that sent two pros), France, Canada, Romania and Serbia, which defaulted a lot. Americans consisted of Washburn, Mathey, plus a demobilized officer who once captained Harvard, "a typically violent" lieutenant (Stanford) and a captain, once a New Jersey titlist. Norris Williams, America's best, was not available. In the prelims, three Americans advanced and two fell to Australians, both in four sets. Washburn survived the first round, as another Australian mastered Mathey in straight sets. In the second round, Washburn won over another American, becoming the sole American remaining for the semis, losing to a Frenchman in four sets. Andre Gobert defeated Wood of Australia in straight sets. In the doubles' prelims, Washburn-Mathey took four sets to overcome Frenchmen and got by Czechoslovakians in five sets in the first round. In the semis, they overcame Australians, again in five, the deciding one, 12–10. Wood and his mate had a much easier time in three. It took them four sets to dispose of Washburn and Mathey.

Reputations pretty much determined the makeup of the American fencing team in the Inter-Allied Olympics, with many West Point athletes or other collegians. Of the nine nations competing, the French tied Italy in foils, winning over Portugal in epee, while Italy downed Portugal in sabers. Romanians easily won in trials for foils over Americans, who made a better showing in the sabers but still lost to Greeks.

The U.S. rugby squad did rather well, with Californians aided by a couple of Americans from English universities. The French overwhelmed Romania, 48–5, as Americans beat the same, 23–0. In the finale, with American youth and passion pitted against French experience, after the first half ended scoreless, the French won, 8–3. Five thousand spectators followed the action at Colombes Field. England, the nation that created the sport, did not compete.

The U.S. soccer eleven lost to Czechoslovakia and Belgium after edging Canada. With the main stadium often filled, eight nations vied, Czechoslovakians, with a more active forward line, overcame the French for the title in a well-played match.

The second-place U.S. rugby squad at the Military Olympics, many from California.

Americans finally found qualified horses, not surprisingly, in remount depots. The French won the cross-country, Lt. Col H.D. Chamberlain (AEF) close in the 55-kilometer. Chamberlain and his mates also tied for second in jumping. A Frenchman won, while Chamberlain tied a Belgian as another American placed fourth. The French won team competition, the U.S. second and Italy third. All participants were army officers, the seven Americans coming from a list of pre-war equestrians. In the total medal count, Italy won the most awards, France and the U.S. second and third.

Some 30,000 or so filled the stadium for the closing ceremonies, the bands playing "The Star-Spangled Banner" and "La Marseillaise." After talking for some time, Pershing handed out awards, giving each recipient a firm handshake. Ross basked amid a huge ovation as he hauled away his prizes. A great cheer went up for Jean Vermeulen, a wounded French war hero who won the modified marathon. Another big cheer greeted Sol Butler.[5]

Colonel Johnson thanked the AAU for sending so many remarkable athletes. He assumed the AAU would send many of those who competed to the regular Olympics in 1920. Johnson praised Australians, Canadians, and New Zealanders in many sports, the Czechs and Greeks in wrestling, an Italian who kissed a Canadian on both cheeks after beating him in boxing

16. The Inter-Allied Military Olympics

and the French winner of the marathon. He reminded everyone that 58 percent of Frenchmen between ages 21 and 31 had either died or been wounded, but he believed they would still compete successfully in the 1920 Olympics.[6]

Antwerp, Belgium, hosted that Olympiad, even though far from recovered from the war. That the Olympics were even held in 1920, especially at Antwerp, provides a positive statement about the human spirit. U.S. athletes, especially collegians, piled up many medals in track and field, Paddock taking gold in the 100-metre and silver in the 200, while Eby secured

Cpl. Robert LeGendre, Georgetown University, 1919 pentathlon winner at the Penn Relays and in the Military Olympics. *Library of Congress: LC-DIG-npcc-00642.*

Lt. Charlie Paddock, University of Southern California record setter, winner of the 100 and 220 at the Military Olympics and the 100-meter at the Antwerp Summer Olympics in 1920. *Courtesy University of Southern California, on behalf of USC Libraries Special Collections.*

silver in the 800-metre. Ross added three gold to his stockpile accumulated the previous year. Robert LeGendre, Georgetown athlete and winner at the Penn Relays that spring and champion in the pentathlon at the military Olympics in '19, had to be satisfied with a bronze at Antwerp.

The U.S. Naval Academy made up for its absence at the Military Olympics by taking gold in the eight-oared event. Eddie Eagan, Yale grad and now a student at Oxford and English amateur titlist, won the boxing middleweight gold, using a style learned in the American army. British boxers won more medals than the U.S. though America won three gold, more than any other nation. The Netherlands overcame Belgium in soccer, while the American rugby squad reversed the previous year's results in a stunning upset of France, Great Britain again not participating. Americans won the most medals in Free Style (catch-as-catch-can) wrestling, though Finland fetched two gold. No Americans—men or women, played tennis at Antwerp, preferring to compete at Forest Hills, the exception being Kumagae, who was usually one of the top ten in the U.S. Lawn Tennis Association rankings. His two silver medals counted for Japan.

17

Legacy of the War

The possible impact of the Great War on athletics raises many questions. Did the Black Sox scandal have anything to do with the decline in betting at horse races in '18? One of the participants thought so. Was there a connection between the scandal and the "fight or work" issue of 1918? None of the eight accused served in the military (three stars in the industrial leagues), while Collins, the only starter who went into the service, apparently took no bribes. Did the penchant for gambling by soldiers and sailors gain more of a foothold because of the war? Did 3,000,000 learning how to box help increase interest in major matches in the 1920s? A likely "yes" in both cases. How come so many top American tennis players (most of them collegians) served in the military? Did amateur baseball receive a boost with the return to civilian life from those who played the National Pastime while in the military? Possibly, but certainly not the growth predicted.

A disproportionate number of former and current college athletes died in the war. One-time major leaguer Eddie Grant was an infielder for Harvard, which also had two from '18 freshmen hockey, one a goal tender who perished behind German lines, three frosh from '17 rowing, one of whom earned the Croix de Guerre and a pole vault record holder, who led a charge. The roll call started when an old quarterback died in September '16, serving in the Coldstream Guards as a lieutenant. A captain on the gridiron early in the century died in action with the infantry in late July '18 after driving ambulances in '16.[1]

Columbia counted twenty, including a '19 fencer, whose plane crashed. Rowing and soccer had the most, three of the former and four in the latter. The captain of '15 football downed three German planes and sustained serious injuries from a crash. Yale honored '06 and '16 crew, the captain of the '16 eleven, a '13 (four sports), two '17 wrestlers, a '16 and a '17 track, including Johnny Overton, plus a '15 swimmer and another '15 crew/football.[2]

Princeton had at least nineteen. John Poe, football player and later University of Virginia coach in the 1890s died charging a machine gun in

'15, serving in the Black Watch. A '98 captain and All-American died from flu about to board a transport home. An outstanding player in '12 died falling from a horse. A tackle from '12 perished at Camp Gordon, probably from the flu. A '13 All-American center perished on a bombing run for the French. A captain, in '13 and recipient of a French cross, died of wounds. The list also included three from baseball and two who helped oar for Harvard in '16. The most prominent of all, Hobey Baker, from football and hockey, died after the Armistice in France flying a defective plane.[3]

Williams College, which had the greatest number of former football players killed in action (10) or dying from accidents or disease (3) had at least ten other former varsity athletes die in the service out of 42 students from the school who perished. It is quite likely that athletes made up a disproportionate share of the losses. One estimate that half the college athletes that were victims of the Great War played football seems high, but hundreds of athletes threw "themselves into the struggle," demonstrating "enthusiasm, spirit and loyalty, initiative and courage."[4]

The war accelerated the movement of athletes as well as their coaches. Collegians showed up by the thousands at military camps which contained athletes and coaches from other schools. This mixing of different ideas and strategies, occurring at a much more rapid rate than normal, transformed almost every athletic activity. As one commentator viewed it, athletic training made good fighters, doing more for sports than "ever happened before." Those receiving such training "will never forget" the competition, the war making "an athletic team of about four million men."[5]

This war and its results were also closely connected to several cultural issues that troubled the nation for some time. During the war era, reporters focused on having the New York legislature repeal the flawed Frawley Act, where promoters paid for certain results while arena owners oversold tickets and money moved underneath numerous tables. The N.Y. legislature, however, would more than likely simply end any kind of boxing. "The hungry tentacles" of state laws might put boxing on its "last legs," a reporter opined. Earlier pugilism looked like it was gaining, as Illinois seemed ready to follow the advice of the commander of an infantry regiment previously stationed on the Mexican border. California, Missouri and Nebraska appeared to be moving forward as well.[6]

In the winter of '19, the manager of the Red Circle Theater in Norfolk, pressured by "certain ministers," canceled a match. Anyone helping at a match for financial gain where gambling took place could incur a year in the Virginia state pen, the use of gloves having no bearing. Such events could continue at the Navy Y and the Army Base, not subject to state law. Six "gentlemen of the U.S. Navy" praised the War Camp Community Service and berated the ministers. Sailors were not "disreputable reprobates"

17. Legacy of the War

and matches harmed no one, including the hundred or so women who regularly watched them.[7]

In Idaho, a minister introduced a bill to meet the "demands of returned soldiers, sailors and marines" who wanted to end mollycoddling. One proposal would legalize 20-round matches using four-ounce gloves. Michigan passed a bill that created a commission and permitted 10-round matches, with no announced winner. A poll of 2,000 convalescing at Fort Sheridan, found only one objecting to legalizing a form of pro boxing. Earlier, it looked like Illinois, as well as Nebraska, might liberalize restraints because of the attitudes of soldiers at the camps getting ready to go to France, but the efforts bore no fruit.[8]

In January '19, several states leaned toward legalizing "the art of self-defense," which produced "the world's greatest soldier." Wisconsin, where the sport had been legal for some time, experienced no corruption. California, Oregon, Minnesota, New Jersey and Nevada, states which allowed matches, considered more liberal rules, such as having 25-round matches in Nevada. The governor vetoed that measure. A columnist relished the defeat of Governor Charles Whitman, whose "pet" commissioner's demand for a bribe of $1,000 to allow a fight in Madison Square Garden caused the New York legislature to end exhibitions. Fans backed the winner, Democrat Al Smith, who found a way to create real boxing.[9]

Pro boxing made gains, but some states waited for the 1930s before authorizing the sport. In January, Iowa's lower house favored boxing because the "boys coming back from the army are all in favor of the sport." But in March it buried a proposal to create a commission for the no-decision form, 41 to 59.[10]

After the Armistice, a "Law and Order" brigade (Protestant ministers), writing to Baker, called a game between two army camps on a Sunday a "disgrace" to the "decent people of Iowa." In May '18, the D.C. press linked a decision to allow pro ball on the Sabbath to the "sacrifices" of soldiers and sailors. One reporter classified the "fanatics and bigots" who opposed this reform as "alien enemies." Griffith arranged a game with Cleveland on Sunday, won by the Senators 1–0 in 12 innings, before over 15,000 paying customers, 2,000 soldiers and sailors coming in for free.[11]

In September '19, ministers demanded the arrest of the Brattleboro (Vermont) Athletics, who played at the fair grounds on a Sunday. When the manager and owner of the accused team called for the arrest of golfers and those who transacted business that day, a pitcher, a golfer and a businessman went to trial. The state attorney insisted that although the 1787 law might run against prevailing sentiment, one could not play sports or conduct business on Sunday. The defense claimed (1) the state had not proved a game took place (the state attorney said it wasn't "a prayer meeting"); (2)

the law dated from fifty years before baseball existed; (3) all receipts went to the Knights of Columbus; (4) doctors told a witness who was gassed three times fighting in at least five different major battles to exercise in the "open air." The prosecutor and judge declared these arguments irrelevant, the defense taking exception to each decision. The trial before jurors from neighboring towns failed to produce a verdict, whereupon the ministers called for an "indefinite suspension," hoping the legislature would rewrite the statute sanctifying Sunday. The state attorney withdrew charges, a reporter declaring an "armistice" on an issue that "stirred up public feeling more than anything else which has happened here in recent years."[12]

In May '19, N.Y. City started major league play on Sundays when the mayor approved an action by alderman allowed by the state. The Southern League now had games on Sunday in Tennessee, the state court accepting the argument that the government could not apply an old law against something that did not exist at the time said law was passed (1803). A Methodist minister, the president of Boston University testified before a legislative committee that he was protecting the interests of those in the military from his university in preventing the Braves and Red Sox from playing on Sunday. His efforts succeeded. Boston, Philadelphia and much of the South would have to wait several years for changes in the law.[13]

The Protestant backlash can also be seen in matters relating to gambling on horse races. General Wood, who had ridden in pursuit of Comanches, stressed the value of horses and called for retaining racing during the war. Another general in '18 blamed the shortage of horses so vital to the Allies on "hostile legislation against horse racing … the most alluring … and wholesome of outdoor sports and pastimes." "Mechanical contrivances" might have changed modern warfare, but army officers would not overlook possible future uses for thoroughbreds—thus the need for legalized betting. When Kentucky's racing commission considered discontinuing during the war, the War Department, particularly the remount service, objected. They considered racing a necessity to keep the army supplied with horses as well as a diversion. In contrast, the Santa Monica Bay Ministerial Union complained to the War Department for locating a camp too near Tia Juana, known for its "sin and iniquity" and racetrack gambling.[14]

Elements of the Protestant clergy had serious issues with gambling at horse races or other sports, playing sports on Sundays and prize fighting. It was almost as if the gains made for prohibition during the war were somehow offset by ground lost on the other three issues.

The war also raised questions about amateurism. In 1916, a Richmond association under rules of the Amateur Athletic Federation, considered banning anyone who played with or against ex-pros. Richmond College agreed not to let students who earned income supervising city playgrounds play against Federation teams. "Not content with its dictatorship in local athletics, the Richmond Amateur Athletic Federation is now trying to meddle in collegiate sports," a local reporter grumbled. The local commission gave up Federation ties in '17, even inviting the Richmond Grays, a semi-pro nine but with a military connection, to play league games. Reporters praised the military for spurning efforts by the Amateur Athletic Union to control sports in army camps.[15]

Americans learned lessons that would be applied in World War II in the political realm with acceptance of an international approach with the United Nations and in the economic, with a G.I. Bill of Rights to cushion a post-war recession. In the athletic realm, instead of letting religious organizations have access to training camps and near battlefields, the military relied on the United Service Organization (USO) for entertainment and took care of athletics itself. Even though a second war required four times as many to serve and losses were greater, major league baseball ran four full seasons. A dozen minor leagues survived through 1945, compared to one in '18. The National Football League survived, although a team or two changed locations. Most major horse races continued, while the Indianapolis Speedway closed, as in the first war. The National Basketball League (centered in the Midwest) got through World War II while the Eastern Basketball League and other associations gave up in the first one. West Point and the Naval Academy competed against each other during the second war, unlike in the first one. Doubtless many other differences or similarities can be detected but it is also clear that those who lived through the Great War and carried on through ensuing times had the ability to adjust to new circumstances.

Appendix: Records, 1916-1919

Baseball

Western Conference (Big 9/10)

1916—Ill. 8-1 (14-3); Ohio St 4-2 (13-2); Purdue 6-5 (12-7); Ind. 4-3 (8-6); Chi 5-4 (12-6) Iowa 2-4 (9-6); Wisc. 4-6 (14-8); N-western 1-9
1917—Ohio St 6-1 (16-1); Ill. 8-3 (12-7); Ind. 5-4 (5-9); N-western 4-4; Iowa 3-5 (4-6); Purdue 3-6 (5-7) Chicago 2-8 (8-10); Wisc. 0-0 (5-1)
1918—Mich. 9-1 (15-1); Ill. 7-3 (14-4); Ohio St 3-2 (8-4); Chi 6-5 (8-5); Iowa 2-3 (7-5); Wisc. 1-5 (3-8) Purdue 1-5 (6-7); Ind. 0-5 (9-7)
1919—Mich. 9-0 (13-1); Ill. 7-4 (10-5); Iowa 5-3 (10-6); Chi. 5-4 (7-6); Ohio St 2-2 (8-3); Ind. 2-5 (13-9) Wisc. 1-6 (7-7); Purdue 0-7 (3-11) overall in parenthesis

Pacific Coast Conference

1916—California 3-0 (13-11-2); Oregon 4-4 (6-6); Oregon Aggies 5-6 (9-9-1); Washington 3-5 (4-5)
1917—Washington 5-0 (7-0); Cal 0-0 (12-8-1); Ore. 0-2 (0-9); Ore. Aggies 0-3 ("abandoned" due to war)
1918—Oregon 6-2 (10-2); Cal. 3-1 (4-4-1); Stanford 1-3 (7-9-1); Ore. Aggies 2-6 (4-6), Washington ("abolished)
1919—Washington 10-0 (10-0); Stanford 2-0 (5-3-1); Ore. Aggies 5-6 (6-7); Washington St 1-5 (10-6) Ore. 1-6 (2-6); Cal. 0-2 (8-5)

Southwest Conference

1916—Texas 10-3 (15-7); Baylor 6-4 (14-7); Texas. A&M 8-7 (17-8); S-western 4-7 (7-10); Rice 2-9
1917—Tex. 4-1 (12-3); Tex. A&M 2-4 (9-5-3); Baylor 1-2 (3-4-1)
1918—Tex. 8-1 (17-4); Tex. A&M 4-4 (14-5); Baylor 1-6 (3-11); Rice 0-2 (6-8)
1919—Tex. 12-0 (21-4); Tex. A&M 4-4 (8-10-2); Baylor 3-5 (7-11); SMU 2-6 (4-10); Okla. St 1-3 (3-10) Okla. 1-5 (6-7)

Basketball

Eastern Intercollegiate

1917—Yale 9–1; Princeton 8–2; Penn 5–5; Dartmouth 4–6, Columbia 3–7, Cornell 1–9

1918—Penn. 9–1, Princeton (8–2), Cornell (7–3), Yale (4–6), Columbia (2–8), Dartmouth (0–10)

1919—Penn. 7–1 (15–1); Yale 4–2 (7–2); Cornell 2–3; Princeton 2–5 (5–5); Columbia 2–6 (3–7)

Western Conference (Big 9/ Big 10)

1917—Minn. 10–2; Ill. 10–2; Purdue 7–2; Wisc. 9–3; Ind. 3–5; Chi 4–8; Ohio. St 3–9; N-western 2–10 Iowa 1–8

1918—Wisc. 9–3; Minn. 7–3; N-western 5–3; Ill. 6–6; Chi. 6–6; Purdue 5–5; Ohio St 5–5; Ind. 3–3; Iowa 4–6 Mich. 0–10

1919—Minn.10–0 (13–0); Chi. 10–2 (21–6); N-western 6–4 (6–6); Mich. 5–4 (18–6); Ill. 5–7 (6–8) Ind. 4–6 (9–8); Purdue 4–7 (6–8); Iowa 4–7 (8–7); Ohio 2–6 (7–12); Wisc. 3–9 (5–11)

Missouri Valley Conference

1917—Kan. St 10–2 (15–2); Mo. 10–4 (12–4); Iowa St 6–4 (12–6); Kan. 9–7 (12–8); Neb. 4–8 (12–10) Washington 1–11 (6–13); Drake 0–4 (5–7)

1918—Mo. 15-(17–1); Kan. St 10–5 (12–5); Kan. 9–8 (10–8); Wash. 4–8 (9–8); Ncb. 4–5 (7–7) 1 Iowa St 1–6 (6–9); Drake 0–10 (1–15)

1919—Kan. St 10–2 (17–2); Mo. 11–3 (14–3); Neb. 10–6 (10–6); Grinnell 5–3 (6–5); Kan. 5–9 (7–9); Iowa St 3–8 (5–11) Washington 2–8 (9–9); Drake 2–9 (10–18)

Northwest Conference

1917—(1) Washington St; (2) Ore. Aggies; (3) Whitman; (4) Washington; (5) Idaho; (6) Mont. U; (7) Ore.

1918—(1) Idaho; (2) Washington St; (3); (4) Montana; (5); (6) Whitman; (7) Washington St; (8) Washington

1919—(1) Oregon; (2) Idaho; (3) Washington St; (4) Whitman; (5) Oregon St

Cal-Nevada League

1918—(1) St Mary's; (2) Stanford; (3) Cal; (4) Nevada; (5) Davis; (6) St Ignatius; (7) Coll. of Pacific

1919—(1) Santa Clara (2) Cal tie; (3) St Ignatius (4) St Mary's (5) Davis; (6) Nev. (7) Coll. of Pacific

Pacific Coast Conference

1917—Washington St 8–1; Cal 5–1; Wash. 7–5; Oregon St 7–6; Stanford 0–6; Ore. 0–8

1919—Oregon 11–3; Washington St 7–5; Cal 2–2; Washington 5–7; Oregon St 3–9; Stanford 0–2

Football

South Atlantic Conference

1916—VPI 4-0 (7-2); Md. St 4-0 (6-2); G-town 2-0 (9-1); W & Lee 1-0 (5-2-2); Catholic 2-1 (4-4) Va. 2-1 (4-5); UNC 2-1 (5-4); G. Wash. 1-1 (3-3-1); Richmond 2-1 (5-4-2); Davidson 1-2 (5-3-1) Hopkins 0-3 (3-6); St John's 1-2 (2-5-1); VMI 1-5 (4-5); W & Mary 0-2-1 (2-4-2); N.C. A&E 0-4 (2-5)

1917—G-town 2-0 (8-1); Richmond 2-1 (4-2-1); W & Lee 2-1 (4-3); Md. St 3-1-1 (5-3-1) N.C. A&E 3-1-1 (6-2-1); VPI 2-1-1 (6-2-1); St John's 1-1 (4-3); Davidson 1-2 (6-4); VMI 1-3-1(4-4-1) Hopkins 0-2 (1-6-2); W & Mary 0-3 (3-5)

1918—VPI 4-0 (7-0); Davidson 2-0 (2-1-1); Md. St 3-0-1 (4-2-1); Richmond 1-0 (3-1-1); G-town 0-0 (3-2) Hopkins 1-0-1 (1-1-1); N.C. St 0-1 (1-3); St John's 0-2 (2-3); Catholic 0-1 (0-1-2); W & Lee 0-2 (1-3) W & Mary 0-2 (0-3); VMI 0-2 (2-4); St John's 0-3 (1-3)

1919—G-town 2-0 (7-3); Md. St 4-1 (5-4); N C St 3-1 (7-2); UNC 3-1 (4-3-1); W & Lee 2-1 (8-1) VMI 4-2 (6-2); Hopkins 0-1-1 (5-3-1); Richmond 2-2-1 (5-2-2); VPI 2-4 (5-4); Va. 1-2-1 (2-5-2) St John's 0-1-1 (3-1-2); W & Mary 1-3 (3-6-1); Catholic 0-1 (1-6-1); Davidson 0-4 (4-6-1)

Southern Intercollegiate

1916—Ga. Tech 5-0 (8-0-1); Tenn. 6-0-1 (8-0-1); Vanderbilt 4-1-1 (7-1-1); Ala. Poly. 6-2 (6-2) Citadel 3-1 (6-1-1); LSU 3-1-1 (7-1-2); Ga. 4-2 (6-3); Tulane 2-1-1 (4-3-1); Ky. 2-1-2 (4-1-2); Ala. 4-3 (6-3) Miss. A&M 4-4 (4-4-1); Sewanee 2-2-2 (5-2-2); Transylvania 2-2 (2-2-); Miss. Coll. 2-3 (4-3) S. Carolina 2-3 (2-7); Clemson 2-4 (3-6); Furman 1-4 (4-3); Centre 0-1-2 (5-1-3); Louisville 0-2-1 (2-3-1) Howard 0-1 (0-1); Wofford 1-2 (2-7); Mercer 0-3 (1-6); Chattanooga 1-4;(3-5); Fla. 0-4 (0-5); Miss. 0-6 (3-6)

1917—Ga. Tech 4-0 (9-0); Auburn 5-1 (6-2-1); Clemson 5-1 (6-2); Centre 1-0 (7-1); Miss. A&M 3-1 (7-1) Sewanee 3-1-1 (4-1-2); Ala. 3-1-1 (5-2-1); Tulane 2-1- (5-3); Vanderbilt 3-2; (5-3); LSU 2-3 (3-5) South Carolina 2-3 (3-5); Wofford 1-2 (5-4); Furman 1-3 (3-5); Fla. 1-4 (2-4); Miss. 1-4 (1-4-1) Howard (Samford) 0-2-1 (1-3); The Citadel 0-2 (3-3); Miss. Coll. 0-4 (0-5)

1918—Ga. Tech 3-0 (6-1); Vanderbilt 2-0 (4-2); Miss A&M 2-0 (3-2); Clemson 3-1 (5-2); Furman 1-3; (3-5-1) Citadel 0-1-1 (0-3-1); Sewanee 0-1 (4-2); Wofford 0-2 (0-3); Auburn 0-2 (2-5); Miss. 0-2 (1-3)

1919—Aub. 5-1 (8-1); Centre 2-0; (9-0); Ala. 6-1 (8-1); Miss. A&M 5-2 (6-2); Ky. 3-1-1 (3-4-1) Ga. Tech 2-1 (7-3); Ga. 4-2-2 (4-2-3); Furman 2-1-1 (6-2-1); Tulane 3-2-1 (6-2-1); Vanderbilt 3-1-2 (5-1-2) Fla. 2-2 (5-3); Wofford 1-1 (3-2-1); G-town Coll. 1-2 (4-3) Miss. 1-4 (4-4); Sewanee 1-4 (3-6) Tenn. 0-3-2 (3-3-3); S. Carolina 0-4 (1-7-1); Transylvania 0-2 (2-4); Mercer 0-1 (0-2);Miss. Coll. 0-4 (3-5-1) Howard 0-4 (3-5-2)

Western Conference (Big 9/Big 10)

1916—Ohio St 4-0 (7-0); N-western 4-1 (6-1); Minn. 3-1 (6-1); Chi 3-3 (3-4); Ill. 2-2-1 (3-3-1) Wisc. 1-2-1 (4-2-1); Iowa 1-2 (4-3); Ind. 0-3-1 (2-4-1); Purdue 0-4-1 (2-4-1)

1917—Ohio St 4-0 (8-0-1); Minn. 3-1 (4-1); Wisc. 3-2 (4-2-1); N-western 4-2

(5-2); Ill. 2-2-1 (5-2-1) Chi 2-2-1 (3-2-1); Ind. 1-2 (5-2); Mich. 0-1 (8-2); Iowa 0-2 (3-5); Purdue 0-4 (3-4)

1918—Ill. 4-0 (5-1-1); Mich. 2-0 (5-0); Purdue 1-0 (3-3); 2 Iowa 2-1 (6-2-1); Minn. 2-1 (5-2-1) N-western 1-1 (2-2-1) Wisc. 1-2 (3-3); Ind. 0-0 (2-2); Ohio St 0-3 (3-3); Chi. 0-5 (4-6-1)

1919—Ill. 6-1(6-1); Ohio St 3-1 (6-1); Chi. 4-2 ((5-2); Minn. 3-2 (4-2-1); Wisc. 3-2 (5-2); Iowa 2-2 (5-2) Mich. 1-4 (3-4); N-western 1-4 (2-5); Indiana 0-2 (3-4); Purdue 0-3 (2-4-1)

Missouri Valley Intercollegiate Conference

1916—Neb. 3-1 (6-2); Mo. 3-1-1 (6-1-1); Iowa St 2-1-1 (5-2-1); Kan. St 1-1-1 (6-1-1) Kan. 1-2-1 (4-3-1); Drake 1-3 (3-5); Washington 0-2 (3-3-1)

1917—Neb.2-0 (5-2); Kan. 3-1 (6-2); Iowa St 3-1 (5-2); Kan. St 2-2 (6-2); Mo. 2-4 (3-5); Washington 1-2 (4-3) Drake 0-3 (5-2)

1918—Washington 2-0 (6-0); Kan. St 1-1 (4-1); Drake 0-1 (3-2); Kan. 1-1 (2-2); Neb. 1-1 (2-3-1) Iowa St. 0-1 (0-2) no official winner

1919—Mo. 4-1-1 (5-1-2); Iowa St 3-1-1 (5-2-1); Neb. 2-1 (3-3-2); Drake 2-2 (4-3); Kan. 1-1-1 (3-2-3) Washington 2-2 (5-2); Kan. St 0-3-1 (4-5-1); Grinnell 0-3 (1-4-1)

The Southwestern Intercollegiate Athletic Conference

1916—Tex. 6-1 (7-2); Baylor 3-1 (9-1); Rice 2-1 (6-1-2); Okla. 2-1 (7-5); Tex. A&M 1-2 (6-3) Ark. 0-2 (4-4); Okla. A&M 0-3 (4-4) S-western 0-3 (3-5-1)

1917—Tex. A&M 3-0 (8-0); Baylor 2-1 (9-1); Rice 1-1 (8-1) Okla. 1-1-1 (6-4-1); Tex. 2-4 (4-4) Okla. A&M 1-2 (4-5); Ark. 0-1-1 (5-1-1)

1918—Tex. 4-0 (9-0); Okla. 1-0 (6-0); Rice 1-1 (1-4-2); Ark. 0-1 (4-2); Okla. A&M 0-2 (4-2); SMU 1-2 (3-3) Baylor 0-2 (0-6)

1919—Tex. A&M 4-0 (10-0); Rice 3-1 (8-1); Okla. 2-1 (5-2-3); Tex. 3-2 (6-3); Ark. 1-2 (3-4) Okla. A&M 0-2 (4-2) Okla. A&M 0-2 (3-3-2); SMU 0-2-1 (5-4-1); Baylor 0-3-1 (5-3-1) *Southwestern a member only in 1916; Rice provisional 1916-1917; SMU joined 1918

Rocky Mountain Conference

1916—Col. Aggies 6-0-1; Colorado College 4-1 (6-1); Denver 3-2 (4-2-1); Utah 2-2 (3-2) Col. Mines 2-2-1 (3-2-1); Wyo. 1-4 (1-4); Colorado 1-5 (1-5-1); Utah Aggies 0-4 (1-5-1)

1917—Denver 4-0 (8-0); Utah St 3-0 (7-0-1); Col. 4-2; (6-2); Col. Mines 2-2 (5-3); Col Coll. 2-3 (3-3) Utah 2-3 (2-4) Col. Aggies 0-6 (0-7-1)

1918—Col. Mines 2-0 (4-0); Denver 3-1 (3-2); Colorado U 1-2 (2-3); Colorado College 1-2 (1-2) Colorado Aggies 0-2 (1-2)

1919—Col Aggies 7-1 (7-1); Utah 4-1 (5-4); Col College 3-1-1 (4-2-1); Utah St 3-2 (5-2); Col. 2-3-1 (2-3-1); Denver 0-4-1 (1-5-1); Col. Mines 0-4-1 (0-4-1) [assumes Wyo. 3-3 (3-5) in league]

Pacific Coast Intercollegiate Athletic Association

1916—Wash. 3-0-1 (6-0-1); Ore. 2-0-1 (7-0-1); Ore. Aggies 0-2 (4-5); Cal 0-3 (6-4-1)

1917—Wash. St 3-0 (6-0-1); Cal 2-1 (4-3-1); Ore. Aggies 1-2-1 (3-2-2); Ore. 1-2 (4-3); Wash. 0-2-1 (1-2-1)
1918—Cal 2-0 (7-2); Ore. 2-1 (4-2); Wash. 1-1 (3-1); Ore. Aggies 0-2 (3-4); Wash. St 0-0 (1-1)
1919—Ore 2-1 (5-2); Wash. 2-1 (5-1); Cal 2-2 (7-2); Wash. St 2-2 (5-2) Stanford 1-1 (4-3) Ore. Aggies 1-3 (4-4-1)

Track and Field

New England Intercollegiate

1916—Dartmouth 50½, Me. 32½, Bowdoin 18, H. Cross 18, MIT 10, Williams 8, Colby 4, Trinity 3, Middlebury 3, Tufts 2, Wesleyan 2, WPI 1
1917—MIT 61; Brown 56; WPI 14; H. Cross and Middlebury 8; Trinity 6; Tufts 5 B.C. 3
1918—MIT 74; Brown 25; H. Cross 13; Bowdoin 13; Williams and Wesleyan 6; B.C. 5; Tufts and Middlebury 2
1919—MIT 37; Wesleyan 19½; Brown 19; N.H. 17½; Williams 11; B.C. 10; Bowdoin 9; H. Cross 8; Me. 6; Amherst 5; Tufts 5; Mass Aggies; Worcester Poly Institute 1

The Middle States (Delaware, New Jersey, New York, Pa.) Intercollegiate

1917—(S. Bethlehem, Pa.) Lafayette 38½; NYU (29); Swarthmore (25¼); Lehigh (18½); Dickinson (15); Del. (12½); Rutgers (6); Gettysburg (5); W & Jefferson (3¼); Stevens (0)
1918—(Easton, Pa.) Lafayette (45); Swarthmore (30¼); Del. (17) (partial)
1919—(Swarthmore, Pa.) Rutgers (48); Swarthmore (33); Lafayette (31+); Muhlenberg (10); Stevens (8+); Del. (8+) NYU (7); Gettysburg (4.17); W & J (3)

Intercollegiate Association of Amateur Athletes of America (IC4A)

1916—Cornell 45; Yale 29; Columbia 22; Stanford 22; Penn 18; Dartmouth 14; Mich. 13; Harvard 11; Princeton 10; Bowdoin 5; Syr. 3; Penn St 2; MIT 1
1918—Cornell 47; Pitt (30), Dartmouth, 26; Princeton 19, Penn 18; MIT 13; Columbia 13; J. Hopkins 5; Lafayette 5; Penn St 5; Amherst 3½; Brown 3; Yale 3 Rutgers 2½; Harvard 2, and Swarthmore 1
1919—Cornell 39½; Penn 29; Mich. 25½; Harvard 23; Dartmouth 14; Yale 13½; Princeton 12; Bowdoin 9 Rutgers 5½; G-town 4; Lafayette 4; Columbia 3 Syr. 3 (21 competed 24 in '16) I

Missouri Valley Conference Outdoors

1917—Mo. 57; Neb 34½; Iowa St 34; Grinnell 18; Kan. 12½; Drake 6; Simpson 1
1918—Mo 62, Neb. 39, Kansas 10, Washington U, 10 Kansas Osteopathy 10; Iowa St 8, Drake 6, Kan. St 6, Baker 5, Fairmount 3+, Westminster 2

Southwestern Intercollegiate Athletic Conference

1916—Tex. 60⅓; Tex. A&M 33⅓; Okla. 17; Okla. A&M 8⅓; Rice 7; Baylor 1

1917—Okla. 56; Okla. A&M (26), Texas (17) Rice (12), SMU (9), Texas A&M (4) and Baylor (2)
1918—Okla. 69; A&M 28; Tex. 20 5/6; SMU 13; Rice 12 Tex. A&M 11 5/6; Baylor 7 later version
1919—Okla. 87 (78); Tex. 34 (37); SMU 16½; Rice 13½; Tex. A&M 9½; Okla. A&M 8; Baylor 5½—different versions

Pacific Coast Conference

1916—California 36; Stanford 31. Ore. Aggies 18; Ore. 12; Santa Clara 11; USC 6 Wash. 5 Wash. St 4 Idaho 2 St Ignatius 1
1919—Cal. 53½; Stanford 38; Washington St 31½; Ore. Aggies 24½; Washington 19½; Ore. 9½

Northwest Conference

1916—Ore. 37; Idaho 29; Ore. Aggies 28; Washington St 22; Whitman 18
1919—Idaho 43; Washington St 41

Chapter Notes

Introduction

1. 2 December 1915, 19 October and 4 November 1916 *N.Y. Times*.
2. 4 December 1917 *Ogden Standard* and 4 January 1917 *Kansas City Times*.
3. 13 June 1917 *Christian Science Monitor* and 15 and 20 January 1917 *Virginian-Pilot*.
4. 9 and 14 October 1916 *El Paso Herald* and 16 June 1916 *N.Y. Times*.
5. 16 December 1916 *Richmond Times Dispatch*, 26 November 1916 and 2 January 1917 *Corpus Christi Caller* and 17 December 1916 *Virginian-Pilot*.
6. 6, 13, 20, 27 November 1916, 18, 22, 23, 25 December 1916 and 2 January 1917 *El Paso Herald*.
7. *The Cactus*, Texas (1917) p. 88 and 29 September 1916 *Dubuque Telegraph Herald*.
8. 24 October and 7 November 1916 *El Paso Herald* and 29 January 1917 *Arizona Republican*.
9. 22 December 1916 *El Paso Herald*.
10. 29 December 1916 *Washington Post*.
11. 4 April 1917 *L.A. Times* and 4 February 1917 *Washington Post*.
12. 6, 27–28 March 1917 *L.A. Times*.

Chapter 1

1. 19 August 1917 *Ledger-Dispatch* (Norfolk), 19 June, 24 September 1917 and 10 May 1918 *L.A. Times*.
2. 3 May 1917 *L.A. Times*, 12, 20 April 1917 *Ledger Dispatch* and 15 April 1917 *Richmond Times Dispatch*.
3. 9 February 1917 *Clinton Herald* (Iowa) and 12 August 1917 *Chicago Tribune*.
4. *The Encyclopedia of Minor League Baseball* (Durham: Baseball America, 1997) pp. 205–211 and 16 May 1917 *Greensboro Daily News*.
5. April–October 1917 *Nashville Globe*.
6. 22 July, 2 September 1917 *Washington Post* and 21, 23 July 1917 *L.A. Times*.
7. *Ball Players in the Great War: Newspaper Accounts of Major Leaguers in World War I Military Service* (Jefferson, N.C.: McFarland, 2013), pp. 90–93; 204–211.
8. 30 July 1917 *L.A. Times*, 23 May, 22 November 1918 *Chattanooga News*, 13 August 1917 *Virginian-Pilot*, 23 November 1917 *Chicago Tribune* and 22 November 1917 *Christian Science Monitor*.
9. 11 October 1917 *Washington Post*.
10. 8 January 1918 *Washington Post*.
11. 6 January 1918 *Chicago Tribune*, 30 June *N.Y. Tribune*, 4 January 1918 *Ball Players*, pp. 129–31
12. 19 August 1918 *Philadelphia Public Ledger*; *Ball Players*, pp. 152–155, 161–63; 26 September 1918 *Sporting News*, 13 August 1918 *Stars and Stripes*.
13. John B. Foster, ed., *Spalding's Official Base Ball Guide: Forty-third Year* (1919) (N.Y.: American Sports Publishing Co., 1919), pp. 127–143, 2 December 1918 *Chicago Tribune* and 26 May 1918 *Atlanta Constitution*.
14. 7 April 1918 *Virginian-Pilot*.
15. 24 May 1918 *L.A. Times*.
16. 28 May 1918 *Atlanta Constitution*.
17. 18 June 1918 *Washington Post*.
18. 22 June 1918 *Christian Science Monitor*.
19. 6 June 1918 *Virginian-Pilot*.
20. 20 July 1918 *Christian Science Monitor*.
21. 5, 9 July 1918 *Christian Science Monitor* and 26 July 1918 *Stars and Stripes*.

22. 20 July 1918 *Virginian-Pilot*, 25 July 1918 *The Sporting News* and 21, 25 July 1918 *Washington Post*.
23. 27 May 1918 *Tacoma Times* and March–Summer 1918 *Nashville Globe*.
24. 24 December 1916 and 30 December 1917 *Washington Herald*.
25. 5 July 1918 *Bemidji Pioneer*.
26. 5 January 1919 *N.Y. Times* and 17 September 1918 *Chicago Tribune*.
27. Alan H. Levy, *Joe McCarthy: Architect of the Yankee Dynasty* (Jefferson, NC: McFarland, 2005), pp. 55–55 and 12 and 16 October 1918 *Ledger-Dispatch*.
28. Rick Huhn, *The Sizzler: George Sisler, Baseball's Forgotten Great* (Columbus: University of Missouri Press, 2004), pp. 73–74; 18 October 1918 *Washington Times* and *Ball Players*, pp. 189–91.
29. 3 October 1918 *Sporting News* and 11 October 1918 *Ledger-Dispatch*.
30. 13 October 1918 *Providence Journal*.
31. 21 October 1918 *Ledger-Dispatch* and 24 February 1919 *Washington Post*.
32. Foster, pp. 295–317, 3 October 1918 *Sporting News* and Marshall Smelser, *The Life That Ruth Built: A Biography* (N.Y.: Quadrangle, 1976), p. 106.
33. 15 August 1918 *Sporting News*.
34. 23 December 1918 *Washington Post*.
35. 5 December 1918 *L.A. Times*.
36. *Ballplayers*, pp. 226–27 and 17 February 1919 *Chicago Tribune*; 7 September 1918 *Washington Times*.
37. 10 April 1919 *Virginian-Pilot* and 6 December 1918 *Washington Post*.
38. *Ball Players*, pp. 38–39.

Chapter 2

1. 8 April, 21 May 1917 *Virginian-Pilot*, 6, 8 April 1917 *Christian Science Monitor* and 7 April 1917 *L.A. Times*
2. *Blue & Gold Yearbook* (1919), p. 169.
3. Edward O. Stiehm, "Athletics in War Time," *Outing* (August 1917), p. 674.
4. *Trinity Ivy* (1920), p. 102.
5. *The Bowdoin Bugle* (1919), p. 162.
6. *The Anselmian*, St. Anselm's (May 1917), p. 30.
7. *The Index* (1919) Mass Aggies, p. 101.
8. 29 May 1918 *Christian Science Monitor*.
9. 11 May 1917 *N.Y. Tribune*.
10. *The Cornellian and Class Book* (1918), p. 509; 30 April 1917 *Hill News* (St. Lawrence) and 8 June 1917 *The Concordien*.
11. 7 April, 12 June 1919 *Washington Post* and 29 May 1918 *Christian Science Monitor*.
12. 29 June 1917 *Denver Post*.
13. *A Record*, Haverford (1918) p. 61 and (1919), p. 9; 28 August 1916, 23 September 1917, 19, 24 August 1919 *N.Y. Times*.
14. *Lanthorn*, Susquehanna (1921), p. 112; *Pandora*, Washington & Jefferson (1919), p. 146, (1920), p. 118 and (1921), p. 127, and 20 May 1919 *Thielesian*, Thiel.
15. *The Comenian*, Muhlenberg (11 April 1917).
16. 7 April, 12 June 1917 *Washington Post*.
17. *The Philomathean Monthly* (April 1918) Bridgewater College, p. 41.
18. 13 May 1917 *Richmond Times Dispatch* and *The Calyx*, Washington & Lee (1920), p. 294.
19. *The Chanticleer*, Trinity (1920), p. 120 and *The Howler*, Wake Forest (1920), p. 154.
20. 19 April 1919 *Washington Herald* and 3 May 1919 *West Virginia Intelligencer*.
21. 24 May 1917 *Fairmont West Virginian*.
22. *The Blue & Gray*, Lincoln Memorial (April-May 1917 and April-May 1918).
23. *Seminole* (1918) University Fla., p. 84.
24. 23 April 1918 *Atlanta Constitution* and *Cyclops*, North Georgia (1919) no pagination.
25. *The Sphinx*, Citadel (1920), p. 155.
26. *Gumbo*, LSU 1918, p. 106.
27. *Redskin* (1919) Okla. A&M, p. 60.
28. *Kaydet*, St. Thomas (1918), p. 120 and (1919), p. 188; *Sagatagan*, St. John's (1919), p. 5; *Viking*, St. Olaf (1919) Image 133 and *Wenonah* Winona Normal (1919), p. 82.
29. *Illio* (1919), p. 260.
30. *Wesleyana* (1919) p. 132; *The McKendrean* (1919) Image 71; *The Decaturian*, Millikin (June 1917), p. 13 and *The Millidek* (1918), p. 120; *Rocketry I*, Augustana (1918), p. 277; *Polyscope*, Bradley (1918), p. 159.
31. 3 May 1918 *The Franklin*.
32. *Tel Buch*, Akron (1918) p. 138; *Reveille*, Kenyon (1920), p. 135 and *The Recensio*, Miami (1919), p. 246
33. *The Zenith*, Simpson (1919), Image

135 and (1920), Image 158, *The Acorn,* Coe (1921), Image 207.
34. *Columbia College Dubuque, Iowa, 1873–1923* (Dubuque: Hardie [1923]), pp. 90–91 and *The Scarlet & Black,* Oberlin (10 May 1917).
35. *The Croaker,* Iowa Wesleyan (1919), Image 92.
36. 8 April, 28 May, 27 July 1917 *Christian Science Monitor* and *Jayhawker,* Kansas (1920), p. 81 and *Royal Purple,* Kansas State (1920), p. 42.
37. *Gray-Maroon,* Bethel (1920), p. 94; *Parnassus,* Fairmount (1917), no pagination; 20 February 1917 *The Ottawan;* and 16 February 1917 *The Topeka State Journal.*
38. *Tatler,* William Jewel (1918), p. 91, *The Rhetor,* Warrensburg (1919), p. 77 and *Sagamore,* Girardeau Normal (1918), p. 98.
39. *Cornhusker,* Nebraska (1920) p. 378, *Blue & Gold Yearbook,* Kearney Normal (1917), p. 170 and *The Peruvian,* Peru Normal (1917).
40. *Utonian* (1918), p. 133.
41. May 1917 *Jamestown Collegian; Pasque,* Northern Normal (1918), p. 107 and 1–7 May 1917 *Mitchell Mirror.*
42. 9 April 1918 *Stanford Daily*
43. *El Rodeo,* USC (1920), p. 272, 6 May 1917 *L.A. Times* and *Metate,* Pomona (1918), p. 60.
44. 13 February 1918 *Evergreen* (Washington State).
45. *Wallulah,* Willamette (1918), p. 159 and (1920), p. 157.

Chapter 3

1. 31 March 1918 *Washington Post* and 31 March, 27 May 1918 *Christian Science Monitor.*
2. Summers, 1918–1919 *The Newport Mirror.*
3. William Robinson, *Forging the Sword: The Story of Camp Devens: New England's Army Cantonment* (Concord N.H., 1920), pp. 144–146.
4. 20 March 1918 *Christian Science Monitor* and 1–8 July 1918 *Providence Evening Bulletin.*
5. 7 July 1918 *N.Y. Times* and *Ballplayers,* pp. 121–22.
6. 10 June 1918 *Norwich Bulletin.*
7. *Ballplayers,* pp. 79–80.
8. Frederick C. Reynolds and William F. McLaughlin, eds., *115th Infantry USA in the World War* (1920), pp. 39, 53, 55, 66, and 67; *The Official History of the 315th Infantry,* comp. Historical Board (1920), pp. 337–342; and *The History of Company C, 314th Field Signal Battalion U.S. Army AEF,* comp. History Committee (Philadelphia: The Shade Printing Co., 1920), p. 5.
9. 4 September 1917 *Washington Times,* 26 May 1918 *Washington Post* and *Ball Players,* pp. 141–145.
10. 17 February and 24 March 1918 *Richmond Times Dispatch,* 26 April 1918 *Bayonet (Trench & Camp).*
11. 15 April *Richmond News Leader (Trench & Camp),* 12 July 1918 *The Bayonet* and 9 July *Richmond Times Dispatch.*
12. 15 April 1919 *N.Y. Times.*
13. 5 September 1919 *Charleston News and Courier.*
14. 4 April 1918 *Sporting News* and 6 June 1918 *Denver Post.*
15. 28 March 1918 *Atlanta Constitution.*
16. 1–31 May 1918 *Atlanta Constitution.*
17. 11 August, 21 September 1918 *Atlanta Constitution.*
18. 5, 13 March, 15 August 1918 *Atlanta Constitution.*
19. 24 February, 3, 22, 24, 25, 30 March, 8 April 1918 "Diary of Bugler Wayne Desilvey," trans. and ed. Phil Reese
20. 8 June, 9 August 1918 *Tampa Daily Times (Trench & Camp).*
21. 14 January 1918 *Chicago Tribune.*
22. John Cutchins and Stewart Scott, *History of the Twenty-ninth Division, "Blue & Gray," 1917–1919* (Philadelphia: MacCallan, 1921), p. 19.
23. *The Red Guidon,* "Soixante Quinze" *Being a complete illustrated history of B Battery, 134th Field Artillery, 1915–1918* (Akron, 1920), pp. 66 and 126.
24. 11 March, 8 July 1918 *New Orleans Picayune (Trench & Camp).*
25. 22 September 1918 *Atlanta Constitution.*
26. 17 March 1918 *N.Y. Times* and *Ball Players* p. 67.
27. July/August 1916, 1–31 July 1917 and July/August 1918 *Bisbee Daily Review.*
28. 19 November 17, 17, 29 December 1917 *El Paso Herald* and 8 August 1918 *Deming Graphic.*
29. 10 June–23 September 1918 *El Paso Herald.*

Notes—Chapter 3

30. 30 March 1918 *Chicago Tribune* and 22 October 1917, 12 August 1918 *El Paso Herald*.
31. 21 September 1918 *N.Y. Times*, 2 September 1918 *Fort Worth Telegram-Star (Trench & Camp)*, October 1918 *Sporting News*, 6 July 1918 *Corpus Christi Caller* and Foster, p. 187.
32. Robert Walston Chubb, *Regimental History, 342nd Field Artillery, 89th Division* (1921), p. 11, *Memoirs of France and the Eighty-Eighth Division*, comp. Edgar J.D. Larson (Minneapolis, 1920), pp. 15, 55 and Foster, p. 186
33. 25 August–3 September 1918 *Omaha Daily Bee*.
34. *History of the 322nd Field Artillery* (N. Haven: Yale University Press, 1920), pp. 175, 411–420, 449; 23 June 1918 *N.Y. Times; Ball Players*, pp. 105–107.
35. Foster, p. 183, 21 April *Chicago Tribune* and October 1918 *Sporting News*.
36. 21 June, 11 August 1918; *Chicago Tribune*, 4 August 1918; *N.Y. Times* and *Ball Players*, pp. 65–67.
37. 7 September 1918 *Christian Science Monitor* and 1 August 1918 *Sporting News*.
38. 19 May 1918 *L.A. Times*, 31 July 1918 *Washington Post*, Alice Henderson, *The Ninety-First: The First at Camp Lewis* (Tacoma: Smith-Kinney Press, 1918), p. 394 and 4 April, 29 May 1918 *Tacoma Times*.
39. 16 August 1917 *L.A. Times*.
40. 15 July, 19 August, 14 September 1918 *L.A. Times*.
41. 10 May 1918 *L. A Times* and *Ball Players*, pp. 14. 67–68 and 77–78.
42. 8, 21 June 1917 *Virginian-Pilot* and 1 July 1917 *Washington Post*.
43. 4 July 1917 *Chicago Tribune*, 11 August 1917 *Virginian-Pilot* and 8 November 1917 *Richmond Times Dispatch*.
44. 12 July 1918 *Christian Science Monitor*.
45. 3, 10 May and 7 June 1918 *Stars and Stripes* and 10, 20 May 1918 *Virginian-Pilot*.
46. 24 May 1918 *Stars and Stripes* and Foster, p. 231.
47. 5 July N Y Times, *Ballplayers*, pp. 200–203 and 4 October 1918 *Chicago Tribune*.
48. 18 August 1918 *Washington Post*.
49. Herman Louser, *The Propeller: 840th Aero Squadron* (1923), pp. 213–224.
50. *The Story of "E" Company, 101st Engineers* (Boston, 1919), p. 90 and 15 May,

16 April 1918 *Chicago Tribune* and James T. Addison, *The Story of the Frist Gas Regiment* (Boston: Houghton-Mifflin, 1919), pp. 29, 35 and 12 May 1918 *L.A. Times*.
51. 5, 19 April, 3 May and 7 June 1918 *Stars and Stripes, The Red Guidon*, pp. 40–41 and William Wright, ed., *A History of the Sixty-Sixth Field Artillery Brigade AEF*, pp. 81, 147, 198.
52. 24 May 1918 *Stars and Stripes* and Foster, p. 231.
53. *An Historical & Technical Biography of the Twenty-first Engineers ...* (N.Y., 1919), p. 122.
54. Henry T. Simpson and George Hull, *The War Story of C. Battery, One Hundred Third U.S. Field Artillery in France, 1917–1919* (Norwood, Mass: Plimpton Press, 1920), pp. 66 and 120
55. 21 June 1918 *Stars and Stripes*, 25 August 1918 *Washington Post* and Desilvey Diary.
56. DeWitt C. Millen, *Memoirs of 591 in the World War* (Ann Arbor, 1932), pp. 46, 59, 60, 62.
57. Jay Lee, *The Artillerymen: Battery E in France, 129th Field Artillery* (Kansas City, 1919) p. 46, James Pollard, *The Forty-Seventh Infantry: A History, 1917, 1918, 1919* (Saginaw, 1919), p. 32, *History of the 58th U.S. Artillery, C.A.C.* (New York, 1919) pp. 22, 23 and 10 November 1918 *L.A. Times*.
58. *A History of the lst U.S. Engineers, Ist U.S. Division* (Coblentz, Germany, 1919), p. 22 and Frederick McKenna, *Battery "A": 103rd Field Artillery in France*, p. 162.
59. Robert Ware Bodfish, et al., *A History of Section 647 US Army Ambulance Service with the French Army*, pp. 14, 23, 37, 44, 89.
60. Charles Dienst, *The History of the 353rd Infantry Regiment* (1921), p. 222 and 25 April 1919; *Ball Players*, p. 82.
61. *Co "A" Twenty-third Engineers AEF* (Chicago 1923, p. 100.
62. 1 Sept 1918 Washington Post and 31 July 1918 Christian Science Monitor.
63. 26 August 1918 *Richmond Times Dispatch*.
64. 8, 15 September 1918 *Richmond Times Dispatch* and 9 November 1918 *L.A. Times*.
65. 22 September 1918 *N.Y. Times*, 26 December 1918 *Sporting News* and *Ball Players*, pp. 213–225.

66. *Ball Players,* p. 9.
67. 3 September, 7 October 1918 and 31 Oct 1919 *Providence Journal,* 22 April 1919 *Virginian-Pilot* and 16 December 1919 *The Arizona Republic.*
68. 2 May 1918 *Christian Science Monitor,* 4 July 1918 *Sporting News* and *Ball Players,* p. 176.
69. Raymond Blaine Fosdick, *Chronicle of a Generation,* pp. 153-54.
70. 17 January 1920 *Ledger Dispatch.*
71. Charles Ryman Herr, Co. F. *History, 319th Infantry* (Flemington, N.J., 1920), pp. 59-60.
72. Ashby Williams, *Experiences of the Great War* (Roanoke: The Stone Printing and Mfg. Co., 1919), p. 195 and *A History of the 313th Field Artillery U.S.A.* (N.Y.: Thomas Y Crowell Co., 1920), pp. 105-110.
73. 28 February, 7, 14 March and 16 May 1919 *Stars and Stripes.*
74. *The 88th Division in the World War of 1914-1918,* pp. 83-84 and Lonnie J. White, *Panthers to Arrowheads: The 36th (Texas-Oklahoma) Division in World War I* (Military History Associates, Inc., 1984), p. 188.
75. U.S. Corps of Engineers *"C" Co. Our Book,* pp. 72-73.
76. Clarence Walton Johnson, *The History of the 321st* (Columbia, S.C.: R.L. Bryan Co. 1919), pp. 7, 83, *History of the Y.M.C.A. in the Le Mans Area* (Portland, Ore., 1920), p. 25, *The Official History of the 315th Infantry,* p. 341, *History of the Sixteenth Engineers (Railway) AEF* (Detroit: La Salle Press, 1939), pp. 320-327 and *History of the 58th U.S. Artillery C.A.C.,* pp. 22, 23, 58-61.
77. 14 May 1918 *L.A. Times.*
78. 26 September 1918 *The Sporting News,* 7 March, 4, 11 April 1919 *Stars and Stripes.*
79. 27 May 1919 *Atlanta Constitution.*
80. 31 March 1919 *Charlotte Observer* and 21 June 1919 *St. Tammany Farmer.*
81. *Ball Players,* pp. 96-97, 110-111, 170-171.
82. Ibid., pp. 100-102, 109, 114-116, 145-150.
83. Ibid., p. 188.

Chapter 4

1. Edward O Stiehm, "Athletics in Wartime," *Outing* (August 1917), p. 675; 6 August 1917 *Virginian-Pilot* and 3 June 1917 *L.A. Times.*
2. 5 November 1917 *Tacoma Times.*
3. *Outing,* p. 724; 22 August 1917 *Washington Post,* 12, 13 July, 22 November 1917 *Christian Science* Monitor, 29 May 1917 *Butte Daily Post.*
4. 22 November 1917 *Christian Science Monitor,* 18 November 1917 *Virginian-Pilot,* 29 October 1917 *Washington Post* and 21 January 1918 *Grand Forks Herald.*
5. 19 September 1918 *Sporting News.*
6. 13 September 1918 *L.A. Times* and 3 October 1918 *Providence Journal.*
7. 9 October 1918 *Ledger-Dispatch* (Norfolk).
8. 19 October 1918 *Ledger-Dispatch.*
9. 22 April 1917 *Richmond Times Dispatch,* 14 April 1917 *Virginian-Pilot* and *Trinity Ivy* (1920), p. 100.
10. *The Mirror,* Bates (1919) pp. 93, 173 and *The Prism,* Maine (1920), p. 135 and 213.
11. 12 October 1917 *Christian Science Monitor.*
12. *Guilielmensian,* Williams, 1920 and earlier yearbooks.
13. 26 November 1918 and 30 September 1919 *Boston University News* and *The Hub* (1921), p. 198.
14. *The Aftermath,* WPI (1919), p. 115.
15. *Salmagundi,* Colgate (1920) p. 169 and *Pedagogue,* Albany State Teachers College (1917), p. 170
16. 19 February 1918 *N.Y. Times.*
17. 1 December 1917 *Christian Science Monitor* and *Scarlet Letter,* Rutgers (1920), p. 144.
18. *Epitome,* Lehigh (1918) p. 362, 11 July 1917 *N.Y. Times* and *The Thielensian* (1918 and 1919).
19. 2 December 1918 *Bridgeport Times and Evening Farmer.*
20. 16 December 1917 *N.Y. Times,* 4 December 1917 *Richmond Times Dispatch* and 10 October 1918 *Washington Post.*
21. 17 August 1917 *Virginian-Pilot,* 15 July 1917 *Chicago Tribune,* 17 August 1917 *Christian Science Monitor,* 17 September 1917 *N.Y. Times.*
22. *The Halcyon,* Swarthmore (1919), p. 213 and (1920), p.185 and *A Record,* Haverford (1918), p. 61
23. 3 February 1918 *N.Y. Times.*
24. *Instano,* Indiana (1919), p. 140 and

(1920), pp.147–151 and *Carontawan*, Mansfield (1919), p. 130.

25. *The Normal School Herald* (January 1917), p. 29 and (January 1918), p. 24 and *The Cumberland*, Shippensburg (1919), p. 111.

26. John M. Carroll, *Fritz Pollard: Pioneer in Racial Advancement* (Urbana: University of Illinois Press, 1992), pp. 120–125.

27. 16 September, 6; 13 October 1918 *Washington Post*.

28. 24 September, 29 November 1917 *Richmond Times Dispatch* and *Kaleidoscope*, Hampden-Sydney (1918), p. 81.

29. *The Yellow Jacket Record*, Randolph-Macon (1919) p. 178.

30. *The ERA* (January/February 1916), p. 218, (November 1916), p. 39 and (October 1917), p. 55.

31. 7 January 1917 *Richmond Times Dispatch* and *Corks and Curls*, University of Virginia (1919), pp. 265–66.

32. 24 June 1917; 7 September; 27 October 1918; 2 April 1919 *Richmond Times Dispatch*; 17 November 1918 *Virginian-Pilot*.

33. *Calyx*, W & L (1919), p. 116.

34. 17 January 1919 *The Cadet*.

35. 11 March 1918 *Atlanta Constitution* and *Chanticleer*, Trinity (1920), p. 135.

36. *The Agromeck*, N.C. State (1919), p. 194 and (1920), p. 232 and 10 November 1919 *Richmond Times Dispatch*.

37. *Murmurmontis*, W.V. Wesleyan (1921), pp. 193–200 and *Monticola*, West Virginia (1920), p. 226.

38. *The Kentuckian*, Kentucky (1919), p. 147.

39. *The Volunteer*, Tennessee (1920), pp. 120–22.

40. *Cap & Gown*, University of the South (1918), p. 68.

41. *The Centennial* Chilowean, Maryville (1919), pp. 160–170 and *Lest We Forget* (1920), Image 181.

42. 23 November 1917 *Nashville Globe*.

43. *Oshihiyi*, Stetson (1920), p. 119.

44. 2 November, 1 December 1917 *Atlanta Constitution* and 27 October–1 November 1917 *Philadelphia Evening Ledger*.

45. *Yamacraw*, Oglethorpe (1920), Image 118 and *Cyclops*, North Georgia Agricultural College (1919), Image 72

46. 17 October 1919 *Orange & Black*, Mercer.

47. *The Jambalaya*, Tulane (1919), p. 322.

48. *The Reveille*, Mississippi A&M, pp. 235 and 245–47 and *Ole Miss* (1919), pp. 101–105.

49. *L-Allegro*, Mississippi College (1919), p. 86.

50. 4 and 6 September 1919 *Charleston News and Courier* and *Taps*, Clemson (1919), p. 136.

51. 15 April 1917 *Chicago Tribune*; 10, 19 September 1917 *Christian Science Monitor*.

52. 19 September 1917 *Christian Science Monitor*, 5 November 1917 *L.A. Times* and *Gopher*, Minn. (1920), pp. 64 and 174.

53. 23 December 1917 *Chicago Tribune*.

54. 4 November 1918 *Rock Island Argus*.

55. 13 September 1918 *Washington Post*, 2 October 1918 *Christian Science Monitor*, 4 June *Chicago Tribune*.

56. 4 November 1918 *Rock Island Argus*.

57. *Arbutus*, Indiana (1920), p. 59.

58. 1 October 1918 *Denver Post; Hawkeye* (1920), pp. 212–223 and 3 December 1918 *Chicago Tribune*.

59. *Ravelings*, Monmouth (1921), p. 87.

60. 22 Nov 1918 *The Stentor*.

61. *Retrospect*, Shurtleff (1918), p. 26 and *The Rambler*, Carthage (1920), p. 104.

62. *Sargasso*, Wabash (1920) p. 61 and Katharine M. Graydon, *Butler College in the World War* (Indianapolis: Alumni Association, 1922), p. 58.

63. *Athena*, Ohio University (1919), p. 193.

64. *The Unionian* (1918) p. 89; *The Sybil*, Otterbein (1919), pp. 104–105 and *Hi-Hi-Ho*, Oberlin (1920), pp. 255–56.

65. *Milestone*, Hope (1918), p. 78 and (1919), p. 79.

66. 26 September, 7 November 1918 *Alma Record*.

67. *Viking*, St. Olaf (1919), Image 136.

68. *Gustavian*, Gustavus-Adolphus (1917), p. 178.

69. *Hilltop*, Marquette (1920), p. 160.

70. *Periscope*, Eau Claire Normal (1917) and (1918), no pagination.

71. 14 September, 22 November 1917 *Christian Science Monitor*.

72. *The Key*, Dubuque University (1919), p. 97 and (1921), p. 111.

73. *Alla Rah*, College of Emporia 1919, p. 74.

74. *Parnassus*, Fairmount Normal (1918), p. 70 and (1919), pp. 31 and 67;

(October 1916) *Parnassus* 1918; 7 December 1919 *N.Y. Tribune*, *The Ottawan* (campus newspaper) (1919), p. 6.
75. 14 March 1918 *Virginian-Pilot*.
76. *Sagamore*, Cape Girardeau Normal (1920), Image 67.
77. *The Rhetor*, Warrensburg State Normal (1919), pp. 74–79.
78. *Coyote*, Nebraska Wesleyan (1918), p. 116 and *Gateway*, Peru Normal (1919), no pagination.
79. *The Ouachitonian*, Ouachita Baptist College (1920), pp. 114–120.
80. 19 December 1918 *The Vista*, Central State Normal.
81. 5 June 1918 *Tulsa Daily World*.
82. *The Trail*, Daniel Baker College (1920), p. 104.
83. *The Mirage*, University of New Mexico (1918), p. 57 and 9 December 1917 *Denver Post*.
84. 11 August, 2 October 1917 *L.A. Times*.
85. *The Pikes Peak Nugget*, Colorado College (1919), pp. 32, 85 and 6 Dec 1918 *Denver Post*.
86. 1 November 1919 *Denver Post*.
87. *Artemisia*, Nevada (1919) p. 135.
88. *Gem of the Mountains* (1920), p. 116.
89. *The Poly*, Billings Poly (1919) p. 99 and *Prickly Pear*, Montana Wesleyan (1918) Image 31.
90. (October 1915) p. 1; (December 1915), p. 7; (November 1916), p. 10; (December 1916), p. 5; (January 1918), p. 9 *Jamestown Collegian*
91. 21 September 1916 *Mitchell Capital*.
92. *Coyote*, University of South Dakota (1921), p. 121.
93. *Blue & Gold Yearbook*, California (1917) p. 146 and (1919), p. 179.
94. Roberta Park, "From Football to Rugby—and Back, 1906–1919: The University of California-Stanford University Response to the 'Football Crisis of 1905,'" *Journal of Sport History* (Winter 1984): 34–38.
95. 14, 21, 15 October, 26 December 1918 *L.A. Times*.
96. 17, 30 October, 11 November, 12 December 1917 *The Polygram*.
97. *Tyee*, Washington (1919), p. 88.
98. 15 February, 13 December 1918 and 22 February 1919 *Pullman Herald*.
99. *Oregana*, Oregon (1919), pp. 133–139.
100. 15 June 1919 *N.Y. Times* and 15 February 1919 *Atlanta Constitution*.

Chapter 5

1. 12 November 1917 *Chicago Tribune*.
2. 3–30 November 1919 *Lake County Times*.
3. 25 November 1918 *Rock Island Argus*.
4. 29 October 1917 *Washington Post* and 28 November 1917 *Weekly Journal Miner* (Prescott, AZ).
5. *Regimental History, Three Hundred and Forty-First Field Artillery* (Kansas City: Union Bank Note Co.), pp. 51, 65 and 4 September 1917 *Washington Times* and *Memoirs of France and the Eighty-Eighth Division*, comp. Edgar J.D. Larson (Minneapolis, 1920), pp. 15, 55.
6. 24 March 1918 *Chicago Tribune*.
7. *An Historical & Technical Biography of the Twenty-first Engineers* (N.Y., 1919), p. 121 and 10 October 1918 *Christian Science Monitor*.
8. *History of the 322nd Field Artillery* (New Haven: Yale University Press, 1920).
9. 2 December 1917 *Chicago Tribune* and 20 September, 16 October 1918 *Christian Science Monitor*.
10. 13 Dec 1918 *Christian Science Monitor*.
11. 11 November 1917 *Atlanta Constitution*, 23 November 1917 *Virginian-Pilot* and 29 May 1918 *Richmond Times Dispatch*.
12. 3 November 1918 *Atlanta Constitution*.
13. 8 December 1918 *Washington Post*.
14. 11, 18 November 1917 *Pensacola Journal* and 26 November 1918 *The News Scinitar* (Memphis).
15. F.C. Reynolds and William P. McLaughlin, *115th Infantry U.S.A. in the World War* (1920), p. 53.
16. 24 August 1917 *Christian Science Monitor*.
17. 16–29 November 1918 *Corpus Christi Caller*.
18. Earl B. Gansser, *History of the 126th Infantry in the War with Germ*any (Grand Rapids, 1920), p. 33, *Red Arrow: Thirty-Second Division: History and Facts*, p. 7; Roy Hollingsworth, *10,000 Miles with the 125th Infantry Supply Train*, p. 24, 12

and 19 November 1917 *Fort Worth Telegram Star* (*Trench & Camp*).
19. 9, 30 November 1917 *El Paso Herald* and *Deming Graphic*.
20. 6 October-26 December 9 *El Paso Herald*.
21. 30 November *Deming Graphic* and 28, 29 November 1918 *El Paso Herald*.
22. 14 October, 2, 9, 16, 23, 30 December 1918 and 6 January 1919 *El Paso Herald*.
23. 16 December, 6 January 1919 *El Paso Herald* and 17 January 1919 *Columbus Courier*.
24. Fredrick Strong, *History of the Fortieth (Sunshine) Division* (Los Angeles: C.S. Huston & Co., 1920), p. 165, 11 October 1917 and 11 February 1918 *L.A. Times*.
25. 30 Jan 1918 *Tacoma Times* and Henderson, *The Ninety-First: The First at Camp Lewis* (Tacoma: Smith-Kinney Co., 1918), p. 398.
26. 8, 23 November 1917 *L.A. Times*.
27. 3 December 1917 *Christian Science Monitor*.
28. 16 November-9 December 1918 *Washington Herald*.
29. 15 October-27 December 1918 and 3 January 1919 *Bayonet* (*Trench & Camp*).
30. 29 November 1917 *Newport News Herald* and 24 November 1917 *Richmond Times Dispatch*.
31. 30 November 1917 *Richmond Times Dispatch* and 10 December 1917, 5 September 1918 *Christian Science Monitor*.
32. William Robinson, *Forging the Sword: The Story of Camp Devens*: New England's Army Cantonment (Concord N.H., 1920), pp. 144-146.
33. 30 Nov-12 December 1917 *Honolulu Star-Bulletin*.
34. 23 December 1917 *Richmond Times Dispatch*.
35. 7 November 1918 *Providence Journal* and 9 December 1917 *Washington Post*.
36. 11 November 1918 *Providence Journal* and 2, 11 November and 2, 9 December 1918 *Christian Science Monitor*.
37. 23 September 1917 Norfolk *Ledger Dispatch*.
38. 27-30 November 1919 *Virginian-Pilot* and 28 November 1919 *N.Y. Times*.
39. 29 November 1918 *Pensacola Journal*.
40. *Our Navy* (March 1918) p. 56 and subsequent issues.

41. 28 November 1918 *New York Times*, 16 December 1917 *Virginian-Pilot*, 26 October, 9, 16 and 28 November 1919 *N.Y. Times*.
42. 3 December 1918 *Chicago Tribune*.
43. 15 December 1918 *L.A. Times*.
44. 19 August, 11 October, 7 and 26 November 1918 *L.A. Times*.
45. 2 January 1919 *L.A. Times*.
46. James T. Duane, *Dear Old 'K'* (Boston, 1922), pp. 21-24.
47. Frederic R. Kilner, *Battery E. in France, 149th Field Artillery, 42nd Division* (Chicago, 1919), p. 18.
48. 3, 10 March 1918 *Chicago Tribune*.
49. James Bennett Nolan, *Reading Militia in the Great War* (Reading, 1921) pp. 43-44, 17 May 1918 *Norfolk Ledger-Dispatch* and 30 November 1917 *Clinch Valley News*.
50. 3 September 1918 *Richmond Times Dispatch*.
51. James Ross and Noel B. Heath, *History of Co. E, 355th Infantry* (Omaha: Waters-Barnhardt Print Co.) p 27, *331st Field Artillery* (Chicago: Rogers Printing Co., 1919), pp. 48, 111, 250, 424 and *Memoirs of France and the Eighty-eighth Division*, comp. Edgar Larson (Minneapolis, 1920), pp. 15 and 55.
52. *Story of the Forty-Seventh Coast Artillery* (Baltimore: George W. King Printing Co., 1919) pp. 9, 44, 56, 62, 63, 66, 83, 84 and *History of the 318th Infantry Regiment of the 80th Division, 1917-1919* (Richmond: The William Byrd Press, 1919), pp. 92-104.
53. *The Story of "E" Company, 101st Engineers, 26th Division* (Boston, 1919) pp. 47, 118 and Benjamin Allison Colonna, *The History of Company B., 311th Infantry in the World War* (Freehold, N.J., 1922) p. 30.
54. *Being the Narrative of Battery A of the 101st Field Artillery* (Boston: Loomis & Co., 1919), pp. 210-11.
55. Frederick McKenna, *Battery "A" 103rd Field Artillery In France* (Providence, 1920), p. 162 and Simpson and Hull, *The War Story of C Battery, One Hundred Third U.S. Field Artillery in France, 1917-1919* (Norwood, MA: Plimpton Press, 1920), pp. 211, 222 and 227.
56. Frederick C. Reynolds and William P. McLaughlin, *115th Infantry U.S.A. in the World War* (Baltimore, 1920), pp. 175, 177.
57. Herman Louser, *The Propeller: 840th Aero Squadron* (1923), pp. 63-64,

1 November 1916 and 1 November 1918 *Xavier Athenaeum*.
58. *History of the Sixteenth Engineers (Railway) AEF* (Detroit: La Salle Press, 1939), p. 321.
59. 24 January 1919 *Stars and Stripes*.
60. 3 April 1919, *The Red and Black*, University of Georgia.
61. 21 January 1919 *Chicago Tribune*.
62. 15 August, 18 January 24 and 28 Feb 1919 Staley to Mary, Letters.
63. 9 April 1919, *Princeton Alumni Weekly*, p. 466.
64. 21, 28 February 1919 *Stars and Stripes* and Christian Bach and Henry Noble Hall, *The Fourth Division: Its Services and Achievements in the World War* (1920), p. 236.
65. 8 March 1919 *Richmond Times Dispatch*.
66. 7 and 21 March 1919 *Stars and Stripes*.
67. John Cuthins and Stewart Scott, *History of the Twenty-Ninth Division, "Blue and Gray," 1917-1919*. (Philadelphia, 1921), p. 251.
68. 28 March 1919 *Virginian-Pilot*
69. 21 March 1919 *Stars and Stripes* and *Regimental History Three Hundred and Forty First Field Artillery* (Kansas City: Union Bank Note Co., 1920), p. 41.
70. Lonnie J. White, *Panthers to Arrowheads: The 36th (Texas-Oklahoma) Division in World War I* (Military History Associates, Inc., 1984), pp. 189-192; Doran L. Cart, "Kansas Football 'Over There,'" *Kansas History: A Journal of the Central Plains* 29 (Autumn 2006): 194-199; 4 April 1919 *Stars and Stripes*; and 31 March 1919 *Richmond Times Dispatch*. Masheet was likely "Carl Masheet" pictured with the 1915 squad in the Oklahoma A&M yearbook for 1916. Other sources claim him to be "Eddie" with either Kendall or Haskell.

Chapter 6

1. *The Mirror*, Bates (1918), p. 147 and *The Bowdoin Bugle* (1919), p. 166.
2. *Grist*, Rhode Island State (1919), p. 99.
3. 13 October 1918 *Richmond Times Dispatch*.
4. 30 January 1918 *Dubuque Daily Telegraph*.
5. *Onondagan*, Syracuse 1921, pp. 204-205.
6. *L'Agenda*, Bucknell (1918), p. 200, 24 May 1917 *The Dickinsonian* and *A Record*, Haverford (1919), p. 90.
7. *Epitome*, Lehigh (1919) p. 355, *Ciarla*, Muhlenberg (1921), p. 92 and *Argo* Westminster (1919), p. 131.
8. *The Record*, Pennsylvania (1918) p. 189.
9. 5 February 1918 *Christian Science Monitor*, *La Vie*, Penn State (1921) p. 353 and *Argo*, Pittsburgh (1919), p. 130
10. 12 June 1918 *Washington Post* and 25 February 1918 *Denver Post*.
11. 12 May 1918 *N.Y. Times*.
12. *The Lucky Bag*, Naval Academy (1921) and 12 June 1918 *Washington Post*.
13. *The Georgetonian* (1 June 1918), p. 31.
14. 29 March, 27 April 1917 *Christian Science Monitor*.
15. *Commodore*, Vanderbilt (1919), Image 116 and *Jambalaya*, Tulane (1920), p. 268.
16. *The Cactus*, Texas (1918), p. 358.
17. *Gopher*, Minnesota (1920), pp. 64 and 479.
18. 21 May 1919 *Grand Forks Daily Herald* and *The Badger*, Wisconsin (1919), p. 186.
19. *The Mac*, Macalester (1920), p. 152.
20. *Polyscope*, Bradley (1918), p. 69, *Ravelings*, Monmouth (1920), p. 84 and *Spectrum*, Northwestern (1919), p. 148
21. *The Mirage*, DePauw University (1920), p., 84; *The Advance*, Indiana State Normal (1919), p. 190, 12 April, 5 May 1917 *Christian Science Monitor* and *De Bris*, Purdue (1919).
22. *Arbutus*, Indiana (1918), pp. 88, 104.
23. *Old Gold*, Iowa State Teachers College (1918), p. 183.
24. 28 May 1916 *Dubuque Telegraph-Herald*, *Clavis*, Dubuque (1920), p. 128 and *The Key*, Dubuque (1921), p. 116.
25. *Sioux*, Morningside (1920), p. 124.
26. *The Hawkeye*, Iowa (1918), p. 404.
27. *Sunflower*, Kansas State (1918), p. 122 and *Coyote*, Kansas Wesleyan (1918), p. 122.
28. *The Cornhusker*, Nebraska (1920), p. 378.
29. *Blue and Gold*, University of California (1919) p. 227.
30. *Oregana* (1919), p. 140.
31. 23 January, 4 February 1918 *Christian Science Monitor*.

32. 7, 15, 22, and 29 March 1918 *Stars and Stripes*.
33. 29 and 31 May and 2 June 1917 *N.Y. Times*; George J. Shively, ed., *Record of S.S.U. 585* (New Haven: The Brock Row Book Shop, 1920; pp. 15, 194, 302, 202; 31 July 1918 *Washington Post;* and 14 October 1917 and 31 May 1918 *Pensacola Journal*.
34. 4 April, 14 July 1918 *Atlanta Constitution*.
35. 22 September, 30 December 1917 and 2 October 1918 *N.Y. Times*.
36. 17 May 1917 *N.Y. Times* and *Our Navy* (1918–1919), passim.
37. 18, 19 April 1918 *Christian Science Monitor*.
38. *The Official History of the 315th Infantry* (1920), p. 352.
39. 15 June 1918 *Christian Science Monitor*, Herman Louser, *The Propeller: 840th Aero Squa*dron (1923), p. 65 and Leslie Baker, *The Story of Company B, 106th Machine gun Battalion, 27th Division, USA* (1920), pp. 37–38.
40. 9 November 1918 *L.A. Times*.
41. 20 May 1919 *N.Y. Times*.

Chapter 7

1. *Violet*, NYU (1918); p. 192; Sub Turri, Boston College (1919), p. 259 and 24 February 1918 *N.Y. Times*.
2. 5 March 1919 *N.Y. Times*.
3. *La Vie*, Penn State (1920), p. 297.
4. *The Record*, Haverford (1920), p. 93 and *The Quittapahilla*, Lebanon Valley (1921), p. 152.
5. *Orbiter*, Bloomsburg State Normal (1919), p. 168 and *Corontawan*, Mansfield State Normal (1918), p 195
6. *The Liberty Bomb*, VMI (1919), p. 199.
7. 30 January 1918 *Charleston News and Courier*.
8. *Ole Miss* (1919), p. 108.
9. *Jambalaya*, Tulane (1919), p. 329.
10. *The Chilowean*, Maryville Normal (1919), p. 165 and *Buccaneer,* East Tennessee State (1919), p. 75.
11. February 1917, *The MAC Record* Michigan State.
12. *Aurora*, Michigan State Normal (1917), p. 199 and *Milestone*, Hope College (1918), p. 79.
13. 17 January 1918 *Index* (the Ka-Col) and 7 March 1918 *Alma Record*.

14. *Gopher*, Minnesota (1918) p. 435 and (1920), p. 64.
15. *Crimson*, Ripon (1918), p. 127 and 26 November 1918 *N.Y. Times*.
16. 5 March 1918 *Ottumna Semi-Weekly Courier*.
17. *Illio*, Illinois (1919), p. 280 and *Syllabus*, Northwestern (1920), p. 48.
18. 9 April 1917 *N.Y. Tribune*.
19. *Ohio Northern* (1918), p. 191, *The Cedras* (1918) p. 83 and *The Bee Gee* (1918) p. 102.
20. 10 January and 12 February 1919 *The Coe College Cosmos*.
21. 5 June 1918 *The Scarlet & Black* (Grinnell).
22. *The Sunflower*, Kansas State (1918), p. 113, 17 May 1918 *The Ottawa Campus* and 28 January 1918 *Topeka State Journal*.
23. *Savitar*, Missouri (1917), p. 382.
24. *Pulse*, Central Wesleyan (1919) p. 105, *The Sou-wester*, Drury (1918) Image 78, 17 February 1919 *Southwest Standard* (Springfield Normal) and *The Rhetor*, Warrensburg State Normal (1919), pp. 77–78.
25. 3 March 1918 *The Redwood* (Creighton), p. 305.
26. 21 February 1919 *Omaha Daily Bee*.
27. *The Kendallabrum*, Henry Kendall College (1917) p. 116, *Kendall Review* (1919).
28. *The Cactus*, University of Texas (1919), p. 256.
29. 26 February 1917 and 5 March 1919 *The Campus*, Southern Methodist University.
30. *Banyan*, Brigham Young University (1918), p. 98 and *Utonian*, University of Utah (1919), p. 95.
31. *Pikes Peak Nugget*, Colorado College (1918), pp. 166 and 173 and 4 May 1917 *Denver Post*.
32. 26 February 1919 *Grand Forks Herald*.
33. *The Ignatian*, St. Ignatius 1918, Image 85, and 1919, Image 101.
34. *Klipsun*, Washington State Normal (1917), p. 51.
35. *Beaver*, Oregon Agricultural (1921), p. 302.
36. *Evening Public Ledger* (Philadelphia) January–March 1917.
37. 14 February 1919 *Philadelphia Evening Public Ledger*.
38. 10, 29 December 1917 *Christian Science Monitor* and *Spalding's Basket-Ball Guide* (1918), pp. 57 and 71–72.

39. 15 February 1918 *N.Y. Times.*
40. Spalding, p. 73 and 342.
41. Spalding, pp. 73–74 and 3 March, 3 April 1918 *Atlanta Constitution.*
42. *Red Guidon* (1920); pp. 128–29.
43. 5 February 1918 *Hawaii Gazette*; 27 January 1919 and Thayer Addison, *The Story of the First Gas Regiment* (Boston: Houghton-Mifflin, 1919), p. 18.
44. 17 January 1918 *Grand Forks Daily Herald* and 4 March *N.Y. Times.*
45. 8 February 1918 *L.A. Times.*
46. Henderson, *The Ninety-First: The First at Camp Lewis* (Tacoma, 1918), p. 400 and 13 December 1917 and 14 February 1918 *Tacoma Times.*
47. *Red Guidon*, pp. 123–125
48. *The Official History of the 315th Infantry* (1920), p. 342.
49. *Company "A" Twenty-third Engineers AEF* (Chicago, 1923), pp. 47 and 101; 3 January 1919 Harry Truman to Bess, Robert H. Ferrell, ed., *Dear Bess: The Letters from Harry to Bess Truman* (N.Y.: W.W. Norton, 1983). p 288 and Frederic R. Kilner, *Battery E in France, 149th Field Artillery, 42nd Division* (Chicago, 1919), p. 84.
50. 28 March and 11 April 1919 *Stars and Stripes.*
51. 18 April 1919 *Stars and Stripes.*
52. 24 December 1916, 10 February 1917 and 11 February 1918 *Charleston News Courier.*
53. 22 September, 1 December 1918 *Atlanta Constitution* and 17 January 1920 *Norfolk Ledger-Dispatch.*

Chapter 8

1. 26 May 1917 *L.A. Times* and 23 May, 12, 23 June and 22 December 1917 *N.Y. Times.*
2. 25, 26 July 1917 *Virginian-Pilot.*
3. 23 May, 5 July, 30 December 1917 *N.Y. Times.*
4. 25, 27 July, 12 August, 16 September and 23 December 1917 *N.Y. Times.*
5. 23 June, 30 December 1917 *Denver Post.*
6. 30 December 1918 *Charleston News and Courier,* 10 June, 9, 12 November 1917, 13 April, 5, 14 August and 3 November 1918 *N.Y. Times.*
7. 30 December 1917 *Richmond Times Dispatch* and 3 November 1918 *N.Y. Times.*
8. 14 April 1917 *Denver Post,* 26 May 1917 *L.A. Times* and 3 November 1918 *N.Y. Times.*
9. 27 May, 19 August, 26 November, and 24 December 1917 and 3 November 1918 *N.Y. Times.*
10. 14 October and 20, 23, 24 December 1917 *N.Y. Times.*
11. 6 January 1918 *Richmond Times Dispatch.*
12. 12 August 1917 *Washington Post* and 28 October, 25 November and 30 December 1917 *N.Y. Times.*
13. 1 April, 23 December 1917 *N.Y. Times*, 13 January 1918 *Washington Post*; (August 1918) *Our Navy* and *Outing*, p. 392
14. 10 July 1918 *N.Y. Times.*
15. 6 October 1918 *N.Y. Times.*
16. 6, 20, 27 October 1918 and 17 June 1919 *N.Y. Times.*
17. 13 June 1919 *Stars and Stripes.*
18. *The Ivy,* Trinity (1920), p. 106.
19. *L'Agenda,* Bucknell (1921), p. 218; *Argo,* Westminster (1920), p. 100; *Pandora,* W. & Jefferson (1919), p. 155.
20. *The Campanile,* Rice (1919), p. 164 and *The Cactus,* Texas (1919), p. 247.
21. *The Bomb,* Iowa State (1921), Image 331 and *Savitar,* Missouri (1920), p. 175.
22. *The Badger,* Wisconsin (1920), p. 233.
23. *Makio,* Ohio State (1920), p. 235.
24. Paul B. Williams, *United States Lawn Tennis Association and the World War* (N.Y., 1921), p. 25.
25. 8 August 1917 *Christian Science Monitor.*
26. 22 July, 3 August 1917 *Washington Post* and 3 September 1918 *D.C. Evening Star.*
27. 30 December 1917 *Richmond Times Dispatch;* 7 July, 3, 4 September 1918 *N.Y. Times* and 21 July 1918 *Washington Post*
28. 6 July 1918 *Christian Science Monitor; Spalding's Lawn Tennis Annual* (1919), ed. Samuel Hardy (N.Y.: American Sport Publishing Co., 1919), p. 27 and 22 October 1918 *L.A. Times.*
29. 1 June 1919 *Virginian-Pilot* and Harry L. Graff, "American Officers' A.E.F. Championships, Cannes" *Spalding's.*
30. 16 June 1919 *N.Y. Times.*

Chapter 9

1. 25 February 1918 *Denver Post.*
2. 10 January 1919 *N.Y. Tribune.*

3. 12 June 1918 *Washington Post* and 8 December 1918 *N.Y. Times; Lucky Bag* (1918) p. 346 and (1920), p. 348.
4. *Tyee*, University of Washington (1919), p. 72.
5. 15 April 1919 *N.Y. Times*.
6. 23 June, 5 September 1916, 13 July 1918 and 2 September 1919 *Richmond Times Dispatch*.
7. *Technique*, MIT (1918), p. 200 and *The Gulielmensian*, Williams (1919), p. 270.
8. *Gopher*, Minnesota (1918), p. 185 and *The Bomb*, Iowa State (1919), Image 128.
9. 15 July 1917 and 6 January 1918 *Chicago Tribune* and Henderson, *The Ninety-First: The First at Camp Lewis*, p. 400.
10. 15 May 1918 *Christian Science Monitor*.
11. 10 May, 19 September 1917 *L.A. Times*.
12. 31 May, 5, 30 July and 23 September 1917 *N.Y. Times*.
13. 6, 11 August 1917 *Charleston News and Courier*.
14. 1 June 1918 *N.Y. Times*.

Chapter 10

1. 31 August 1918 *Chicago Tribune*.
2. 22 September 1917 *Ledger-Dispatch; Indiana Weekly Messenger* (Letter W.J. Stark, Pennsylvania, 11 October 1917) and 5 April 1918 *Richmond Times Dispatch*.
3. 11 April 1918 *Richmond Times Dispatch*.
4. 18 November 1917 *Chicago Tribune*; 6 July, 29 December 1917 and 10 February 1918 *Virginian-Pilot*; 21; and 28 May 1918 *Atlanta Constitution*.
5. 3 February 1918 *N.Y. Times* and 11, 20 June 1917 *L.A. Times*.
6. 12 May 1917 *Denver Post*.
7. 5-6 July 1916-1919 *Tonopah Daily Bonanza*.
8. *The Official History of the 315th Infantry*, pp. 351-353 and 14, 15 March 1918 *Washington Post*.
9. 21 and 27 October, 27 November 1917, 4 and 30 January, 13 February and 11 June 1918 *Tacoma Times*; 31 July 1918 *Washington Post* and Henderson, *The Ninety-first: The First at Camp Lewis* (Tacoma: Smith-Kinney Co., 1918), p. 393.
10. 28 March 1918 *Stars and Stripes*.
11. 27 October 1917 and 9, 27, 28 March, 8 September and 6 October 1918 *Atlanta Constitution*.
12. Paul Schmidt, *Co. C, 127th Infantry (32nd Div.) in the World War*. p. 14; H.C. Brown, *History of E Co., 37th U.S. Engineers* (Boston: Ellis Co., 1919) p. 21; Lloyd Staley, 1 May 1918, *Letters from the Front* and Proctor M. Fiske, comp. and ed., *History of the Three Hundred Fiftieth Regiment of U.S. Infantry* (Cedar Rapids: The Lawrence Press, 1919), p. 86.
13. Herman W. Louser, *The Propeller: 840th Aero Squadron* (1923), p. 69.
14. Evan Alexander Edwards, *From Doniphan to Verdun: The Official History of the 140th Infantry* (Lawrence, Kan. The World Co., 1920) p. 38 and 17 June 1918 *Denver Post*.
15. *The Official History of the 315th Infantry*, p. 348 and *History of the 322nd Field* Artillery, pp. 68-70, 270, 300.
16. John Cutchins and Stewart Scott, *History of the Twenty-ninth Division, "Blue and Gray," 1917-1919*. (Philadelphia, 1921), p. 252.
17. 6 October 1918 *Washington Post*
18. 3 January 1919, Harry Truman to Bess, Ferrell, ed., *Dear Bess*, p. 288.
19. *The Story of "E" Company, 101st Engineers, 26th Division*, p. 94 and Joseph Glass, et al., *The Story of Battery D, 304th Field Artillery*, p. 88.
20. 4 December 1918 and 26 February 1919 *Washington Post* and William L Peterson, *Company History "D," 55th Engineers, AEF*.
21. 12 December 1918 *Washington Post*, 13-14 December 1918 *Norfolk Ledger Dispatch*, 27 December 1919 *Stars and Stripes* and 13 December 1918 *Denver Post*.
22. 24 December 1918 *Washington Post* and *Our Navy* (February 1919), p. 44.
23. *Our Navy* (July 1918) p. 20 and (January 1919), p. 48.
24. 12 January 1919 *Chicago Tribune*.
25. 26 May 1919 *Ledger-Dispatch*.
26. 21 April 1919 *Virginian-Pilot* and *The 88th Division in the World War* (Google), p. 84.
27. "Bushy" Graham was an Italian-American using an alias, about 16 years old in '19; a photo of Patterson's opponent shows someone much older. 25 April and 30 May 1919 *Stars and Stripes* and 10 August 1918 *N.Y. Times*
28. *History of the Y.M.C.A in the Le*

Mans Area (Portland, Ore. 1920), p. 26, *Our Navy* (Feb 1919), p. 44, and *115th Infantry*, p. 189.
  29. 4 July 1919 *Charleston News and Courier*.
  30. 18 May 1919 *Virginian-Pilot*.
  31. 20 January 1918 *Hawaiian Gazette* and 13 October 1918 *N.Y. Times*.
  32. 17 August 1918 *N.Y. Times*.
  33. 14, 16, 23, and 26 January 1920 *N.Y. Times*.
  34. 8 June 1919 *Richmond Times Dispatch*.
  35. 11 June 1920 *Richmond Times Dispatch*.
  36. 24 December 1916, 9 January and 16 March 1919 *N.Y. Times*.
  37. *Jack Rabbit,* South Dakota State (1921), Image 58.
  38. 5 February, 30 March 1918 *Christian Science Monitor* and *De Bris* (1918), p. 200.
  39. 19, 30 January, 10 February 2, 20 March and 27 November 1918 *N.Y. Times*.
  40. 3 February 1918 *Atlanta Constitution*.
  41. 16 February and 12 March 1918 *N.Y. Times*.
  42. 30 September 1917 *Virginian-Pilot*.
  43. 25 April, 2 May 1919 *Stars and Stripes*.
  44. Clarence Johnson, *History of 321st Infantry* (Columbia, S.C.: R.L. Bryan Co., 1919), pp. 84–85.
  45. 3 Feb 1918 *N.Y. Times*.

Chapter 11

  1. 31 May, 23, 12, 17 June, 23 September, 17 November, 9 and 30 December 1917 *N.Y. Times* and 4, 11 August 1917 *Virginian-Pilot*.
  2. 9 December 1917 *L.A. Times* and 31 March, 28 September 1918 *N.Y. Times*.
  3. 3 June, 29 July, 18 August and 15 September 1918 *N.Y. Times* and 5 July 1918 *Seattle Star*.
  4. 5 July 1917 *Tacoma Times*; 5 July 1918 *Seattle Star*; 5 July 1917 *Arizona Republican*; 18 October 1918 *L.A. Times* 4 March 1918 *Denver Post*.
  5. 11–18 November 1917, October-November 1918, and 2–9 November 1919 *Arizona Republican*, and Don Radbruch, *Dirt Track Auto Racing, 1919–1941: A Pictorial History* (Jefferson N.C.: McFarland, 2004), passim.

  6. 4, 5 August 1918 *Omaha Daily Bee* and 4 September 1917 and 3 September 1918 *Evening Star* (D.C.).
  7. 4 September 1917 and 3 September 1918 *Evening Star*.
  8. 13, October 1916; 14 October 1917, 6, 16 October 1918 *Richmond Times Dispatch*.
  9. 5 July 1918 *Richmond Times Dispatch* and 5 July 1917 *Arizona Republican*.
  10. 31 May, 5 July and 4 September 1916; 31 May, 5 July and 3 September 1917; and 31 May 1918 *Harrisburg Telegraph*.
  11. 19 July and 12 October 1919 *N.Y. Times*.
  12. 5 July and 2–4 September 1918 *Philadelphia Evening Public Ledger*, 2 and 9 July, 17 September 1917 *N.Y. Times* and 2 September 1919 *Motorcycling and Bicycling*.
  13. 2 and 9 July, 17 September 1917 *N.Y. Times*.

Chapter 12

  1. 17–28 January and 18 February 1918 *N.Y. Times*.
  2. 28 January, 9 and 17 February *N.Y. Times*.
  3. 20 January, 3–5, 17–19, 24 February 1918 *N.Y. Times* and 21 January 1918 *Grand Forks Daily Herald*.
  4. *Guilielmensian* Williams (1920, p. 287.
  5. *The Howitzer,* West Point (1919) p. 240.
  6. 29 December 1917 *Christian Science Monitor*
  7. 3 March 1917, 6 March 1918 and 10 March 1919 *Seattle Star*.
  8. 25 February 1918 *Denver Post*.
  9. 19 February 1918 *South Bend Times*.
  10. 21 January and 5 February 1918 *Barre Daily Times*.

Chapter 13

  1. 2 and 23 October 1917 *Washington Post* and 12 May 1917 *L.A. Times*.
  2. 24 July 1917 *L.A. Times* and 30 December 1917 *N.Y. Times*.
  3. 17 October 1918 *Atlanta Constitution*.
  4. 18 June and 1–30 September 1917 *Watertown News* and 28 June and 1–30 Sept 1918 *Watertown Weekly Leader*. 1–15 Oct 1916; 1–15, 1917 *Norwich Bulletin*.
  5. 10 September *Winchester Star*; 11

Oct 1917; 4, 8, 11 1919 *Richmond Times Dispatch*.
   6. 9 October 1918 *N.Y. Times*, 23 February 1919 *Providence Journal*, 4 August and 14 October 1918 *Washington Post*.
   7. 5 October 1918 *Denver Post*.
   8. 26 February 1919 *Tulsa Daily World*.
   9. William Elmer Bachman, *The Delta of the Triple Eleven* (Hazelton, Penn.: Stanford Sentinel Print, 1920), pp. 105-197 and *Official History of the 315th*, p. 340.
   10. *History of the 318th Infantry Regiment of the 80th Division, 1917-1919* (Richmond: The William Byrd Press, 1919), pp. 92-104 and 31 May and 5 July, 30 July and 23 September 1917 *N.Y. Times*.
   11. 1, 15, and 25 October, 20 November 1916, 21 and 24 November 1918 *N.Y. Times*
   12. "C" *Battery Book, 306th F.A. 77th Division, 1917-1919* (Brooklyn, 1920), p. 107-108.
   13. *Outing* (June 1917), p. 394 and (August 1917), p 720.
   14. 5, 7, 11, 17, 22, and 25 July and 1, 2 September, 30 December 1917 and 6 January and 1 September 1918 *N.Y. Times*.
   15. 13 September, 6 October 1918 *L.A. Times*.
   16. 3 November 1918 *Atlanta Constitution*; and *Red Guidon* (1920), p. 123.
   17. 19 October 1918 *Denver Post*.
   18. 22 January 1919 *Philadelphia Evening Public Ledger*, 16 and 22 December 1919 *N.Y. Times*, 15 June 1919 *N.Y. Tribune*
   19. 20 October 1917 *Daily Capital Journal* (Salem, Ore.); 3 November 1917 *East Oregonian*; 3 March 1918 *Bisbee Daily Review*
   20. 5 June 1918, *The Bismarck Tribune*.

Chapter 14

1. 25 August 1919 *N.Y. Times*.
2. *La Vie*, Penn State (1919), p. 352 and (1921), p. 372.
3. *The Record*, Haverford (1919), p. 85.
4. 29 December 1918 *N.Y. Times*.
5. *Oriflamme*, Franklin & Marshall (1921) p. 218; *Epitome*, Lehigh (1919), p. 363 and *The Halcyon* Swarthmore (1918), p. 233 and (1919), p. 239.
6. *La Vie*, Penn State (1920), p.298 and (1921), p. 372.
7. Col. Wait C. Johnson and Edward Brown, eds., *Official Athletic Almanac of the American Expeditionary Force, 1919: A.E.F. Championships: Inter-Allied Olympics* (N.Y.: American Sports Publishing Co. 1919), p. 117.

Chapter 15

1. 11 October 1916 *Richmond Times Dispatch*.
2. 23 December 1917 *N.Y. Times* and 10 October 1918 *Denver Post*.
3. Steven A. Riess, *City Games: The Evolution of American Urban Society and the Rise of Sports* (Urbana: University of Illinois Press, 1991), p. 74; 4 and 11 May 1917 *Celena Democrat* (Ohio).
4. 5 December 1918 *El Paso Herald* and 29 January 1917 and 12 March 1918 *Brattleboro Daily Reformer*.
5. 1, 7 February 1918 and 5 May 1919 *Rock Island Argus*.
6. 15 January 1919 *South Bend Times*.
7. 17 March, 8 and 21 April 1918 *The Daily Missoulian*.
8. 17, 30 January and 17 January 1919 *Grand Forks Daily Herald*.
9. 27 January, 8 February and 3, 5 March 1918 *N.Y. Times*.
10. *Cap & Gown* (1919), p. 172 and 24 March 1918 *N.Y. Times*.
11. 5 March 1918 *N.Y. Times*.
12. 1, 29 July 1917 and 30 January 1918 *Denver Post*.
13. July 1917 *Outing* (1917), p. 422.

Chapter 16

1. The first part of this chapter discusses the origin and organization of the games and the construction of the stadium. *The Inter-Allied Games, Paris 22nd June to 6th July* (Games Committee, 1919), pp. 1-176.
2. 5, 21 June 1919 *N.Y. Times*.
3. 26 June 1919 *L.A. Times*.
4. The rest of the chapter contains a summary from Baseball to the Tug of War. *Inter-Allied Games*, pp. 180-331.
5. *Ibid.*, p. 336.
6. 10 August 1919 *N.Y. Times*.

Chapter 17

1. 11 August, 29 December 1918 *N.Y. Times*.
2. 9 October 1918 *Providence Journal*.

Notes—Chapter 17

3. 10 June 1917 *Virginian-Pilot*; 27 November 1917 *L.A. Times*; 30 December 1918 *Washington Post*; and 3 January 1919 *Stars and Stripes*.

4. 10 December 1918 *Denver Post*.

5. 29 December 1918 *N.Y. Times*.

6. 20 February, 28 January 1919 *Washington Herald*.

7. 11 February 1919 *Virginian-Pilot*.

8. 27 February 1919 *The Daily Gate City and Constitutional Democrat*; 14 May 1919 *Grand Forks Daily Herald*; 30 April 1919 *Rock Island Argus* and 30 December 1917 *Washington Herald*.

9. 11 January 1919 *Denver Post*.

10. 20 January 1917 *Clinton Advertiser*.

11. Nancy Bristow, *Making Men Moral: Social Engineering During the Great War* (N.Y.: N.Y. University Press, 1997), p. 186 and 15, 20 May 1918 *Washington Herald* and 28 May 1918 *Sporting Life*.

12. 23–26 September 1919 *Brattleboro Daily Reformer*, 28 July and 27 September 1919 *Bennington Evening Banner*.

13. 27 April 1919 *Virginian-Pilot* and 2 April 1919 *Charleston News and Currier*.

14. 2 May 1917 *Free-Trader Journal* (Ottawa, IL), 8 February 1918 *Washington Post*, and 26 March 1917 *L.A. Times*

15. 21 April 1916 *Richmond Times Dispatch*.

Bibliography

Bristow, Nancy. *Making Men Moral: Social Engineering During the Great War*. N.Y.: NYU Press, 1997.

Carroll, John M. *Fritz Pollard: Pioneer in Racial Advancement*. Urbana: University of Illinois Press, 1992.

Cart, Doran L. "Kansas Football Over There." *Kansas History: A Journal of the Central Plains* 29 (Autumn 2006): 194–199.

The Encyclopedia of Minor League Baseball. 2nd edition. Lloyd Johnson and Miles Wolff, eds. Durham: Baseball America, 1997.

Graff, Harry L. "American Officers' A.E.F. Championships, Cannes." *Spalding's Lawn Tennis Annual*. Samuel Hardy, ed. N.Y.: American Sports Publishing, 1919.

Graydon, Katharine, *Butler College in the World War*. Indianapolis: Alumni Association, 1922.

Huhn, Rick. *The Sizzler: George Sisler, Baseball's Forgotten Great*. Columbus: University of Missouri Press, 2004.

Levy, Alan H. *Joe McCarthy: Architect of the Yankee Dynasty*. Jefferson, N.C.: McFarland, 2005.

Mennell, James. "The Service Football Program of World War I: Its Impact on the Popularity of the Game." *Journal of Sport History* 16 (Winter 1989): 248–260.

Park, Roberta. "From Football to Rugby—and Back, 1906–1919: University of California–Stanford University Response to the Football Crisis of 1905." *Journal of Sport History* (Winter 1984): 5–40.

Radbruch, Don. *Dirt Track Auto Racing, 1919–1941: A Pictorial History*. Jefferson, N.C.: McFarland, 2004.

Reiss, Steven A. *City Games: The Evolution of American Urban Society and the Rise of Sports*. Urbana: University of Illinois Press, 1991.

Smelser, Marshall. *The Life That Ruth Built: A Biography*. N.Y.: Quadrangle, 1976.

Spalding's Official Base Ball Guide: Forty-third Year (N.Y.: American Sports Publishing Co., 1919.

Spalding's Official Football Guide, 1919. N.Y. American Sports Publishing Co., 1919.

Stiehm, Edward O. "Athletics in War Time." *Outing* (August, 1917): 672–680.

Williams, Paul B. *United States Lawn Tennis Association and the World War*. N.Y., 1921.

Government Sources

U.S. Department of the Interior, Bureau of Education, Bulletin, 1919, No. 22. A Survey of Higher Education, 1916–1918–by Samuel P. Capen and Walton C. John. Washington: Government Printing Office, 1919.

U.S. Department of the Interior, Bureau of Education, Bulletin 1922 No. 28. Statistics of Universities, Colleges, and Professional Schools, 1919–1920. Washington: Government Printing Office, 1922.

U.S. Department of the Interior, Bureau of Education Bulletin 1920, No. 34 Statistics of Universities, Colleges, and Professional Schools, 1917–1918 by H.R. Boner. Washington: Government Printing Office, 1921.

U.S. War Department. *Student Army Training Corps*. 2nd Edition. October 1918.

Primary Sources

Ball Players in the Great War: Newspaper Accounts of Major Leaguers in World War

I Military Service. Comp. Jim Leeke. Jefferson, N.C.: McFarland, 2013.

"Diary of Bugler Wayne Desilvey." Phil Reese, ed., worldwarI.com/dbc/desilvey.htm.

Ferrell, Robert H., ed. *Dear Bess: The Letters from Harry to Bess Truman, 1910–1959,* N.Y.: W.W. Norton, 1983.

Fosdick, Raymond Blaine. *Chronicle of a Generation: An Autobiography.* N.Y.: Harper, 1958.

Staley, Lloyd M. to Mary B. Gray. "Letters Home from the War." u.arizona.edu/~rstaley/wwlettri.htm.

Military Histories

Addison, James Thayer. *The Story of the First Gas Regiment.* Boston: Houghton-Mifflin, 1919.

Bach, Christian and Henry Noble Hall. *The Fourth Division: Its Services and Achievements in the World War.* 1920.

Bachman, Elmer. *The Delta of the Triple Eleven.* Hazelton, Pa.: Standard Sentinel Print, 1920.

Baker, Leslie. *The Story of Company B, 106th Machine Gun Battalion 27th Division USA,* 1920.

Being the Narrative of Battery A of the 101st Field Artillery. Boston: Loomis & Co., 1919.

Bodfish, Robert Ware. *A History of Section 647 U.S. Army Ambulance Service with the French Army.* Worcester: Stobbs, 1919.

Brown, Herbert C. *History of E Co. 37th Engineers.* Boston: Ellis, 1919.

C Battery Book, 306th, Field Artillery, 77th Division, 1917–1919. Brooklyn: Braunworth, 1920.

Chubb, Robert Walston. *Regimental History, 342nd Field Artillery, 89th Division.* 1921.

Co. "A" Twenty-third Engineers AEF. Chicago, 1923.

Colonna, Benjamin Allison. *The History of Company B, 311th Infantry in the World War.* Freehold, N.J., 1922.

Cutchins, John A., and Stewart George Scott, Jr. *History of the Twenty-ninth Division, "Blue and Gray," 1917–1919.* Philadelphia: MacCallan, 1921.

Dienst, Charles. *The History of the 353rd Infantry Regiment.* Wichita, Kan., 1921.

Duane, James T. *Dear Old 'K'.* Boston, 1922.

Edwards, Evan Alexander. *From Doniphan to Verdun: The Official History of the 140th Infantry.* Lawrence, Kan.: The World, 1920.

The 88th Division in the World War of 1914–1918. N.Y. Wynkoop-Hallenbeck-Crawford Co., 1919

Fiske, Proctor M. ed. *History of the Three Hundred Fiftieth Regiment of U.S. Infantry.* Cedar Rapids: Lawrence Press, 1919

Gansser, Earl B. *History of the 126th Infantry in the War with Germany.* Grand Rapids, 1920.

Glass, Joseph et. al. *The Story of Battery D, 304th Field Artillery from September 1917-May 1919.*

Henderson, Alice Palmer. *The Ninety-first: The First at Camp Lewis.* Tacoma: Smith-Kinney Co., 1918.

Herr, Charles Ryman. *Co. F. History, 319th Infantry.* Flemington, N.J., 1920.

An Historical & Technical Biography of the Twenty-First Engineers, Light Railway, U.S. Army. N.Y.: [McConnell] 1919

The History of Company C, 314th Field Signal Battalion, U.S Army AEF. Comp. The History Committee. Philadelphia: Shade Printing, 1920

A History of the 1st Engineers, 1st U.S. Division. Coblentz, Germany, 1919

History of the Sixteenth Engineers (Railway) AEF. Detroit: La Salle Press, 1939.

History of the 58th U.S. Artillery CAC. N.Y., 1919.

A History of the 313th Field Artillery USA. N.Y. Thomas Y. Crowell, 1920.

History of the 318th Infantry Regiment of the 80th Division, 1917–1919. Richmond: William Byrd Press, 1919.

History of the 322nd Field Artillery. New Haven: Yale University Press, 1920.

History of the Y.M.C.A in the Le Mans Area. Portland, Ore.: Arcade Press, 1920.

Hollingsworth, Roy. *10,000 Miles with the 125th Infantry Supply Train.* [University Mich., 1932]

The Inter-Allied Games, Paris 22nd June to 6th July 1919. The Games Committee, [1920].

Johnson, Clarence Walton. *The History of the 321st. with a Brief Historical Sketch of the 81st Division.* Columbia, S.C.: R.L. Bryan Co., 1919.

Kilner, Frederic R. *Battery E in France,*

149th Field Artillery, 42nd Division. Chicago, 1919.
Lee, Jay. *The Artillerymen: Battery E in France, 129th Field Artillery.* Kansas City, Mo.
Louser, Herman W. *The Propeller: Aero Squadron.* 1923.
McKenna, Frederick Ambrose. *Battery "A": 103rd Field Artillery in France.* Providence: Livermore & Knight, 1919.
Memoirs of France and the Eighty-eighth Division. Edgar J.D. Larson, comp. Minneapolis, 1920.
Millen, Dewitt C. *Memoirs of 591 in the World War.* Ann Arbor, 1932.
Noland, James Bennett. *Reading Militia in the Great War.* Reading, Pa., 1921.
Official Athletic Almanac of the American Expeditionary Force, 1919: A.E.F. Championships: Inter-Allied Olympics. Col. Wait C. Johnson and Elwood Brown, eds. N.Y.: American Sports Publishing Co., 1919.
Official History of the 315th Infantry, 1917-1919 (79th Div.) Historical Board, comp., 1920
Peterson, William L. *Company History "D," 55th Engineers AEF.* 1919.
Pollard, James. *The Forty-Seventh Infantry: A History, 1917, 1918, 1919.* Saginaw, 1919.
Red Arrow: Thirty-Second Division: History and Facts [American Legion Post 361, 1934].
The Red Guidon, "Soixante Quinze": Being a Complete Illustrated History of B Battery, 134th Field Artillery, 1915-1918. Akron, 1920.
The Red Guidon, 328th Field Artillery (85th Division). 1919.
Regimental History, Three Hundred and Forty-First Field Artillery. Kansas City: Union Bank Note Co., 1920.
Reynolds, Frederick C., and William P. McLaughlin. *115th Infantry U.S.A. in the World War.* Baltimore, 1920.
Robinson, William. *Forging the Sword: The Story of Camp Devens; New England's Army Cantonment.* Concord, N.H., 1920.
Ross, James, and Noel B. Heath. *History of Co. E, 355th Infantry.* Omaha: Waters-Barnhardt Print Co.
Schmidt, Paul. *Co. C, 127th Infantry (32nd Division) in the World War.*
Simpson, Henry T. and George Hull. *The War Story of C Battery, One Hundred Third U.S. Field Artillery in France, 1917-1919.* Norwood, Mass: L. Plimpton Press, 1920.
Shively, George J. ed. *Record of S.S.U. 585.* New Haven: Brook Row Book Shop, 1920.
The Story of Company B, 106th Machine Gun Battalion, 27th Division USA. 1920.
The Story of "E" Company 101st Engineers, 26th Division. Boston, 1919.
The Story of the Forty-Seventh Coast Artillery. Baltimore: George W. King Printing, 1919.
Strong, Fredrick. *History of the Fortieth (Sunshine) Division.* Los Angeles: C.S. Huston, 1920.
331st Field Artillery, United States Army. Chicago: Rogers Printing, 1919.
White, Lonnie J. *Panthers to Arrowheads: The 36th (Texas-Oklahoma) Division in World War I.* Military History Associates, Inc., 1984.
Williams, Ashby. *Experiences of the Great War.* Roanoke: Stone Printing and Mfg., 1919.
Wright, William ed. *History of the 66th Field Artillery Brigade.* Denver, 1919.

College and University Archives (visited by author)

Illinois: Knox College (Galesburg); Lincoln College; Quincy University (St. Francis)
Iowa- Coe College (Cedar Rapids); Loras College (Dubuque College); St. Ambrose College (Davenport); Wartburg College (Waverly)
Kentucky: Centre College (Danville); Georgetown University (College); Transylvania University (Lexington)
Maryland: Washington College (Chestertown)
Massachusetts: Boston University; Fitchburg State University (State Normal); Northeastern University
Nebraska, Doane College (Crete); Hastings College; Kearney State University (State Normal); Midland University (College), Fremont; Wayne State University (State Normal)
New Jersey, Seton Hall University (Newark)
New Hampshire: St. Anslem's (Manchester)
New York: Hamilton College (Clinton); The State University at Albany SUNY (New York State Teachers College); St.

Bonaventure University (Olean); Union College (Schenectady)

North Carolina: Belmont Abbey College; Mars Hill University (College)

North Dakota; Black Hills University (Spearfish State Normal); North Dakota State University (Fargo); Jamestown University (College)*; Valley City University (State Normal) *could not access archives but archivist very helpful

Pennsylvania: California State University (State Normal); Geneva College (Beaver Falls); Grove City College; Juniata College (Huntingdon); St. Francis University (Loretto); Shippensburg State University (State Normal); Slippery Rock State University (State Normal); Thiel College (Greenville); Waynesburg College

Rhode Island: University of R.I. (State College)

South Dakota–Dakota Wesleyan University (Mitchell); Sioux Falls College (University)

Tennessee-Carson-Newman University (College), Jefferson City; East Tennessee State University (State Normal); Fisk University (HBU Nashville); King College (Bristol); Lincoln Memorial University (Harrogate); Milligan College (Elizabethtown); Tusculum University (College), Greeneville.

Vermont; Norwich University.

Virginia: Bridgewater College; College of William and Mary; Emory and Henry College; Hampton University (Normal & Industrial); Lynchburg College; Randolph-Macon College (Ashland); Roanoke College; Shenandoah University (Collegiate Institute); Winchester, Dayton; University of Virginia (Charlottesville).

Index

Ada Normal School (Okla.) 77
Adair, Perry (golfer) 135, 136
Adam, Albert (football) 57
Adrian College (Mich. basketball) 124
Akron Indians (pro football) 86
Alabama Poly (Auburn) 26, 66, 67, 68, 88
Albany State Teachers College (N.Y.) 60, 165
Albert Hall (London) 153
Albion College (Mich.) 72, 111
Alexander, Fred (tennis) 141, 142
Alexander, Grover (baseball) 12, 50
Alexandria Bay 148
Alexandria Cardinals (baseball) 16
Alhambra (Ogden, Utah) 150
Allegheny College (Pa.) 131
Allentown, Pa. 46
Alma College (Mich.) 72, 124
Alva Normal School (Okla.) 77, 127, 128
Amateur Athletic Union 85, 104, 116, 122, 124, 128, 159, 166, 188, 197
Amateur Baseball Federation (Richmond, Va.) 196
Amateur Fencing League 181
American Amateur Hockey League 166
American Association (baseball) 15, 39
American Automobile Association 160
American Basketball League 130
American Football Conference (soccer) 176
American Henley (crew) 144, 145
American Hockey League 165
American League (roller polo) 181
American Legion 156
American Library Association 38
American Polo Association 170
American Power Boat Association 148
American University (D.C.) 132
America's Cup (yachting) 147
Amherst College (Mass.) 21, 105, 135, 177
angling 180
Archangel 154
archery 180
Arizona Airdrome arena (boxing) 150
Arizona School of Mines 32
Arizona State College *see* Tempe Normal

Arkansas Baptist College 77
Arkansas College 127
Arkansas First District Agricultural School (Jonesboro) 65, 77
Armour Institute (Ill.) 69, 87
Army *see* West Point
Army & Navy League (France) 46
Arundel (crew) 145
Atlanta Athletic Club 122
Atlanta Auditorium (boxing) 152
Atlanta Crackers 16, 39, 50
Atlanta Cubs (Black) 39
Atlanta University (HBU) 67
Atlantic Fleet title (1915) 5
Auburn University *see* Alabama Poly
Augustana College (Ill.) 29, 76, 124
Australia (boxing) 154

Babcock & Wilcox (N.J. soccer) 176
Babe Ruth's All Stars 18
Baker, Hobart (Princeton athlete) 194
Baker, Newton (Sec. of War) 20, 25, 37, 54, 88
Baker University (Kan.) 75, 113, 126
Baldwin-Wallace College 111
Baltimore City College (lacrosse) 174
Baptist Hill (Nashville, Negro League) 10
Barbarians (Cal. soccer) 176
Barrow, Edward (baseball mgr.) 15
Barry, Jack (baseball) 11, 36
Bartols, John (track) 107
Baseball Players Fraternity 6
Baston, Bert (Minn. athlete) 68
Bates College (Me.) 20, 21, 56, 57, 104, 165
Battenberg Cup (crew) 145
Battle Axe (Richmond Va. baseball) 16
Baylor University (Tex.) 7, 27, 78, 109
Beckett, John (football) 86, 91, 101
Belgium (soccer/water polo) 13, 188, 189
Bellevue College (Neb.) 127
Bellows, Franklin 124
Belmont (horse racing) 169
Beloit College (Wisc.) 30, 69, 73, 110, 124
Bemidji, Minn. (baseball) 16
Bender, Charles A. "Chief" (baseball) 17

225

226　Index

Bender, F (Carlisle football)　101, 103
Bennett College (N.C. HBC)　25
Bennington Track (D.C.)　161
Benson Oval Track (Omaha)　161
Bensonhurst Yacht Club (N.Y.)　147
Benton, Rube (baseball)　39
Benz, Christian　129
Berea College (Ky.)　108
Bernard twins (Chester and Lester)　126
Berry, Howard (U Pa. athlete)　23, 39, 60, 94, 107
Bethany College (W. Va.)　25, 64, 92
Bethel College (Kan.)　31
Bethlehem Steel (soccer)　176
Bezdeck, Hugh (football)　61
Biddle College (HBC)　25
Big Nine (Western Conference)　6
Big Six (Ohio track)　111
Big Ten (Western Conference)　84, 123, 124
Big Three (Harvard, Princeton, Yale)　54, 114, 165
billiards　178
Billings Poly (Montana)　80
"Billy Sunday" (horse)　172
Birmingham-Southern College　66
Bisbee, Ariz. (baseball)　41
Bjurstedt, Molla (tennis)　141
Black, Clinton　86, 131
Black Sox scandal　193
"Black Thunderbolt" (black pitcher)　41
Bloomsburg State Normal School (Pa.)　18, 23, 61, 120, 121
Blue Mountain League (soccer)　176
Board of Boxing Control　156
Bodine, Earl (football)　73
Boeling, John (baseball)　16, 38
Bohler, Fred (basketball)　130
Boston Athletic Association　116, 117
Boston Athletic Club　104, 115
Boston Braves　10, 12, 14, 35, 36, 37, 94
Boston College　62, 119, 165
Boston Navy Yard　33
Boston Red Sox　5, 12, 15, 18, 36, 37
Boston University　59, 119, 165, 196
Bowdoin College (Me.)　20, 21, 57, 104
bowling　179, 180
Bowling Green, Ohio　125
Boynton, Benny "Purple Streak" (football)　57
Bradley Institute (Ill.)　29, 110, 176
Brattleboro, Vt (bowling)　179
Brattleboro Athletics (Vt. sabbath dispute)　195
Braves Field (Boston)　37, 59, 94
Breck, Lt. H.C. (tennis)　143
Breed, Glenn (auto racer)　161
Brickley, Charles (football)　94
Bridgewater College (Va.)　24
Brigham Young University (Utah)　114
British Army (boxing)　154
British Open (golf)　135

British Prisoner of War Fund　44
Brooklyn (National League)　5, 11, 12
Brooks, Belvidere (Williams football)　58
Brown, Elwood (YMCA)　48
Brown University (R.I.)　21, 38, 57, 88, 157
Browne, Mary (tennis)　141
Bucknell University　106, 120, 139
Buena Vista College (Iowa)　74
Burr, Alex　53
Butler, Solomon　75, 112, 125, 185
Butler University (Ind.)　71, 92, 125, 184

Cactus Alley (El Paso bowling)　179
Caddock, Earl (wrestler)　158, 159
Cadore, Leon (baseball)　11, 39, 50
Cal/Nevada League (basketball)　129
Caledonian Club (curling)　164
California Institute of Technology　115
California Polytechnic School (San Luis Obispo)　83
California State Normal (Pa.)　61
Camden, N.J. armory (basketball)　130
Camp, Walter, Jr.　40, 88
Camp, Walter, Sr.　35, 36, 93, 159
Camp Meade Handicap (horse race)　168
Campbell, Tom (track)　186
Canada　46, 166, 172, 189
Canton Bulldogs (pro football)　85
Cape Cod (fox hunting)　170
Cape Girardeau State Normal　31, 75, 76
Capital City League (Nashville Negro League)　39
Carleton College (Minn.)　28, 73, 110, 114, 115
Carlisle Institute (Pa.)　23, 39, 174, 186
Carman, Clarence (motorcyclist)　163
Carnegie Tech (Pittsburgh)　106, 107
Carpentier, Georges (boxer)　15, 153, 155, 156
Carroll College (University in Wisc.)　73, 110, 124
Carson-Newman College (Tenn.)　63
Case Institute (Ohio)　125
Cassidy, Ken (basketball)　75, 126
Carthage College (Ill.)　71
Catholic University　24, 62, 77, 92, 108, 121, 131
Central Association (baseball)　30
Central State Normal School (Okla.)　24, 77
Central States Bowling Tournament　179
Central Wesleyan College (Mo.)　126
Centre College (Ky.)　25, 26, 64, 65, 108, 123
Chamberlain, Lt. Col. H.D. (equestrian)　190
Chapman, Ralph (football)　69
Chapman, Ray (baseball)　36
Chappell, Larry (baseball)　52
Charleston (S.C.) City League (baseball)　39
Charleston (S.C.) YMCA (volley ball)　134
Chattanooga College　67
Chemawa Indian School (Ore.)　83, 91
Chevrolet, Arthur (auto racer)　160
Chevrolet, Gaston (auto racer)　160
Chevrolet, Louis (auto racer)　160

Cheyenne, Wyoming (rodeo) 172
Chicago AAU (wrestling championships 1918) 159
Chicago Athletic Association 116
Chicago Cubs 12, 15, 32, 38
Chicago White Sox 11, 12, 18, 19, 40
Chicago Yacht Club 147
Chicago YMCA School 70, 110
Chilocco Indian School (Okla.) 27, 113, 127
Chinese University (baseball) 32
Churchill, Winston 44
Churchill Downs (horse racing) 169
Cincinnati Reds 11, 12, 18, 35
(Cirque de Paris (boxing arena) 154
The) Citadel: Military College of South Carolina 27, 68
City College of New York 120, 121, 131, 145, 175
Clarendon (Alexandria Va. baseball) 16
Clark, George 102
Clark, Win (baseball) 38, 94
Clarke, Justin (baseball) 38, 49
Clemson College (S. Carolina) 26, 27, 68, 108, 109, 122, 146
Cleveland Indians 13, 36, 40
Cobb, Capt. Ty 17
Cody, Josh 50, 65, 88
Coe College (Iowa) 30, 75, 112, 125
Colby College (Me.) 21, 57, 104
Colgate University 21, 59, 92, 101, 106, 131, 145, 165, 180
College of Charleston 27
College of Emporia (Kan.) 75, 113
College of William & Mary 24, 63, 121
College of Wooster (Ohio) 72, 111, 112
Collins, Eddie (baseball) 12, 193
Colonial Dames (crew) 145
Colorado Agricultural College 79
Colorado College 32, 79, 80, 114, 128
Colorado School of Mines 32, 79, 80, 114
Colorado Teachers 32, 79, 80
Colored Intercollegiate Athletic Conference 62
Columbes Field (France) 189
Columbia University 6, 21, 106, 107, 135, 140, 144, 145, 146, 157, 158, 180, 181, 193
Comiskey, Charles 11, 18
Commission on Training Camp Activities 47, 98, 138
Connecticut Agricultural College 57
Connecticut League (baseball) 39
Connecticut Valley track meet 104
Cooper Memorial College (Kan,) 113
Copper League (N. Mexico) 18
Copper Queens (N. Mexico baseball) 18, 41
Corinthian Yacht Club 147
Cornell College (Iowa) 30, 73, 74, 112, 125
Cornell University 22, 35, 87, 90, 106, 117, 135, 144, 171, 174
Coronado Club (polo) 171
Corpus Christi, Tex. 6, 42

Cox, Gov. James (Ohio) 179
Craft, Molly (baseball) 38
Crane Junior College (Ill.) 69
Crawford, Sam (baseball) 43
Creek Nation 39
Creighton University 32, 76, 125, 127
Crescent Athletic Club (N.Y.) 131, 132, 175, 180
Crescents (N. Orleans) 122
Cricket League (lacrosse) 175
croquet 180
Crowder, Maj. Gen. Enoch (War Department) 13
Cumberland College (Ky.) 123
Cumberland University (Tenn.) 6
Cunnha, George (swimmer) 147
Curry, Irby (football) 65

Dahlonega see North Georgia
Dakota Wesleyan College 33
Dallas Athletics (soccer) 175
Dalton, Jack (football Naval Ac.) 62
Danbury, Conn. (horse racing) 168
Daniel Baker College (Tex.) 78
Daniels, Josephus (Sec. of Navy) 37, 96
Dartmouth College (N.H.) 21, 57, 87, 93, 104, 106, 107, 120, 135, 140, 165
Davidson College 25, 108, 122
Davis, Dwight (tennis) 141, 143
D.C. League (basketball) 121
Decatur Baptist (football) 78
DeHart, Jimmy 96
Delaware College 62, 106, 107, 120
Dempsey, Jack (boxer) 150, 156, 157
Denver bowling 179
Denver trapshooting 181
Denver University 32, 75, 79, 114, 128
De Oro, Alfredo (billiards) 178
De Palma, Ralph (auto racer) 160, 161
DePauw University (Ind.) 30, 69, 71, 110, 111
Des Moines College 112
Des Moines, Western League (baseball) 42
Detroit Heralds (basketball/football) 85, 87, 133
Detroit Rayl (basketball) 132
Detroit Tigers 12
Devaney, Mike (track) 116, 117
Dickinson College 107
Dickson, Byron (football coach) 94
Dietz, William (football Washington St) 83, 96
Dobie, Gilmour (football coach) 62, 102
Dodge City Motorcycle Speedway (Kan.) 163
Dorias, Gus 85, 125
Dougherty, Bud (football coach) 33
Douglass, Addison (U Minn. basketball) 109
Drake Relays 112
Drake University (Iowa) 112, 13, 125, 126
Drew, Howard (track) 112, 186
Drexel Institute 107, 120

228 Index

Driscoll, John (Northwestern) 28, 38, 69, 85, 96, 97, 132
Drury College (Mo.) 76, 114, 126
Dubuque College (Iowa) 30, 74, 75, 125
Dubuque German College & Seminary/ Dubuque College 74, 125
Ducote, Richard (football) 60
Duke of Wellington 56
Duke University see Trinity University
Duluth Curling Club 164
Duluth, Wisc. shipbuilding 16
Dunbartan Club (D.C.) 142
Dundee, Johnny (boxer) 150, 156
Dunn, Jim (baseball) 13

Eagan, Lt. Edward (boxer) 188, 192
Earlham Coll. (Ind.) 71, 111, 125
East Central University of Oklahoma see Ada Normal
East Lake Country Club (Ga.) 136
East Stroudsburg State Normal School (Pa.) 61
Eastern Collegiate Basketball Association 35, 120
Eastern Collegiate Swimming Association 145
Eastern Intercollegiate (track) 106
Eastern League (pro basketball) 130
Eastern Michigan Normal (soccer) 176
Eastern Virginia Intercollegiate Conference 24, 62, 121
Eau Claire State Normal 73, 74
Ebbet's Field 156
Eby, Earl (track) 117, 186
Eckersall, Walter (reporter) 70, 76, 87, 97
Edinboro State Normal (Pa.) 61
El Paso bowling 179
Elberfeld, Norman (baseball mgr.) 16, 89
Elon College 25
Emergency Fleet Corporation 16
Emory & Henry College (Va.) 63
Emporia State Normal School 75, 113
Erskine College (S. Carolina) 27, 68
Eureka College (Ill.) 124
Evangelical Lutheran Synod 70
Evans, Chic (golfer) 137, 139
Exterminator (horse) 169

Faber, Urban (baseball) 30, 43
Fairbanks, Douglass (actor) 9, 172
Fairmont State Normal (W. Va.) 25, 108
Fairmount College (Wichita St U) 31, 75, 113
Fall River Rovers (soccer) 176
Far Eastern Olympics 48
Fargo College (N. Dakota) 81, 129
Federal League (baseball) 6
Felsch, Oscar (baseball) 17
fencing 180–81
Fenway Park 15, 59
"Fight or Work" 13

Fish, Hamilton (football) 101
Fisher, Joe (boxer) 155
Fisk University (HBU) 66, 67
flu 56, 63, 64, 65, 69, 82
"Flying Dutchman" 150
Foch Field (Coblentz football) 103
Fordham University 31, 59, 61, 62
Forest Hills (tennis) 141
Fort Hays Normal School (Kan.) 75, 113, 126
Fort Wayne Friars (pro football) 85
Fosdick, Raymond 47, 48, 49
Foster, Reuben (Black baseball entrepreneur) 10
Fourth Liberty Loan 169
fox hunting N.Y. and Va. 170
Frank, Charley (baseball mgr.) 16
Franklin & Marshall University (Pa.) 120, 175
Franklin College (Ind.) 30, 70, 125
Franklin Field (Philadelphia) 106
Frawley Act (N.Y. boxing) 194
Frazee, Harry (baseball owner) 11
French University Baseball League 50
Frey, John (football) 99
Friedman, Marty (basketball) 130, 133
Friel, William (umpire) 48
Friends Reconstruction 23
Friends University 75, 113
Frisch, Frankie (baseball) 21, 22, 60
Fuel Administration 60
Fulton, Fred (boxer) 149
Fultz, David (baseball) 6, 18
Furman University (S. Carolina) 27, 68

Gallaudet College for the Deaf (D.C.) 24, 62, 64, 121
Gans, Joe "Young" (Black boxer) 150, 155
Gardiner, Robert (golf) 136, 138
Gardiner, W.J. (Carlisle, army football) 86
Garfield, Harry A., (Fuel Administrator) 145
General Order #241 (Inter-Allied Games) 183
Geneva College (Pa.) 61, 120
George Washington University (D.C.) 62, 121
Georgetown College (Ky.) 65, 108
Georgetown University (D.C.) 24, 38, 59, 62, 64, 94, 101, 121, 131, 140, 186
Georgia Tech 6, 26, 60, 64, 65, 66, 68, 88, 108, 109, 135, 140
G.I. Bill of Rights (WW II) 197
Gibbons, Mike (boxer) 149, 152
Gipp, George 70
Glazner, Charles (baseball) 50
Glockson, Norm (baseball) 38
Gobert, Andre (tennis) 189
Gold Cup (motorboating) 148
Gonzaga University 83, 96
Gooch, Robert (football) 63
Goodwin, Marv (baseball) 40
Gordon, Willie (track) 116
Gordon State Coll. 67
Goullet, Arthur (bicyclist) 163

Index 229

Governor's Island N.Y. 186
Gowdy, Hank (baseball) 10, 11, 19
Graham, Bushy (boxer) 155
Grand Alleys (N. Dakota) 180
Grand Circuit (harness racing) 168
Grand Fleet (British) 44
Grand Forks (bowling) 180
Grant, Eddie (baseball, KIA) 52, 193
Gravesend Bay 147
Great Northern 184
Greater Omaha All-Stars 42
Greb, Harry (boxer) "Human Windmill" 154
Greco-Roman wrestling 173
Greeley, Colorado (shooting) 181
Greystock Churchmen (basketball) 130
Griffen, Clarence (tennis) 141
Griffith, Clark (baseball) 12, 14, 19, 38, 92, 95
Grinnell College (Iowa) 30, 69, 75, 112, 113, 125
Guilford, Jessie (golfer) 136
Guilford College (N.C.) 25, 121
Gustavus-Adolphus College (Minn.) 73, 124
Guyon, Joe (football) 66, 84

Hagen, Walter (golfer) 136
Halas, George 28, 29, 85, 96, 124, 132
Hall, Henry (ski jumper) 166
Hall, Sherman (fencer) 181
Hamlin College 73, 114, 124
Hammond (Ind.) (football) 85
Hampden-Sydney College (Va.) 62, 114
Hampton Normal & Industrial (Va.) 62, 63
Hanover College (Ind.) 71
Harkness Gold Trophy 160
Harkness Handicap 161
Harlan (Steel League baseball) 17
Harley-Davidson 162
Harnsworth Trophy (motorboating) 148
Harris, Joe (baseball) 53
Harrison Park (N. Jersey) soccer championship 176
Hart, Eddie (football player) 100
Hartford (baseball) 35
Harvard University 6, 21, 50, 57, 59, 65, 90, 104, 105, 106, 135, 140, 142, 143–145, 157, 165, 174, 180, 181, 189; alumni (squash) 180
Haskell Institute (Kan.) 31, 39, 75
Haugen, Anders (Norwegian skier) 162, 166
Haugen, Lars (Norwegian skier) 162, 166
Haughton, Maj. Percy (baseball) 53, 93, 103
Haverford College (Pa.) 23, 24, 61, 103, 120, 173, 174, 175
Haverford Cricket Club 143
Hayes, Michael Joseph (Colgate) 59, 165
Hearne, Ed (auto racer) 162
Heisman, John (football) 6, 66
Helms Foundation 130
Hempstead, Harry (baseball owner) 13
Henderson, John 100
Henderson-Brown College (Ark.) 77, 127

Hendricks, John C. (baseball mgr.) 48
Hendrix College (Ark.) 27, 77, 127
Henley Regatta 188
Henry, John (baseball) 14
Henry Kendall College (U of Tulsa) 77, 85, 127
Hercules Co. 132
Herman, Pete (boxer) 149
Hermann, August (baseball commissioner) 13, 14, 15
Highland Park College (Iowa) 30, 112
Hillsdale College (Mich.) 72
Hindenburg Line 59, 64
Hinton, Bobby 108
Hiram College (Ohio) 140
Hitchcock, Tom, Jr. (polo) 169, 171
Hitchcock, Tom, Sr (polo) 169, 171
Hobart College (N.Y.) 174
Hobbes, Warren (track) 104
Hohenzollern, Wilhelm ("Kaiser Bill") 13, 21, 107, 110
Holman, Nat 175
Holy Cross College (Mass) 21, 57, 58, 104, 119
Hooper, Harry (baseball) 15
Hoover, Herbert (Food Administrator) 60
Hope College (Mich.) 72, 123
Hoppe, William (billiards) 178
Horey, Fred (auto racer) 162
Hornsby, Rogers 14, 15, 17
"Hosier Giant Killer" 149
Hotel Astor (fencing) 180
Housatonic River (Conn.) 180
Howard University (D.C.) 24, 62, 63
Hoyt, Charles (track, Grinnell) 66, 112
Hucles, Henry (Va. Union University) 63
Hudson River Yacht Club (motorboating) 148
Huston, Tillinghast (baseball) 7, 9, 48, 50, 99
Hutchinson, Jock (golfer) 136

Idaho boxing 195
Illinois Athletic Club (Chicago) 123, 125, 128, 147
Illinois Wesleyan 28, 124
Indian Flexible (motorbike) 162
Indiana Conference Athletic League (basketball) 125
Indiana State Meet (track) 111
Indiana State Normal (Muncie) 111
Indiana State Normal (Terre Haute) 36, 111
Indiana State Normal School (Pa.) 18
Indiana University 20, 30, 69, 110, 111, 125, 147
Indianapolis Motor Speedway 8
Industrial Workers of the World 41
Inland Empire 130
Inter-Allied Olympics (France) 112, 183
Inter-Aviation League (baseball) 42
Intercollegiate Association of Amateur Athletes of America (IC4A) 106, 117
Intercollegiate Golf Association 135

Intercollegiate Soccer Football League 174, 175
Intercollegiate Wrestling 158
Interlake Yachting Association 148
"International Ball Game" 13
International League (baseball) 9, 15, 18, 39
International Motor Contests Association 161
International Olympics 1920 (Antwerp) 192
International Skating Union 165
Iowa State 111, 112, 113, 125, 140, 146, 157
Iowa State Teachers College 112
Iowa Wesleyan College 31, 125
"Iowa Whirlwind" v "Iowa Cyclone" (military boxing) 153

Jackson, Joe (baseball) 16, 17
Jacobson, William (baseball) 38
James Millikin University (Ill.) 70, 124
Jamestown, N. Dakota 180
Jamestown College (N. Dakota) 33, 81, 129
Janvrin, Harold (baseball) 36
Japanese baseball collegians 28
Jasper Jewels (pro basketball) 130
Jenkins, Joe (baseball) 53
Jewish Welfare Board 38, 76
Joffre, Joseph (French commander) 11
Johns Hopkins University 145, 174
Johnson, Jack (boxer) 156
Johnson, Col. Wait (Inter-Allied Olympics) 142, 183, 190
Johnson, Walter (baseball) 40
Jones, Bobby (golf) 135
Johnson, Bancroft (baseball) 9, 11, 18, 19
Jones, Harry (Ada Normal) 77
Jones, John Paul (track) 106
Jonesboro Aggies (First Agricultural District, Ark.) 65
Juarez, Mexico 7

Kahanamoku, Duke (swimmer) 147
Kalamazoo College (Mich.) 28, 72, 73, 124, 128
Kalamazoo Normal School (Mich.) 61, 72, 123
Kansas City Speedway 160
Kansas Intercollegiate Athletic Association 75
Kansas State Agricultural College 31, 93, 113, 126, 181
Kansas State Normal 113, 126, 158
Kansas Wesleyan 113, 114
Kathryn III (motorboat) 148
Kaw, Eddie (Cornell) 50, 99, 100
Kearns, Jack (boxing) 156
Keene, Foxhall (polo) 170
Kentucky College for Women 123
Kentucky Derby 169
Kentucky State Association (baseball) 25
Kentucky Wesleyan College 123
Kenyon College (Ohio) 30, 132
Keokuk, Iowa volley ball 134

Kerin, Jack (umpire) 48
Kerrigan, Tom (golf) 138
Keswick Club (Va. fox hunting) 170
Keystone Club (motorcycling) 161
Kilbane, Johnny (boxer) 149
King Albert (Belgian) 103
"King of the Dirt Track" (auto racing) 161
Kingfisher College (Okla.) 127
Klepfer, Ed (baseball) 38, 53
Klutztown State Normal (Pa.) 121
Knights of Columbus 38, 47, 48, 98, 154, 156, 196
Knox College (Ill.) 30, 69, 110
Kramer, Frank; (bicyclist) 163
Kumagae, Ichiya (tennis) 142

La Crosse State Normal 28, 74, 124
Lafayette College (Pa.) 106, 175
Lafitte, Maj. Ed (baseball) 45
Lake Erie Put-In-Bay 148
Lake Forest College (Ill.) 30, 69, 124
Lake Placid (ice skating) 164
Lake St James (France) 187
Lake Shore Club 137
Lakewood Gun Club 181
Larchmont Club 147
Larned, William (tennis) 142
La Roche, Chester (football) 56
La Rochelle (France) 49
Larsen, Clinton (track) 114, 116
Lathrop Cup (Stanford/Cal.) 176
Laubis, Herman (swimming) 147
Laurel Park (horse racing) 168, 169
"Law & Order Brigade" 191
Lawrence, Mass (roller polo) 181
Lawrence University (Wisc.) 73
Lebanon Valley College (Pa.) 120
Le Gendre, Robert (track) 186, 191, 192
Le Gore, Harry (football) 101
Lehigh University (Pa.) 23, 31, 60, 61, 90, 94, 107, 120, 131, 157, 158, 174, 175
Le Mans France (boxing) 155
Lenoir College (N.C.) 121
Leonard, Benny (boxer) 149, 152
Levinsky, Barney "Battling" (boxer) 149
Lewis, Duffy (baseball) 43
Lewis, Ed "Strangler" (wrestler) 158, 188
Lewiston, Maine (roller polo) 181
Lewiston, Montana (boxing) 180
Liberty Handicap (Cincinnati) 161
liberty loans 12
Liberty Theater, Ft Myer 150
"Liberty Tournament" Vt. (golf) 136
Lincoln Memorial University (Tenn.) 26
Lincoln University (Pa. HBU) 61, 63
Lineaweaver, William (motorcyclist) 161
Lipton, Sir Thomas 147
Little 5 Conference (Ill.) 29–30, 70, 73, 110, 124
Little 7 Conference (Iowa) 113

Index

Little 19 Conference (Ill.) 28
Little Rock College 77, 127
Little Rock Travelers (baseball) 16, 41
Liversedge, Henry (track) 118
Lobert, Hans (baseball) 17, 18, 22
Lombard College (Ill.) 30, 71
Long Branch, N.J. (ice yachting) 164
Long Island Sound 147
Loomis, Henry (track) 116
Loras College *see* Dubuque College
Los Angeles Country Club 136
Los Angeles State Normal School 82
Louisiana Industrial Institute (Ruston) 67
Louisiana State Normal (Natchitoches) 122
Louisiana State University 26, 27, 67, 68, 108, 109, 122
Lowell, Mass (roller polo) 181
Luther College (gymnastics) 173
Lyons (France) 50

Macalester College (Minn.) 73, 110, 114
"Machine Gun Joe" (boxer) 151
Machine Gun Polo Club 171
Mack Men (Phil. A's) 11, 17, 36, 37, 38, 40, 41, 42, 47, 51
Mackinac Island 187
Madison Square Garden 116, 149, 158, 169, 195
Mahan, Eddie (football) 93, 100
Mahseet, Carl (football) 103
Main Line League (Phil. baseball) 12
Maine State League (college) 20, 21
Manhasset Bay Club 147
Mann, Leslie (baseball) 15
Mansfield State Normal School (Pa.) 61, 121
Maranville, Walter (baseball) 11, 36, 37, 38, 95
Marietta College (Ohio) 132
Marquette University 73, 76, 87
Marseille (France) 49
Marshall College 25, 64
Martin, Bob (boxer) 155, 188
Maryland Board of Health 169
Maryland State College of Agriculture 24, 108, 121, 174
Maryland State Fair (horse racing) 168
Maryville College (Tenn.) 26, 123
Massachusetts Agricultural College 21, 59, 105, 119, 165
Massachusetts Golf Association 137
Massachusetts Institute of Technology 12, 104, 106, 140, 157
Mathey, Dean (tennis) 143, 189
Matthewson, Capt. Christy (baseball) 17, 21, 33, 48
Maxwell Club (amateur baseball Detroit) 40
Mayer, Eugene (U Va. football) 63
Mays, Carl (baseball) 18
McCarthy, Joe (baseball) 17
McClean, Bobby (ice skater) 164
McCormick, Harry (baseball) 48
McFarland, Packey (boxer) 149

McGill University (Canada) 165
McGillivray, Perry (swimming) 147
McGoorty, Eddie (boxer) 149, 153
McKendre College (Ill.) 28
McLaughlin, Maurice (tennis) 142
McLean, Warden 143
McMillin, Alvin (Centre College) 65
McMinnville College (Ore.) 115
Meadowbrook Athletic Club 105, 116
Meadowbrook Country Club 170
Meehan, Willie (boxer) 154
Mercer University (Ga.) 26, 77
Meredith, Ted (track) 107
Metropolitan District N.Y. (wrestling) 158
Metropolitan Golf Association (N.Y.) 136
Metzger, Sol (football coach) 61
Miami University (Ohio) 30, 72, 111, 125
Michigan (boxing) 195
Michigan Agricultural College 8, 28, 72, 92, 96, 99, 101, 123, 125, 131, 140, 146
Michigan Intercollegiate Athletic Association 28, 73
Michigan State Normal 123
Middle States Regatta (crew) 145
Middle States Intercollegiate (track) 106
Middlebury College (Vt.) 56, 106
Midwest Catholic league (baseball) 30
Milburn, Devereux (polo) 171
Military Preparedness Committee AAA 160
Miljus, Milligan (baseball) 51
Miller, Cedric (football) 102, 103
Miller, Hugh (baseball) 53
Miller, Jack (baseball) 37
Millersville State Normal (Pa.) 61, 121
Milligan, Marcus (baseball) 26
Millrose Athletic Club 104, 116
Millsaps College (Miss.) 26, 122
Milwaukee State Normal 110
Minesweepers (Norfolk) 38
Minneapolis Millers (baseball) 16
Minnesota Agricultural College 124
"Minnesota Shift" 70
minor leagues Classes A-D. 10
"Miracle of the Marne" 11
Miss Detroit II and *Miss Detroit III* (motorboats) 148
Miss Minneapolis (motorboat) 148
Mississippi A&M 26, 67, 68, 108, 109, 122
Mississippi College 68, 122
Missoula, Montana City Bowling League 179
Missouri Inter-collegiate Conference 31, 113, 126
Missouri School of Mines (Rolla) 76, 114, 126
Missouri Valley Conference 31, 74, 76, 125
Missouri Wesleyan College 76
Molesworth, Carleton (baseball mgr.) 16
Monmouth College (Ill.) 29, 69, 110, 124
Montana State College 32, 80, 124, 128
Montana Wesleyan 80
Montreal Canadiens (ice hockey) 166

Moore, Billy (football) 101
Moore, Pal (boxer) 154
Moran, Frank (boxer) 149
Moravian College (Pa.) 140
Morehouse College (HBC-Atlanta) 67
Morningside College (Iowa) 31, 75, 112, 113, 125
Morris-Brown College (HBC-Atlanta) 39, 64, 66, 67
Morris -Harvey College alumni (W. Va.) 25
Morton, Guy (baseball) 41
Mt. Pleasant, Frank (football) 88
Mt. St. Joseph College (Md.) 131
Mt. Union College (Ohio) 92, 125
Mucks, Arlie (track) 110, 116
Muhlenberg College (Pa.) 20, 107
Murray, Robert (tennis) 141, 142
"Muscular Christianity" 5

Nashville Ramblers (semi-pro basketball) 127
National Archery Association 178
National Association of American Billiards 178
National Baseball Federation 50
National Basketball League 197
National Collegiate Athletic Association 54
National Commission (baseball) 15
National Football League 197
National Rifle Association 182
Nebraska State Normal School (Peru) 76
Nebraska Wesleyan College 75, 113
New Bedford Whalers (roller polo) 181
New England Intercollegiate (track) 104, 105
New England League (pro baseball) 39
New England League (roller polo) 181
New Hampshire State 21, 57, 116
New Jersey boxing 156, 195
New Jersey League (baseball) 39
New London, Conn. (baseball) 37, 94
New London, Conn. (crew) 144
New Mexico College of Agriculture and Mechanic Arts 32, 78, 79, 114, 128
New Mexico Military Institute (Roswell) 74, 78, 114
New Mexico School of Mines 32
New Mexico State University *see* New Mexico College of Agriculture and Mechanic Arts
New Orleans (baseball) 40
New York Athletic Club 92, 116, 147, 181
New York City (pool parlors) 179
New York Footballers Protective Association (soccer) 176
New York Giants 11, 40
New York Jockey Club 169
New York State Intercollegiate (track) 106
New York State League (soccer) 175
New York Teachers College 59
New York University 92, 120, 173
Newberry College (S. Carolina) 27, 68

Newell, Kirk (football) 88
Newport, Rhode Island (polo) 170
Newport News Shipbuilders 16, 45
Newport Trojans (R.I. baseball) 16
Newark Velodrome 163
Nightingale, Gordon (track) 104
Norfolk Va. (military wrestling) 159
Norfolk Va. Light Artillery Blues 87
Norfolk, Va. Tars (baseball) 16
North Carolina A&E (State) 64, 108, 121
North Carolina A&T (HBC) 25
North Carolina League (pro baseball) 10, 39
North Dakota State College 33, 73, 80, 81 129
North Dakota State Normal (Ellendale) 33
North Dakota University 33, 73, 110, 114, 129
North Georgia Agricultural College (Dahlonega) 26, 67
North Texas Soccer League 175
North Texas State Normal 78, 127
Northern Arizona Normal 128
Northern Normal (Aberdeen) 33
Northern State Normal (Aberdeen S. Dakota) 33
Northwest Association (wrestling) 158
Northwest Intercollegiate Conference: Western Div. (baseball) 33
Northwest Ohio 127
Northwestern College (Ill.) 69, 110, 124
Northwestern College (Wisc.) 73
Northwestern League (baseball) 10
Northwestern Oklahoma State University-Territorial Normal *see* Alva State Normal
Northwestern Swimming League 146
Northwestern University (Ill.) 28, 69, 84, 92, 110, 111, 112, 124, 135, 146, 165
Norwich (Conn.) All-Stars 37
Norwich University (Vt.) 56, 93

Oahu League (football) 93
Oberlin College (Ohio) 72, 109, 111, 112, 132, 141
Occidental College 79, 82, 115, 117, 141
O'Day, Hank (umpire) 48
O'Dowd, Mike (boxer) 149, 153
Oglethorpe College 26, 39, 67, 88, 109
Ohio Collegiate Conference 72, 125
Ohio National Guard 11
Ohio Northern Coll. 125
Ohio State League 39
Ohio State University 30, 38–9, 66, 68, 69, 110, 111, 112, 125, 146
Ohio University 71, 198
Ohio Wesleyan College 30, 111, 146, 176
Oklahoma A&M College 77, 92, 109, 127, 158
Oklahoma Baptist 127
Oldfield, Barney (auto racer) 160, 161
Oldring, "Rube" (baseball) 17
Oliphant, Elmer (West Point) 22, 50, 64, 165
Oliver, Ruth Law, (aviatrix) 178
Olympic Club 115, 146

Index

Omaha Balloonists 126
Omar Khayyam (race horse) 169
Omtvedt, Ragnar (ski jumper) 166
Oregon Agricultural College 7, 33, 34, 83, 97, 115, 129, 158, 176
Oregon State Penitentiary 34
Ottawa University (Kansas) 31, 75, 113
Otterbein College (Ohio) 72
Ouachita Baptist College 27, 76
Ouimet, Francis (golfer) 137, 138
Overton, John (track) 105, 116
Oyster League (S. Carolina volley ball) 133, 134

Pacific Coast Conference (baseball) 33, 145
Pacific Coast Conference (track) 115, 139
Pacific Coast Hockey League 166
Pacific Coast International League (baseball) 16
Pacific Coast League (baseball) 10, 43
Pacific Northwest Bowling Congress 143, 180
Pacific University 115
Paddock, Lt. Charley (track) 115, 185, 186, 191
Palmer College (Fla.) 26
Panama-Pacific (golf) 188
Pappan, Louis (basketball) 127
Pasadena High School 115
Patterson, Leo (black boxer) 155
Patton, Lt. George (polo) 7
Pawtucket, R.I. soccer championship 176
"Pearl of the Riviera" (tennis) 142
Peck, Bob (football) 94, 95
Pelham Parkway (bike race) 163
Pelham Country Club 141
Pell, Clarence (racquets) 180
Penn College (Iowa) 113
Penn Relays 107
Penn State League (baseball) 13
Penn State University 23, 57, 107, 120, 131, 149, 157, 158
Pennock, Herb (baseball) 36, 45
Pershing, Gen. John 13, 48, 100, 160, 183
Pershing Stadium 183
Petersburg Normal & Industrial (Va. HBC) 63
Pfeffer, Jeff (baseball) 31
Philadelphia As (baseball) 11
Phillips University (Okla.) 27, 77, 127
Phoenix motorcycling 162
Pickford, Mary (actress) 91
Pierce, Maj. Palmer E. 7
Pine Village (Indiana pro football) 85
Pinehurst N.C. (golf) 136
Pipp, Wally (baseball) 12
Pittsburg Normal (Kan.) 113, 114
Pittsburgh A.A. 116
Pittsburgh A.C. (ice hockey) 165, 166
Pittsburgh Pirates 12, 35, 61
Poe, John (Princeton athlete) 193
Pollard, Fred (football) 61, 85

Polo Grounds 9, 37, 92
Pomona College 82, 115, 141
Ponce de Leon Park (Atlanta) 26, 39
pool parlors 179
Pores, Charles (track) 116
Port Breeze Motordrome (Pa. motorcycling) 162
Portland Rosebuds (ice hockey) 166
Portsmouth Virginia Truckers (pro baseball) 26
Portugal (fencing) 189
Potomac Boat Club 144
Pottstown, Pa. motorcycling 162
Pratt Institute (N.Y.) 120
Preakness (horse race) 169
Presbyterian College (S. Carolina) 27, 68
Price, Ivan (Washington St basketball) 130
Princeton University 21, 35, 50, 54, 90, 91, 100, 101, 105, 120, 144, 145, 157, 165, 173, 175, 182, 193
Professional Golf Association 135
Providence Gold Bugs (roller polo) 181
Providence Steamrollers (pro football) 94
Providence YMCA 116
Purdue University 28, 30, 69, 90, 110, 111, 125

Quadrangular League (college baseball) 26
Queen City Giants (baseball) 16
Queen City Yacht Club 148
Queen Elizabeth (Belgian) 49, 103
Queen's Club (England) 44, 142
quoits 181

Racine, Wisc. (pro football) 85
Racing Club, Colombes France 46, 143, 189
racquets 180
Raftery, William (football coach) 64, 66
Randolph-Macon College (Va.) 24, 62, 121, 139
Rautenbush, William (golf) 138, 188, 189
Ray, Joie (track) 104, 116
Raycroft James, Commissioner, Army Camps 20, 35, 130, 131, 155
Reading Motorcycle Club 162
Reading Steel Casting Co. 17
Red Bank, N.J. (ice yachting) 164
Red Circle Park (Norfolk 38
Red Circle Theater (Norfolk) 194
Red Cross 11, 13, 45, 96, 136, 137, 138, 141, 142, 152, 170, 171, 178, 180
Red Lake, Minn. (baseball) 16
Redlands University 115
Reed College (women's basketball) 130
Rensselaer Polytechnic Institute 104, 106, 165
Reserve Officer Training Corps (ROTC) 7, 25
Rhode Island State College 21, 57, 119
Rice, Charles (Maine track) 104, 105
Rice, Grantland (columnist) 6
Rice, Sam (baseball) 37
Rice Institute (Tex.) 27, 109, 127

Index

Richards, Alma (track) 118
Richards, Vincent (tennis) 141, 142
Richmond Amateur Athletic Federation (baseball) 197
Richmond Amateur Commission (baseball) 16
Richmond College (Va.) 62, 108, 121, 139
Richmond Grays (baseball) 197
Rickenbacker, Eddie (auto racer) 160, 161
Rickey, Maj. Branch (baseball owner) 17, 53
rifle shooting 182
Rio Grande Park (El Paso) 7, 78
Ripon College (Wisc.) 73, 110, 124, 132
Ritchie, Pvt. Willie (boxer) 149, 150
River Falls Sate Normal School (Wisc.) 28, 73
Riverside Park (N.Y.) 148
Riviera League (baseball, France) 49
Roanoke College 24, 121
Robertson, Davis (baseball) 11, 38
Robeson, Paul (football) 60, 94
Rochester College 106
Rochne, Knute (football) 69
Rock Island, Ill. bowling 179
Rock Island Independents (pro football) 85
Rocky Mountain Conference (baseball) 32, 79, 114
roller polo 181
Rollins College (Fla.) 66
Romania 13
Romneys (Utah) 32, 80
Roosevelt, Franklin (Asst. Sec. Navy) 7, 96
roque 180
Rose Polytechnic (Ind.) 71
Ross, Clarence (Black baseball player) 41
Ross, Norman (swimmer) 146, 147, 187, 192
Royal Air Force 154
Royal Flying Corps (soccer) 175
rugby-Inter-Allied Olympics 189
"Russian Lion" (wrestling) 159
Rutgers College 21, 59, 61, 94, 96. 173
Ruth, George Herman 5, 15, 17
Ruth's All-Stars 18
Ryan, Paddy (track) 118, 186

Sacred Heart School (Colorado) 32
St. Ambrose College (Iowa) 30, 75, 115
St. Anselm's Coll. (N.H.) 21
St. Columba (pro basketball) 131
St. Ignatius College (S Francisco) 115, 129
St. John's College (Md.) 24, 108
St. John's College (Minn.) 28
St. Lawrence College 22, 106
St. Louis Browns (baseball) 12, 36
St. Louis Cardinals 37
St. Louis University 73, 75, 76, 125
St. Mary's (Kan.) 31
St. Mary's College (Oakland Cal.) 146
St. Michael's College (Vt.) 119
St. Olaf College (Minn.) 28, 73, 87, 110, 124, 176

St. Thomas College (Minn.) 28, 73, 110, 124
St. Viator's 75
Salem College (University in W. Va.) 108
Salem Witches (roller polo), 181
Salt Lake City 150
"Sammies" 13
San Francisco 156
Santa Clara University see University of Santa Clara
Santa Monica Bay Ministerial Union 196
Saranac Lake (ice skating) 164
Saratoga (horse racing) 169
Schauer, Alexander (baseball) 16
Schmader, Andy (boxer) 154
Schuylkill River 144, 145
Schwab Charles (financier, industrialist) 176
Scott, Jim 11, 43
Sea Bird 148
Sea Gold Cup 148
Sea Island Regatta (yachting) 148
Sears-Roebuck (Texas soccer) 175
Seattle Mets (ice hockey) 166
Second Liberty Fund 117
Seibold, Harry "Socks" (baseball) 37
Seton Hall College (N.J.) 21, 120
Severn River 144
Sewanee (college) 26, 65, 108, 109, 123
Sewanee Athletic Club (Va.) 63
Shaman, Ralph (baseball) 51
Shaw University (N.C. HBU) 25
Shawkey, Bob (baseball) 12
Sheehan, Tom (baseball) 42, 48
Sheepshead Bay (L. Island track) 160, 162
Sherman Indians 82
Shippensburg State Normal School (Pa.) 61, 120
Shurtleff College (Ill.) 70, 76
Simpson, Robert (track) 109, 112, 186
Simpson College 30, 112, 113
Sims, Admiral William 13, 44
Sisler, George (baseball) 17
Slater, Fred (black football player) 70, 71
Smith John (baseball) 21
Smith, Pat (football) 55, 86, 87
Soccer Football League 175
Soldiers Tobacco Fund 17
South Africa (boxing) 154
South Atlantic Conference 24, 63
South Atlantic Intercollegiate Athletic Association (track) 107, 121
South Bend, Ind. bowling 179
South Carolina Oyster League (volley ball) 133
South Coast Yacht Club (Cal.) 147
South Dakota State College 81, 92, 114, 124
South Dakota University 72, 81, 82, 101, 112, 113, 114
Southeast Louisiana 27
Southeast Missouri State University see Cape Girardeau Normal

Southeast New England army (baseball) 36
Southern College (Fla.) 66
Southern Collegiate Association 26, 84, 108, 109
Southern Golf Association 135
Southern Methodist University (Tex.) 78, 127, 128
Southern New England League (soccer) 176
Southern Rowing Association 145
Southwest Louisiana Industrial Institute (Lafayette) 27, 67
Southwest Military Baseball title 41
Southwest New England Army title 36
Southwest Patriotic Tournament 126
Southwestern Oklahoma Normal 127
Southwestern University (Texas) 78, 128
Speaker, Tris (baseball) 36
Spencer, Arthur (bicyclist) 163
spinal meningitis (S. Carolina) 122
Spokane Canaries (ice hockey) 166
Spokane Indians (baseball) 33
Sporting Club (London) 7
"Sporting Fraternity" 5
Spring Hill College (Ala.) 27, 66, 67
Springfield Normal (S-west Missouri State) 114, 126
Springfield YMCA School (Ma.) 59, 93, 104
squash 180
Stagg, Amos Alonzo (football coach) 55
Staley, Lloyd (football) 100
Stanford University 7, 33, 82, 96, 140, 142, 144, 146, 157, 165, 176
Stanley Cup (ice hockey) 166
Staunton Military Academy (Va.) 64, 72
Steamboat Springs, Colorado (ski jumping) 166
Steel League (baseball) 37
Steelton (baseball) 17
Stengel, Casey (baseball) 12, 37
Sterling College *see* Cooper Memorial College
Stetcher, Joe (wrestler) 158
Stetson University 66, 122
Stevens Institute of Technology (N.J.) 21, 60, 94, 106, 120
Stevens Point Normal School (Wisc.) 124
Stewart Ed (football coach Nebraska, Camp Gordon) 88
Stinson, Katherine (aviatrix) 178
Stockholm Olympics (1912) 7
Stonebraker, Homer (college basketball) 125
Street, Charles "Gabby" (baseball) 52
Strupper, Ed (football) 84, 88
Student Army Training Corps *see* U.S. Army
Student Navy Training Corps *see* U.S. Navy
Sullivan Island (S. Carolina) 148
Sunday, Billy (preacher) 9
Sunday Blue Laws 191
Susquehanna College (Pa.) 23

Swarthmore College (Pa.) 23, 61, 94, 120, 174, 175
Sylvester, William (track) 185, 186
Syracuse University 6, 22, 59, 60, 68, 69, 74, 82, 94, 106

Tacoma Club (boxing) 150
Tacoma Tigers (baseball) 16
Talladega Institute (Ala.) 66, 67
Tarkio College (Mo.) 31, 113
Taylor, Billy (auto racer) 160
Taylor, Major (bicyclist) 163
Tempe Normal (Ariz. State University) 32, 79, 128
Temple University 120
Tener, John (baseball commissioner) 11
Terre Haute Normal (Ind.) 30
"Terrible Swedes" (football) 70
Teschner, Edward (track) 118, 185
Texas A&M 6, 109, 122, 127
Texas Christian University 28, 78
Texas Intercollegiate 127
Texas School of Mines (El Paso) 78, 114
Texas State League (pro baseball) 39, 40
Texas State Normal 27
Thiel College (Pa.) 23, 60
Thistle Club (curling) Yonkers 164
Thomas, Claude (baseball) 45
Thomas, Fred (baseball) 15
Thomson, Fred 91, 117, 186
Thorpe, Jim 85, 87, 107, 141
Three I League (baseball) 41
Throckmorton, Harold (tennis) 141
Throop College (Cal. Inst. of Technology) 82
Thousand Island Yacht Club 148
Thurman, Alan (U. Va.) 63, 88
Tilden, Bill (tennis) 141, 142
Toledo 156
Toney, Fred (baseball) 11
Transylvania U (Ky.) 25, 26, 108
trapshooting (skeet), "America's Favorite Pastime" 181
Travers, Jerome (golf) 136
Trinity University (Conn.) 20, 56, 104, 105, 140
Trinity University (Duke U) 25, 64
Trinity University (Texas) 78
Troy, Bun (baseball) 53
Truman, Captain Harry (artillery) 133, 153
Tufts University 6, 59, 72
Tulane University 27, 67, 68, 95, 109, 119, 122, 140
Tunney, Gene (boxer) 155
Turner, Bradford (Williams football) 59
Tusculum College (Tenn.) 123
Tuskegee Institute (Ala. HBC) 67

Undines (crew) 148
Union College (Tenn.) 65
Union University (N.Y.) 22, 106

236 Index

Uniontown Oval (Pa. motorcycling) 162
United Nations 147
United Service Organization (WW II) 197
United States Armies: First 100; Second 101; Third 132; Occupation 19, 46
United States Army airfields: Carlstrom (Fla.) 40; Dorr (Fla.) 40; Dick (Tex.) 42; Kelly (Tex.) 27, 42, 89; Langley (Va.) 92; Mather (Cal.) 96, 97; Mineola (N.Y.) 59, 92, 171; Mitchell (N.Y.) 171; Park (Tenn.) 89, 123; Payne (Miss.) 67, 89; Presidio Aviation 115; Rockwell (Cal.) 96; Selfridge (Mich.) 86, 87
United States Army Ambulance Corps (Allentown, Pa.) 48, 57, 61, 94, 117, 131, 141, 147
United States Army camps (divisions in parentheses): Beauregard (La. 39, 17) 67, 89, 138, 169; Benning (Ga.) 50, 121; Bowie (Tex. 36) 41, 42, 89; Cody (N. Mexico 34, 97) 90; Cotton (Tex.) 7; Custer (Mich. 85, 14) 42, 72, 86, 123, 132; Devens (Mass 26, 76, 12) 18, 36, 57, 59, 88, 93, 94, 115, 130, 137; Dix (N.J. 78) 88, 92, 107, 115, 117, 131; Dodge (Iowa 88, 92, 19) 28, 43, 60, 70, 74, 82, 86, 87, 101, 125, 126; Doniphan (Okla. 35) 77; Fremont (Cal. 41) 33, 92, 115, 129, 176; Funston (Kan. 89 10) 47, 50, 86, 103, 126, 138; Gordon (Ga. 82, 5) 16, 19, 39, 50, 60, 65, 66, 67, 87, 88, 152, 194; Grant (Ill. 86) 42, 46, 73, 87, 149, 188; Greene (N.C. 3, 4) 16, 64, 131, 171; Greenleaf (Ga. 35, 39, 88, 143; Hancock (Ga. 28) 39, 40, 41, 46, 61, 87, 88, 94; Harry Jones (Ariz.) 41, 79; Humphreys (Va.) 40, 41, 50; Jackson (S. Car. 81) 17, 38, 50, 63, 116, 122; Jessup (Atlanta) 39, 50; Johnston (Fla.) 40–41; Kearny (Cal 40, 16) 43, 90, 96, 138; Las Casas (Puerto Rico) 138; Leach American University (D.C.) Chemical Warfare 92; Lee (Va. 80) 24, 38, 56, 63, 92, 94, 132, 149, 169; Lewis (Wash. 91, 13) 43, 83, 91, 96, 132, 143, 172, 176; Logan (Tex. 5, 15) 78; Mabry (Tex..) 78; MacArthur (Tex. 33) 72, 89; McClellan (Ala. 29, 6) 39, 87, 88; Meade (Md. 79) 91, 94, 107, 117, 121, 131, 133, 150, 169; Merritt (N.J.) 93; Perry (Lake Erie rifle range) 182; Pike (Ark 87) 41, 73, 75, 76; Polk (N.C.) 64; Sevier (S. Carolina) 20, 13) 39, 41; Shelby (Ala. 38, 101) 16, 40, 67, 87, 89, 169; Sheridan (Ala. 37, 9) 40, 41, 89, 133; Sherman (Ohio 83, 84, 95, 96) 42, 61, 82, 87, 132; Taylor (Ky. 84) 30, 65, 69, 71, 87, 132; Travis (Tex. 90, 18) 39, 41, 78; Upton (N.Y. 77) 11, 88, 92, 138, 151, 165; Wadsworth (S.C. 27, 96) 41, 59; Warden McClean Ft. Oglethorpe 143; Wheeler (Ga. 31) 39, 152, 171
United States Army coast defense (artillery): California (Long Beach) 82, 83; Maine 94; Narragansett Bay 36; Virginia 47th 98

United States Army divisions: 1st "The Big Red One" 57; 2nd "Indian Head" 101; 3rd "Rock of the Marne" 50, 101, 148; 4th "Ivy" 101; 5th "Red Devils" "Red Diamond" 101, 117; 6th "Red Star" 49, 100, 159, 177; 7th "Hourglass" 42, 49, 101; 13th "Lucky 13th" 96; 26th "Yankee" 45, 93, 97, 99; 28th "Keystone" 40, 101; 29th "Blue-Gray" 40, 87, 99, 102, 152, 153; 31st "Dixie" 39; 32nd Mich. 1916 6; 32nd "Red Arrow" 89, 152; 33rd "Prairie" 101 117, 158; 34th "Red Bull" "Sandstorm" 41; 35th "Santa Fe Trail" 46, 100, 117, 133, 152, 159; 36th "Texas" 42, 49, 100, 101, 133; 37th "Buckeye" 99; 40th "Sunshine" 90; 41st "Sunset" 45; 42nd "Rainbow" 55, 97, 101; 76th "Liberty Bell" 133; 77th "Statue of Liberty" 117, 118; 78th "Lightning" 99, 101, 133; 79th "Cross of Lorraine" 37, 91; 80th "Blue Ridge" 38, 49, 99, 102, 133, 169, 170, 176; 81st "Wildcat" 50, 64, 102, 153, 159; 82nd "All-American" 39, 152; 85th "Custer" 42, 75, 98; 86th "Blackhawk" 50; 88th "Fighting Blue Devils" 42, 49, 86, 87, 98, 101, 152, 154, 169; 89th "Rolling W" 50, 86, 98, 101, 117; 91st "Wild West" (fir tree) 91; 96th "Deadeye" 130; 97th "Trident" 41, 90
United States Army forts and domestic posts: Adams (R.I.) 5; Bayard (N. Mex.) 18, 41; Benjamin Harrison (Ind.) 40, 64, 69; Bliss, (Tex.) 7, 41, 78, 89, 90, 138; Crook (Omaha) 42, 127; Douglas (Ariz.) 90; Ethan Allen (Vt) 56; Greble (R.I.) 94; Huachuca (Ariz.) 41; Jefferson Barracks (Mo.) 43; Kamehameha (Hawaii) 93; Kearny (R.I.) 57, 119; MacArthur (Cal.) 43; McKinley (Me.) 57, 59; McPherson (Atlanta) 39, 50, 116, 152; Moultrie (S. Carolina) 39; Myer (Va.) 24, 63, 132; Oglethorpe (Ga.) 41, 65, 87, 108; Omaha (Neb.) 127; Ontario (N.Y.) 32; Plattsburg Officer Training (Mo.) 7, 54, 141, 142, 171; Presidio (Cal.) 45; Reading Pennsylvania Militia 97; Riley (Kan.) 31, 42, 86; Root (Ark.) 89; Rosecrans (Cal.) 95; Schofield Barracks (Hawaii) 93; Shafter (Hawaii) 93; Sheridan (Ill.) 45, 86, 87, 97; Slocum (N.Y.) 92, 131; Snelling (Minn.) 74; Taliaferro (Tex.) 14; Terry (N.Y.) 37; Totten (N.Y.) 5
United States Army Student Army Training Corps (SATC) 2, 34, 55–84
United States Army units: 4th Cavalry 93; 7th Cavalry 7; 10th Cavalry 90; 15th Cavalry 41; 22nd Regimental Armory (N.Y.) 114; 24th Inf. Reg. (Black) 90; 25th Inf. Reg. (Black) 90; 26th Engineers 45; 27th Reg. 165; 63rd Reg. 129; 129th Field Artillery 33; 112th Ordnance 76; 186th Aero Squadron 45; 311th Field Artillery (Norfolk Light Artillery Blues) 87; 315th Inf. Reg. 133; 318th

Inf. Reg. 38, 99; 319th Inf. Reg. 38; 321st Inf. Reg. 50; 342nd F. Artillery 86; 361st Inf. Reg. 130; 362nd Inf. Reg. 91; 369th Inf. Reg (Black) 50; 371st Inf. Reg. (Black) 88; 809th Pioneers (Black combat engineers) 47, 50, 140, 155; 840th Aero Squadron 45, 99, 117; Base Section 2 (France) 143; Headquarters Le Mans 101, 176; Quartermaster Corps 142; St. Nazaire Service of Supply 101; Tours Intermediate (basketball) 101, 103

U.S. Bowling Congress 179

U.S. Football Association (soccer) 176

U.S. Golf Association 135, 136, 138

U.S. Lacrosse League Northern & Southern Divisions (colleges) 174

U.S. Lawn Tennis Association 142, 143

U.S. Marines: Barracks D.C. 92; League Island 12, 94; Mare Island 33, 43, 80, 82, 86, 91, 97, 101, 130; Parris Island 37, 41; Quantico 37, 62, 64, 83, 92

U.S. Naval Academy (Md.) 7, 20, 22, 23, 24, 35, 59, 107, 108, 144, 145, 146, 157, 173, 180, 192

U.S. Navy: Balboa Park (Cal.) Naval Training 43, 96, 132; Boston Navy Yard 94, 116; Bremerton Sailors 155; Bumpkin Island (Mass) 36, 37, 93; Cape May (N.J.) 131; Charleston Naval Training 27; Charleston Navy Yard (S. Carolina) 27, 68, 94; Charlestown Navy Yard (Mass) 93, 115, 122; Chicago Naval Reserves 97; Cleveland Naval Reserves 60, 75, 96; Coast Naval Reserves (Cal.) 43; Coast Naval Reserves (La.) 43; D.C. Navy Yard (Gunners) 62; Great Lake Reservists (football) 75; Great Lakes Naval Training (baseball) 38, 42, 43, 62; Great Lakes Naval Training (football) 69, 85, 86, 96, 97, 116, 126, 132, 147, 149, 156, 157; Great Lakes Naval Training/Reservists 116, 126, 132, 147, 149, 156, 157, 159, 166; Gulfport Naval Reserves and Training 66; Hampton Roads Operating Base 38, 94, 95; Harvard Naval Radio School 37, 93; Hoboken Naval Transport (football) 94; League Island Navy Yard (Philadelphia) 57, 61, 64, 95, 97, 107; Mare Island Naval Training 43; Municipal Pier (Chicago) 37, 69, 96; Naval Coast Defense Reserves 142; Newport (R.I.) Naval Reserves 35, 37, 86, 94, 119, 120; Newport Naval Training 35, 59, 93, 94, 95; Newport Torpedo Station 94, 131; Norfolk Naval Air Station 38; Norfolk Naval Training Station 45; Omaha Naval Recruiting 42; Pacific Coast Naval Reserves 43; Pelham Bay Naval Training Station 22; Pelham Naval Reserves (N.Y.) 116, 120, 131; Pensacola Air Station 67; Pensacola Naval Training Station 95; Portland Naval Reserves 56; Rockaway Naval Air Station (N.Y.) 131; Rockwell Aviation 132; Rumford Naval Rifle Range (R.I.) 94; St. Helena Armed Guards/Naval Training (Norfolk) 38, 62, 94; San Diego Air Station 95; San Diego Naval Training 95; San Pedro Naval Reserves 128; San Pedro Sub Base 43, 96, 97; University of Washington Naval Training 132; Washington (D.C.) Navy Yard-gun factory 62, 127

U.S. Navy Naval Districts: First 93, 166; Second 119; Third 94; Fourth 38, 94; Fifth 38, 43, 94, 95

U.S. Navy ships: *Arizona* 94, 95, 145; *Arkansas* 145; *Granite State* 37, 97, 116; *Illinois* 95, 154; *Kentucky* 95; *Michigan* 95; *New Mexico* 95; *Nevada* 96; *New Hampshire* 5, 95; *New York* 145; *North Carolina* 152; *Ohio* 95; *Oklahoma* 145; *Oregon* 96; *Pennsylvania* 38, 95, 145, 154; *Utah* 96; *Wisconsin* 145; *Wyoming* 5

U.S. Navy troop ships: *George Washington* 152; *Great Northern* 185; *Mauretania* 152; *Rotterdam* 48

U.S. Navy Student Navy Training Corps (SNTC) 57, 71

United War Workers Campaign 38, 48, 56, 68, 80, 83, 137, 178

University of Alabama 26, 109

University of Arizona 32, 79, 89, 92, 114, 128

University of Arkansas 27, 76, 127, 158

University of Buffalo 123

University of California 33, 82, 96, 115, 129, 132, 141, 145, 146, 157, 165, 176

University of California, Davis 114

University of California, Southern Branch 82

University of Central Missouri *see* Warrensburg Teachers College

University of Central Oklahoma *see* Central State Normal School

University of Chicago 28, 68, 69, 90, 109, 110, 111, 112, 124, 131, 134, 140, 157, 186

University of Colorado 32, 79, 80, 90, 128

University of Detroit 62, 72, 89

University of Dubuque *see* Dubuque German College & Seminary/Dubuque College

University of Florida 26, 66

University of Georgia 26, 88, 109, 121

University of Idaho 32, 33, 80, 114, 115, 128, 130, 132, 157

University of Illinois 6, 28, 109, 124, 125, 132, 135, 146, 173

University of Iowa 31, 68, 69, 112, 113, 125

University of Kansas 31, 90

University of Kentucky (State) 25, 26, 65, 108, 109, 123

University of Louisville 123

University of Maine 21, 56, 104, 105, 119

University of Maryland *see* Maryland State College of Agriculture

University of Michigan 23, 28, 42, 68, 72, 74, 87, 94, 97, 99, 106, 109, 110, 111, 117, 123, 140

University of Minnesota 68, 73, 96, 101, 109, 110, 111, 124, 140, 146, 173
University of Mississippi 26, 109, 122
University of Missouri 6, 31, 68, 76, 109, 112, 113, 126, 140
University of Montana 32, 33, 80, 114, 128, 129
University of Nebraska 32, 74, 88, 89, 90, 95, 110, 113, 126
University of New Mexico 32, 78, 79, 114, 120
University of Nevada 124
University of New Hampshire *see* New Hampshire State
University of North Carolina 64, 104, 108, 122
University of North Georgia *see* North Georgia Agricultural College
University of Notre Dame 29, 30, 31, 39, 42, 50, 69, 72, 82, 87, 89, 92, 96, 109, 110, 111, 112, 123, 125
University of Oklahoma 27, 77, 92, 109, 127, 140
University of Omaha 76, 126
University of Oregon 6, 33, 61, 83, 84, 86, 96, 114, 115, 130, 158, 176
University of Pennsylvania 60, 61, 94, 106–107, 120, 143, 144, 145, 156, 158, 173, 174, 175, 180, 181
University of Pittsburgh 23, 88, 96, 107, 120, 131
University of San Francisco *see* St. Ignatius College
University of Santa Clara 33, 80, 82, 115, 132
University of South Carolina 27, 88, 108, 122
University of Southern California 33, 79, 144
University of Tennessee 26, 87, 108, 123
University of Texas 6, 27, 76, 78, 90, 97, 101, 109, 127, 140, 158
University of the South *see* Sewanee
University of Tulsa *see* Henry Kendall College
University of Utah 32, 79, 90, 114, 128, 132
University of Vermont 22, 56, 105, 119
University of Virginia 63, 90, 108, 121, 123, 140, 169, 194
University of Washington 7, 33, 83, 91, 92, 97, 102 115, 126, 130, 132, 157, 158
University of Wisconsin 28, 140, 157, 165, 173, 176
University of Wisconsin, Eau Claire *see* Eau Claire State Normal
University of Wisconsin, La Crosse *see* La Crosse State Normal
University of Wisconsin, Milwaukee *see* Milwaukee State Normal
University of Wisconsin, Stevens Point *see* Stevens Point Normal School
University Sports Club 117
Utah State College 32, 80, 114, 128
Utica, N.Y. curling 164

Valley City N. Dakota bowling 180

Valley City Normal (N. Dakota) 33, 81
Van Cortland Park (N.Y.) 104, 106
Vancouver Millionaires (ice hockey) 166
Vanderbilt University 65, 89, 108, 109, 121
Verdun 13, 46, 133, 153
Vermeulen, Jean (French) marathon winner 190
Victoria "Fragments" 176
"Victory Fleet" (track) 184
Vidal, Gene (West Point) 82, 186
Villa, Pancho 6
Villanova College (Pa.) 23
Virginia Boat Club (Richmond) 145
Virginia Christian College (Lynchburg) 63
Virginia League (pro baseball) 6, 26, 38
Virginia Military Institute 62, 64, 108, 121, 123
Virginia Normal & Industrial Institute (HBC) 92
Virginia Polytechnic Institute 24, 63, 89, 108, 121
Virginia State Fair (auto/horse racing) 161, 168, 169
Virginia State University *see* Petersburg Normal & Industrial Institute
Virginia Union University (HBU) 24, 63, 92
Visitacion Valley California 115
Vitagliano, Nina (woman auto racer) 161
Vollmer, Herbert (swimmer) 145, 147
Von Kolnitz, Fritz (baseball) 19, 39, 88

Wabash (pro football) 85
Wabash College (Ind.) 30, 71, 111, 112, 125
Wagner, Honus 38, 48
Wahpeton State Science School (N. Dakota) 81
Wake Forest University 25, 64, 108, 122
Walden University (HBU Tenn.) 66
Walker, A.L. (golf) 135
Walker, Frank (baseball) 45
Wallace, Carl (track) 110
Wanderers (N.Y. ice hockey) 168
Wanner, Kennedy (Jamestown College) 21, 129
War Camp Community Service 38, 95, 194
Warner, Glenn (football) 6, 60
Warrensburg Teachers College (Mo.) 31, 76, 126
Washburn, Watson (tennis) 141, 143, 189
Washburn College (Kan.) 75, 126
Washington & Jefferson College (Pa.) 23, 61, 70, 85, 120, 123, 140
Washington & Lee (Va.) 24, 61, 62–4, 66, 88, 121, 123, 140
Washington College (Md.) 24
Washington State College 32–33, 83, 91, 92, 96, 114, 115, 129–30, 132, 158, 182
Washington State Normal 130
Washington University (St. Louis) 18, 74, 93, 126
water polo 145, 146

Watertown, Wisc. Fair (horse racing) 168
Watters, Doug (tennis) 140, 143
Webb, H. M (boxing) 153
Webster, Pearl (Black baseball) 53
Wells, Billy (boxer) 154
Wesleyan University (Conn.) 20
West Point Military Academy 24, 59, 70, 165, 180
West Virginia Institute (HBC) 66
West Virginia University 25, 38, 57, 64, 65, 92, 107, 108, 123
West Virginia Wesleyan College 25, 64, 65, 108
Westchester State Normal (Pa.) 61
Western Amateur Golf Association 138
Western Association (baseball) 124
Western Catholic League 75
Western Collegiate 107
Western Conference 27, 30, 31, 39, 109, 111, 112, 124
Western Conference (gymnastics) 173
Western Conference (swimming) 151
Western Conference (tennis) 140
Western Conference (wrestling) 157
Western Golf Association 135, 136
Western League (baseball) 42
Westminster College (Pa.) 140
Weyand, Alex (football) 90
Wheelock, Joel (football) 95
Whip Po Will (motorboat) 148
White Sulphur Springs (golf) 136
Whiting Owls (pro basketball) 123
Whitman, Gov. Charles (N.Y.) 195
Whitman College (Ore.) 33, 80, 83, 115, 130
Whitney, Howard 136
Whitney, Wilmot 102
Whittier College (Cal.) 79, 82
Wichita State University *see* Fairmount College
Wild West Rodeo (L. Angeles) 172
Wilde, Jimmy (British boxer) 154
Willamette University (Ore.) 33, 83, 115
Willard, Jess (boxer) 149, 155, 156
William Jewell College 31, 89, 126

Williams, Claude (baseball) 17
Williams, Richard Norris (tennis) 141, 142, 143, 189
Williams, Rufus (black boxer) 5
Williams College (Mass) 21, 53, 57, 105, 119, 135, 140, 145, 165, 194
Wilson, Pres. Woodrow 32, 56, 161
Wimbledon (tennis) 143
Winchester Fair (Va.) 168
Wingo, Absalom (baseball) 26, 39
Winn, Gen. Frank 103
Winona Normal (Minn.) 28
Wisconsin commission 28
Wisconsin Intercollegiate 73
Wisconsin mining school 7
Withington, Dr. Paul 86, 103, 187, 188
Wofford College (S. Carolina) 27, 68
Wood, Gar (motorboating) 148
Wood, Gen. Leonard 9, 12, 20, 196
Wood, Pat (tennis) 143
Wooster College (Ohio) 72, 111, 112
Worcester, Mass (roller polo) 181
Worcester Polytechnic Institute (Mass) 59
Wrenn, Robert (tennis) 142
wrestling Greco-Roman 188
Wyoming University 80, 132

Xavier College 99

Yacht Racing Association (Jamaica Bay) 148
Yale University 8, 20, 21, 63, 94, 99, 104, 105, 106, 119, 120, 135, 139, 144, 145, 157, 165, 174, 180; alumni 180
Yankton College (S. Dakota) 82, 113, 129
York College (Neb.) 21, 56, 75, 86, 88, 101
Yost, Fielding (football) 55, 68
Young Men's Christian Association 5, 16, 38 43, 48, 85, 131, 134, 183
Young Women's Christian Association 38, 1.
Younger, Monk (football) 63

Zbyszko, Wladek (wrestler) 158
Zuppke, Robert (football) 69